This book offers timely analysis on many of the key questions confronting stake-holders working on statelessness, and will be an invaluable resource for a growing global civil society coalition committed to tackling the problem.

Chris Nash, *Director, European Network on Statelessness*

This outstanding book, enriched by a collective as well as separate and insightful chapters by its editors and incisive chapters by its distinguished contributors, illuminates both theoretical and practical aspects of statelessness as the dark side of modernity.

Engin Isin, *Professor of International Politics, School of Politics and International Relations (SPIR), Queen Mary University of London (QMUL) and University of London Institute in Paris (ULIP)*

Understanding Statelessness

Understanding Statelessness offers a comprehensive, in-depth examination of statelessness. The volume presents the theoretical, legal and political concept of statelessness through the work of leading critical thinkers in this area. They offer a critique of the existing framework through detailed and theoretically-based scrutiny of challenging contexts of statelessness in the real world and suggest ways forward.

The volume is divided into three parts. The first, 'Defining Statelessness', features chapters exploring conceptual issues in the definition of statelessness. The second, 'Living Statelessness', uses case studies of statelessness contexts from States across global regions to explore the diversity of contemporary lived realities of statelessness and to interrogate standard theoretical presentations. 'Theorising Statelessness', the final part, approaches the theorisation of statelessness from a variety of theoretical perspectives, building upon the earlier sections. All the chapters come together to suggest a rethinking of how we approach statelessness. They raise questions and seek answers with a view to contributing to the development of a theoretical approach which can support more just policy development.

Throughout the volume, readers are encouraged to connect theoretical concepts, real-world accounts and challenging analyses. The result is a rich and cohesive volume which acts as both a state-of-the-art statement on statelessness research and a call to action for future work in the field. It will be of great interest to graduates and scholars of political theory, human rights, law and international development, as well as those looking for new approaches to thinking about statelessness.

Tendayi Bloom is a Lecturer in Politics and International Studies at The Open University, UK.

Katherine Tonkiss is a Lecturer in Sociology and Policy at Aston University, UK.

Phillip Cole is Senior Lecturer in Politics and International Relations at the University of West of England, UK.

Routledge Studies in Human Rights
Series Editors: Mark Gibney
UNC Asheville, USA
Thomas Gammeltoft-Hansen
The Danish Institute for Human Rights, Denmark
and Bonny Ibhawoh
McMaster University, Canada

www.routledge.com/series/RSIHR

The Routledge Studies in Human Rights series publishes high quality and cross-disciplinary scholarship on topics of key importance in human rights today. In a world where human rights are both celebrated and contested, this series is committed to create stronger links between disciplines and explore new methodological and theoretical approaches in human rights research. Aimed towards both scholars and human rights professionals, the series strives to provide both critical analysis and policy-oriented research in an accessible form. The series welcomes work on specific human rights issues as well as on cross-cutting themes and institutional perspectives.

1   **Human Rights and the Dark Side of Globalisation**
    Transnational Law Enforcement and Migration Control
    Edited by Thomas Gammeltoft-Hansen and Jens Vedsted-Hansen

2   **A Genealogy of the Torture Taboo**
    Jamal Barnes

3   **Sovereignty, State Failure and Human Rights**
    Petty Despots and Exemplary Villains
    Neil Englehart

4   **Understanding Statelessness**
    Edited by Tendayi Bloom, Katherine Tonkiss and Phillip Cole

Understanding Statelessness

Edited by
Tendayi Bloom,
Katherine Tonkiss
and Phillip Cole

LONDON AND NEW YORK

First published 2017 by Routledge

2 Park Square, Milton Park, Abingdon, Oxfordshire OX14 4RN
52 Vanderbilt Avenue, New York, NY 10017

Routledge is an imprint of the Taylor & Francis Group, an informa business

First issued in paperback 2018

British Library Cataloguing in Publication Data
A catalogue record for this book is available from the British Library

Library of Congress Cataloging in Publication Data
Names: Bloom, Tendayi, editor. | Tonkiss, Katherine, 1983–, editor. |
Cole, Phillip, editor.
Title: Understanding statelessness: lives in limbo / Edited by Tendayi
Bloom, Katherine Tonkiss and Phillip Cole.
Description: New York: Routledge, 2017. | Series: Routledge studies in
human rights | Includes bibliographical references and index.
Identifiers: LCCN 2017013917 | ISBN 9781138711235 (hardback) |
ISBN 9781315200460 (ebook)
Subjects: LCSH: Statelessness
Classification: LCC K7128.S7 U525 2017 | DDC 342.08/3–dc23
LC record available at https://lccn.loc.gov/2017013917

ISBN: 978-1-138-71123-5 (hbk)
ISBN: 978-0-367-13860-8 (pbk)

Typeset in Times New Roman
by Wearset Ltd, Boldon, Tyne and Wear

Printed in the United Kingdom
by Henry Ling Limited

Photo 1 Abul Kalam by the Naaf river in Bangladesh.

My home is not far from here, you just cross the Naaf river and my home is on the riverside. It is just two miles but for me it feels more like two million miles which I will never be able to cross.

My Rohingya guide, Abul Kalam points towards the other side of the river as we return home after a long day of work.

Contents

List of illustrations   xii

Notes on contributors   xiii

Foreword   xx

MATTHEW GIBNEY

Acknowledgements   xxiii

1 **Introduction: providing a framework for understanding statelessness**   1

TENDAYI BLOOM, KATHERINE TONKISS AND PHILLIP COLE

PART I

Defining statelessness   15

2 **Worthy of rights: statelessness as a cause and symptom of marginalisation**   17

LINDSEY N. KINGSTON

3 **Contexts of statelessness: the concepts 'statelessness *in situ*' and 'statelessness in the migratory context'**   35

CAIA VLIEKS

4 **Unpacking statelessness**   53

LAURA VAN WAAS AND AMAL DE CHICKERA

5 **The state and the stateless: the legacy of Hannah Arendt reconsidered**   70

BRAD K. BLITZ

PART II
Living statelessness   85

 6 **Challenging the disunity of statelessness in the Middle East
    and North Africa**   87
    ZAHRA AL BARAZI AND JASON TUCKER

 7 **Race-based statelessness in the Dominican Republic**   102
    JILLIAN BLAKE

 8 **Statelessness, ungoverned spaces and security in Kenya**   117
    OSCAR GAKUO MWANGI

 9 **Citizenship, gender and statelessness in Nepal: before and
    after the 2015 Constitution**   135
    SUBIN MULMI AND SARA SHNEIDERMAN

10 **Members of colonised groups, statelessness and the right to
    have rights**   153
    TENDAYI BLOOM

11 **Recognition, nationality, and statelessness: state-based
    challenges for UNHCR's plan to end statelessness**   173
    KELLY STAPLES

PART III
Theorising statelessness   189

12 **Why end statelessness?**   191
    KATJA SWIDER

13 **Realising the rights of stateless persons: the doctrine of
    fiduciary duty and the role of municipal government**   210
    DAVID PASSARELLI

14 **The right to family: protecting stateless children**   227
    PATTI TAMARA LENARD

15 **Statelessness and the performance of
    citizenship-as-nationality**   241
    KATHERINE TONKISS

16 **Insider theory and the construction of statelessness** 255
PHILLIP COLE

Index 268

Illustrations

Photo 1 Abul Kalam by the Naaf river in Bangladesh v
SAIFUL HUQ OMI

Photo 2 Rasha Khalil. Born and lives in Borj El Barajneh Camp
for Palestinian Refugees, Beirut, Lebanon 15
JOHN HALAKA

Photo 3 Camp near Anse a Pitre in Haiti 85
LOGAN ABASSI

Photo 4 Three Stateless Dalit in Nepal 134
GREG CONSTANTINE

Photo 5 Photographer's father in Boudhanath, Nepal 189
LODOE LAURA

Photo 6 Two Boys in a Caravan Near Rome 267
DENIS BOSNIC

Contributors

Logan Abassi was always torn between the image seen, remembered and then reproduced. When he was eight, an uncle gave him a point and shoot camera. After completing a degree in journalism, Logan embarked on a freelance career that took him to North Africa, Scandinavia, North, Central and South America and finally to the Caribbean. In 2004 he flew to the Dominican Republic, then overland into a country undergoing a frightening and all too often lethal *coup d'état*. At the border, a heavily armed border guard explained to him that 'they' would slit his throat and steal his stuff. Ten years later, despite the ominous warnings, he still has those original cameras with which he documented the sad and tragic events that shook Haiti. After free-lancing in Haiti, Logan was recruited by Reuters where he provided both video and photographic coverage of the developing story in Haiti until the end of 2006, when he started with the United Nations as the chief photo-grapher. For almost ten years Logan has worked to visually portray the complexities and dynamics of life in Haiti.

Zahra Al Barazi is a co-founder and senior researcher at the Institute on State-lessness and Inclusion. Her work has mostly focused on the understanding of statelessness and nationality in the Middle East and North Africa region. She has conducted substantive research on the interlink between discrimination, forced displacement and statelessness. Zahra has worked as a consultant for UNHCR, the Open Society Justice Initiative and Amel House of Human Rights on related human rights issues, and is a Board member of the Syrian Legal Development Programme. She is currently enrolled as a PhD student at Tilburg University.

Jillian Blake is an Immigration Lawyer at Blake & Wilson Immigration Law, PLLC in Alexandria, Virginia. Her practice focuses on removal (deportation) defence and asylum, mainly for immigrants and refugees from Latin Amer-ican countries. She holds a JD from the University of Michigan Law School and is a member of the Maryland Bar. She also holds an MA in international relations from the Johns Hopkins School of Advanced International Studies (SAIS), where she concentrated on international economics and Latin Amer-ican Studies.

Brad K. Blitz received his PhD from Stanford University. He is currently Professor of International Politics at Middlesex University, London and Senior Fellow at the Global Migration Centre at the Graduate Institute, Geneva. A former Jean Monnet Chair, he is widely regarded as a leading expert on refugees and stateless persons, migration, human rights and international politics. A comparative political scientist by training, he has worked extensively in former Yugoslavia and the former Soviet Union and acted as an advisor and consultant to UNDP, UNICEF, the UN Office of the High Commissioner for Human Rights (OHCHR), the World Bank, OSCE, Council of Europe, DFID, and several NGOs. Recent publications include *Statelessness in the European Union: Displaced, Undocumented and Unwanted* (Cambridge University Press, 2011) and *Statelessness and Citizenship: A Comparative Study on the Benefits of Nationality* (Edward Elgar Publishing, 2011). In November 2013, he completed a major study of the benefits of birth registration for Plan International. He is also the author of *Migration and Freedom: Mobility, Citizenship and Exclusion* (Edward Elgar Publishing, 2014; reprinted 2016) which was nominated for three awards. He is currently Principal Investigator for the ESRC-DFID funded EVI-MED project on refugee and migrant reception systems in the Mediterranean, and the EU Commission project INFORM which seeks to understand how asylum seekers access legal and procedural information.

Tendayi Bloom is a lecturer in Politics and International Studies at The Open University, UK and conducts research into the nature of noncitizenship from a political and legal theory perspective and from a policy perspective. She began work on this project as a Research Fellow at the United Nations University Institute on Globalization, Culture and Mobility, Spain, and the majority of her work on it was conducted as Postdoctoral Associate and Lecturer at the Global Justice Program, Yale University, US. She is co-editor (with Katherine Tonkiss) of *Theorising Noncitizenship*, a December 2015 special issue of *Citizenship Studies* (republished as a book, Routledge, 2016), which forms the precursor to the current volume. Alongside theoretical work, Tendayi leads a team producing an ASAP report examining the relationship between global development objectives and the situation of statelessness.

Denis Bosnic specialises in documentary portraiture photography and has worked on a number of projects related to human rights issues and marginalised communities. His work is influenced by his own experience of being a refugee. Bosnic was born in pre-war Sarajevo, Bosnia and Herzegovina, in 1986. In the 1990s, his family fled the Balkan Wars. As a result, he developed an intense interest in issues of human rights, forced displacement and marginalised communities. He specialises in collaborating on long-term projects with NGOs and media, focusing on telling strong stories through portraiture and documentary-style reporting. He is currently based in Rome, Italy, but is always on the move.

Amal de Chickera has researched, advocated, written, spoken, delivered training and served as an expert on statelessness and related issues for the UN, NGOs and academia, since 2008. As a human rights lawyer, he is particularly interested in the nexus between statelessness and discrimination and its implications on access to other rights. Before co-founding the Institute, Amal provided the lead on the Equal Rights Trust's statelessness work. He was also one of the co-founders of the European Network on Statelessness, and is a founding member of Stages – a Sri Lankan theatre group.

Phillip Cole is Senior Lecturer in Politics and International Relations at the University of West of England, Bristol and a Visiting Professor in Applied Philosophy with the Social Ethics Research Group, University of South Wales. He has written extensively on the ethics of international migration and his books include *Philosophies of Exclusion: Liberal Political Theory and Migration* (Edinburgh University Press, 2000) and, co-authored by Christopher Heath Wellman, *Debating the Ethics of Immigration: Is There a Right to Exclude?* (Oxford University Press, 2011). He is currently a trustee for the Welsh Refugee Council.

Greg Constantine is an independent documentary photographer from the USA. For the past 11 years he has dedicated himself to photographing and exposing the stories of stateless people around the world. His project 'Nowhere People' has produced three books including *Kenya's Nubians: Then & Now* (2011) and the critically acclaimed books, *Exiled To Nowhere: Burma's Rohingya* (2012) and *Nowhere People* (2015). Work from 'Nowhere People' has been exhibited in over 35 cities around the world. In early 2017, Constantine was awarded his PhD by Middlesex University in the UK. He continues to collaborate with numerous organisations to highlight the struggles of stateless people and the need for solutions to this global issue (www.nowherepeople. org).

John Halaka is a Visual Artist, Documentary Filmmaker and Professor of Visual Arts at the University of San Diego, where he has taught since 1991. He received his MFA in the Visual Arts from the University of Houston in 1983 and his BA in Fine Arts from the City University of New York Baccalaureate Program, with Brooklyn College as home school. Halaka's artwork has been exhibited and his films have been screened nationally and internationally. He is the recent recipient of a Fulbright Research Fellowship that enabled him to develop the second phase of the project 'Portraits of Denial & Desire' in Lebanon.

Saiful Huq Omi is an award-winning Bangladeshi photographer. He initially studied telecoms engineering, before taking up photography in 2005. His photos have appeared in numerous publications, including: *Asian Photography*, the *New York Times*, *Newsweek* and *Time*. His work has been exhibited in galleries from Bangladesh to Zimbabwe and has received numerous awards. The photograph included in this book is part of a larger project that won him a Magnum Foundation Emergency Fund grant. Saiful Huq Omi is represented by Polaris Images, and published his first photo book, *Heroes Never Die – Tales of Political Violence in Bangladesh*, in 2006. In a 2010 interview with UNHCR he observed:

> What is very important for me is knowing in my heart that the lives of the people I photographed are at least a little different than the day before they were photographed. There are many different goals, as a person, as an artist, but this is what I want to do with my life: I want to change lives.

Lindsey Kingston is an Associate Professor of International Human Rights at Webster University in Saint Louis, Missouri, USA. She directs the university's Institute for Human Rights and Humanitarian Studies, which includes its undergraduate and graduate human rights programmes. Kingston is also a World Social Science Fellow, an editor for *Human Rights Review* and an alumna of the Social Science Doctoral Program at Syracuse University's Maxwell School of Citizenship and Public Affairs. Her research has taken her to fieldwork sites including the Canadian Arctic territory of Nunavut, Rwanda and throughout Eastern Europe. Her work has been published in journals such as *The Journal of Human Rights, Forced Migration Review, Human Rights Review* and *The Journal of Human Rights Practice.*

Lodoe Laura is a multidisciplinary artist living and working in Toronto, Canada. Through photography, performance, printmaking and video, she has examined themes of cultural crossover, collective memory and the intersection of cultural and political practice. Lodoe Laura holds a BFA in Photography from Ryerson University, and is an MA Candidate in the Film and Photography Preservation and Collections Management programme at Ryerson University.

Patti Tamara Lenard is Associate Professor of Applied Ethics in the Graduate School of Public and International Affairs, at the University of Ottawa. Her current research focuses on the moral questions raised by migration across borders, and she is particularly interested in the challenges posed by 'non-standard' migrants, including child migrants, victims of trafficking, stateless individuals and foreign fighters. She is the author of *Trust, Democracy and Multicultural Challenges* (Penn State, 2012) and her work has been published in a range of journals, including *Political Studies, Politics, Journal of Moral Philosophy* and *Contemporary Political Theory*. She is the co-editor, with Christine Straehle, of *Health Inequalities and Global Justice* (Edinburgh University Press) as well as *Legislated Inequality: Temporary Labour Migration in Canada* (McGill-Queen's University Press).

Subin Mulmi is an Advocate of Law working at the Forum for Women, Law and Development (FWLD), a non-profit human rights organisation in Nepal, and an independent researcher who has conducted research on issues of citizenship, statelessness and the rights of women. He is the co-author of

Acquisition of Citizenship Certificate in Nepal: Estimation and Projection (FWLD, 2015) and *Legal Analysis of the Citizenship Law of Nepal* (FWLD, 2016). A human rights lawyer working on issues of gender equality and statelessness, he is currently engaged in research on women's economic empowerment in Nepal and the status of civil registration in Nepal.

Oscar Gakuo Mwangi is an Associate Professor at the Department of Political and Administrative Studies, National University of Lesotho. His research interests are in comparative politics, especially in the areas of democratisation, governance, conflict and security, and environmental politics in eastern and southern Africa. The research interests are mainly in the context of statehood, particularly state collapse and state fragility. He is the author of several published book chapters as well as articles in internationally refereed journals such as *African Security Review*, *The Journal of Modern African Studies*, *Journal of Southern African Studies*, *Politics, Religion and Ideology*, *The Round Table: The Commonwealth of International Affairs* and *Review of African Political Economy*. His teaching areas are in the fields of Comparative Politics, International Relations and Political Economy. He also taught Political Science at the University of Nairobi.

David Passarelli is based in Tokyo, Japan and Oxford, UK. He is Executive Officer of the United Nations University (UNU). Since 2016, he has been engaged in the strategic coordination of UNU's chairmanship of the Global Migration Group. He has contributed to the research programme of the United Nations University Institute on Globalization, Culture and Mobility as an Honorary Associate Research Fellow, working predominantly on issues related to statelessness and irregular migration. He is completing a doctoral degree at the Oxford Department of International Development, Oxford University, where his research focuses on the rights of irregular migrant children to education.

Sara Shneiderman is Assistant Professor in Anthropology and the Institute of Asian Research at the University of British Columbia. She is the author of *Rituals of Ethnicity: Thangmi Identities Between Nepal and India* (University of Pennsylvania Press, 2015). A socio-cultural anthropologist working in the Himalayan regions of Nepal, India and China's Tibetan Autonomous Region, her research explores the relationships between political discourse, ritual action and cross-border mobility in producing ethnic identities and shaping social transformation. Current research projects include an ethnography of 'post-conflict' state restructuring in Nepal, with a focus on citizenship, territory and religiosity, and an exploration of trans-Himalayan citizenship across the historical and contemporary borders of India, China and Nepal.

Kelly Staples is Lecturer in International Politics at the University of Leicester. She was awarded her PhD by the University of Manchester in 2008 for a thesis on statelessness and political theory, the starting point for her 2012 book, *Retheorising Statelessness: A Background Theory of Membership in World Politics* (Edinburgh University Press, 2012). She has also published articles on recognition, statelessness and migration. Her current research is on subjectivity in international relations, and on the meaning of international protection.

Katja Swider is a Doctoral Researcher at the law faculty of the University of Amsterdam, working on her PhD thesis 'Statelessness Identification in Europe'. The thesis is supervised by Professor René de Groot and Professor Leonard Besselink and funded by the Netherlands Organisation for Scientific Research (NWO). Katja holds an LLM degree in European Law from Leiden University and an LLM in Legal Research from the University of Utrecht. In addition to studying statelessness, Katja supports NGOs, lawyers and governments in addressing statelessness in practice. She advises national stakeholders on drafting statelessness-related legislation, supports legal practitioners in litigating cases on statelessness and participates in various advocacy initiatives in this field. Katja has previously volunteered for the Dutch Red Cross as a legal advisor for victims of human trafficking. Since 2014, she has been an Advisory Committee member of the European Network on Statelessness.

Katherine Tonkiss is a Lecturer in Sociology at Aston University. She is interested in noncitizenship, particularly in terms of identity and belonging, and has explored these issues from both theoretical and applied perspectives in scholarly journals including *Citizenship Studies* and the *Journal of Ethnic and Migration Studies*. Katherine's book, *Migration and Identity in a Post-National World*, was published by Palgrave Macmillan in 2013. In it, she explores the implications of open borders migration rights for the negotiation of identity and belonging. This analysis has gone on to underpin her collaborative work with international colleagues on the theoretical conceptualisation of noncitizenship. She is also interested in political and policy-oriented perspectives on migration, and is currently researching the policy narratives of migration charities in the UK and Australia as well as exploring the implications of 'superdiversity' for policy and governance in Europe.

Jason Tucker is a postdoctoral researcher at the Malmö Institute for Studies of Migration, Diversity and Welfare (MIM), Malmö University, Sweden. He received his PhD from the University of Bath in 2014, which considered global citizenship and statelessness in Lebanon. Following this he has worked on statelessness for UNHCR, civil society, and as an independent researcher. His current research focuses on the indefinite statelessness of refugees in Denmark and Sweden. He is also working on research that explores the development of UNHCR's policy relating to stateless refugees and the long-term impact of the refugee 'crisis' on statelessness in Europe.

Caia Vlieks is a PhD candidate and lecturer at Tilburg Law School in the Netherlands. She also obtained her master's degrees in international and European public law and legal research *cum laude* in Tilburg. Both of her prize-winning master's theses were on the issue of statelessness in Europe. Her PhD research focuses on European legal instruments addressing the prevention and resolution of statelessness against the backdrop of the changing conceptions of nationality and citizenship. She is also an individual member of the European Network on Statelessness (ENS), and has published for instance on the protection of stateless persons under the Dutch 'no-fault' policy and on litigating for statelessness determination under the European Convention on Human Rights.

Laura van Waas is Co-Director of the Institute on Statelessness and Inclusion and an Assistant Professor at Tilburg Law School in the Netherlands. Laura is the author of *Nationality Matters – Statelessness under International Law* (2008), an in-depth analysis of the international normative framework relating to statelessness, alongside numerous other academic publications on nationality and statelessness. She has worked for UNHCR on several successive statelessness projects: drafting public information materials, developing training programmes and delivering training on statelessness, and undertaking comparative regional research of statelessness situations. She has also been commissioned to undertake research or provide training for a number of other international organisations.

Foreword

Matthew J. Gibney

In a 1970 essay entitled 'Prisoners of War', the political theorist Michael Walzer characterised the plight of the stateless refugee in paradoxical terms. Those without a state, Walzer suggested, experienced both 'a special kind of helplessness' and 'an unaccountable and peculiar freedom' (Walzer 1970, 147). The 'helplessness' of the stateless stemmed from the fact that lacking the protections and standing associated with formal membership in a political community, they were subject to the caprice of those who ruled over them. Their 'freedom', on the other hand, was evident in the fact that they were unencumbered by any of the obligations and duties of citizenship.

For Walzer, this paradox was largely theoretical and basically nugatory in practice. The actual conditions faced by the stateless – impoverishment, desperation, insecurity – showed all too well the 'wretchedness' of the freedom associated with their plight. Theirs was a kind of freedom, Walzer writes, that anyone would rapidly exchange for the 'membership and protection' of a state, in spite of the many 'restraints' membership imposes.

It is a welcome feature of this work, deftly edited by Tendayi Bloom, Katherine Tonkiss and Phillip Cole, and with an impressive and thoughtful group of contributors, that it helps us to see unblinkingly the paradox that Michael Walzer clearly identified but promptly closed down. The chapters of this volume illuminate this paradox by taking the important but often ignored phenomenon of statelessness seriously both as a source of danger and precariousness – of helplessness, to put it in Walzer's terms – and as a site of struggle and questioning of the relationship between individuals and political authority.

There is, of course, no doubting the hardships that are typically associated with statelessness, and this work fulfils a desperate need to understand them better. Statelessness is often a tracer of the existence of marginalised ethnic and social groups that face discrimination, violence and rejection. The exclusion of their members from formal recognition as citizens in the country where they have made their lives typically represents a crowning injustice on the top of many others. The stateless face a more general injustice inflicted upon them by the international system of states, too, of course. No matter where they are they must live under the authority of a state, yet they have no (practically enforceable) entitlement to citizenship anywhere.

Yet to follow Walzer and characterise the stateless as 'helpless' seems strangely shy of the mark. It ignores the fact that when people have been stateless for an extended period (and some groups, it is worth noting, have been stateless for generations) they have no choice but to get on with their lives as best they can. They must eke out a living, make themselves a home, and, in some cases, sustain a sense of collective identity. Inevitably, they must, as communities, also strive politically to articulate and protect their interests and needs in the face of state power. This has led some groups of stateless people, such as the Palestinians and the Kurds, into becoming significant actors in international politics.

Walzer's characterisation also seems ill-fitted to describe those vulnerable people who, in desperation, have used statelessness as a way to improve their situation. Consider, for example, that some asylum seekers have in recent years destroyed their passports and even burnt off their own fingerprints to prevent their deportation from Europe. In situations like these, an informal form of statelessness (the concealment of nationality) has offered refugees and migrants a rough and ready way of foiling attempts by states effectively to confine them to countries where they do not want to be. As Audrey Macklin has noted, statelessness confounds states because it creates people who have no 'return address' (2015, 4).

This last example offers one powerful reason why, in spite of the evident dangers of a life without citizenship, the association between statelessness and freedom has stubbornly refused to disappear in the years since Walzer wrote. When Walzer described the stateless as escaping citizenship's 'restraints', he had in mind the onerous duties that sometimes come with citizenship. The most important of these – still operative in many countries – is the duty to undertake military service (and *in extremis* even to die for the state). The fact that this duty has lain behind the exodus of young men from Eritrea in recent years reminds us of how severe the price of citizenship can still be.

Yet perhaps the most salient contemporary 'restraint' provided by citizenship lies not in the obligations such membership imposes but in the way nationality binds people – often unwillingly – to particular territories, preventing them from moving to another country. This restraint, cemented in place by a world of sovereign states jealously controlling immigration, would perhaps matter little if citizenship in the world's poorer countries delivered more. But in many states citizenship does not even guarantee an individual's basic human rights, let alone ensure he or she will be able to live their life with a semblance of economic security. In a world of egregious inequalities between states, citizenship itself can be a form of imprisonment as much as a site of freedom.

The key point is that if being stateless is virtually always worse than being a citizen somewhere, the gap between the two can be quite small. For this reason, the challenge is not simply to decry the fact that states unjustly refuse to recognise some people as their own or to articulate the rights of people everywhere to enjoy state membership somewhere. It is to generate empirically honest accounts of the lived experience of those who *lack* – as well as those who *possess* – citizenship and to use them to consider how individual states and, perhaps, the state system itself need to be rethought to make membership more meaningful, secure and legitimate. I can think of no better starting point for this difficult task than the insightful chapters that follow.

References

Macklin, A. (2015) 'Introduction', in Macklin, A. and Baubõck, R. *The Return of Banishment*, EUI Working Paper, No. 14.

Walzer, M. (1970) *Obligations: Essays on Disobedience, War and Citizenship*. Cambridge, MA: Harvard University Press.

Acknowledgements

This project was made possible through the hard work and commitment of many people and we would like to extend our thanks to all of them – both those we have named below and those we have not referred to by name.

It has been wonderful to work with such a committed team of authors and artists – and such an interesting group of individuals. Their expertise, enthusiasm, dedication and collegiality have been crucial, both to the quality of their individual chapters, and to the way the book has come together as a whole. Despite hectic schedules and across multiple time zones, they have worked hard to ensure a coherent and cohesive book, receptive to comments and generous with suggestions. Everyone's commitment to the project and generosity has been inspiring and each contribution plays a vital role within the resulting volume.

The book as you see it today would not have been possible, however, without the thoroughness, tirelessness and diligence of Janina Pescinski. Her work as an exemplary copyeditor, reference-checker and much more throughout the production of this book has been crucial to ensuring the quality of the text in its current form. All of the authors, artists and editors are indebted to her and we take this opportunity to thank her publicly.

The idea for this book emerged out of a series of panels at the United Nations University Institute on Globalization, Culture and Mobility 2014 Conference on Statelessness and Transcontinental Migration in Barcelona and we would like to thank all those who participated in the conference for their generous debate and discussion of the issues involved. The work was further developed at the European Consortium for Political Research Annual Conference in 2015, held at the Université de Montréal in Canada, where the book project again benefited from an engaged and challenging discussion. The chapters in this book have been presented to audiences around the world and we thank everyone that has listened to, read, commented upon them and given time in other ways to help us bring the book to completion.

Finally, the book you are reading would have been impossible without Lydia de Cruz, Matt Deacon, Tony Hirst, Nicola Parkin, and their many behind-the-scenes colleagues at Routledge. Everyone involved in this project is grateful to them for their patience, their flexibility, and their good humour throughout the process.

Thank you.

1 Introduction

Providing a framework for understanding statelessness

Tendayi Bloom, Katherine Tonkiss and Phillip Cole

Formerly man had only a body and soul. Now he needs a passport as well, for without it he will not be treated as a human being.

(Stefan Zweig in *The World of Yesterday*, recalling the words of a Russian émigré)

Introduction

The above quotation from author Stefan Zweig is possibly his most famous, often cited when talking about statelessness (e.g. see Pouilly 2007, p. 19). However, it is most usefully seen in the context of the text directly preceding it. Before recalling the words above, Zweig reflects on how at one time he was an Austrian citizen, never questioning that he should be treated by officials and law enforcers alike as a gentleman and as 'a citizen in good standing' (Zweig 1964, p. 413). Back then, Zweig recounts, he had reflected on the beauty in statelessness, in not being beholden to any country. He recalls that he only really understood the folly of this on the day he experienced the visceral reality of statelessness for himself. It was on the day that he found himself no longer an Austrian citizen, petitioning an English official for papers (Zweig 1964, p. 413). From that moment on, he was treated with suspicion, 'because all countries were suspicious of the sort of people of which I had suddenly become one, of the outlaws, of the men without a country' (Zweig 1964, p. 413). From one day to the next, Zweig was transformed from someone with a strong relationship with a member of the community of States to someone with no such relationship. In that transition, Zweig was confronted with a realignment of his position in the world – of the assumptions about his eligibility for rights and for legal personhood. It was at that moment, Zweig recounts, that he was reminded of these words which had been told to him some years before, and which he had not fully understood at the time.

For those of us with a functioning and protective citizenship, it is hard to imagine quite how important this is for our lives, and indeed it is even uncomfortable to do so. Perhaps this is one reason why statelessness has been so understudied, under-acknowledged and allowed to continue to cause problems for those affected. Yet in order to understand statelessness it is important to consider what it means for stateless persons, how persons become stateless and how they experience their statelessness. It is also important to examine how statelessness is created, how it persists and why it brings with it the deprivations it does. While much of the recent literature, both scholarly and practitioner-focused, has built upon the assumption that citizenship acquisition is the principal appropriate remedy for the problems associated with statelessness, this book finds the situation to be more complex. It focuses on understanding contemporary statelessness in historical and geographical terms. It explores how to move forward in such a way that most relieves the difficulties experienced by stateless persons, and at the same time emphasises the rational autonomy and individuality of stateless and potentially stateless persons themselves. The inclusion in this volume of six carefully selected photographs provides another route through which to challenge existing discourses and explore the reality of statelessness today.

The purpose of this introductory chapter is to locate the contents of the book which follows within wider discourses on statelessness and noncitizenship, to explain the contributions of the book's chapters to the study of statelessness from this perspective and to draw on these contributions to offer a call-to-action agenda for future research which can continue the project of building questions of statelessness into the theorisation of rights and justice and, in turn, the question of justice into policy approaches based upon a deeper understanding of statelessness as it is lived today.

Statelessness: a pressing concern

The standard definition categorises a person as 'stateless' if he or she is a noncitizen everywhere. For the most part, statelessness in this book is understood in this way, though with examination also of the implications of stateless spaces (e.g. Mwangi, this volume) and stateless peoples (e.g. Bloom, this volume), for example. Statelessness is complex and multi-faceted, and this book finds that there is no singular appropriate way to respond. Part of the reason for this is that statelessness arises for many different reasons in different contexts and at different times. For example, members of some groups found themselves stateless when the construction of the modern State system after the World Wars failed to accommodate them, such as members of the Roma community in Europe or Kurds in the Middle East. Others are stateless in the aftermath of empire and decolonisation, such as Palestinians and the Tamils of Northern Sri Lanka. In some regions women experience discrimination in this or other areas which can lead to statelessness in unexpected ways, particularly when combined with administrative problems (Al Barazi and Tucker, this volume; Mulmi and Schneiderman, this volume). Still others fall into statelessness because of a mismatch in citizenship laws, or because of international events such as State collapse, or changes in law. There are also laws which permit the removal of individuals' citizenship through denationalisation, potentially rendering them stateless (Gibney 2013).

It is generally agreed that for the most part statelessness carries with it privations and vulnerabilities that are deeply problematic, arising from the exclusion of stateless persons from the formal apparatus of States. Yet at the same time, and often neglected in debates around statelessness, it is more than merely a status of victimhood. As contributions in this book demonstrate, stateless persons should not be generally seen as passive victims of circumstance; rather, their diverse and complex ways of engaging with States and asserting claims need to be recognised. Stateless persons often navigate new forms of individual–State relationships, and examining those strategies of stateless persons draws attention to the diversity of forms of such relationships that exist, and the diversity of levels of membership that shape our political reality (Passarelli, this volume). A further complexity in the study of statelessness is that it intersects with other sources of exclusion, such as xenophobia (Kingston, this volume), which may act as a driving force of racialised policies towards some citizens (Blake, this volume). For others, aspects of statelessness arise in the claiming of memberships in the face of colonisation (Bloom, this volume).

Basic information about the global situation of statelessness is not comprehensive, with data notoriously sparse. The United Nations High Commissioner for Refugees (UNHCR), within whose mandate stateless persons fall, keeps the most thorough global data, providing figures on reported numbers of stateless persons in 78 countries around the world (UNHCR 2015), though even data for these countries are unlikely to catch everyone affected in the countries concerned (ISI 2014). For example, these data may miss information relating to some groups whose members experience entrenched statelessness, responsibility for which is extremely contentious and difficult to address. While it is important to look beyond numbers, they can help to frame the situation. While UNHCR extrapolates from its data for 78 countries that there are probably at least ten million stateless persons globally (UNHCR 2015 – extrapolating from 3.7 million individuals 'recorded by governments and communicated to UNHCR'), others argue that the number is probably significantly higher (ISI 2014), and little is known of their circumstances. With so little basic knowledge available, the paucity of theoretical literature is part of a wider gap in understanding. In turn, while statelessness remains under-discussed, the pressure and resources for better reporting and analysis will also remain weak. Frustratingly, we know that there are stateless persons, but the various and complex forms statelessness can take evade our current ways of accounting for it and theorising about it.

In 2014, UNHCR launched its ten-year #IBelong Campaign to end statelessness by 2024, and several initiatives aimed at improving data on statelessness have been developed, including the ISI *The World's Stateless* report (ISI, 2014) and the forthcoming Academics Stand Against Poverty (ASAP) Report on Statelessness and Development. Each of these tries in different ways to develop a better overview of statelessness and to mainstream consideration of how statelessness impacts upon human rights and development respectively. In this book, then, the intention is not only to provide a re-examination of the theoretical approaches to statelessness but to offer analyses of contexts of statelessness

which are insufficiently understood in the literature and which challenge ortho-
doxy in the debates surrounding statelessness.

The state of statelessness research

It is possible to trace out three key moments in thinking about statelessness:
(1) after the end of the Second World War, with statelessness as exception; (2) at
the beginning of the twenty-first century, with statelessness as phenomenon; and
(3) more recently, with statelessness seen as endemic in, or even symptomatic
of, modernity.

In the aftermath of the Second World War, concern about statelessness was
most famously enunciated by Hannah Arendt, herself both a political theorist
and a stateless person. Indeed, Arendt's work is often taken as the 'canon' for
contemporary theorisations of statelessness. However, as is argued in this book,
it is necessary to look beyond Arendt's 'right to have rights' to re-examine the
relevance of her work to contemporary debates about statelessness (Blitz, this
volume). In the 20 years or so after the end of the Second World War, which
was also an important period of decolonisation and global refocusing, the discourse around statelessness seems to have included a sense of surprise. That is,
statelessness is seen as an exceptional aspect of a unique moment in history, and
something that can be fixed. This thinking is evidenced, for example, in the
works of Paul Weis (a Harvard academic and lawyer) and Gerrit Jan van Heuven
Goedhart (the first High Commissioner for Refugees), who were involved in the
drafting of the Statelessness Conventions (van Heuven Goedhart 1955; Weis
1961, 1962; for discussion see also Goodwin-Gill 2011).

In the 1990s and 2000s a new global landscape was developing. This was the
period after the dissolution of the Soviet Union, and then the period after the 9/11
attacks in the US. In the late 2000s, a new discourse around statelessness was
beginning to emerge, coinciding with, but distinct from, developments in theorisations of migration. For migration scholars, 2008 is known for Joseph Carens'
symposium and special issue of *Ethics and International Affairs* considering the
rights of irregular migrants, and this was also a key time for renewed engagement
with statelessness. Within a widening discourse challenging the assumed scope of
liberal theory's *demos* were a number of important papers from around the same
time (e.g. Gibney 2006; Frelick and Lynch 2005; Goris *et al.* 2009). Emerging at
the end of that period, Kelly Staples' 2012 book, *Retheorising Statelessness*, can
be seen as the first book-length sustained attempt to use statelessness to critique
the contemporary global framework. Meanwhile, others were drawing attention
to the wider problems associated directly with the non-membership of stateless
persons (e.g. Sawyer and Blitz 2011; Blitz and Lynch 2012), and to localised
meanings of statelessness on the ground following crises including the break-up
of the Soviet Union and of Yugoslavia (e.g. Blitz and Otero-Iglesias 2011).
Added to this, processes of denationalisation were becoming the subject of sustained theoretical consideration as a specific and increasingly prominent form of
statelessness (Gibney 2013; Hidalgo 2014).

The years from 2013 to 2016 have seen a substantial realignment of global approaches to citizenship and migration. This has included the development of a new approach to statelessness, including new global agreements and commitments. The 2014 UNHCR campaign mentioned above can be seen as part of this. This has involved a rethinking of systems inherited from the past, with increasing numbers of theorists and activists seeing statelessness as endemic rather than exceptional. This book sits within this third wave, but takes it a step further. Overall it characterises statelessness as perhaps even arising from the very structure of the international State system rather than a problem that can be solved by that system. Statelessness challenges the structure of the international State system and perhaps even the foundations of liberal political theory itself, so that we must look beyond the limits of these frameworks if we are going to begin to address those challenges.

Theorising statelessness

Statelessness poses a considerable challenge for dominant understandings of State-based liberal justice. It is deeply problematic for liberal understandings of justice that a significant proportion of the world's population lives in a situation of disenfranchisement constructed by the liberal State system that was supposed to ensure universal rights and shared development (Cole, this volume). This deep and troubling challenge may account for the scarcity of discussions of statelessness in the political theoretical literature, but failing to talk about a problem as fundamental as this will not make it any less pressing. This book then also emerges out of a worry in the minds of the authors that the continuation of statelessness not only represents a troubling exclusion from rights and development for the individuals concerned but also, if not properly addressed, undermines the project of liberal political theory itself.

Theoretical disciplines in the social sciences concerned with rights and justice have been slow to address the implications of statelessness for rights, human development and the nature of States and individual–State relationships. This includes analysing statelessness not only in the abstract, but in light of its varied causes and consequences in different geographical regions. Crucially, it also requires a critical approach to the common discourses around statelessness. This book adopts a political theory which engages with a range of social sciences and humanities disciplines in order to understand the realities of statelessness today.

While few political theorists have engaged directly with statelessness, there is a broad and growing analysis of membership, identity and citizenship within the discipline. Work examining exclusions arising from migration in particular provides a useful basis for thinking about statelessness from the perspective of political theory. In this field, theorists have drawn attention to the inability of work on ethics and justice to take into account the questions raised by migration. For example, this includes critiquing the ethics of controlling migration, which can be viewed as excluding persons from access to basic rights on arbitrary grounds (Carens 1987, 2013; Risse 2008; Verlinden 2010) and the contradictions of the liberal state in permitting such exclusion (Bosniak 2008; Cole 2000; Rubio-Marin 2000). These concerns have been taken up by sociologists examining the dynamics of marginalisation and exclusion perpetuated by contemporary citizenship regimes (Isin 2004; Nyers 2006; Rygiel 2011; Sigona 2005, 2012), and by cosmopolitan theorists who have sought the extension of citizenship and justice beyond state boundaries to better account for the rights of migrants, particularly in the context of vast and dramatic global inequalities of wealth and resources (Bauböck 2007; Cabrera 2010; Caney 2006; Pogge 2010). However, the focus has predominantly been on migration, and on lack of status insofar as it is a consequence of this.

This book also sits within this theoretical tradition but moves away from the prior emphasis on migration. It follows on the heels of another volume, *Theorising Noncitizenship* (Tonkiss and Bloom 2015, republished in 2016), which can be seen in many ways as this book's precursor. That book sought to re-examine the structures that allow such forms of disenfranchisement and dehumanisation to occur. Building upon this, the current volume applies this approach to the question of statelessness and contributes to a burgeoning literature examining statelessness (e.g. Aggarwal 2014). It draws on the real-world experience of statelessness to deconstruct assumptions and consider the ways in which the liberal State system both theoretically and in reality contributes to the exclusion of stateless persons from considerations of rights and justice.

Structure of the book

The three parts of this book carry the reader through three broad ways of thinking about the topic. First, the book presents the theoretical, legal and political concept of statelessness through the work of leading critical thinkers in this area. Then, it offers a critique of the existing framework through the in-depth and theoretically-based presentation of some particularly challenging contexts of statelessness in the real world. The final section of the book provides chapters that offer some suggested ways forward, based on the foregoing analyses. Each chapter offers an original and challenging approach to thinking about statelessness, contributing in different ways to the development of a theoretical approach that can better support more just policy development. Collectively, the chapters are designed to define statelessness, to explore how it is lived in the real world and to examine the consequences of this for how we think about rights and justice both in this context and more broadly. The book is divided accordingly into three sections, with each focusing on one of these dimensions, though all of the chapters do, to a greater or lesser extent, engage across all three. Recognising that thinking about statelessness must cut across multiple disciplines, the collected chapters are also deliberately interdisciplinary and transdisciplinary in nature, bringing together a diverse range of legal, sociological, applied and theoretical perspectives, as well as visual artists, to contribute to the understanding of statelessness from as broad a knowledge base as possible.

The book opened with a photograph, taken in Bangladesh by Saiful Huq Omi. In it, Huq Omi's colleague, collaborator and guide, Abul Kalam, himself a

Rohingya human rights activist, indicates towards Myanmar, where his family lives. Kalam is telling Huq Omi that because he is stateless and because he is Rohingya, travelling from Bangladesh to Myanmar, where he has family, is impossible.

Part I: defining statelessness

This first part contributes primarily to the definition of statelessness as a concept. The section opens with a triptych photograph of Rasha Khalil, taken in Borj El Barajneh Palestinian Camp, Beirut, produced by visual artist John Halaka. Khalil has explained to Halaka the impact that being born stateless has had on her life. Khalil has developed a puppet theatre for children living in Borj El Barajneh and sees this as an important way both to deal with the difficulties of statelessness and to maintain her sense of Palestinian identity, as well as that of the children with whom she works. The situation for stateless Palestinians is sometimes considered to be an archetypal case of statelessness. As becomes clear in this first section, this is part of a now complex and diverse global landscape of statelessness.

Lindsey Kingston begins the written contributions to this part of the book by building on the notion that statelessness is primarily structural. She argues that it is in fact both a symptom and a cause of marginalisation. In this way, she shows how a right to citizenship itself may be insufficient in addressing deprivations faced by stateless persons. Kingston demonstrates how, for the most part, statelessness primarily affects those who already fall within marginalised groups, suffering systematic discrimination. From this position she argues that stateless persons require an active and mutually beneficial relationship with a government, and that nationality law can only provide a first step in a journey towards this. Kingston's chapter demonstrates the complex nature of deprivation and the ways in which different structural barriers intersect to exclude stateless persons, highlighting the shortcomings of a simplistic legal definition.

This is not, of course, to diminish the importance of analysing the legal definition of statelessness as the deprivation of citizenship, and the following two chapters turn their attention to this. The first of these, from Caia Vlieks, considers a critical distinction in the literature on statelessness between statelessness *in situ*, where it is experienced by a person in his or her 'own country', and statelessness in the migratory context, where statelessness is experienced by persons who have migrated. Crucially, Vlieks shows that these two forms of statelessness call for different responses, while at the same time demonstrating that there are difficulties in applying the definition of each statelessness concept in individual cases.

The 'slipperiness' of the concept of statelessness is picked up by Laura van Waas and Amal de Chickera. They provide a detailed analysis of the conceptual blurring of statelessness and related sources of marginalisation, arguing for the central importance of the legal definition of statelessness in order to locate it as a distinct issue requiring a specific and targeted response. On first reading, the chapters by both Vlieks and van Waas and de Chickera may appear to be at odds with that of Kingston, and the following one of Brad K. Blitz, and there are certainly some useful moments of contention. However, for the project as a whole, the issues of the legal, political and social realities of statelessness do not need to be seen as mutually exclusive. Instead, they usefully speak to each other, demonstrating the importance of an interdisciplinary research agenda for statelessness which can examine the phenomenon from a range of perspectives – and which can bring together insights from across disciplinary specialism and focus in order to develop the most appropriate response.

It is traditional to begin thinking about statelessness by considering the world of Hannah Arendt, but in the final chapter of this part Blitz does not take a typical approach to Arendt's treatment of statelessness. While acknowledging that her work has been central to the definition of statelessness and appropriate responses to the challenges it presents, Blitz's chapter offers a critical reading of work by Arendt and her contemporaries alongside an analysis of contemporary realities of statelessness. Counter to Arendt's legal approach, Blitz defines statelessness as structural, requiring solutions beyond the simplistic reform of nationality law. His focus on the potential for contestation and change within the States in which stateless persons live sets the scene for the remainder of the book.

Part II: living statelessness

Having set out some critical issues in the conceptual definition of statelessness from a range of disciplinary perspectives, the second part of the book develops this through in-depth analyses of the particular challenges raised through some localised situations of statelessness. It examines the theoretical issues that arise through consideration of the realities of statelessness in very different contexts across global regions and in different local frameworks. Logan Abassi's photograph of a kite being flown in a camp for displaced persons from the Dominican Republic on the outskirts of a town called Anse a Pitre in the north-eastern part of Haiti helps to open the discussion. The camp is home to many former residents of the Dominican Republic who have been identified as being of Haitian heritage. This includes persons deported from the Dominican Republic, including those who are stateless or at risk of statelessness.

The six chapters of this part offer contextual analyses of different dimensions of contemporary statelessness. It raises issues of race, governance, indigeneity, nationality, gender and colonisation, as well as the implications of conflict. It also examines the relevance, and relative success, of regional or global approaches. Each chapter uncovers aspects relating to the specifics of the case, but it is found that these also raise broader questions relating to statelessness in the twenty-first century.

The first chapter, from Zahra Al Barazi and Jason Tucker, presents the evolving and complex situation of statelessness in the Middle East and North Africa region (MENA). In this region, statelessness often arises as a dynamic response to a constellation of features. For example, while gender discrimination in passing on citizenship makes the children of mothers married to foreign husbands stateless in several countries, the effects of conflict and human mobility exacerbate this situation as children displaced with their mothers may struggle to prove their fathers' nationalities. This region is also home to several minority groups who experience inherited statelessness, both with and across MENA States, such as groups of Kurds and Palestinians. Al Barazi and Tucker explain that there is not a coherent approach to the complex situation of statelessness in the MENA region and suggest ways in which examining this could help in fostering a deeper understanding of statelessness more generally.

Following this, Jillian Blake's chapter examines the situation for persons identified as being of Haitian descent living in the Dominican Republic, which involves an interplay of race, national identity, indigeneity and illegality to define people out of rights. Blake argues that the Dominican Republic government has used the notion that people are 'passing through' to remove their citizenship and that this fits within a wider discussion of race and citizenship in the Dominican Republic and in the Caribbean. This is followed by Oscar Mwangi's analysis of the situation for Somalis living in Kenya, including Kenyan citizens of Somali heritage, Somali refugees and stateless people of Somali heritage. Mwangi argues that in this Kenyan case there are stateless spaces and there is statelessness as experienced by those living in spaces beyond the control of the State or the State system. He explores the impact of this upon formally stateless persons, but also upon those who have formal Kenyan citizenship.

Both Mwangi and Blake show how the tension between the 'migratory' and '*in situ*' contexts of statelessness can derive more from definition than facts on the ground. They show how a complex understanding of race and nationhood interplay with this in the construction of outsiderness and so statelessness. Mwangi takes this further, drawing attention also to how the fact of statelessness among Somalis and the way in which stateless Somalis are treated within the Kenyan political context affects many more individuals' connection to the Kenyan State, with implications also for broader questions about sovereignty and national security. He shows the dynamic interplay of governance, space and security in the construction of statelessness.

This is followed by a photograph produced by Greg Constantine. Taken in Nepal, this image shows three Dalit people who walk long distances carrying bundles of firewood to sell at market. The Dalit community is one of several vulnerable groups whose members are often stateless in Nepal. This image also sets the scene for the next chapter. Subin Mulmi and Sara Shneiderman present a context of statelessness in Nepal which is uncontroversially characterised as *in situ*. They argue that it is relatively novel to apply the language of statelessness to the populations that are most at risk of statelessness in Nepal, such as orphans, mentally ill persons and divorced women. Their analysis draws attention to a potential mismatch between official citizenship policies and those who are actually able to call upon their citizenship status. In doing so, they raise uncomfortable questions for the relationship between the construction of the Nepali nation and the construction of the Nepali citizenry. Importantly, Mulmi and Shneiderman also show how it is the most vulnerable Nepali 'citizens' who find themselves actively excluded from the citizenship rights that are often seen in liberal theory as intended to protect precisely those most vulnerable persons.

The remaining chapters of this part draw more explicit attention to the active rights-claiming and political structures associated with stateless populations. This starts with Tendayi Bloom's analysis of specific questions raised by contexts of colonisation, which examines the political nature of citizenship and statelessness in settler States, with a focus on those of North America. While not claiming that the people she describes are *stateless*, Bloom argues that there is a tension between the rights entitlements tied to citizenship and reinforcement of the status quo. She argues that members of colonised groups may face a pseudo choice between statelessness, or partial statelessness (with its associated vulnerabilities), and embracing an imposed colonial citizenship (and its associated rights). Bloom uses this to demonstrate the critical importance of disrupting simple binary assumptions in academic studies of statelessness as well as the need to examine what citizenship, noncitizenship and statelessness mean for the individuals concerned, prioritising individual rights-claiming over citizenship.

Kelly Staples completes this part with an examination of the UNHCR approach to statelessness, specifically analysing the agency's Global Action Plan on Statelessness. Through her analysis, Staples demonstrates that the approach underpinning the plan, particularly with regard to identification, registration and documentation, overlooks significant challenges relating to the persistent stigmatisation of, and discrimination against, minority populations. She argues as a result that it is necessary to challenge the 'myth' that the State system can ever provide a universal equal status of citizenship. Through her chapter Staples demonstrates the intersecting and interrelated dynamics of marginalisation and exclusion in the contemporary State system, and she suggests that new ways are needed both to research statelessness and, based on this, to come to understand it.

Part III: theorising statelessness

The final part of the book offers a response. It draws from the first two parts to suggest a series of theoretical reflections on the position of statelessness within political theory. It opens with a photograph taken by Lodoe Laura. It shows her father looking through the lens of her camera at the most important Tibetan Buddhist monument outside Tibet. In the absence of a Tibetan citizenship, many Tibetans are stateless, while others have complex relationships with other citizenships outside Tibet. This image begins this final part of the book, in which a lens is turned on theory itself.

In the first chapter of this part, Katja Swider follows on from Staples' chapter to offer a direct critique of citizenship acquisition as the principal remedy for the problems associated with statelessness. Staples takes an institutional overview and Swider's analysis provides a bridge between this and the theoretical framing of the chapters of the final part. Drawing on experiences of statelessness in the Netherlands, Latvia and the post-Soviet space, Swider identifies problems inherent in international policy goals which prioritise the reduction of statelessness over the identification and protection of stateless persons, and the ways in which these two sets of goals can come into tension in the real world.

This is followed by David Passarelli's presentation of how the duty of municipal authorities towards stateless persons within their jurisdictions can be seen as a form of fiduciary duty. For the most part, municipal authorities do not have the jurisdiction to control State membership, nor do they wield the power of the State itself. As such, the municipal authority is a particularly interesting site for constructing obligation. In focusing on this level, Passarelli consciously strips away the tools that can usually be used by political theorists and others in order to understand the obligation of a political entity towards stateless persons. He argues that it is the very vulnerability itself and the person's physical presence and participation that activates a fiduciary obligation in the municipal authorities.

Focusing on the situation of stateless children, and in particular children who are stateless in a migratory context, Patti Lenard draws on moral theory concerning the vulnerability of children to present a systematic argument that such children should have easy access to citizenship and that this in turn requires that their parents also have access to a regularised status. She then works to establish a right to citizenship for both children and parents on the basis of both the vulnerability of children and the right to family unity, giving rise to citizenship rights for their parents as derivative from those of their children. In focusing on the situation of children in the migratory context in particular, Lenard's chapter offers a normative theorisation of the theme of vulnerability running throughout the volume.

Katherine Tonkiss and Phillip Cole then take a step further back, to look at stateless populations in general and the implications for political theory of acknowledging and addressing the fact of their existence. Tonkiss takes as her focus the role of nationality in defining, researching and theorising statelessness. She exposes the ways in which academic literature and international law in this area both explicitly and implicitly assume the interchangeability of nationality and citizenship. Tonkiss argues that this leads them to support the performance of what she terms 'citizenship-as-nationality', which she presents as problematic in the context of statelessness. She proposes that an alternative post-national frame for examining statelessness could respond to the challenges found in the specific cases considered throughout this volume. In interrogating the notion of national citizenship at the heart of discourses on statelessness, Tonkiss reveals the critical importance of exposing such ideas to critique in the theorisation of statelessness.

In the final chapter, Phillip Cole adopts what he terms a 'radically theoretical' perspective to expose and interrogate the assumptions about the political systems in which we live which sit at the heart of political theory and to problematise these from the perspective of statelessness. He takes liberal political theory itself as the object of inquiry and seeks to offer an alternative vision which could better account for the rights of stateless persons. Cole plays upon the problematics that are illustrated throughout the book to develop a more radical vision. He argues that liberal political theory is a theory of privileged 'insiders' with access to citizenship, while the interests of those on the outside (the stateless) are left behind. To end the volume, therefore, Cole uses the analysis of statelessness to turn his lens on theory itself and offers a radical vision to shape future theoretical work in the field.

The book ends with a photograph by Denis Bosnic which shows two boys looking out through the window of their family caravan which sits in a trailer park on the outskirts of Rome in Italy. Their father's birth in Macedonia was never registered, leaving him stateless. As a result their parents have been unable officially to marry and their father unable to work. He does not appear on the record of their birth. The children are registered as if their mother had been single. While the boys have Romanian citizenship, through their mother, the family struggles both economically and in other ways because of their father's statelessness. What future are these boys looking out upon?

A call to action

Political theory and philosophy can sometimes be accused of being abstract or navel-gazing, so as to be of little use in solving contemporary political challenges. The contributors to this book think otherwise. They wield political theoretic tools, alongside those from the social sciences, law, humanities and visual art, to address directly the situation of statelessness and the challenges it poses for individuals and for liberal political frameworks. Its primary guiding question concerns whether, and if so how, political theory can engage with and account for the rights of stateless persons. This book should not be seen as a finished project. Instead, it is a call to action. Its contributors argue that liberal political theory and policymaking based on liberal political theoretical foundations cannot, as currently understood, successfully address the question of statelessness.

First, statelessness must be seen as both a structural problem and a legal one. It can be seen both as the *lack* of any citizenship, and as the *positive* exclusion located within multiple intersecting structural barriers. Second, statelessness and citizenship are upshots of the same institutional structure and are necessary upshots of this structure as it is currently constructed. A genuine attempt to address the privations associated with statelessness will need a re-examination of the structures within which it is constructed and within which such privations and vulnerabilities arise. Though this is important for the protection of currently stateless persons in the interim, addressing statelessness merely by offering citizenship to specific stateless persons is insufficient in the longer term. Third, then, the legal definition is important, within the current context, for mobilising support for change and action across international institutions. The legal definition, along with the Conventions within which it sits, is vital for ensuring protections and rights are in place for currently stateless persons. However, this must be done alongside a longer term critical examination of statelessness.

In the longer term, then, it is necessary to re-examine the binary assumptions inherent in existing discourse around citizenship, noncitizenship and statelessness, and to recognise the complex reality of individuals' relationships with States, with regional and local political entities. This will require revisiting the language used to discuss these concepts and the tools employed. It will also require breaking down existing limits to political imagination, including through the introduction of new voices and new forms of engagement.

As discussed in the opening paragraph of this chapter in relation to the writings of Zweig, the condition of stateless persons is often treated as anomalous and they are improperly labelled as objects of suspicion. We hope with this volume to break down these assumptions and to show that stateless persons and their experiences within liberal frameworks are a critical factor in mainstream political theory. By keeping stateless persons voiceless in political theory and policymaking, the global community is losing an essential resource for building a more just world and limiting political theoretical imaginations to the vagaries of the precise State-based framework that history has provided.

References

Aggarwal, A. (2014) *Statelessness and 'Right to Have Rights'. Importance of Citizenship in Protecting Human Rights of Stateless Communities.* Norderstedt: German National Library.

Bauböck, R. (2007) The rights of others and the boundaries of democracy. *European Journal of Political Theory*, 6(4), pp. 398–405.

Blitz, B. K. and M. Lynch (2012) *Statelessness and Citizenship: A Comparative Study on the Benefits of Nationality.* Northampton: Edward Elgar.

Blitz, B. K. and M. Otero-Iglesias (2011) Stateless by any other name: refused asylum seekers in the United Kingdom. *Journal of Ethnic and Migration Studies*, 37(4), pp. 657–673.

Bosniak, L. (2008) *The Citizen and the Alien: Dilemmas of Contemporary Membership.* Princeton: Princeton University Press.

Cabrera, L. (2010) *The Practice of Global Citizenship.* Cambridge: Cambridge University Press.

Caney, S. (2006) *Justice Beyond Borders.* Oxford: Oxford University Press.

Carens, J. (2013) *The Ethics of Immigration.* Oxford: Oxford University Press.

Carens, J. (2008) The rights of irregular migrants. *Ethics and International Affairs*, 22(2), pp. 163–186.

Carens, J. (1987) Aliens and citizens: the case for open borders. *The Review of Politics*, 49(2), pp. 251–273.

Cole, P. (2000) *Philosophies of Exclusion.* Edinburgh: Edinburgh University Press.

Frelick, B. and M. Lynch (2005) Statelessness: a forgotten human rights crisis. *Forced Migration Review*, 24(1), pp. 65–66.

Gibney, M. (2013) Should citizenship be conditional? The ethics of denationalisation. *The Journal of Politics*, 75(3), pp. 646–658.

Gibney, M. (2006) Who Should be Included? Noncitizens, Conflict and the Constitution of Citizenry. Centre for Research on Inequality, Human Security and Ethnicity Working Paper No. 17 September 2006.

Goodwin-Gill, G. (2011) Convention on the Reduction of Statelessness. *United Nations Audiovisual Library of International Law.* New York: United Nations.

Goris, I., J. Harrington and S. Köhn (2009) Statelessness: what it is and why it matters. *Forced Migration Review*, 32(6), pp. 4–6.

van Heuven Goedhart, G. J. (1955) Address by Dr Gerrit Jan van Heuven Goedhart, United Nations High Commissioner for Refugees, on the occasion of the award of the 1954 Nobel Prize for Peace to UNHCR, 10 December.

Hildago, J. (2014) Self-determination, immigration restrictions and the problem of compatriot deportation. *Journal of International Political Theory*, 10(3), pp. 261–282.

ISI (2014) *The World's Stateless.* Oisterwijk: Wolf Legal Publishers.

Isin, E. (2004) The neurotic citizen. *Citizenship Studies*, 8(3), pp. 217–235.

Nyers, P. (2006) The accidental citizen: acts of sovereignty and (un)making citizenship. *Economy and Society*, 25(1), pp. 22–41.

Pogge, T. (2010) *Politics as Usual: What Lies Behind the Pro-poor Rhetoric.* Cambridge: Polity.

Pouilly, C. (2007) Stateless achievers. *Refugees*, 147(3), pp. 18–19.

Risse, M. (2008) On the morality of immigration. *Ethics and International Affairs*, 22(1), pp. 25–33.

Rubio-Marin, R. (2000) *Immigration as a Democratic Challenge: Citizenship and Inclusion in Germany and the United States.* Cambridge: Cambridge University Press.

Rygiel, K. (2011) Bordering solidarities: migrant activism and the politics of movement and camps at Calais. *Citizenship Studies*, 15(1), 1–19.

Sawyer, C. and B. K. Blitz (2011) *Statelessness in the European Union: Displaced, Undocumented, Unwanted.* Cambridge: Cambridge University Press.

Sigona, N. (2012) 'I have too much baggage': the impacts of legal status on the social worlds of irregular migrants. *Social Anthropology*, 20(1), pp. 50–65.

Sigona, N. (2005) Locating 'the Gypsy problem'. The Roma in Italy: stereotyping, labelling and 'nomad camps'. *Journal of Ethnic and Migration Studies*, 31(4), pp. 741–756.

Staples, K. (2012) *Retheorising Statelessness: A Background Theory of Membership in World Politics.* Abingdon: Routledge.

Tonkiss, K. and T. Bloom (2016) *Theorising Noncitizenship.* London: Routledge.

Tonkiss, K. and T. Bloom (2015) *Theorising Noncitizenship.* Special Issue of *Citizenship Studies*, 19(2).

UNHCR (United Nations High Commissioner for Refugees) (2015) *UNHCR Global Trends 2015.* Available at: www.unhcr.org/uk/statistics/unhcrstats/576408cd7/unhcr-global-trends-2015.html [Accessed 26 February 2017].

Verlinden, A. (2010) Free movement? On the liberal impasse in coping with the immigration dilemma. *Journal of International Political Theory*, 6(1), pp. 51–72.

Weis, P. (1962) The United Nations Convention on the reduction of statelessness, 1961. *The International and Comparative Law Quarterly*, 11(4), pp. 1073–1096.

Weis, P. (1961) The convention relating to the status of stateless persons. *The International and Comparative Law Quarterly*, 10(2), pp. 255–264.

Zweig, S. (1964) *The World of Yesterday.* Lincoln: University of Nebraska Press.

Part I

Defining statelessness

Photo 2 Rasha Khalil. Born and lives in Borj El Barajneh Camp for Palestinian Refugees, Beirut, Lebanon.

Source: from the Series: Portraits of Denial & Desire. Digital Photograph. 70×42 inches. 2014 ©. Artist: John Halaka. Reproduced with permission from the Artist.

When I speak with an elder from my village, it's as if I am living in the village in the moment he is describing. I would cry with them when they spoke of their pain and laugh with them when they spoke of their joy. It's as if I was living the moments they were describing … I remember my grandparents' stories as if they were memories that I lived.

(Rasha Khalil)

Defining statelessness

2   Worthy of rights

Statelessness as a cause and symptom of marginalisation

Lindsey N. Kingston

Introduction

Statelessness is recognised not only as a violation of the 'right to a nationality' outlined by international human rights frameworks, but also as a root cause of additional rights abuses and threats to human security. Political theorist Hannah Arendt (1973) associated citizenship with 'the right to have rights', while statelessness has been equated with Giorgio Agamben's (1998) concept of 'bare life', impeding human dignity and the recognition of full personhood.[1] Today, scholars and advocates posit the acquisition of legal nationality as a solution to statelessness, stressing the existing guidelines laid out by international conventions in 1954 and 1961. In November 2014, the United Nations High Commissioner for Refugees (UNHCR) launched a ten-year 'I Belong' campaign to eliminate statelessness globally; their focus is on achieving a 'critical mass' of states party to the statelessness conventions and eliminating barriers to legal nationality for children and minorities (UNHCR 2014b).[2] Indeed, the main strategies for combatting statelessness tend to be primarily focused on gaining (or regaining) legal status for those who do not currently have citizenship of any state – including the work of major actors such as the UNHCR, Plan International, the European Network on Statelessness, and the Institute on Statelessness and Inclusion.

Although such work is vital and well-intentioned, the current legalistic focus on citizenship provision tends to ignore important, subtle realities about the nature of marginalisation and rights abuses. While I assert that legal nationality is an essential prerequisite for the mere possibility of enjoying a variety of basic human rights, this chapter also contends that a narrow emphasis on citizenship acquisition is misguided; legal status is only one step in a long journey towards full rights protection.[3] The ways by which individuals are rendered stateless – including denationalisation, exclusionary citizenship laws, and inequalities that obstruct registration and naturalisation – often serve to discriminate against minority populations and create structural barriers to their full protection under the law. I argue that statelessness is both a *cause* of marginalisation as well as a *symptom* of it. That is, most stateless populations lack legal nationality because they are part of a marginalised group that faces systematic discrimination and oppression from the start. Their circumstances are greatly harmed by their statelessness, yet the acquisition of legal nationality alone will not ensure their access to human rights. Instead, individuals must have legal status as well as *functioning citizenship*; they require an active and mutually beneficial relationship with a government in order to be full members of a political community and to access their fundamental rights (Kingston 2014).[4] By viewing statelessness as both a cause and symptom of marginalisation and abuse, we begin to unravel the complex relationships and political contexts that make this condition so dangerous. From this perspective, we must expand our understanding of citizenship to more critically consider the process of recognising claimants of human rights in the first place.

Statelessness as a cause of marginalisation

Existing research shows that the condition of statelessness, which is a human rights violation that constitutes a breach of international law, is a root cause of other rights abuses. Put simply, stateless individuals are vulnerable to a variety of human rights violations because their lack of legal status puts them in a precarious position within state society. They are frequently unable to access political membership or call upon governments to protect their most basic needs and entitlements. As noted in the UNHCR's (2014a) *Global Action Plan to End Statelessness*, 'statelessness has serious consequences for people in almost every country and in all regions of the world', including issues such as denied identity documentation, employment, education, and health care. The UNHCR also ties statelessness to instances of forced displacement, political and social tensions, and impaired economic and social development of states (p. 6). Studies from around the world support these claims, linking lack of legal nationality to violations including denied health rights (Kingston *et al.* 2010), human trafficking (Rijken *et al.* 2015), arbitrary detention and inequality before the law (McBride and Kingston 2014), and denied economic rights to livelihood and safe working conditions (Kanapathipillai 2009). Furthermore, individuals who are already vulnerable to abuse and exploitation face a 'compound deprivation' when they cannot access legal nationality. Brad K. Blitz (2011) writes that such deprivations for children 'have long-standing consequences in terms of [their] social, economic, and personal development', often leading to social problems including poverty, infant mortality, labour exploitation, and human trafficking (p. 50).

Current case studies of traditionally stateless groups worldwide highlight the human rights impacts of statelessness, and perhaps one of the most startling is that of Burma's Rohingya.[5] State-sanctioned discrimination against the Rohingya is entrenched in the country's 1982 Citizenship Law, which fails to recognise the Muslim ethnic group as a 'national race' worthy of legal nationality and creates the condition of statelessness (Human Rights Watch 2013). The Rohingya are therefore denied a range of human rights protections available to citizens, including the rights to a basic education and employment. The perpetuation of direct violence, including murders and rape, has been equated with ethnic cleansing and crimes against humanity by human rights observers (Human Rights Watch

2013). Some contend that the violence is a warning of impending genocide (Al Jazeera 2014). Many of Burma's 1.1 million Rohingya live in 'a state of apartheid', clustered into concentration camps and subjected to pervasive human rights violations. In the first three months of 2015 alone, an estimated 25,000 Rohingya fled the country in boats – many of whom became stranded in unseaworthy vessels (Schiavenza 2015). The displaced face a myriad of threats, including chronic malnutrition and physical abuse by unscrupulous smugglers known for killing or abandoning charges who could not pay their steep fees. Those caught by the Thai government face so-called 'soft' deportation, when they are moved out of detention cells and put in wooden boats headed towards the Andaman Sea – towards smugglers and, for those who can't pay ransom for passage, into indentured servitude[6] on Thai farms and fishing vessels (Perlez 2014).

Stateless populations around the world – including many European Roma and Palestinians, ethnic Haitians in the Dominican Republic, hill tribe peoples in northern Thailand, and Kenya's Nubians – are similarly denied their 'right to a nationality' and are unable to access the rights protections available to citizens. In extreme cases, such as that of Burma's Rohingya, the stateless face government-sanctioned violence that prompts massive forced displacement. Other cases may result in fewer (or no) cases of direct violence, but nevertheless create vast inequalities that obstruct rights protection and human development. These negative impacts represent a form of 'structural violence' – the systematic ways in which a social institution or structure kills people slowly by denying them access to basic necessities. They are social harms resulting from the pervasive and persistent impact of economic, political, and cultural violence in societies (Galtung and Höivik 1971, p. 73). For instance, Laura van Waas (2011) notes that while the majority of human rights are (at least ideally) guaranteed under international law regardless of nationality, there are still 'a number of citizens' rights dressed up as human rights' (p. 26). Those without legal nationality are frequently denied the right to participate in government, freedom of movement, and economic rights. Some citizenship theorists argue that 'citizenship is a divider' between citizen members and an excluded category of non-members, which includes the stateless. 'In the contemporary world, the inequalities associated with this exclusive dimension of citizenship weigh heavily,' Matthew J. Gibney writes (2011, p. 41).

Indeed, research on formerly stateless populations shows that the acquisition of legal nationality leads to significant human rights gains. A recent comparative global study on the benefits of nationality highlighted the positive impacts that formerly stateless individuals enjoyed when various governments provided citizenship to some minority populations (Blitz and Lynch 2011). For instance, findings from Slovenia, Sri Lanka, Mauritania, and Kenya illustrated how resulting documentation was essential for accessing public services, lessening risks for police brutality and deportation, and having a chance to participate politically in their society (Lynch and Blitz 2011, p. 204). Although citizenship benefits were not evenly distributed across the case studies, the acquisition of nationality had life-changing consequences for some formerly stateless individuals, such as young people who were able to acquire university education and gain employment (Lynch and Blitz 2011, p. 205). A 2014 qualitative study of formerly stateless refugees in the United States' New York State highlighted three key obstacles for stateless individuals: inequalities related to recognition and membership, denied educational opportunities, and serious impediments to employment and livelihoods. By comparing life as stateless individuals and then as US citizens (or green card holders), the Bhutanese-Nepali and Karen interview respondents showed that legal nationality and status are indeed important for accessing resources, political membership and identity, physical security, and other benefits (Kingston and Stam 2015).

Importantly, however, the acquisition of legal nationality does not *guarantee* equality and respect for human rights; the fact that positive gains are distributed unevenly across formerly stateless groups shows us that citizenship alone is not enough. Rather, the granting of legal nationality to marginalised groups is just one essential step in the process ensuring that rights are upheld universally. Put simply, 'the granting of citizenship does not absolve state responsibility to ensure all persons can access and enjoy their human rights' (Lynch and Blitz 2011, p. 205). In the United States, for instance, interviews with resettled refugees highlight that citizenship is important – but not sufficient – to guarantee the full protection of rights; the struggle does not end with the attainment of legal status. Bhutanese-Nepali and Karen individuals living in New York State continue to struggle with issues such as unemployment, poverty, and the inability to access higher education. While the granting of US citizenship or green cards is a positive development, additional state measures are necessary for ensuring that resettled refugees can enjoy their rights and participate as full members of their new society (Kingston and Stam 2015). Similarly, a study of Nubians in Kenya highlighted how increasing access to ID cards among formerly stateless populations was not sufficient for attaining equal recognition and rights. Data from eight months of semi-ethnographic observation and more than 100 interviews showed that Nubians experienced and interpreted their position within the Kenyan political community as unequal and marginalised. While access to government-issued identification meant that many Nubians could no longer be categorised as stateless, 'it does not make sense to categorize them as full citizens either' (Balaton-Chrimes 2014, p. 15).

More broadly, even within the category of citizens we see that some legal nationalities hold more political sway and provide greater human rights protections. For instance, freedom of movement is greatly impacted by one's country of citizenship. The financial firm Arton Capital ranks the world's most powerful passports based on the global mobility they provide, measured by the ability to visit foreign countries without a visa. Arton, which specialises in helping wealthy individuals obtain multiple citizenships, ranked the United States and the United Kingdom as the top most powerful passports in 2015, followed closely by France, South Korea, and Germany. Perhaps not surprisingly, the bottom-ranked countries included developing countries where human rights violations are often prevalent, including South Sudan, the Palestinian Territories, and Burma (Passport Index n.d.). These mobility-related inequalities reflect differences in 'mobility citizenship', which Steffen Mau (2010) understands as encompassing both the right to be mobile as well as the right to stay in a given territory – rights, notably, that are threatened for stateless individuals. Unequal protection of mobility, due in part to differences in passport power, is one way that membership within the international community is impacted by what Ayelet Shachar (2009) calls the 'birthright lottery'. She contends that birthright citizenship in an affluent society is a form of property inheritance, allowing people born in wealthy countries such as the United States to transfer the elite enjoyment of human rights to children purely by accidental circumstances of birth.

These inequalities and human rights challenges begin to problematise the prevailing view that the negative ramifications of statelessness can be solved simply by providing legal nationality. Surely statelessness can be linked to a plethora of deeply harmful social injustices and rights violations, and researchers who have taken up this cause in recent years have made a strong case for respecting and protecting the 'right to a nationality' globally. What was once a forgotten human rights issue (Kingston 2013) has garnered the attention of the UNHCR and has entered important debates about migration, rights protection, and human trafficking. Yet the reason that statelessness is so deeply harmful is not because all people yearn for this theoretical concept of 'citizenship', but rather because they want and need the practical protections and social goods that come with citizenship – or at least citizenship when the relationship between citizens and the state is a functioning one. Sadly, legal status alone cannot guarantee the stability of that relationship or ensure that human rights will be upheld. Instead, legal nationality is an essential prerequisite for the attainment of human rights – but it is not sufficient if other vital factors are missing. With the understanding that the 'right to a nationality' must indeed be protected and that statelessness creates human rights risks that should not be tolerated within the international system, we must move this conversation forward by refocusing statelessness as a symptom, in addition to being a cause, of marginalisation.

Statelessness as a symptom of marginalisation

The causes of statelessness vary widely around the world, but discrimination often plays a significant role in determining who gets counted as a citizen and who does not. Discriminatory deprivation of legal nationality 'fundamentally describes the situation where a state withholds or withdraws the nationality of an individual on the basis of a distinction that is deemed unreasonable and untenable, such as on the grounds of some immutable characteristic like skin color' (Van Waas 2008, p. 95). Such practice constitutes 'arbitrary deprivation of nationality'; it is closely related to the unlawful or illegal deprivation of citizenship, as well as deprivation of nationality that is not accompanied by due process, including review and appeal (Van Waas 2008, pp. 94–95). While some of the more technical causes of statelessness (such as oversights related to marriage, divorce, and state succession) may be relatively easy to remedy with the correct policy changes, most cases are far more complex. Ways of rendering an individual stateless – including denationalisation, exclusionary citizenship laws, and inequalities that obstruct registration and naturalisation – help us understand how lack of legal nationality serves as a symptom of existing discrimination and marginalisation. Recent case studies highlight how these processes have been used to oppress certain identity groups around the world. Notably, minority groups are often targeted with various methods for denying legal nationality as part of a broader process of marginalisation; it is a process that does not begin with statelessness, and cannot end simply by providing citizenship status.

Denationalisation serves as a stark example of statelessness as a symptom of marginalisation because it constitutes stripping a citizen of their previous legal nationality, often during times of conflict, with the aim of 'purifying' communities of minority groups. Historically, perhaps the most well-known denationalisation campaign occurred around the Second World War when Nazi Germany revoked legal nationality from minority groups in the years leading up to the Holocaust.[7] More recently, cases such as the denationalisation and forced migration of ethnic Nepalis living in Bhutan during the 1970s and 1980s highlight how statelessness has been used as a tool to marginalise minority groups. Arbitrary deprivation of nationality began with a 1977 law that created more stringent requirements for those seeking Bhutanese nationality, followed by additional legislation in 1980 and 1985 that introduced punitive measures against Bhutanese nationals who married foreigners and further constrained citizenship requirements (Hutt 2003). During this time, the Bhutanese government became increasingly focused on enforcing a distinct national identity in line with its 'one nation, one people policy'. The king issued a 1989 degree requiring all citizens to observe the traditional Drukpa code of values and dress, for instance, and the Nepali language was removed from school curricula in southern Bhutan. Any protest against these policies was met with swift government action, including arrest, torture, rape by security forces, and even death (Human Rights Watch 2007). Bhutanese-Nepalis began fleeing Bhutan en masse to neighbouring Nepal in 1990, often under severe pressure from the government. Those who were categorised as 'non-nationals' under a 1988 census were told to leave the country or go to jail; security forces destroyed homes and intimidated many Bhutanese-Nepalis into signing 'voluntary migration forms' (Human Rights Watch 2007). Many Bhutanese-Nepalis recall being summoned to local government offices on the pretext of getting new or updated identity papers, only to have their existing documents – including citizenship cards – confiscated without replacement (Kingston and Stam 2015). Most Bhutanese-Nepalis who fled Bhutan ended up in refugee camps in Nepal, where they remained for more than 18 years before finally being resettled elsewhere (UNHCR 2013).

In addition to denationalising unwanted populations, discriminatory citizenship laws are also used to block minorities from accessing legal nationality – even in cases where the minority population has lived in a country for generations. In Thailand, for example, many members of so-called 'hill tribes' are stateless as a result of the 'combined operation of nationality, civil registration and immigration policies' despite the fact that the original Thai Nationality Law allowed any child born on Thai soil to acquire *jus soli* nationality (Rijken *et al.* 2015, p. 30). Many hill tribe children were overlooked by civil registration processes because they lived in remote locations or simply due to lack of interest in gaining legal nationality, but increasing government attention to the uplands beginning in the 1950s made legal nationality a necessity (Rijken *et al.* 2015; see also Scott 2009). In 1972, changes to the Nationality Law placed restrictions on the *jus soli* principle, requiring parents to have permanent residency status for the child to qualify for Thai nationality and thereby blocking many hill tribe families from citizenship. In the meantime, a complicated array of colour-coded identity cards was issued to non-citizens; children born to card holders were barred from *jus soli* entitlement. Although a 2008 amendment to the Thai Nationality Law has the potential to provide citizenship to those who were negatively impacted by the 1972 provision (provided that they have evidence of birth and domicile in Thailand, as well as good behaviour in the country), 'there remains a question of whether [hill tribe members] can satisfy the evidentiary requirements', since many individuals lack any form of documentation (Rijken *et al.* 2015, p. 32).

Statelessness throughout the European Union is frequently linked to migration and ethnic marginalisation, particularly related to tens of thousands of stateless Roma. For instance, Romani families that fled Bosnia and Herzegovina during the Yugoslav conflicts of the 1990s were often unable to access legal nationality in other parts of Europe. The process of EU enlargement has forced many to return to Bosnia and Herzegovina, where they are frequently no longer counted as citizens. In 2011 the European Commission requested that Balkan countries stop the influx of asylum seekers (who have benefited from a visa-free regime in the past), and accelerated asylum procedures have often led to rejected appeals and forced returns of stateless Roma. Critics have responded to these decisions by arguing that such obstacles to legal status within the European Union are part of a broader cycle of anti-Roma discrimination in wealthier European states. An estimated 5,000 Roma in Bosnia and Herzegovina lack identification documents, rendering them de facto stateless and blocking them from basic rights such as education, healthcare, and social assistance (de Verneuil 2014). Political unrest in nearby Slovenia during the 1990s facilitated statelessness that has continued for decades. The discriminatory 1991 Citizenship of the Republic of Slovenia Act and the 1991 Alien Act led to the erasure of 25,671 would-be Slovenian citizens from the country's permanent register (including the destruction or invalidation of their documentation) and severely limited the rights of non-citizens living within the territory (Zorn 2011). Similarly, statelessness in Estonia has been linked to discrimination against certain cultural and ethnic groups (including Russian speakers), despite national laws barring such forms of discrimination (Vetik 2011).

Inequalities that obstruct registration and naturalisation further institutionalise state-sanctioned discrimination. Statelessness is a condition that millions of children are born into, due to their parents' inability to register live births and secure birth certificates. Birth registration is 'the continuous, permanent and universal recording within the civil registry of the occurrence and characteristics of birth', which 'establishes the existence of a person under law, and lays the foundation for safeguarding civil, political, economic, social and cultural rights' (Office of the United Nations High Commissioner for Human Rights 2014, p. 9). Despite legal guarantees,[8] an estimated 230 million children under the age of five have never been registered (UNICEF 2013, p. 6) and face human rights risks as a result.[9] Discrimination in birth registration is a way that statelessness and lack of documentation are perpetuated within families. In many cases, parents are required to present their own identity documents in order to register their children; this is impossible for stateless individuals and undocumented migrants. Some states refuse to register the children of non-citizens, and these issues are exacerbated in times of conflict and emergencies (Office of the United Nations High Commissioner for Human Rights 2014, pp. 24–25). Discrimination against women also impedes birth registration and exacerbates statelessness, particularly if mothers are unmarried or fathers are missing (Plan International 2012, p. 10).

In some cases, various human rights challenges intersect to create obstacles for birth registration; recent data suggests that ethnic minorities living in isolated rural areas and/or facing poverty are less likely to access birth registration than their non-minority, wealthier counterparts (UNICEF 2013, pp. 22–29). Families may be unable to pay the direct or indirect costs of registration, such as transportation costs or having to miss work, and some face illegal bribery demands or late fees (Office of the United Nations High Commissioner for Human Rights 2014, p. 23). These challenges occur around the world, and the case of India illustrates just one example of how many poor families may not fully understand the benefits of registration or lack the resources necessary to register their child with the state. Plan India observed that 'Children in Difficult Circumstances' – including street children, children from 'backward castes', children of the urban poor and migrants/refugees, and nomadic children – faced significant challenges to birth registration. Millions of these children lacked state-issued documentation, making them automatically vulnerable 'to the quiet discrimination and dangers that come from being "invisible"' (Plan India 2009, p. 14). When Plan India launched its five-year Universal Birth Registration campaign in 2006, it focused specifically on creating awareness and combatting the legal and administrative hurdles that prevented families from registering births (Plan India 2009).

Inequalities in naturalisation processes continue discrimination into adulthood. The most dramatic example in recent news comes from the Dominican Republic, where Dominican-born people of Haitian descent have long faced discrimination in government policies and were rendered stateless in 2013 by a high court ruling (this is addressed in detail in Blake, this volume). The Dominican Republic again made international headlines in 2015, when authorities reportedly set up processing centres and bus fleets ahead of a 17 June deadline for naturalisation registration (Human Rights Watch 2015). Critics argued that only

300 of the 250,000 Dominican Haitians applying for residency permits had received them – raising alarms of impending 'ethnic purging' and mass forced deportations (Democracy Now 2015).

It is no coincidence that the causes of statelessness frequently overlap, or that the human rights consequences of statelessness are often similar across geographical space and identity groups. Traditionally, citizenship has signified inclusion within a bounded group and the enjoyment of a range of basic rights. In his foundational work, T. H. Marshall (1965) contends that basic human equality is associated with full political membership, or citizenship, and that such membership cannot be fully attained until every citizen enjoys the full range of rights. From this perspective denying citizenship to minorities is a way to exclude them from society and its protection, thereby building inequalities and hierarchies of recognition into the state system. Lack of legal nationality is therefore one tool in a broader process of discrimination against marginalised groups. It is symptomatic of the structural violence levelled against minority groups that the government has deemed dangerous, impure, and/or unwanted within the territory. In addition to denying or stripping an individual of the legal status that (theoretically, at least) grants them full membership in the political community, statelessness also denies state protections against human rights violations outlined in international law. In some cases, statelessness provides governments with the opportunity to deport or incarcerate unwanted minorities, to deny them access to vital social services, and to block their participation in formal sectors such as legal employment and public education. Lack of legal nationality is frequently used as a rationale for ignoring or violating the rights of minorities, yet statelessness doesn't occur in a vacuum; *certain* people are stateless because they were deemed unworthy of membership and rights in a given community. Statelessness and the human rights consequences that result are symptoms of deeply embedded systems of discrimination.

Yet it is imperative to remember that the concept of statelessness exists along a spectrum of recognition and political belonging; we cannot simply say that stateless individuals are marginalised and citizens are not. Political theorist Elizabeth Cohen (2009) warns against idealising citizenship and argues that citizenship itself is a gradient category. Definitions of citizenship are often driven by normative assumptions but don't reflect reality. Many individuals fit on a spectrum somewhere between full and noncitizenship, making them *semi-citizens*. The circumstances of migrants and children, for instance, illustrate situations of semi-citizenship in which a person may hold legal nationality but cannot access their full range of rights. Closely related to this perspective is Iris Marion Young's (1990) concept of 'differentiated citizenship', which identifies injustices within the structure of state society and illustrates how those with so-called 'full' citizenship are not always treated as such. For instance, freedom of movement and state-issued documentation are sometimes denied to citizens who engage in activism against state interests. Anti-apartheid activist-citizens were regularly refused passports by the South African government, blocking them from engaging in activism internationally (Associated Press 1986). More recently, the Chinese government revokes passports of Tibetan activists in order to control movement and intensify regional control (International Campaign for Tibet 2015). The government similarly detained and barred Chinese citizen and artist-activist Ai Weiwei from travelling internationally in 2011, finally returning his passport in July 2015 (Phillips 2015). These examples highlight the fact that even so-called 'full citizens' do not always enjoy functioning citizenship and corresponding rights protection – and that states sometimes use legal nationality and its protections to marginalise certain groups or individuals.

Reflections and next steps

Recognising that statelessness is both a cause and a symptom of marginalisation exposes the weaknesses that are built into the entire human rights system. In particular, there are two key problems at the heart of this discussion: First, human rights language contends that fundamental rights belong to all human beings, regardless of citizenship or legal status: 'All human beings are born free and equal in dignity and rights' (United Nations General Assembly 1948, Article 1). When Arendt was critiquing international human rights and reflecting on her experiences as a stateless refugee following the World Wars, the prevailing assumption was that everyone had membership to a state; statelessness was cast 'as an unwelcome yet anomalous condition' that 'did not need to raise any questions about the ordering principles of the international system itself' (Gündoğdu 2015, p. 11). Today, the international community's broad acceptance of human rights standards – including the universality of rights based on personhood rather than legal status – risks turning the human rights challenges faced by noncitizens into 'unfortunate exceptions' to norms that detach rights from citizenship (Gündoğdu 2015). Yet ten to 15 million people around the world face situations of statelessness,[10] while countless others suffer human rights consequences stemming from their lack of functioning citizenship; clearly noncitizenship (or semi-citizenship) can no longer be viewed as an unfortunate exception to the rule. Instead, hierarchies have been created based on legal status, identity group, and even the relative power of specific passports. The modern human rights regime dictates that all people belong to a 'human family' and 'should act towards one another in a spirit of brotherhood' (United Nations General Assembly 1948, Preamble & Article 1), but realistically it takes more than personhood to access fundamental rights. The idealistic insistence that citizenship does not matter simply perpetuates the suffering of those without functioning citizenship; those who hold rights in theory but often have no duty-bearing state willing (or able) to offer protection. It is vitally important that the international community critically considers how a person's relationship with a state impacts his or her ability to enjoy basic human rights.

Second, human rights centre on legal protections of the individual, which limits our understanding of political membership – as well as narrows our approaches to tackling the problem of statelessness. Studies of statelessness tend to be 'dominated by legal scholars and typically [evoke] an implicit liberal tradition of citizenship' that may ignore post-statelessness inequalities (Balaton-Chrimes 2014, p. 16). Liberalism's emphasis on the value of autonomy makes it an individualistic political doctrine, paying little attention to how a person's world view and circumstances are influenced by others. As a result, liberalism holds a 'thin' notion of citizenship, which is operationalised primarily through legal status such as formal citizenship (Balaton-Chrimes 2014, p. 17) rather than participatory membership within a society. Kelly Staples (2012) avoids using terms such as 'nationality' and 'citizenship' and instead writes about 'membership', offering an interpretation of belonging that doesn't rely on legal status alone. She argues, in part, that the human rights discourse is limited 'by its need to hold on to the fiction that the importance of citizenship (or membership) has been eroded' in the face of universal human rights norms (Staples 2012, p. 7). Indeed, human rights are based on a kind of altruism that emphasises respect for fellow human beings – but citizenship is not about such altruism. Instead,

> it is about acknowledging the community's goals as one's own, choosing them, and committing oneself to them.... Citizenship is exclusive: it is not a person's humanity that one is responding to, it is the fact that he or she is a fellow citizen, or a stranger.
>
> (Oldfield 1990, p. 8)

It is a mistake to conceptualise citizenship in thin terms such as a 'fixed or static concept signifying passive legal relationships between individuals and their respective states', because citizenship is an evolving concept that involves politics and society – 'a series of habits, dispositions, and practices' that an individual is politically situated within (Schattle 2012, pp. 13–14). In other words, protecting an individual's 'right to a nationality' by granting her or him legal citizenship does not necessarily alter their position (or lack thereof) in society. People are bound by the complexities of their political community, including its prejudices and inequalities, and full membership within that society requires more than legal status.

While the first problem – the decoupling of rights and nationality – remains prevalent within the international community, it is also true that increasing attention to statelessness is changing the ways that some actors view this relationship. The value of birth registration and legal nationality for children has been acknowledged by major NGOs, led by Plan International's (n.d.) 'Count Every Child' universal birth registration campaign. Connections between statelessness and human rights abuse – particularly in relation to situations with high media coverage, such as the forced migration of Burma's Rohingya – have been noted by human rights watchdogs and journalists. In recent years, statelessness initiatives have formed to reform nationality legislation and advocate within the United Nations system; for instance, the European Network on Statelessness (n.d.) and the Institute on Statelessness and Inclusion (n.d.), both based in the European Union and led primarily by legal scholars. The UNHCR recognises statelessness as a cause of human rights violations and a cause of forced displacement and conflict; it has more than tripled its expenditures on statelessness since 2009, which includes the launch of its 'I Belong' campaign to eliminate statelessness in a decade (UNHCR 2014a, p. 6). Its 2014 Global Action Plan centres on actions to 'resolve existing situations of statelessness, prevent new cases of statelessness from emerging, and better identify and protect stateless persons' (UNHCR 2014a, p. 4). The UNHCR's campaign has set the global agenda for combatting statelessness and focuses on ten strategic priorities – almost all centred on the legal acquisition of citizenship (UNHCR 2014a).

These actions to eliminate statelessness are vitally important, but they fail to address the second problem outlined above and instead perpetuate thin notions of citizenship. Despite the laudable intentions of the UNHCR's 'I Belong' campaign, for instance, its legalistic approach tends to 'flatten' the problem of statelessness and posit the acquisition of legal nationality as its sole aim. Yet existing data shows that the granting of citizenship 'ameliorates many, but not all, of the complex problems that have roots in economic inequality, systemic discrimination and other forms of injustice' (Lynch and Blitz 2011, p. 207). Simply, the granting of legal nationality is not enough to stop the pervasive human rights threats that have mobilised recent (albeit still limited) attention to statelessness. There remains a need 'to incorporate greater care to ensure the underlying causes are addressed by citizenship campaigns', including proactive steps to educate government officials and stateless persons about responsibilities for human rights protection (Lynch and Blitz 2011, p. 207). Perhaps this includes renewed discussion regarding international forms of documentation, which would shift dependence away from state-issued identity documents – therefore limiting opportunities for governments to use passports as a form of social control.[11] In many cases, proactive steps must also include rooting out corruption that garners benefits from the trafficking and exploitation of marginalised groups, including stateless populations, and local-level discrimination that blocks some individuals from accessing their rights.

At a deeper level, there is a need to push discussions beyond thin notions of citizenship to more seriously address the question: What does it mean to be a member of a political community? That is, aside from legal nationality and the documentation that goes with it, what makes an individual recognised as a person worthy of rights within our state-centric society? For instance, Gibney's (2011) discussion of 'precarious residents' (including unlawful migrants and asylum seekers awaiting status determination) provides an interesting potential starting point. He offers recommendations for ensuring rights protection and political membership outside the bounds of traditional citizenship: First, one potential standard for defining membership is the principle of *choice*. Membership should be available to anyone who chooses to live in a state. A second approach is to emphasise the role of individuals as *subjects* of state power; a state can only legitimately rule if the people consent to such rule. Third, the principle of *societal membership* contends that membership of a state should be composed of those who have a significant stake in the success and future of that society. All three of these approaches extend membership beyond thin, legal notions of citizenship and instead privilege the values of autonomy, democracy, and community. These alternative approaches to membership also extend the social goods of voice (freedom of expression and political participation) and security (security of residence or presence in a state), which are often limited or denied entirely to the stateless and those without functioning citizenship (Gibney 2011). The international community needs to engage with such theoretical approaches in order to fill some of the protection gaps built into our current human rights system.

My intention in writing this chapter is not to deny the value of current actions aimed at eliminating statelessness, but rather to suggest additional, complementary approaches for combatting this complex problem. Rather than relying solely on legal strategies to provide nationality, I believe a multi-faceted plan is necessary for alleviating the harms of statelessness – both as a cause of human rights abuse, and as a symptom of it. Critics may contend that focusing on legal status will at least reduce some of the ill effects of statelessness, but in the long term I believe this strategy simply puts a temporary bandage on widespread issues of structural inequality. If we acknowledge that the denial of legal nationality is simply one tool to marginalise unwanted populations (and unfortunately that 'tool box' of discrimination is vast), then we must also acknowledge that providing legal nationality will not stop the suffering of currently stateless people. Governments bent on oppressing minority populations will not simply accept these groups as full citizens because the state accedes to the UN Statelessness Conventions or closes loopholes in its nationality laws. Rather, human rights advocates must continue actions to eliminate statelessness as a legal issue while also rooting out the social and political forces that facilitate such structural violence. We have, quite simply, the classic 'chicken or the egg' causality dilemma: People are discriminated against because they are stateless, and they are stateless because they are discriminated against. It is a frustratingly complex problem that calls into question what it means to belong to a political community, how we recognise personhood and claimants of human rights, and how we structure fair and equitable societies.

Notes

1 Arendt is discussed further in Blitz, this volume.
2 This is discussed further in Staples, this volume.
3 Scholarship on statelessness is complicated, in part, by a limited vocabulary that makes it difficult to adequately discuss notions of membership and status. As Katherine Tonkiss rightly notes in this volume, the terms 'nationality' and 'citizenship' are often used interchangeably within the statelessness literature despite vital differences between these concepts. She seeks to problematise this interchangeability and advocates for a post-national approach to understanding belonging and rights. In this chapter and in my other work, I use the terms 'citizenship' and 'legal nationality' to connote state-sanctioned, recognised legal status. At the same time, I recognise that not all nations constitute nation-states (consider identity groups without their own nation-states, such as the Kurds) and that legal status alone does not constitute full membership in a given society. As this chapter outlines, such legal status does not guarantee the full enjoyment of supposedly universal and inalienable human rights.

4 Article 1 of the 1954 Convention relating to the Status of Stateless Persons sets out the international legal definition of a stateless person as being 'a person who is not considered as a national by any State under the operation of its law'. From this definition, a stateless person is simply one who does not have legal nationality of any country. The concept of functioning citizenship problematises that legalistic definition of statelessness by arguing that legal status alone cannot guarantee the political membership that is often assumed in discussions of legal nationality and citizenship. If we approach 'citizenship' as a relationship between an individual and a state that is necessary for human rights protection, then legal status is a prerequisite for attaining rights but it is certainly not sufficient on its own. Such a relationship must be functioning in the sense that individuals are acknowledged as full members of the political community, which includes their full enjoyment of human rights and non-discrimination by the state (see Kingston 2014).

5 The country's military-led government officially changed the state's name from 'Burma' to 'Myanmar' in 1989, but the author continues to use the term 'Burma' in solidarity with Burmese human rights advocates and the country's pro-democracy movement. This group is considered 'traditionally stateless' here in the sense that the Rohingya have inherited statelessness because of discrimination against their identity group. As this chapter will soon discuss, the causes of statelessness are often complex and perpetuated through denationalisation, exclusionary citizenship laws, and inequalities that obstruct registration and naturalisation.

6 It is noteworthy that state-sanctioned discrimination often fuels human smuggling, as well as contributes to cases of human trafficking. The United States Department of Homeland Security (n.d.) contends that smuggling and trafficking are 'distinct criminal activities', with smuggling centring on transportation and the deliberate evasion of immigration laws. While stateless populations such as the Rohingya may initially pay human smugglers to transport them to other countries, the situation transforms into one of human trafficking when long-term exploitation (including indentured servitude to pay smuggling debts) begins. Trafficking includes the 'recruitment, harboring, transportation, provision or obtaining of a person for labor or services, through the use of force, fraud or coercion for the purpose of subjection to involuntary servitude, peonage, debt bondage or slavery' (United States Department of Homeland Security n.d.).

7 The German Reich Citizenship Law of 1935 (one of the so-called 'Nuremberg Race Laws') defined a citizen of the Reich as an individual 'of German or related blood', and only citizens constituted 'the sole bearer(s) of full political rights in accordance with the law' (United States Holocaust Memorial Museum n.d.). Notably, the Law for the Protection of German Blood and German Honour was passed on the same day; it was based on the assertion that 'purity of German blood is the essential condition for the continued existence of the German people', and it outlawed (among other things) marriage between Jews and non-Jews (United States Holocaust Memorial Museum n.d.).

8 Birth registration and the right to be recognised as a person before the law are recognised under various international legal instruments, including Article 24 of the International Covenant on Civil and Political Rights and Article 7 of the Convention on the Rights of the Child.

9 Lack of registration creates vulnerabilities to a range of human rights abuses, including: the inability to access education and health care, child labour and child soldiering, early and forced marriages, and human trafficking (Office of the United Nations High Commissioner for Human Rights 2014).

10 Estimates of the number of stateless persons worldwide vary greatly, due in large part to the challenges associated with researching undocumented and vulnerable populations. These challenges include definitional issues, gaps in data collection tools, and lack of adequate data collection (see: Van Waas et al. 2014). The United Nations High Commissioner for Refugees (n.d.) notes that it 'cannot provide definitive statistics on the number of stateless people around the world' but estimates the total to be

'up to at least 10 million'. A recent report from the Institute on Statelessness and Inclusion contends that the true tally is likely closer to 15 million (Van Waas *et al.* 2014; Institute on Statelessness and Inclusion 2014).

11 The international community has been grappling with issues of documentation for a century. During the interwar period, certificates of identity (commonly referred to as 'Nansen passports') were issued by the League of Nations to allow stateless refugees to travel internationally. Later termed 'travel documents' in 1938, these passports represented the international community's first attempt to provide documentation that was not legitimised by any one state. Yet attempts to rally political support for 'world citizenship' (and, for instance, UN-issued identity documentation) have not received meaningful support.

References

Agamben, G. (1998) *Homo Sacer: Sovereign Power and Bare Life.* Stanford: Stanford University Press.

Al Jazeera (2014) UN calls for 'full Rohingya citizenship'. [online] 30 December. Available at: www.aljazeera.com/news/americas/2014/12/un-calls-full-rohingya-citizenship-myanmar-monks-rakhin-2014123044246726211.html [Accessed 7 August 2015].

Arendt, H. (1973) *The Origins of Totalitarianism. New Edition.* New York: Harcourt, Brace, Jovanovich.

Associated Press (1986) S. Africa refuses passport for anti-apartheid activist. *Los Angeles Times.* [online] 26 November. Available at: http://articles.latimes.com/1986-11-26/news/mn-15689_1_anti-apartheid-activist [Accessed 28 August 2015].

Balaton-Chrimes, S. (2014) Statelessness, identity cards, and citizenship as status in the case of the Nubians of Kenya. *Citizenship Studies*, 18(1), pp. 15–28.

Blitz, B. K. (2011) Neither Seen nor Heard: Compound Deprivation among Stateless Children. In Bhaba, J. (ed.) *Children Without a State: A Global Human Rights Challenge.* Cambridge, MA: MIT Press.

Blitz, B. K. and Lynch, M. (eds) (2011) *Statelessness and Citizenship: A Comparative Study on the Benefits of Nationality.* Cheltenham: Edward Elgar.

Cohen, E. F. (2009) *Semi-Citizenship in Democratic Politics.* Cambridge: Cambridge University Press.

De Verneuil, M. (2014) Romani Migration Resulting in Statelessness: The Case of Bosnia and Herzegovina. *Roma Rights: Journal of the European Roma Rights Centre*, pp. 27–33. [online] Available at: www.errc.org/cms/upload/file/roma-rights-1–2014-going-nowhere-western-balkan-roma-and-eu-visa-liberalisation.pdf?utm_medium=email&utm_campaign=Roma+Rights+1+2014%3A+Going+Nowhere%3F+Western+…&utm_source=YMLP&utm_term= [Accessed 28 August 2015].

Democracy Now (2015) The Dominican Republic's 'Ethnic Purging': Edwidge Danticat on Mass Deportation of Haitian Families. [online] 17 June. Available at: www.democracynow.org/2015/6/17/the_dominican_republics_ethnic_purging_edwidge [Accessed 11 August 2015].

European Network on Statelessness (n.d.) Mission Statement. [online] Available at: www.statelessness.eu/about-us/mission-statement [Accessed 12 August 2015].

Galtung, J. and Höivik, T. (1971) Structural and direct violence: a note on operationalization. *Journal of Peace Research*, 8(1), pp. 73–76.

Gibney, M. J. (2011) The Rights of Non-citizens to Membership. In Sawyer, C. and Blitz, B. K. (eds) *Statelessness in the European Union: Displaced, Undocumented, Unwanted.* Cambridge: Cambridge University Press.

Gündoğdu, A. (2015) *Rightlessness in an Age of Rights: Hannah Arendt and the Contemporary Struggles of Migrants.* Oxford: Oxford University Press.

Human Rights Watch (2015) Dominican Republic: Thousands at Risk of Expulsion to Haiti. [online] 30 June. Available at: www.hrw.org/news/2015/06/30/dominican-republic-thousands-risk-expulsion-haiti [Accessed 11 August 2015].

Human Rights Watch (2013) 'All You Can Do is Pray': Crimes against Humanity and Ethnic Cleansing of Rohingya Muslims in Burma's Arakan State. [online] Available at: www.hrw.org/sites/default/files/reports/burma0413webwcover_0.pdf [Accessed 7 August 2015].

Human Rights Watch (2007) Discrimination against Ethnic Nepali Children in Bhutan: Submission from Human Rights Watch to the Committee on the Rights of the Child. [online] Available at: www.hrw.org/news/2007/10/03/discrimination-against-ethnic-nepali-children-bhutan [Accessed 10 August 2015].

Hutt, M. (2003) *Unbecoming Citizens: Culture, Nationhood, and the Flight of Refugees from Bhutan.* Oxford: Oxford University Press.

Institute on Statelessness and Inclusion (n.d.) What We Do. [online] Available at: www.institutesi.org/about/whatwedo.php [Accessed 12 August 2015].

Institute on Statelessness and Inclusion (2014) The World's Stateless. [online] Available at: www.institutesi.org/worldsstateless.pdf [Accessed 9 November 2015].

International Campaign for Tibet (2015) 'A Policy Alienating Tibetans': The Denial of Passports to Tibetans as China Intensifies Control. [online] Available at: www.savetibet.org/policy-alienating-tibetans-denial-passports-tibetans-china-intensifies-control/ [Accessed 28 August 2015].

Kanapathipillai, V. (2009) *Citizenship and Statelessness in Sri Lanka: The Case of the Tamil Estate Workers.* London: Anthem Press.

Kingston, L. N. (2014) Statelessness as a lack of functioning citizenship. *Tilburg Law Review*, 19 (Special Issue), pp. 127–35.

Kingston, L. N. (2013) 'A forgotten human rights crisis': statelessness and issue (non) emergence. *Human Rights Review*, 14(2), pp. 73–87.

Kingston, L. N. and Stam, K. R. (2015) Recovering from statelessness: resettled Bhutanese–Nepali and Karen refugees reflect on lack of legal nationality. R&R under review at *The Journal of Human Rights.*

Kingston, L. N., Cohen, E. F., and Morley, C. P. (2010) Limitations on universality: The 'right to health' and the necessity of legal nationality. *BMC International Health & Human Rights*, 10(11). [online] Available at: www.biomedcentral.com/content/pdf/1472–698X-10–11.pdf [Accessed: 4 August 2015].

Lynch, M., and Blitz, B. K. (2011) Summary and Conclusions. In Blitz, B. K. and Lynch, M. (eds) *Statelessness and Citizenship: A Comparative Study on the Benefits of Nationality.* Cheltenham: Edward Elgar.

McBride, K. A. and Kingston, L. N. (2014) Legal invisibility and the revolution: statelessness in Egypt. *Human Rights Review*, 15(2), pp. 159–175.

Marshall, T. H. (1965) *Class, Citizenship, and Social Development: Essays by T.H. Marshall.* New York: Doubleday.

Mau, S. (2010) Mobility citizenship, inequality, and the Liberal State. *International Political Sociology*, 4(4), pp. 339–361.

Oldfield, A. (1990) *Citizenship and Community: Civic Republicanism and the Modern World.* London: Routledge.

Passport Index (n.d.) Passport Power Rank. [online] Available at: www.passportindex.org/byRank.php [Accessed 9 August 2015].

Perlez, J. (2014) For Myanmar Muslim minority, no escape from brutality. *New York Times*. [online] 14 March. Available at: www.nytimes.com/2014/03/15/world/asia/trapped-between-home-and-refuge-burmese-muslims-are-brutalized.html?_r=0 [Accessed 7 August 2015].

Phillips, T. (2015) Ai Weiwei free to travel overseas again after China returns his passport. *Guardian.* [online] 22 July. Available at: www.theguardian.com/artanddesign/2015/jul/22/ai-weiwei-free-to-travel-overseas-again-after-china-returns-his-passport [Accessed 28 August 2015].

Plan India (2009) Count Every Child: Ensuring Universal Birth Registration in India. [online] Available at: https://plan-international.org/files/global/publications/campaigns/count-every-child-india.pdf [Accessed 11 August 2015].

Plan International (n.d.) Birth Registration. [online] Available at: https://plan-international.org/what-we-do/child-participation/birth-registration [Accessed 12 August 2015].

Plan International (2012) Mother to Child: How Discrimination Prevents Women Registering the Birth of their Child. [online] Available at: https://plan-international.org/files/global/publications/campaigns/mother-to-child-how-discrimination-english [Accessed 11 August 2015].

Rijken, C., van Waas, L., Gramatikov, M., and Brennan, D. (2015) The Nexus Between Statelessness and Human Trafficking in Thailand. Oisterwijk: Wolf Legal Publishers. [online] Available at: www.institutesi.org/Stateless-Trafficking_Thailand.pdf [Accessed 28 August 2015].

Schattle, H. (2012) *Globalization and Citizenship*. Lanham: Rowman & Littlefield.

Schiavenza, M. (2015) Asia's Looming Refugee Disaster: Hundreds of Burma's Rohingya Muslims adrift at sea – and nobody wants to take them. *The Atlantic.* [online] 17 May. Available at: www.theatlantic.com/international/archive/2015/05/asias-looming-refugee-disaster/393482/ [Accessed 7 August 2015].

Scott, J. C. (2009) *The Art of Not Being Governed: An Anarchist History of Upland Southeast Asia.* New Haven: Yale University Press.

Shachar, A. (2009) *The Birthright Lottery: Citizenship and Global Inequality.* Cambridge: Harvard University Press.

Staples, K. (2012) *Retheorising Statelessness: A Background Theory of Membership in World Politics*. Edinburgh: Edinburgh University Press.

UNICEF (2013) Every Child's Birth Right: Inequalities and Trends in Birth Registration. [online] Available at: www.unicef.org/mena/MENA-Birth_Registration_report_low_res-01.pdf [Accessed 11 August 2015].

United Nations General Assembly (1948) The Universal Declaration of Human Rights. [online] Available at: www.un.org/en/documents/udhr/ [Accessed 29 August 2015].

United Nations High Commissioner for Human Rights (2014) Birth Registration and the Right of Everyone to Recognition Everywhere as a Person Before the Law. [online] Available at: https://plan-international.org/files/geneva/resources-page/publications/ohchr-birth-registration-report/birth-registration-and-the-right-of-everyone-to-recognition-everywhere-as-a-person-before-the-law [Accessed 11 August 2015].

UNHCR (United Nations High Commissioner for Refugees) (n.d.) Stateless People Figures. [online] Available at: www.unhcr.org/pages/49c3646c26.html [Accessed 9 November 2015].

UNHCR (United Nations High Commissioner for Refugees) (2014a) Global Action Plan to End Statelessness, 2014–24. [online] Available at: www.unhcr.org/stateless-campaign2014/Global-Action-Plan-eng.pdf [Accessed 4 August 2015].

UNHCR (United Nations High Commissioner for Refugees) (2014b) UNHCR Launches 10-year Global Campaign to End Statelessness. [online] Available at: www.unhcr.org/545797f06.html [Accessed 3 August 2015].

UNHCR (United Nations High Commissioner for Refugees) (2013) Refugee Resettlement Referral from Nepal Reaches Six-Figure Mark. [online] Available at: www.unhcr.org/517a77df9.html [Accessed 10 August 2015].

United States Department of Homeland Security (n.d.) Human Trafficking and Smuggling. U.S. Immigration and Customs Enforcement. [online] Available at: www.ice.gov/factsheets/human-trafficking [Accessed 9 November 2015].

United States Holocaust Memorial Museum (n.d.) Nuremberg Race Laws: Translation. [online] Available at: www.ushmm.org/wlc/en/article.php?ModuleId=10007903 [Accessed 10 August 2015].

Van Waas, L. (2011) Nationality and Rights. In Blitz, Brad K. and Lynch, M. (eds) *Statelessness and Citizenship: A Comparative Study on the Benefits of Nationality*. Cheltenham: Edward Elgar.

Van Waas, L. (2008) *Nationality Matters: Statelessness under International Law.* Antwerp: Intersentia.

Van Waas, L., De Chickera, A. and Al Barazi, Z. (2014) The World's Stateless: A New Report On Why Size Does and Doesn't Matter. *European Network on Statelessness.* 15 December. [online] Available at: www.statelessness.eu/blog/world%E2%80%99s-stateless-new-report-why-size-does-and-doesn%E2%80%99t-matter [Accessed 9 November 2015].

Vetik, R. (2011) The Statelessness Issue in Estonia. In Sawyer, C. and Blitz, B. K. (eds) *Statelessness in the European Union: Displaced, Undocumented, Unwanted.* Cambridge: Cambridge University Press.

Young, I. M. (1990) *Justice and the Politics of Difference.* Princeton: Princeton University Press.

Zorn, J. (2011) Non-citizens in Slovenia: Erasure from the Register of Permanent Residents. In Sawyer, C. and Blitz, B. K. (eds) *Statelessness in the European Union: Displaced, Undocumented, Unwanted.* Cambridge: Cambridge University Press.

3 Contexts of statelessness

The concepts 'statelessness *in situ*' and 'statelessness in the migratory context'

Caia Vlieks

Introduction[1]

In academic literature and reports, a distinction is often drawn between stateless-ness in the migratory context and statelessness *in situ* (e.g. Gyulai 2012; Manly 2012; Van Waas and Neal 2013). This distinction is used to address two dif-ferent contexts in which statelessness arises. The first concept – statelessness in the migratory context – encompasses stateless persons who are migrants or have a migratory background. The second comprises stateless populations who are 'in their own country', meaning that they have 'significant and stable ties (through birth, long-term residence, etc.)' with a country (Gyulai 2012, p. 279). It has fur-thermore been said that the type of (legal) response that is necessary to address statelessness may differ depending on the aforementioned contexts of stateless-ness (Gyulai 2012).

This chapter intends to answer the following question: To what extent are the concepts of statelessness *in situ* and statelessness in the migratory context as described in (academic) literature supported in international law, and how can they be defined and evaluated? The chapter focuses on Europe primarily, even though the issues discussed may be applicable to other parts of the world. It first describes how the concepts are used in (academic) literature. Next, the support for the distinction in international law is evaluated by systematising and analys-ing international legal instruments for references to these concepts or, more generally, making a distinction between the situations that these notions represent. For the second part of the evaluation, the definitions of the two con-cepts are applied to some cases of stateless persons in Europe before coming to final definitions and a conclusion, identifying problems that real cases pose for the definitions. Note that whenever this chapter speaks of statelessness, in prin-ciple it refers to *de jure* statelessness, that is, statelessness according to a strict legal definition (see Kingston; de Chickera and van Waas, this volume).

Contexts of statelessness in literature

When examining selected literature that includes a distinction between stateless-ness *in situ* and statelessness in the migratory context (ACVZ 2013; ENS 2013;

Gyulai 2012, 2014; Kochovski 2013; Manly 2012, 2014; Månsson 2013; Mreka-jova 2012; Nikolic 2013; Van Waas and Neal 2013) it is evident that the two contexts of statelessness reflect a difference in attachment to a country. This is articulated in many of the definitions used in these documents, demonstrating that consensus exists. The reasons for making a distinction between the two concepts also highlight this difference in situation that stateless persons can find themselves in: the concepts sometimes seem to be used to characterise the way(s) in which statelessness arises as a phenomenon in a country (e.g. ACVZ 2013; Van Waas and Neal 2013). However, the main reason for making a distinction between the two 'contexts' of statelessness is the difference in response that the distinct situations represented by the two concepts require (ENS 2013; Gyulai 2012, 2014; Manly 2012, 2014). In this regard, it should be kept in mind that there are two ways of responding to statelessness from a legal perspective: (1) statelessness determination and a protection status (as well as access to facilitated naturalisation, which is required under Article 32 of the 1954 Convention Relating to the Status of Stateless Persons (1954 Convention)) – for persons who are stateless in the migratory context – or (2) recognition of nationality – for persons who are stateless *in situ*.

Turning to the question of how the distinction between the two concepts is being made in the literature, the definitions are helpful again. Most striking is that those used for statelessness *in situ* are usually more elaborate than the definitions of statelessness in the migratory context. In fact, the latter context is sometimes simply defined by mentioning 'stateless migrants'. In order to shed more light on how to draw the distinction between the two concepts, it therefore seems worthwhile to consider the definitions of statelessness *in situ* first.

A number of words and phrases are used by almost all authors in the definition of statelessness *in situ*, mainly the notions of 'own country' and '(significant/ strong) ties' (e.g. Gyulai 2012, 2014; Van Waas and Neal 2013). Also, the duration of the relationship with, or stay in, that country – thus, in other words, the ties of a person to a country – is an element that is frequently encountered in these definitions (see also Gibney 2014). It is evident that statelessness *in situ* concerns stateless persons who have considerable ties to the country they live in. Whether a person is stateless *in situ* seems dependent on how strong, significant or old these ties are. Based on the literature review, the concept of *in situ* statelessness can be defined as encompassing persons who are stateless in their 'own country', who have meaningful and long-established ties to the country they live in.

Turning to statelessness in the migratory context, it would appear that if the distinction between the two contexts indeed should be drawn on the basis of the ties of a person to a country, stateless migrants would not have such significant ties to the country they live in. This is acknowledged by Gyulai (2014) and in a report by the European Network on Statelessness (ENS 2013) by the inclusion of the element of 'no or relatively weak ties of a stateless person to the country he or she lives in' in the definition. Furthermore, the fact that it concerns a migratory context is a recurring element in explanations of this concept.

Statelessness in the migratory context can, on the basis of the outcomes of the literature review, be defined as including stateless persons who are migrants, or have a migratory background, and who have no (or no significant) ties to the country they live in (yet). Considering this definition and the definition of the *in situ* context, it may be possible that a person who is at first stateless in the migratory context can transition to being stateless *in situ* when the ties with a country have grown sufficiently strong. However, the exact point when someone transitions from one context into the other is hard to pinpoint and will be dependent on the circumstances of the individual(s) concerned. Hence, this remains quite a grey area. The part below headed 'Contexts of statelessness: a practical perspective' attempts to clarify this further.

International legal instruments: support for the two contexts of statelessness?

This part examines whether, and if so to what extent, international legal instruments – in the broad sense, so including 'soft' law – support the distinction between statelessness *in situ* and statelessness in the migratory context.

UNHCR guidance on the 1954 Convention

In its foreword and introduction on the background of the 1954 Convention, the UNHCR *Handbook on the Protection of Stateless Persons* (Handbook) discusses the different contexts in which statelessness can arise (UNHCR 2014). This Handbook provides states with guidance on the implementation of the 1954 Convention and can be classified as 'soft' law. Similar to the findings in the literature review, the Handbook's explanations (UNHCR 2014, para. 1) of the two contexts of statelessness make visible again that statelessness in the migratory context, or – as the Handbook puts it – 'in migratory situations' is not really defined; only an example is given here. However, the characteristics of statelessness *in situ* included in the Handbook (UNHCR 2014, para. 1) are more elaborate and include the following elements: 'never crossed borders', 'in their "own country"', 'in country of their long-term residence', 'country of their birth'.

Part II of the Handbook raises the issue of populations that are stateless *in situ* in the context of statelessness determination procedures. On this matter, the Handbook says that statelessness determination procedures can help states in complying with the obligations under the 1954 Convention. However, these procedures are not considered to be appropriate for stateless populations in a 'non-migratory context' which 'remain in their "own country"' (UNHCR 2014, para. 58). The Handbook presents a belief that statelessness determination procedures, which have the objective to grant an individual a status as a stateless person, are not suitable for populations which are stateless *in situ* 'because of the long-established ties to [a certain] country' (UNHCR 2014, para. 58). As was seen in literature as well, it is evident that the strong attachment of a stateless person to a state is where the distinction between the two contexts of statelessness is drawn, and the reason why is not only related to these ties but also to the difference in response that they warrant. On the matter of how to fulfil obligations with regard to people who are stateless *in situ* under the 1954 Convention then – if it is not appropriate to use statelessness determination procedures – the Handbook provides further guidance (UNHCR 2014, para. 58):

> Depending on the circumstances of the populations under consideration, States might be advised to undertake targeted nationality campaigns or nationality verification efforts rather than statelessness determination procedures.

The Handbook gives more information on these forms of response (UNHCR 2014, paras 59–60), and also remarks that in practice the procedural requirements of these responses will be comparable to the ones set for statelessness determination procedures.

In Part III of the Handbook a distinction is again made between 'individuals in a migratory context' (UNHCR 2014, paras 144–163) and 'individuals in their "own country"' (UNHCR 2014, paras 164–165) when discussing the appropriate status for stateless persons at the national level. The characteristics of statelessness in the migratory context are again not elaborated; the Handbook really concerns itself with the type of status that stateless persons in this context should get at the national level, which often, depending on their circumstances, involves a residence permit. In the considerations on statelessness *in situ* this context is again characterised further: it can include stateless persons 'who are long-term, habitual residents of the state, which is often their country of birth'; who have a 'profound connection with the state in question, often accompanied with an absence of links with other countries' (UNHCR 2014, para. 164). It is also considered that statelessness *in situ* arises as a consequence of denial of nationality – even when the person in question is born in the state and has resided there for his or her whole life. Another reason for statelessness appearing in this context, according to the Handbook, is that persons belonging to a certain community that 'has fallen out of political or social favour' are stripped of nationality (UNHCR 2014, para. 164). Being stateless in their 'own country', the Handbook says that persons who are stateless *in situ* should have the right to enter that country and reside there (UNHCR 2014, para. 166). Also, their connection to the state demands that they be fully integrated into society. It is therefore no surprise that the Handbook concludes that the proper status for persons who are stateless *in situ* is the nationality of the country involved. The status that persons who are stateless in their 'own country' should be able to obtain as a minimum, for instance where the only option for receiving adequate protection is to go through a statelessness determination procedure, would be permanent residence with facilitated access to nationality (UNHCR 2014, para. 165).

In concluding this part, it seems that the UNHCR guidance on the 1954 Convention, an international soft law instrument, confirms some of the findings of the literature review. First, it is evident that the definition of statelessness *in situ* is more elaborate than that of statelessness in the migratory context. Second, the elements used to characterise the first concept are similar to the ones used in literature. Also, the reason for making the distinction is that a difference in attachment to a state exists between the two contexts, which justifies a different response.

The UDHR and the Nottebohm case

Another source of law to be discussed is Article 15 of the Universal Declaration of Human Rights (UDHR), which guarantees the right to a nationality. In order to claim their right to a nationality, stateless persons may be able to rely on Article 15. Even though this instrument has influenced the entire United Nations (UN) human rights system, this specific Article lacks specification and, therefore, enforceability. In relation to Article 15, it has been argued that it is not surprising that, with no widely ratified international treaty defining or constraining criteria for granting nationality, the principle of a 'genuine and effective link' from the *Nottebohm* case (1955) has emerged as a guideline for state practice in granting nationality, thus ensuring the right to a nationality to a certain extent (Adjami and Harrington 2008, p. 106).

The *Nottenbohm* case concerned a dispute between Liechtenstein and Guatemala, in which Liechtenstein wanted Guatemala to recognise Friedrich Nottebohm as a Liechtenstein national. It has been pointed out that the definition of nationality used in this case (*Nottebohm* 1955) could provide good arguments for claiming nationality through facilitated naturalisation for persons who are stateless *in situ*, as they have a genuine connection to the state they live in (Mrekajova 2012, p. 18). This attachment could be established for instance when a person has been born on the territory of the state or has resided on the territory of the state for a reasonable amount of time. Similar to these factors, the judgment (*Nottebohm* 1955) sums up a number of characteristics that can help in establishing the strength of the ties of a person with a country:

> Different factors are taken into consideration, and their importance will vary from one case to the next: the habitual residence of the individual concerned is an important factor, but there are other factors such as the centre of his interests, his family ties, his participation in public life, attachment shown by him for a given country and inculcated in his children, etc.

These factors resemble the characteristics used in definitions of statelessness *in situ*. As such, the *Nottebohm* judgment seems to support a distinction being drawn between persons with and without a meaningful – or, in the words of the judgment, genuine – connection to a certain country. The case also demonstrates that the characteristics used in the definitions of statelessness *in situ* have roots in international law. However, it should be remembered that this study concerns stateless persons, and stateless persons lack a legal bond to a state. So indeed, as Rubenstein and Lenagh-Maguire (2014) observe, *Nottebohm* recognises 'an effective, social dimension' to nationality. However, as they also rightly point out, the judgment implies that where a formal – *de jure* – nationality is existent, but a true link is absent, an individual is not considered to have an effective nationality (when the formal dimension of nationality was acquired via naturalisation). They (Rubenstein and Lenagh-Maguire 2014, p. 270) continue:

> *Nottebohm* does not provide a solution in the reverse where there is ample evidence of the social connection between an individual and a state, but formal citizenship is lacking as a matter of domestic law. That task falls most often to human rights law as invoked by individuals seeking some of the benefits of nationality from a nation state that either refuses to grant them legal status, or conversely labels them with a citizenship they do not want to retain.

As such, the *Nottebohm* case cannot be seen as truly reinforcing a distinction between statelessness *in situ* and statelessness in the migratory context, as the case does not support granting citizenship to stateless persons with social attachment to a state. Still, as was found above, the case does demonstrate some support for making a distinction between persons with a genuine connection to a country and persons with no (or no meaningful) links to a state in the general sense, and shows that factors that are being used in the definitions of statelessness *in situ* are similar to those employed in the considerations of the *Nottebohm* case.

'Own country' under the International Covenant on Civil and Political Rights

The concept of 'own country' is explicitly mentioned in Article 12(4) of the International Covenant on Civil and Political Rights (ICCPR). On this Article and the notion of 'own country', the UN Human Rights Committee (UN-HRC) has provided further interpretation in a General Comment on Article 12, which says that the scope of this concept is broader than the country of nationality, and names 'special ties to a country' as a defining factor in establishing 'own country' (UN-HRC 1999, para. 20). It furthermore explicitly mentions stateless persons arbitrarily deprived of the right to acquire the nationality of the country of long-term residence. This consideration corresponds with statelessness *in situ*, as is evidenced by the characteristic of long-term residence. Furthermore, it supports a distinction being made between stateless persons who are long-term residents and have special ties to a country, and stateless persons who do not possess these characteristics – i.e. persons who are 'mere aliens' or who are, in other words, stateless in the migratory context – in terms of ensuring the right to enter one's own country.

Further guidance on the concept of 'own country' has been provided by the interpretations of the UN-HRC in its communications, which reaffirm the findings above (*Nystrom v. Australia* 2011, para. 7.4, see also Rubenstein and Lenagh-Maguire 2014). It is demonstrated, for instance, that a distinction can be made between stateless persons with (i.e. stateless *in situ*) and without (i.e.

stateless in the migratory context) strong personal and emotional links to a country as concerns the right to enter one's 'own country' (see also Rubenstein and Lenagh-Maguire 2014).

The concept of 'own country' under the ICCPR can be considered as supporting a distinction between stateless persons with (i.e. *in situ*) and without (i.e. in the migratory context) strong personal and emotional links to a country as concerns the right to enter one's 'own country', and hence a distinction between the two contexts of statelessness. In terms of the response to stateless persons – either statelessness determination (for stateless migrants) or recognition of nationality (for persons who are stateless *in situ*) – it seems that the concept of 'own country' cannot be said to truly reinforce this, as it only concerns the right to enter one's own country under the ICCPR. However, when remembering the lack of specification and enforceability of the right to a nationality in the UDHR and the fact that the latter instrument is an aspirational document that has inspired the entire UN human rights system, including the ICCPR, it may be said that the concept of 'own country' to a certain extent contributes to defining the content of the right to a nationality under international law. Taking this point of view, one could argue that a stateless person who is in his or her 'own country' according to the definitions used under the ICCPR should be granted nationality, while a stateless person who lacks the special ties to the country he or she is in should not be given citizenship (but should receive protection from the state). In this manner, the concept of 'own country' under the ICCPR can also be seen as supporting the distinction between the two contexts of statelessness being made because they entail a difference in response.

Regional legal instruments

At the regional level, more specifically in the Americas and in Europe, legal instruments can be found that relate to the issue discussed in this chapter.

The Inter-American Court of Human Rights (IACtHR) has observed, with regard to the right to a nationality as ensured by Article 20 of the American Convention on Human Rights (ACHR), that 'a foreigner who develops connections in a State cannot be equated to a person in transit' (*Yean and Bosico* v. *the Dominican Republic* 2005, para. 157) in a case concerning stateless persons. According to the IACtHR, the former should have their nationality recognised. This demonstrates direct support for a difference in responding to statelessness in the migratory context and statelessness *in situ*. Also, the interpretations of the IACtHR show that the state should respect a reasonable temporal limit in order to distinguish between the two contexts of statelessness (*Yean and Bosico* v. *the Dominican Republic* 2005, para. 157). Furthermore, it demonstrates the human rights dimension of this issue by relying on the function that a nationality has: nationality is a requirement for the exercise of specific rights and has evolved into being a human right (*Yean and Bosico* v. *the Dominican Republic* 2005, paras 137–139). For a more detailed discussion of the Dominican Republic example, see Blake, this volume.

At the European regional level, the Council of Europe (CoE) Convention on the Avoidance of Statelessness in Relation to State Succession reaffirms the value that is attached to the broad variety of connections of a person to a certain country in terms of recognition of nationality by international law and provides guidance on how to establish the attachment of a person to a country in the context of state succession. The usage of the term 'appropriate connection' in Article 5 of this instrument also appears helpful when defining the contexts of statelessness, as this assessment is similar to the method employed for determining who is stateless *in situ*. This indicates that stateless persons in a situation of state succession can be incorporated in the context of statelessness *in situ*.

The European Convention on Nationality's (ECN) formal definition of nationality does not seem to concern itself with whether a strong connection exists between the person and the state or rely on the international legal principles of 'genuine and effective link'. However, as Krūma (2013, pp. 46–47) says, it can be argued that the ECN supports the principle of effective link as a guideline on defining nationality and provides for compelling examples under Articles 6, 7(e) and 18 of the ECN, which demonstrate this. As such, the ECN appears to attach value to a certain tie of a person to a country, for instance a tie of long-term residence. This underlines that the ties of a person to a country are instrumental in determining his or her 'right' to acquire a nationality and what the proceedings ought to be.

Despite the absence of the right to nationality in the European Convention for the Protection of Human Rights and Fundamental Freedoms (ECHR), the case of *Andrejeva* v. *Latvia* (2009) seems to acknowledge that the ties of a person to a country can matter in relation to the protection that a stateless person can receive under the ECHR. More specifically, the European Court of Human Rights (ECtHR) recognised in this case that where a stateless person has had stable legal ties to a particular country, and to no other country, the state in question should treat this person in the same manner as a national where it concerns social security (*Andrejeva* v. *Latvia* 2009, para. 88), and perhaps beyond (ENS 2014d, pp. 23–24). As such, the case can be deemed to support a distinction between statelessness *in situ* and statelessness in the migratory context, and – to some extent – also the need for a different response depending on the context of statelessness. Moreover, the definition of statelessness *in situ* could benefit from the considerations of the ECtHR in the *Andrejeva* case, as it concerned a person who appeared to be stateless *in situ*. The ECtHR observed that Latvia was 'the only State with which [the applicant] had any stable legal ties and thus the only State which, objectively, could assume responsibility for her' (*Andrejeva* v. *Latvia* 2009, para. 88).

Summary

There is support in international legal instruments for making a distinction between *in situ* and migratory statelessness. The instruments discussed above provide, to different extents, an indication as to how the distinction is to be drawn. Individual decisions will depend on a broad range of factors indicating the strength of the ties between the person and the country in question. The guidance on the 1954 Convention addresses the two concepts and the difference in response they require. This is based upon a difference in the nature of the attachment of the persons concerned to the state. The Convention, then, explicitly and directly reinforces the distinction between the two contexts of statelessness. Furthermore, support seems to be found in (the interpretations of) the concept of 'own country' and (the interpretations of) the right to a nationality under the ACHR, as well as in the Council of Europe Convention on the Avoidance of Statelessness in Relation to State Succession in the usage of the term 'appropriate connection', and the ECHR, which refers to 'stable legal ties', to some extent. This support seems to be linked to human rights law, which was demonstrated for instance by the interpretations of the ACtHR on the matter. Also, the principle of nationality under international law, with its strong emphasis on genuine and effective ties of a person to a country, indirectly demonstrates why it is important – even when it concerns persons that lack nationality – to distinguish between persons with and without meaningful links to a country, because it seems that persons with those ties have a better reason for claiming the nationality of a country than persons who do not (yet) have such ties (even though they may still claim the protection of a state). In this regard, this study has examined a couple of important international instruments to demonstrate this, but does not claim to be exhaustive. In relation to the concept of nationality mentioned here, note that Chapter 15 examines the conflation of 'nationality' and 'citizenship' in the discussion of statelessness.

It is particularly helpful to look at the characterisations of the two concepts in the UNHCR guidance on the 1954 Convention because of its direct and explicit link with the two contexts of statelessness. When comparing the factors to be taken into account according to UNHCR, the important yet obvious characteristic that is lacking in the working definitions formulated on the basis of the literature review is that stateless persons *in situ* are in a non-migratory situation. As this factor was encountered in the literature as well, and can help to provide more clarity, it is added to the definition. Furthermore, the duration of the ties to a country as a differentiator between *in situ* and migratory statelessness is a factor that is visible in the interpretations of the IACtHR for example. Family ties as a characteristic for defining statelessness *in situ* are also found in various instruments, including the *Nottebohm* case, the concept of 'own country' under the ICCPR and the CoE Convention on the Avoidance of Statelessness in Relation to State Succession. However, given the fact that, according to the definition, the ties of a stateless individual to a country have to be meaningful for the person to be considered stateless *in situ*, it is not required to specify this further in the definition. Furthermore, as there is support in international legal instruments for the distinction between the two contexts of statelessness and for the ties that a person has or does not have to a country as the differentiator between the two, no further adjustments to the working definitions are deemed necessary. Thus, statelessness *in situ* is defined as encompassing persons who are in a non-migratory situation and remain stateless in their 'own country', and who have meaningful and long-established ties to the country they live in. Statelessness in the migratory context is defined as concerning stateless persons who are migrants, or have a migratory background, who have no (or no significant) ties to the country they live in (yet).

Contexts of statelessness: a practical perspective

In order to apply the concepts of statelessness *in situ* and statelessness in the migratory context, definitions were formulated on the basis of the findings of this study so far in the summary of the last section. These definitions are applied to three cases of stateless persons in Europe (ENS 2014a, 2014b, 2014c) in order to come to a provisional understanding of the practical workability of the contexts of statelessness. These cases are based on the testimonies of stateless persons and were collected by the European Network on Statelessness (ENS), a civil society alliance with members in 39 European countries, across Europe as part of their campaign to protect stateless persons in this region. The real names of the interviewees are not used to protect their identity (see also ENS 2014e).

Case I: Isa (ENS 2014a)

Isa was born in Kosovo – Former Yugoslavia. He fled to Belgrade following the 1999 conflict, but because he didn't have any papers proving his identity, was never registered as an internally displaced person.

His very first document, his birth certificate, was issued in 2013 when he was 29. This was only possible due to a new procedure introduced in 2012. Up till then Isa lived a life of an invisible. He did not attend school, he did not have health insurance and the only pieces of evidence about his residence are the statements of his common-law spouse and his neighbours.

However, despite managing to register his birth with the birth registry, Isa remains stateless without a nationality. He cannot 'inherit' his father's nationality since his father doesn't have any (his father was born in Macedonia and lived in Kosovo since the 1980s, but has never had his nationality officially registered) or his mother's (she left Isa when he was only two weeks old and Isa doesn't know if she held any nationality at the moment of his birth). Without nationality, Isa remains deprived of rights and services. He says:

'I cannot get married, recognise paternity of my children, visit my family in Kosovo. I cannot work legally, receive social welfare assistance or register for health insurance. To be without documents and a nationality is as if you never existed in this world.'

Serbia currently lacks a procedure to recognise Isa's statelessness and regularise his status. Meanwhile, the only option open to Isa now is to try to acquire Serbian nationality through the naturalisation procedure. Unfortunately, the outcome of the procedure remains uncertain because Isa cannot

provide any written proof of his residence, which is one of the legal requirements. So he remains stuck in a vicious circle and facing a life in limbo.

Isa is one of the persons who remained stateless after the dissolution of Yugoslavia. In order to understand his situation, it is important briefly to discuss the
break-up of Yugoslavia. When Yugoslavia dissolved, the countries mentioned in
Isa's case came into being: the Republic of Serbia, the Socialist Republic of
Macedonia and the currently partially recognised Republic of Kosovo. In the
states that succeeded Yugoslavia, many persons were left stateless. As was presented earlier, persons left stateless in their (new) state after state succession can
be referred to as stateless *in situ*. The starting point for assessing Isa's case thus
appears to be the definition of statelessness *in situ*. First of all, Isa is indeed stateless in a non-migratory context; he has not crossed borders by fleeing to another
state – at least, not to another country that is not a state that succeeded Yugoslavia, the country in which he was born. As such, he remains stateless in his 'own
country', as he has considerable and long-term ties to Yugoslavia through birth.
Arguably, one of the states that succeeded Yugoslavia should therefore have
granted Isa nationality. Remember furthermore that in literature 'long-established
ties to a country' have been specified as including long-term habitual residence
or residence at the time of state succession. Also, that Isa is stateless *in situ* is
evident when recalling the difference in response that the two contexts of statelessness entail. Similar to what, for instance, Manly (2012, 2014) has held, the
appropriate response to Isa's statelessness is not a statelessness determination
procedure; rather states are advised to undertake targeted nationality campaigns
or nationality verification efforts. On the basis of the facts presented in the case
of Isa above, the conclusion may thus be that he is stateless *in situ*. Given this
finding, it might be helpful to include 'residence at the time of state succession'
in the definition of this context of statelessness.

Case II: Luka (ENS 2014b)

Luka was born in Ukraine, then still a part of the former USSR. After
growing up in an orphanage, he moved to Slovakia in 1991 when he was
only 15. Given the circumstances of his childhood Luka never had any
documents from the Ukrainian state confirming his nationality.

During his stay in Slovakia Luka was repeatedly detained, last time in
2010, when he spent 14 months in the detention centre. He was released based
on the decision of the court that his expulsion from Slovakia is not possible
and was granted tolerated stay. Police repeatedly verified and investigated the
possibility of an administrative expulsion to Ukraine, however Ukraine never
confirmed his identity nor his citizenship. Although Luka doesn't have any
travel document, the Slovak authorities simply recorded his citizenship as
'undetermined'. All the evidence however suggests that he is indeed stateless.

Luka has an 8-year-old son who is a Slovak citizen and who lives with him and his mother – Luka's partner. Luka is unable to register himself officially as the father in his son's birth certificate because he does not possess any identification document.

In 2013, when Luka tried to submit an application for extension of his tolerated stay, he was asked to submit new documents from the Ukrainian embassy confirming that Ukrainian embassy refuses to issue him with replacement travel document. Although the police had at that time already enough proof confirming that Ukraine did not accept Luka as its citizen they still refused to accept his application. Instead they issued Luka with a fine of €80 for the misdemeanour of illegal stay. One week later he was given another fine, this time of €160.

After living in Slovakia for over 20 years, Luka is still not recognised as being stateless and his tolerated stay status still doesn't allow him to work or to have health insurance. He cannot marry his partner and he cannot be registered officially as the father of his son.

Source: www.statelessness.eu/faces-of-statelessness/luka, reproduced with the permission of the European Network on Statelessness (ENS)

The case of Luka presents a dilemma. Yes, Slovakia was never part of the USSR, so the qualification as stateless *in situ* in a similar manner to Isa does not apply here, and he appears to be in a migratory context. However, part of then-Czechoslovakia was annexed by the USSR and the relationship between Czechoslovakia and the USSR was very close, making the situation slightly more complicated. What makes the case even more difficult is the fact that Luka's ties to Ukraine appear to be practically non-existent; he has no (family) ties to Ukraine as he grew up in an orphanage and moved to Slovakia when he was only 15 years old. Using the current working definitions of this chapter, Luka would not be stateless *in situ*, because he is in a migratory situation, but would also not be a stateless migrant, because his ties to Ukraine are non-existent and his ties to Slovakia are significant through his duration of residence and his family there.

It is therefore feasible to look beyond these definitions, because they may have flaws in them, and consider definitions that were encountered earlier in this chapter in law and literature. Particular consideration is given to the concept of 'own country' and the significant ties that this entails, as well as the criterion of non-migratory situation. Recall, for instance, that 'own country' has been interpreted by the UN-HRC as inviting consideration of factors such as long-standing residence, close personal and family ties and intentions to remain, as well as the absence of such ties elsewhere. That this interpretation is correct is underlined in the UNHCR Guidance on the 1954 Convention, which notably mentions the absence of ties elsewhere. When applying this to the case of Luka, it is clear that he has long-standing residence and close personal and family ties through his partner and son. Furthermore, his intention to remain can be seen in that he has a partner and a son. Lastly, ties to Ukraine are – besides being born there as an orphan – absent, as noted above. Pursuant to the concept of 'own country' as used in the definition of stateless *in situ* and as interpreted in international legal instruments, this would thus appear to label Luka as stateless *in situ*. But, what of the non-migratory factor of the definition? Some definitions in literature have included this factor, or have referred to it in a different manner, for example by saying that statelessness *in situ* concerns a situation in which persons have been stateless for decades or generations, or that it is the country where the ancestors of the person in question are from (e.g. Van Waas and Neal 2013). The fact that statelessness *in situ* concerns a non-migratory situation is acknowledged in international legal instruments as well, mainly by the Handbook, by saying that this concept is applicable to stateless persons 'who have never crossed borders' (UNHCR 2014). So, when applying this to Luka's case, the conclusion can only be that he has crossed borders and that he has not been in the country for generations, which would point to him being stateless in the migratory context. As such, this case reveals a contradiction in the definition of stateless *in situ*, namely between the concept of 'own country' and the non-migratory factor of the definition. The concept of 'own country' appears to be more inclusive, i.e. broader than what is meant by the notion of statelessness *in situ*. The only way to solve this is to weigh the two and maybe approach the case from an entirely different perspective.

This chapter proved that the difference between the two contexts of statelessness articulates a difference in attachment to a state which warrants a difference in response. Therefore it is helpful to ask whether it is appropriate for Luka to have to go through a statelessness determination procedure and receive a corresponding protection status. Or would this be disproportionate and does Slovakia need to recognise him as a national? The principle of proportionality can thus play an important role in this process. When looking at the case from this perspective, it appears that it is not unfair to ask Luka to obtain a status as a stateless person through a statelessness determination mechanism; he has not been in the country for generations. Even though the facts of the case demonstrate that it is obvious that Luka does 'deserve' to obtain the nationality of Slovakia at some point, this is not out of the question when using statelessness determination procedures, as the connected status to this should provide for a possibility of (facilitated) naturalisation after a certain number of years.

When considering the case again, it indeed appears that Luka is in a different situation than that which is meant by the concept of statelessness *in situ*. As such, the proper characterisation of his case would be to use the notion of statelessness in the migratory context. Luka's case, nonetheless, has demonstrated that the definition of statelessness *in situ* is not as inclusive as the notion of 'own country' in international law, to which the definition of the former refers. Still, the concept of 'own country' proved to be an element in the definition that was helpful to some extent, as it could aid in establishing the significance of the ties of a (stateless) person to a country. The notion of 'own country' should therefore not necessarily be eliminated from the definition. However, it is important to incorporate an element into the definition that can help in weighing the concept of 'own country' and the non-migratory factor in a sort of proportionality test that considers the difference in response.

Case III: Sarah (ENS 2014c)

Sarah was born and raised in the Democratic Republic of Congo. Until the age of 18 she possessed both Congolese and Rwandan nationality as her father is Rwandan and her mother is Congolese.

In 2001, during the conflicts between the two neighbouring countries, Sarah's parents were arrested on allegations of spying on the Congolese government. At the age of 15 Sarah was left on her own. She stayed with family friends for a year, but soon realised that she had nowhere to go. More and more she felt that her life was in danger if she stayed in Congo. After a year of her parents being put into jail, in 2002, when Sarah was only 16, she decided to flee to the Netherlands. On her arrival she applied for a residence permit for unaccompanied minor asylum seekers. Her application was rejected and the process of repatriation commenced. However two days prior to her return to Kinshasa, Congo the Dutch Repatriation & Departure Service announced that the Laisser-Passer needed for her deportation and previously granted by the Congolese authorities had been withdrawn for unknown reasons. This suspended the deportation process and Sarah was allowed to stay.

In order to regularise her status Sarah applied for a Dutch 'no-fault residence permit', a one year residence permit for those who cannot leave the Netherlands through no fault of their own. As part of her application she had to acquire proof of identity documentation from the Congolese authorities and it was at this point Sarah for the first time realised that she was stateless. The Congolese Embassy in the Netherlands stated that she automatically lost her Congolese nationality at the age of 18, stating that people with dual nationality are ought to opt for one nationality when they turn 18. Sarah was not aware of this. She contacted the Rwandan Embassy several times to try and obtain identity documents from them. However, she was told that she cannot be recognised as a Rwandan citizen because she was not born in Rwanda, and has no close links to the country.

Now, 12 years later, Sarah is still stuck in the same situation, unable to (re)acquire original Congolese or Rwandan identity documents. Because the Netherlands currently has no procedure to recognise or regularise stateless persons, Sarah has no solution in sight.

Source: www.statelessness.eu/faces-of-statelessness/sarah, reproduced with permission of the European Network on Statelessness (ENS).

Even though Sarah has been in the Netherlands for a considerable time, her story demonstrates that she fled from Congo to the Netherlands, making her a migrant. She thus seems to be stateless in the migratory context. Is it true then that she has no or no significant ties to the Netherlands (yet)? The answer appears to be 'yes'. The case above does not mention any meaningful ties to the Netherlands, whereas ties (through her parents) to Rwanda and Congo can be observed. Sarah has also actually lived in the latter country, and she seems to have the strongest connection to it. As such, Sarah is stateless in the migratory context.

Definitions and conclusions

This chapter demonstrates that in literature a consensus exists on the concepts of statelessness *in situ* and statelessness in the migratory context and what they entail. It was seen that the two concepts represent a difference in attachment to the state a person lives in, and that this difference in attachment requires a difference in response. By considering the attachment (i.e. the ties of a person to a country) one can thus draw a distinction between the two contexts of statelessness. More importantly, international legal instruments explicitly and implicitly support this distinction and how it is made. An important finding in this regard was the fact that the notion of nationality in international law supports a distinction being made on the basis of the ties of a person to a state, as people with significant connections have a better reason for claiming the nationality of a country than persons with no (or not yet) such ties, even though they may still claim protection of a state.

Still, in the spectrum extending from being a 'full' citizen or national to migrant (for discussion of the relationship between national and citizen see Tonkiss, this volume), somewhere a distinction between statelessness *in situ* and statelessness in the migratory context can indeed be made. The case study helped in uncovering how to do that. While applying the concepts to the cases, it appeared that the working definitions of the concepts could be fine-tuned. An important finding was that the notion of 'own country' – which is referred to in the definition of statelessness *in situ* – in international law is broader than the concept of statelessness *in situ*. As such, using 'own country' in the definition seems contradictory. However, the case studies proved that drawing a line between the two contexts of statelessness is a process of weighing the different facts of a case against the definitions of the two contexts of statelessness. Particularly helpful in this exercise was the usage of a proportionality test, especially when employing this in relation to the response that a context required; i.e. is it in a certain case proportional to ask a person to resort to a statelessness determination procedure, or should he or she have his or her nationality recognised by the state in question? This implies that the goal in terms of this proportionality test is to ensure that a stateless person is able to acquire a nationality that is in line with his or her personal and social situation (cf. Hirsch Ballin 2014). Eventually, it proved possible to apply the concepts of statelessness *in situ* and statelessness in the migratory context to the cases using working definitions of these concepts that did not go beyond the meaning of these contexts as indicated in the literature and legal instruments studied. Consequently, the concepts can be reformulated as follows:

- Statelessness *in situ*: persons who are (usually) in a non-migratory situation and remain stateless in their 'own country', often since birth – who are long-standing residents or were residents at the time of state succession, who have close personal and family ties to the country in question and intentions to remain, as well as no such ties elsewhere – which warrants a different response than to stateless migrants, as the former should be granted nationality.
- Statelessness in the migratory context: statelessness persons who are migrants, or have a migratory background, who have no (or no significant) ties to the country they live in (yet), and should, as a consequence, be able to obtain the protection of the state they live in (as well as access to facilitated naturalisation) through determination of statelessness.

  The latter is no requirement, but a characterisation that can help in distinguishing between the two contexts as it concerns the proper response to this context of statelessness.

Within the two categories of stateless persons, it might be possible to make further distinctions that could better address the situation of a certain type of stateless population, e.g. within the context of statelessness *in situ* one could distinguish persons who remained stateless after state succession. In this regard, it should be remembered, though, that it would be impossible to have a label that would exactly fit every type of situation that a stateless person finds himself or herself in. Also, it is undesirable to have other qualifications for contexts in which statelessness arises from a legal perspective, because international legal instruments support and sometimes even explicitly refer to statelessness in the migratory context and/or statelessness *in situ*. Furthermore, these instruments – some more clearly than others – reinforce the difference in response that these contexts entail. Thus, using the two contexts of statelessness can provisionally be evaluated positively. Still, it must be admitted that applying the concepts of statelessness *in situ* and statelessness in the migratory context to particular cases remains a challenging exercise, as the facts of each case have to be weighed bearing the principle of proportionality in mind and using the definitions of the two contexts of statelessness.

Note

1 This chapter is based on the author's prize-winning Master's Thesis 'Contexts of Statelessness: A Study of the Concepts "Statelessness *in situ*" and "Statelessness in the Migratory Context" in Europe', which was written to complete the Research Master in Law at Tilburg University in August 2014. The author is grateful to Professor Ernst Hirsch Ballin and Laura van Waas for their comments and guidance during the process of writing the Master's Thesis. Any omissions or mistakes remain the author's own.

References

ACVZ (Adviescommissie voor Vreemdelingenzaken) (2013) *Geen land te bekennen. Een advies over de verdragsrechtelijke bescherming van staatlozen in Nederland* (No

Country of One's Own. An Advisory Report on Treaty Protection for Stateless Persons in the Netherlands). [online] Available at: http://acvz.org/wp-content/uploads/2015/05/04-12-2013_GeenLandTeBekennen.pdf [Accessed 10 November 2015].

Adjami, M. and Harrington, J. (2008) The scope and content of Article 15 of the Universal Declaration of Human Rights. *Refugee Survey Quarterly*, 27(3), pp. 93–109.

Andrejeva v. *Latvia* (2009) App. No. 55707/00. European Court of Human Rights. 18 February.

ENS (European Network on Statelessness) (2013) Statelessness Determination and the Protection Status of Stateless Persons. A Summary Guide of Good Practices and Factors to Consider when Designing National Determination and Protection Mechanisms. [online] Available at: www.statelessness.eu/sites/www.statelessness.eu/files/attachments/resources/Statelessness%20determination%20and%20the%20protection%20status%20of%20stateless%20persons%20ENG.pdf [Accessed 20 November 2015].

ENS (2014a) Isa – Faces of Statelessness. [online] Available at: www.statelessness.eu/faces-of-statelessness/isa [Accessed 27 November 2015].

ENS (2014b) Luka – Faces of Statelessness. [online] Available at: www.statelessness.eu/faces-of-statelessness/luka [Accessed 27 November 2015].

ENS (2014c) Sarah – Faces of Statelessness. [online] Available at: www.statelessness.eu/faces-of-statelessness/sarah [Accessed 27 November 2015].

ENS (2014d) *Strategic Litigation: An Obligation for Statelessness Determination under the European Convention on Human Rights?* ENS Discussion Paper 09/14.

ENS (2014e) Still Stateless, Still Suffering. Why Europe Must Act Now to Protect Stateless Persons. [online] Available at: www.statelessness.eu/sites/www.statelessness.eu/files/ENS_Still_Stateless_Still_Suffering_online%20version_2.pdf [Accessed 22 December 2015].

Gibney, M. (2014) Statelessness and Citizenship in Ethical and Political Perspective. In Edwards, A. and van Waas, L. (eds) *Nationality and Statelessness under International Law*, pp. 44–63. Cambridge: Cambridge University Press.

Gyulai, G. (2012) Statelessness in the EU Framework for International Protection. *European Journal of Migration and Law*, 14(3), pp. 279–295.

Gyulai, G. (2014) The Determination of Statelessness and the Establishment of a Statelessness-specific Protection Regime. In Edwards, A. and van Waas, L. (eds) *Nationality and Statelessness under International Law*, pp. 116–143. Cambridge: Cambridge University Press.

Hirsch Ballin, E. M. H. (2014) *Citizens' Rights and the Right to Be a Citizen* (Developments in International Law Vol. 66). Leiden/Boston: Brill Nijhoff.

Kochovski, I. (2013) Statelessness and Discriminatory Nationality Laws: The Case of the Roma in Bosnia and Serbia. LLM Thesis, Tilburg University. [online] Available at: http://arno.uvt.nl/show.cgi?fid=132633 [Accessed 26 November 2015].

Krūma, K. (2013) *EU Citizenship, Nationality and Migrant Status: An Ongoing Challenge*. Leiden/Boston: Martinus Nijhoff Publishers.

Manly, M. (2012) UNHCR's mandate and activities to address statelessness in Europe. *European Journal of Migration and Law*, 14(3), pp. 261–277.

Manly, M. (2014) UNHCR's Mandate and Activities to Address Statelessness. In Edwards, A. and van Waas, L. (eds) *Nationality and Statelessness under International Law*, pp. 88–115. Cambridge: Cambridge University Press.

Månsson, M. (2013) Reduction of Statelessness and Access to Nationality: The Need for EU Legislation. The Showcase of Stateless Roma in Slovenia. LLM Thesis, Lund University. [online] Available at: http://lup.lub.lu.se/luur/download?func=downloadFile&recordOId=3800897&fileOId=3812335 [Accessed 26 November 2015].

Mrekajova, E. (2012) Naturalization of Stateless Persons: Solution of Statelessness? LLM Thesis, Tilburg University. [online] Available at: http://arno.uvt.nl/show.cgi?fid= 127305 [Accessed 26 November 2015].

Nikolic, N. (2013) *De jure* Statelessness in Serbia. A Critical Analysis of the Legal Framework with Regards to Combating Statelessness and the Protection of Stateless Persons. Master's Thesis, University of Gothenburg, University of Roehampton, University of Tromsø. [online] Available at: http://munin.uit.no/handle/10037/5307 [Accessed 26 November 2015].

Nottebohm (Liechtenstein v. *Guatemala)* (1955) ICJ Reports 1955, p. 4, General List, No. 18.

Nystrom v. *Australia* (2011) Comm. No. 1557/2007, CCPR/C/102/D/1557/2007.

Rubenstein, K. and Lenagh-Maguire, N. (2014) More or Less Secure? Nationality Questions, Deportation and Dual Nationality. In Edwards, A. and Van Waas, L. (eds) *Nationality and Statelessness under International Law*, pp. 264–291. Cambridge: Cambridge University Press.

UN-HRC (1999) CCPR General Comment No. 27: Article 12 (Freedom of Movement). CCPR/C/21/Rev.1/Add.9.

UNHCR (2014) *Handbook on the Protection of Stateless Persons under the 1954 Convention relating to the Status of Stateless Persons*. Geneva: UNHCR.

Van Waas, L. and Neal, M. (2013) Statelessness and the Role of National Human Rights Institutions, *Tilburg Law School Legal Research Paper Series No. 022/2013*. [online] Available at: http://papers.ssrn.com/sol3/papers.cfm?abstract_id=2356166 [Accessed 24 November 2015].

Yean and Bosico v. *the Dominican Republic* (2005) Inter-American Court of Human Rights. 8 September.

4   Unpacking statelessness

Amal de Chickera and Laura van Waas[1]

Introduction

Statelessness is a concept of international law, defined by a UN treaty that was adopted over half a century ago (Convention Relating to the Status of Stateless Persons 1954, Art. 1). Nevertheless, the term remains a slippery one. It denotes a human rights problem of massive proportions, global reach and significant consequence. Yet the word is little-used and poorly understood in the public arena, scoring under half a million 'hits' on Google and often failing to register with the average person-in-the-street in terms of its meaning. It succeeds in conjuring up images of dislocation and exclusion, yet falls short of communicating the full human impact of the phenomenon. It is perceived by some as a narrow, technical, legal concept, yet embraced by others as a broad descriptor for a lack of belonging or a situation of rightlessness. In short, there appears to be something both irresistibly compelling yet inherently unsatisfying about the term. This is reflected in – or perhaps explained by – the way in which scholars, policy makers and commentators alike have struggled for several decades to get a firm grip on it, leading at times to highly divergent uses in spite of the existence of an international legal definition.

In the aftermath of hurricane Katrina, one commentator observed that 'those escaping the deluge ... were frequently labelled "refugees" by media reports ... these persons were not, strictly speaking, refugees ... in many respects they were adrift and functionally stateless' (Inniss 2007, p. 331). This statement, which first points out the incorrect use of the term 'refugee' and then goes on to incorrectly apply the term 'stateless' to a non-statelessness situation, is emblematic of wider confusion around and misapplication of the term statelessness.

That the term statelessness has proven to be somewhat 'elusive' has been identified as one reason for the relative lack of mobilisation of stakeholders, historically, to tackle the issue – as compared to other significant human rights challenges (Kingston 2013, p. 81). Today, however, an international movement to address statelessness is emerging, exemplified by numerous national, regional and UN-level initiatives, including the Global Campaign to End Statelessness by 2024 which was launched by the Office of the United Nations High Commissioner for Refugees (UNHCR) at the end of 2014 – also known as the #ibelong campaign.[2] This changing context demands a careful reappraisal of the question of terminology: A shared understanding of definition will be critical to meeting the new level of ambition with which the problem of statelessness is being confronted, since definition determines approach and this ultimately shapes the outcome of collective efforts in this field.

This chapter looks at the historic evolution and contemporary understanding of statelessness with a view to identifying overlap, complementarity and divergence. While acknowledging that many words enjoy multiple meanings across different contexts and disciplines – with statelessness likely to remain a term-of-art that can be usefully embraced in a diversity of ways – the discussion centres on how the concept is defined and understood as a legal term, recognising that the obligations of states are anchored in international law. The chapter unpacks the discourses relating to 'de facto statelessness' and 'ineffective nationality', and positions these within the broader context of the challenge of 'protection' under contemporary human rights law. It also looks at the blurring of conceptual boundaries between statelessness and related phenomena, commenting on the implications of a failure to distinguish statelessness as a distinct issue for the effectiveness of remedial measures. With the underlying aim of supporting and informing real-world efforts to address this global human rights challenge, this chapter argues that a greater awareness and application of the legal definition of statelessness in related research design, publications and debate is essential.

Defining statelessness

Legal history traces the origins of statelessness back to the genesis of the modern system of nation-states (Kubben 2014). The adoption of the first national laws regulating access to citizenship of the nation-state set the parameters for inclusion and exclusion, with the by-product that some people gained dual nationality while others were left with none (for discussion specifically of the relationship between citizenship and nationality see Tonkiss, this volume). By the nineteenth century, international lawyers had already explicitly identified both of these anomalies as a concern, calling the latter 'inhumane' (Bluntschli 1872), 'embarrassing' (Hall and Pearce Higgins 1880) and 'a blemish in international law' (Oppenheim 1912). The term *statelessness* was introduced into legal doctrine as shorthand for the situation of people who were otherwise – rather poignantly – described as 'destitute of nationality' (Oppenheim 1912, pp. 387–390). In 1930, with the adoption under the auspices of the League of Nations of the *Convention on Certain Questions Relating to the Conflict of Nationality Laws* and the *Protocol Relating to a Certain Case of Statelessness*, the concept of statelessness made its first appearance in multilateral treaties aimed at reducing the incidence of this phenomenon (third preamble).

It was not, however, until after the Second World War that a process got underway that would lead to the agreement of a definition of statelessness – or, rather, of a 'stateless person' – for the purposes of international law. In 1948, the Economic and Social Council of the newly formed United Nations requested a study of 'the existing situation in regard to the protection of stateless persons' (Economic and Social Council 1948, Resolution 116, p. 18). The resulting UN *A Study of Statelessness*, published the following year, construed its focus more broadly than the situation of people who are 'destitute of nationality' to consider also people who 'without having been deprived of their nationality [...] no longer enjoy the protection and assistance of their national authorities'. Two distinct but related concepts, *de jure* statelessness and de facto statelessness, were thereby introduced. Subsequently, the study pointed out that 'a considerable majority of stateless persons [*de jure* and de facto] are at present refugees' and devoted extensive attention to the situation of refugees (UNHCR 1949).

An Ad Hoc Committee took up the task of drafting a convention to address the vulnerability of these two distinct, but related and sometimes overlapping, categories of so-called 'unprotected persons'. It prepared a *Draft Convention Relating to the Status of Refugees* and an accompanying *Draft Protocol thereto Relating to the Status of Stateless Persons*. The former, adopted in 1951, defined and established the status of 'refugee' as an international legal status to which various rights are attached (Convention Relating to the Status of Refugees 1951, art. 1). According to the definition enshrined in this instrument, a refugee is considered to be in need of international protection because he or she has fled his or her country due to a well-founded fear of persecution on one of a number of particular grounds. Consideration of the latter text – the protocol – was delayed, but it was ultimately adopted in 1954 as a stand-alone instrument with a view to regulating and improving the status of stateless persons who are not also refugees and are therefore not covered by the 1951 Refugee Convention (Convention Relating to the Status of Stateless Persons 1954).

Article 1(1) of what thus became the *1954 Convention Relating to the Status of Stateless Persons* (1954 Convention) contains a definition of a stateless person:

> The term 'stateless person' means a person who is not considered as a national by any state under the operation of its law.

While many other instruments – treaties and soft law – adopted before and since employ the terminology of 'statelessness' or 'stateless person', this is the only international document which provides a definition, establishing what is to be understood by 'stateless person' as a concept of international law (Convention on the Reduction of Statelessness 1961, Art. 7). As is evident from the citation above, the definition is also singular in the sense that it establishes one international status, that of 'stateless person', which hinges solely on whether a person enjoys the legal bond of nationality. The separate notions of *de jure* and de facto statelessness, while discussed in the earlier UN Study and debated within the drafting process of the convention text, were not reflected in the definition adopted.

In short, for the purposes of international law, it is a person's status under domestic law which is pivotal to determining whether he or she is 'stateless'. The question, quite simply, is this: Is he or she recognised as a national by any state? How or when the person acquired a nationality, whether that nationality is under threat of withdrawal, where the person finds him or herself (i.e. whether he or she has migrated or been displaced) and even what the quality of the nationality is in terms of the rights which attach to it under the states' domestic legislation or in practice – none of these are relevant to a finding of statelessness (UNHCR 2014). On the face of it, this seems a logical and straightforward approach to definition. Nevertheless, as discussed below, the concept of statelessness remained much debated and subject to divergent uses, both within legal doctrine and across other disciplines.

Debating statelessness

The 1954 Convention was drafted at a time when international human rights protection was in its infancy. The Universal Declaration of Human Rights (UDHR) had only recently been adopted, affirming 'the equal and inalienable rights of all members of the human family' (UNGA 1948, first preamble). Other binding human rights covenants and conventions were yet to be elaborated and human rights monitoring bodies yet to be established at the level of the UN. The individual was not yet a direct subject of international law, with his or her protection deriving instead from the reciprocal relationships of states. Therefore, nationality was central to a person's status and protection, opening the door to rights and entitlements under domestic law and creating a link between the individual and international law through his or her attachment to a state. In this context, the 1954 Convention asserted its purpose of responding to the UN's 'profound concern for stateless persons' and assuring them the widest possible exercise of the fundamental rights and freedoms contained within the UN Charter and UDHR (second preamble). The *raison d'être* of this instrument was thus to ensure that those who lacked nationality were protected internationally despite there being no benefit of reciprocity attached to such protection.

However, the line between protected and unprotected does not always align neatly with the formal boundary demarcated by nationality. What of those individuals who, as discussed in the 1949 UN Study, 'without having been deprived of their nationality [...] no longer enjoy the protection and assistance of their national authorities'? As the text of the 1954 Convention was being debated there was – and to this day there remains – concern about the position of those whose situation and needs are analogous to that of a person without a nationality, except that they continue to enjoy this legal bond. In many instances, such individuals will be protected under the 1951 Convention regime adopted to regulate the status of refugees. Yet there may still be 'unprotected persons' whose situation falls outside both the 'stateless person' and the 'refugee' definitions, and thereby beyond the scope of application of the two conventions designed to remedy the protection gap.

It was on this basis that a non-binding recommendation was included within the Final Act of the 1954 Convention, asking contracting states to consider also extending the rights set out in the instrument to persons who do not fall within the definition but who nevertheless – and for valid reasons – have been left without national protection (Robinson 1955, pp. 11–13). As a result, although the definition of a stateless person contained within the 1954 Convention is singular and under international law there is no qualifier of *de jure* attached to it (if you meet the definition, you are 'stateless'), legal doctrine continued to discuss two different 'types' of statelessness: *de jure* – those who meet the definition in the 1954 Convention – and de facto – those who hold a nationality but whose situation is nonetheless cause for concern, which is also (partly) tailored for in the Final Act. The concept of de facto statelessness thus became part and parcel of the international lexicon of statelessness. However, it has remained a vague and elastic notion, which was variously used to describe those who actually were stateless and those who had a nationality but had various challenges in accessing rights.

The emergence of the notion of de facto statelessness accompanied and spurred on criticism of the legal definition of statelessness. While there have been various articulations of such critique, it can be broadly categorised into four areas. First, the challenge of doctrinal development: Statelessness suffered a long period of neglect following the adoption of the UN conventions, during which there was little doctrinal development or guidance on the interpretation of statelessness and perhaps as a result, a narrow, legalistic view taken on the definition. Second, the challenge of proof: A person may be a national but lack proof of, or be unable to establish, that nationality, yet may equally be unable to establish statelessness (a negative), a problem which the definition was seen to leave unaddressed. Stuck in a situation where they cannot prove their nationality and equally cannot prove their statelessness, such persons are denied the protection of the state and also that of the international framework. Third, the challenge of connection and/or belonging: A person may be a national but lack any real *connection* to the state of nationality, such that this nationality is essentially meaningless and does not reflect the true (experience of) belonging or associated rights. Finally, and connecting the above, the challenge of access to rights: This line of critique addresses the fact that the 'quality and attributes of citizenship are not included, even implicitly, in the definition' (Batchelor 1995, p. 232). In other words, while the core concern that the UN intended to address was articulated as one of *protection*, the definition focused on *status* (i.e. the possession or absence of a nationality) without considering the quality of that status or the nexus between status and protection (for more discussion on this, see Kingston, this volume).

In fact, these concerns are interrelated and mutually reinforcing in that most commentators considered the most reliable route to rights to lie in effective nationality of the state with which a person has true connections (see Vlieks, this volume). With all four lines of critique, de facto statelessness was often mooted as the catch-all solution which could be utilised to overcome the definitional shortcomings and conceptual limitations of 'statelessness'.[3] For example, de facto stateless persons have variously been defined and described as 'those with an ineffective nationality or those who cannot prove they are legally stateless'

(UNHCR 1995, para. 6); 'persons who ... might have legal claim to the bene-fits of nationality but are not, for a variety of reasons, able to enjoy these bene-fits' (Weissbrodt and Collins 2006, pp. 251–252); those who 'are unable to obtain proof of their nationality, residency or other means of qualifying for cit-izenship and may be excluded from the formal state as a result' (Blitz 2009, p. 7); those who possess 'a legally meritorious claim for citizenship, but (are) precluded from asserting it because of practical considerations such as cost, circumstances of civil disorder, or fear of persecution' (Milbrandt 2011, pp. 7–8); a person who 'might, like the undocumented migrant, be out of the territory of her state of membership and lack protection because she is unable for some reason to avail herself of the protection of the state in which she is residing' and someone who

> may never have left his national territory but, because of the unwillingness or incapacity of his state, experiences an existence that is tantamount to statelessness in its absence of basic protection and rights ... (like) many internally displaced people, oppressed minorities and marginalized social groups
>
> (Gibney 2014, p. 47)

and those 'whose irregular immigration status renders them de facto stateless – stateless in the sense that despite having a nationality, they cannot turn to the state in which they live for protection or assistance' (Bhabha 2011, preface).

A rights based approach to key questions

With the benefit of time, we are now better positioned to reflect both on the historical growth in appeal of the notion of de facto statelessness and frustration with the limitations of the definition of statelessness. A long lens view which contextualises this against the development of international human rights law and critiques it from the same perspective, throws out a few issues for discussion.

First, it is important to remember that both 'statelessness' and 'de facto state-lessness' are terms which were born out of the pre-justiciable human rights era, but which now must find a place in a world where the international applicability and position of justiciable human rights law is largely uncontroversial. In such a world, nationality should be less fundamental to the enjoyment of protection and rights. States have obligations – which are no longer based on reciprocity – to promote and protect the human rights of all persons subject to their jurisdiction, be they stateless or otherwise. To contend that protection and enjoyment of rights is not forthcoming, either because the individual is stateless or because he or she does not enjoy an effective nationality, is to undermine the nature of rights as inherent to every human being and revert to the pre-justiciable human rights world order, in which the individual only had a place vicariously, through his or her state. In today's human rights world, the statelessness treaties are no longer the only instruments that benefit stateless persons. Yet they remain relevant as part of the mosaic of international human rights law, within which they play a more specific role which complements other human rights treaties. For example, many of the civil, political, social and economic rights contained in the 1954 Convention are more strongly articulated in subsequent treaties which also benefit from the jurisprudence and authoritative observations, comments and recommendations of treaty bodies. That these rights are also articulated in the 1954 Convention adds little. Instead, the true value of the Convention lies in the few key obligations it imposes on states, in relation to the provision of identity documentation, administrative assistance, facilitated naturalisation, etc., which have not been replicated and improved upon by other human rights treaties (Van Waas 2008). In other words, to contend that the term statelessness and the international statelessness regime must also cover those who have a nationality but cannot enjoy its benefits, is to ignore the advances of international human rights law which obligates all states to protect human rights regardless of the status of the holder.

Second, there is a question regarding a logical leap which sees the right to a nationality and statelessness as two sides to the same coin, and thereby expects the term statelessness to be of relevance to all persons whose right to a nationality has been compromised. Statelessness is perhaps the most extreme violation of this right, but there are others as well, and not everyone whose right to a nationality is violated in some way is necessarily stateless or relevant to the statelessness discourse. This is important because de facto statelessness is most commonly viewed as the lack of an *effective* nationality, the argument being that a right only in name, and not in substance, is no right at all (Córdova 1954). However, the statelessness conventions did not set out to protect all those whose right to a nationality has been violated, but rather to address one very specific and extreme manifestation of the violation of the right to a nationality. Consequently, it is perhaps unfair to critique the definition of statelessness on the basis that it does not cover those who have a nationality which is ineffective. A useful way to look at this may be by analogy with another right. The right to education is not merely the right to gain admission to a school; it is also the right to a certain standard of education, accessibility and non-discrimination in enjoying education, etc. In other words, while it is straightforward to assess that a child who does not go to school is being denied her right to an education, children who do attend school might also face challenges of varying degrees in their enjoyment of the right to an education. These are two connected but different problems, which require different strategies to address them. A state may embark on a drive to build new schools, make existing schools more accessible and ensure that entry requirements are not discriminatory and that people see the value in sending their children to school. All of these will contribute to addressing the (relatively) narrower problem of children not having access to education. Overhauling an entire system to ensure it is standardised and of high quality no matter what or where the school is, is a more long-term and complicated project. Similarly, identifying those who have no nationality to protect them and to ultimately ensure that they acquire a suitable nationality is the narrower task that the statelessness conventions set out to fulfil. Ensuring that all people have access to and enjoyment of the protection and minimum rights associated both with citizenship and with being human is the more long-term and complicated object of the international human rights movement at large.

A third and related issue is that of scope. It is clear that stateless persons are a group who lack protection, in part, because of their lack of a status. It is also clear that there are other groups that face very similar challenges even though they have the status that stateless people lack. It does not necessarily follow that all persons who face the same protection challenges should be protected by utilising the same tools. Another analogy may be drawn from the field of human trafficking. Human trafficking is a very specific type of crime, which causes immense exploitation and harm. However, not all persons who suffer such harm related to their work and/or migration are victims of trafficking. To extend the trafficking regime so that it protects against all such types of exploitation would be fundamentally to change its nature and broaden its scope, perhaps to the point where it becomes meaningless.

Fourth, there is the reality that many of the legitimate criticisms of the definition of statelessness have been taken on board and grappled with in expert meetings facilitated by the UNHCR (in 2010 and onwards), resulting in the publication of extensive and authoritative guidelines on the interpretation of the definition (in 2012 and onwards; for more discussion of the UNHCR position on statelessness see Staples, this volume). These guidelines address many (though not all) of the concerns related to proof and scope, have broadened our understanding of statelessness and have shown that many people previously envisaged to be de facto stateless are actually stateless, or at risk of statelessness. For example, central to the 'new' interpretation of the definition is that an assessment of both law and practice is required to determine whether a person 'is considered as a national under the operation of the law' (Convention Relating to the Status of Stateless Persons 1954, art. 1). In other words, a person who meets all the legal requirements to be recognised as a national of a state may still be stateless if, in practice, the competent authorities of the state do not recognise him as such. This more progressive understanding of statelessness covers many persons who also fit within some of the definitions of de facto statelessness referred to above, even though by very definition it should be impossible to be both stateless and de facto stateless. From a legal and protection perspective, applying the broader definition to 'statelessness' and accordingly narrowing down the definition of 'de facto statelessness' is both logical and desirable, as the former status comes with a protection status attached to it. Thus, for example, defining de facto stateless persons as those who have 'a legally meritorious claim for citizenship, but (are) precluded from asserting it because of practical considerations such as cost, circumstances of civil disorder, or fear of persecution' (Milbrandt 2011, pp. 7–8) is problematic, as many such persons would actually fit under the progressive interpretation of the legal definition of statelessness.

A combination of the evolution of international human rights law and our broader, more progressive understanding of the definition of statelessness means that some of the criticisms of the definition of statelessness no longer hold true and, equally, that the term de facto statelessness is less relevant today than it was even five years ago. It can still be a powerful term if used sparingly, for it conveys to a state that its treatment of or indifference towards its citizens is so appalling that they may as well be stateless. But it is merely a descriptor, with emotive value, which has no rights or obligations attached to it. Therefore, using it expansively, particularly in relation to persons who may well be stateless or at risk of statelessness, can be counterproductive.

This is not to say that the term has no place, or that we can be fully satisfied with our present understanding of the definition of statelessness or with the level of protection that international human rights law affords to stateless and similarly vulnerable people. This will be further explored below.

Unpacking nationality

In order to grapple meaningfully with statelessness, it is also important to look at the meaning of nationality and citizenship. In the world of justiciable human rights, which core elements of the content of nationality are not accessible by law to the stateless? A secondary question would be 'which elements are not accessible in practice?' But this would take us into the terrain of standard human rights violations, as both those who have a nationality and those who do not can be denied their basic human rights.

International law does allow for a certain degree of differential treatment between nationals and non-nationals, to the disadvantage of stateless persons. For example, key political rights such as the right to vote or stand for election and to perform certain public functions may be restricted to a country's citizens (International Covenant on Civil and Political Rights 1976, Art. 25). Furthermore, developing countries can limit non-nationals' enjoyment of economic rights in certain circumstances (International Covenant on Economic, Social and Cultural Rights 1976, Art. 2). Under limited conditions, differential treatment of non-nationals in the pursuit of a legitimate aim is also acceptable, as long as it complies with the principle of proportionality (Office of the High Commissioner for Human Rights 2006). However, any restrictions on the rights of non-nationals 'must be construed so as to avoid undermining the basic prohibition of discrimination' (CERD 2004, para. 30).

Thus, there is a qualitative drop in the level of protection and enjoyment of certain rights that international human rights law affords to stateless persons. All other challenges in accessing rights that stateless persons face (and there are many) are not sanctioned under international law and, therefore, should be treated in the same way as any human rights violation against any person. This is because 'the ground of nationality should not bar access to ... rights ... [which] apply to everyone including non-nationals, such as ... stateless persons.' (Committee on Economic, Social and Cultural Rights 2009, para. 30) Accordingly, if an individual is denied the right to vote on the basis of his/her statelessness – as unfortunate (and undemocratic) as this may be – human rights law will provide little immediate relief for him. On the other hand, if a stateless person is unlawfully detained the problem lies not with his statelessness but with the discriminatory and arbitrary immigration detention regime which fails to identify and protect the stateless individual. This is a human rights violation which must be addressed through human rights law.

A second and related issue is the question of when a nationality becomes 'ineffective'. If a continuum was to be drawn from 'nationality' to 'statelessness' at which point would nationality turn 'ineffective' and at which point would it be so ineffective that it is akin to statelessness? According to Goris *et al.*

> although individuals who have legal citizenship and its accompanying rights may take both for granted, what they enjoy is one extreme of a continuum between full, effective citizenship and *de jure* statelessness, in which individuals have neither legal citizenship nor any attendant rights.
>
> (Goris *et al.* 2009, p. 4)

While there is a certain appeal to the idea of a continuum (particularly from a social sciences perspective), this question too is one of limited significance in the human rights context where most rights are not contingent on nationality, but rather on our common humanity. In fact, exploring the content of nationality that is attached to the right to a nationality under international law, Edwards concludes that 'the right to a nationality, as it is expressed as a human right, remains largely framed as a procedural right' and that 'there is no agreed substantive minimum content of nationality as a matter of international law' (Edwards 2014, p. 42). In the absence of an internationally agreed substantive minimum content of nationality, it becomes near impossible objectively to draw a line on a spectrum beyond which statelessness can be assumed on the basis of 'ineffective nationality'. The more appropriate line of scrutiny may therefore be 'effective human rights protection'. However, this question does take us into the territory of one of the remaining grey and problematic areas of the definition of statelessness – an area where the term de facto statelessness (or similar ones) still resonates strongly. This is the question of when should a person be determined to be stateless in the face of silence from his or her state (De Chickera 2014).

Let us take the case of a person in immigration detention whose country refuses to acknowledge that he is a citizen and does not cooperate with his removal. At what point is it safe to say that the person is stateless, and at what point is he merely a person whose nationality is ineffective? Authoritative Guidelines issued by UNHCR on the basis of expert meetings are only partially helpful on this point. The question of whether a person is stateless is one of both fact and law:

> Where the competent authorities treat an individual as a non-national even though he or she would appear to meet the criteria for automatic acquisition

of nationality under the operation of a country's laws, it is their position rather than the letter of the law that is determinative in concluding that a State does not consider such an individual as a national.

(UNHCR 2014, para. 37)

Accordingly, sustained denial of consular protection can be evidence of statelessness (and not merely de facto statelessness). The Guidelines proceed to state that:

Conclusions regarding a lack of response should only be drawn after a reasonable period of time. If a competent authority has a general policy of never replying to such requests, no inference can be drawn from this failure to respond based on the non-response alone. Conversely, when a State routinely responds to such queries, a lack of response will generally provide strong confirmation that the individual is not a national.

(UNHCR 2014, para. 41)

This in turn raises two questions. First, what is a 'reasonable period of time' and second, is it satisfactory that two different standards apply, not based on the individual's situation and lack of protection, but rather on the historical behaviour of a state?

The Guidelines state that six months is a reasonable period of time within which to decide if a person is stateless, and that this can be extended to a maximum of one year if this is likely to result in a substantive response (UNHCR 2014, para. 75). Therefore, on the one hand, if a state as a matter of practice never responds to such queries, the failure to respond should not be construed as evidence of statelessness; on the other, the six-month process of identification of statelessness should be extended to one year only if this is likely to result in a substantive response from the state being asked. The contradiction here is that the Guidelines both caution against jumping to any hasty conclusions based on the habitual non-responsiveness of states and recommend that the timeframe for determining statelessness only be extended if the state in question is likely to be responsive (i.e. is not a habitually non-responsive state). This contradiction can place the individual in a situation of limbo, neither recognised as stateless nor confirmed as having a nationality. This remaining grey area demands greater attention, both in terms of what it means to the definition of statelessness and the process of identifying stateless persons. Until this happens, the notion of de facto statelessness will continue to resonate, though perhaps the more appropriate terminology would be to identify such persons as being at 'risk of statelessness' (European Network on Statelessness 2015).

Clarifying conceptual boundaries

We draw this chapter to a close by moving beyond the question of definition and into the question of outcome and approach. Why is it so important to have a clear understanding of what the law means by the term 'stateless'? And how will this allow us to strengthen protection for the stateless and non-stateless alike? The benefit of identifying and addressing statelessness where this is the dominant protection-related characteristic (for example, stateless people in their own country) is obvious, but it is when statelessness coincides with other characteristics that the importance of a precise approach to, and understanding of, statelessness becomes more evident. Not surprisingly, this is also when statelessness is most likely to be overlooked, or overstretched, both with problematic consequences.

Statelessness and refugeehood

Statelessness is often caused by discrimination, which can escalate to persecution, forcing stateless persons to flee their homes and seek refuge elsewhere. Refugees can also be at heightened risk of statelessness, with poor laws, poor implementation and discriminatory sociopolitical attitudes, resulting in the children of refugees, in particular, being at risk of statelessness (Al Barazi and van Waas 2015; see also Al Barazi and Tucker, this volume). This dual nexus between statelessness and refugees is becoming increasingly significant, as the nature of conflict, violence and displacement evolves. Indeed, there are currently at least 1.5 million stateless refugees and former refugees (Institute on Statelessness and Inclusion, 2014). Be it the Syrian crisis or the Rohingya problem, it is critical to understand, identify and respond to statelessness situations to ensure they do not escalate to persecution (or if they do, that stateless refugees are protected), and forced migration situations to ensure they do not escalate to statelessness. Similarly, identifying statelessness *among* refugees, so that durable solutions for them will include the (re)acquisition of an appropriate nationality, is crucial to their long-term and intergenerational well-being. In this context, failing to distinguish between refugees and stateless persons is problematic, as is the failure to distinguish 'stateless refugees' from non-stateless refugees.

Statelessness and irregularity

Persons in an irregular migration context can also be stateless, or at heightened risk of statelessness. The discussion above on the grey area around non-cooperation of states is an example of how persons who had (or thought they had) a nationality can end up being stateless due to their irregular migration status. Victims of trafficking and smuggling who end up living irregular and exploited lives in third countries are likely to be particularly vulnerable in this regard. However, it is important to recognise that while irregular migration can cause statelessness, the majority of irregular migrants do have a nationality. It would be a disservice to them to consider them to be stateless, when in reality they have a country which is under an obligation to extend consular protection to them while abroad and to accept their return. Thus, failing to distinguish between irregular migrants and stateless persons is problematic, as is the failure to distinguish *stateless* irregular migrants.

Statelessness and absence of an 'own' state

While most stateless people are not recognised as nationals by the state(s) with which they have strong ties, there are other stateless people who are recognised as belonging to an entity and/or ethnicity which has no state. The Kurds are probably the best-known example of a nation without a state, but other groups exist. While many Kurds would be stateless, many others have the nationality of another country. It is important to be able to distinguish the *stateless* among those without an *own* state.

Statelessness and lack of documentation?

Finally, the lack of documentation and corresponding proof of legal identity is a significant challenge that both the stateless and non-stateless face. While many stateless persons do not have documentation, many others do. Similarly, the majority of those who do not have documentation do hold a nationality, though it could be more difficult to prove. Failing to distinguish between the stateless and those who lack documentation, and the failure to distinguish *stateless* persons who lack documentation, can lead to the wrong solutions and frameworks being pursued, with little or even negative gain.

Conclusion

This chapter has looked at the definition of statelessness and explored interpretations of de facto statelessness and (in)effective nationality. The main objective in doing so has been to promote greater awareness, understanding of, and consensus around the progressive interpretation of the legal definition of statelessness, and correspondingly to argue for the term de facto statelessness to be used more sparingly and narrowly. The basis for this argument is a human rights one, which requires us to approach statelessness as a human rights issue and to view both the stateless and those in a statelessness-like situation as subjects (and beneficiaries) of international human rights law. The impetus for the argument has been our growing sense that the lack of a common understanding of what constitutes statelessness ultimately undermines the effectiveness and impact of research and advocacy carried out to address statelessness. While conscious (and appreciative) of the fact that the legal definition of statelessness should not bind all academic endeavour on the subject, we hope this chapter will contribute to a more constructive discourse that is built on a theoretical approach which acknowledges the need to find legal solutions to legal problems as defined under international law. If this is the common starting point, even the broader and different philosophical and sociopolitical understandings of statelessness will in some way relate back to the legal definition as well, thus contributing to our collective efforts to address this phenomenon.

We have also looked at some of the remaining gaps and grey areas in the legal definition of statelessness and have argued that it is in these areas that the term de facto statelessness has the strongest resonance. That such gaps remain is perhaps the most significant argument in favour of retaining the term de facto statelessness in relation to 'persons outside the country of their nationality who are unable or, for valid reasons, are unwilling to avail themselves of the protection of that country' (Massey 2010, p. 61). However, this is also why we must continue to apply minds and expertise to the definition of statelessness, to find clarity amidst the greyness and achieve an interpretation of the definition that is suitably inclusive, comprehensive and progressive.

As a final thought, we turn our attention to solutions to statelessness – for the fundamental purpose of this endeavour must surely be to solve one of the most unnecessary human tragedies of the twenty-first century. As stated above, the 'effectiveness' of one's nationality has no strong bearing on whether a person is determined to be stateless or not. However, when securing a nationality for a stateless person, every effort must be made to ensure that it is an 'effective' one. To go back to our analogy of the right to education, while access to schools and access to good quality education are two different but interrelated problems, it makes no sense to build new schools which do not have the capacity or facilities to provide a good education. Similarly, while those who have an ineffective nationality are not stateless, it makes little sense to provide stateless people with a nationality that is ineffective. To quote (and draw from the wisdom of) one of the earlier studies on statelessness,

> Any attempt to eliminate statelessness can only be considered as fruitful if it results not only in the attribution of a nationality to individuals, but also in an improvement of their status. As a rule, such an improvement will be achieved only if the nationality of the individual is *the nationality of that state with which he is, in fact, most closely connected*, his 'effective nationality', if it *ensures for the national the enjoyment of those rights which are attributed to nationality under international law*, and the *enjoyment of that status which results from nationality under municipal law*.
>
> (Hudson 1952, p. 20)

Notes

1 The authors are Co-Directors of the Institute on Statelessness and Inclusion (www. InstituteSI.org). We wish to thank Maria Jose Recalde Vela for her extensive research assistance with this chapter and Zaid Clor for editing the references.

2 See for more information http://ibelong.unhcr.org/. Among relevant regional initiatives are the *Brazil Declaration and Plan of Action* agreed by Latin American and Caribbean states in December 2014 which includes a chapter on statelessness, the *Abidjan Declaration* endorsed by ECOWAS Heads of State in February 2015, the Action Statement agreed at the European Network on Statelessness' regional campaign conference *None of Europe's children should be stateless* in June 2015, and the European Union's *Conclusions of the Council and the Representatives of the Governments of the Member States on Statelessness* adopted in December 2015. At the national level, civil society movements to address statelessness have emerged in various countries including Nepal, Malaysia, Kuwait, Côte D'Ivoire and the Dominican Republic.

3 Please note that other descriptors and terms have also been used instead of, or in addition to, de facto statelessness. These include terms such as 'normatively stateless' (Gibney 2014); 'functionally stateless' (Inniss 2007); 'effectively stateless' (Bhabha 2011); and 'unreturnable persons' (UNHCR/Asylum Aid 2011).

References

Al Barazi, Z. and van Waas, L. (2015) Statelessness and Displacement: Scoping Paper. Norwegian Refugee Council and Tilburg University. [online] Available from: www. nrc.no/arch/_img/9197390.pdf [Accessed 2 February 2016].

Batchelor, C. (1995) Stateless persons: some gaps in international protection. *International Journal of Refugee Law*, 7(2), p. 232.

Bhabha, J. (ed.) (2011) *Children Without a State, A Global Human Rights Challenge.* Cambridge, MA: MIT Press.

Blitz, B. K. (2009) *Statelessness, Protection and Equality.* Oxford: Refugee Studies Centre.

Bluntschli, J. C. (1872) *Das Modern Völkerrecht.* Nördlingen: Beck'schen.

CERD (Committee on the Elimination of Racial Discrimination). (2004) *General Recommendation 30: Discrimination Against Non-Citizens.* UN Doc. CERD/C/64/Misc.11/rev.3.

Committee on Economic, Social and Cultural Rights. (2009) *General Comment No. 20: Non-Discrimination in Economic, Social and Cultural Rights (Article 2, Para 2 of the International Covenant on Economic, Social and Cultural Rights).* UN Doc. E/C.12/GC/20.

Convention on the Reduction of Statelessness. (1961) UNTS, vol. 989, no. 14458, Art. 7. [online] Available from: https://treaties.un.org/pages/showDetails.aspx?objid=0800000 280035afb [Accessed 2 February, 2016].

Convention Relating to the Status of Refugees. (1951) UNTS, vol. 189, no. 2545, Art. 1. [online] Available from: https://treaties.un.org/pages/showDetails.aspx?objid=0800000 28003002e [Accessed 2 February 2016].

Convention Relating to the Status of Stateless Persons. (1954) UNTS, vol. 360, no. 5158, 3rd and 4th preambles. [online] Available from: https://treaties.un.org/pages/show Details.aspx?objid=0800000280032b94 [Accessed 2 February 2016].

Córdova, R. (1954) International Law Commission. Nationality Including Statelessness – Third Report on the Elimination or Reduction of Statelessness. [online] Available from: http://legal.un.org/ilc/documentation/spanish/a_cn4_81.pdf [Accessed 2 February 2016].

De Chickera, A. (2014) A Question of 'If' and 'When'. European Network on Statelessness. [online] Available from: www.statelessness.eu/blog/question-if-and-when-is-someone-stateless [Accessed 2 February 2016].

Economic and Social Council. (1948) *Resolution 116 (VI) Report of the Second Session of the Commission on Human Rights. 6th session.* [online] Available from: www.un. org/en/ga/search/view_doc.asp?symbol=E/RES/116(VI) [Accessed 2 February 2016].

Edwards, A. (2014) The Meaning of Nationality in International Law: Substantive and Procedural Aspects. In: Edwards, A. and van Waas, L. (eds) *Nationality and Statelessness under International Law.* Cambridge: Cambridge University Press.

European Network on Statelessness. (2015) Protecting Stateless Persons from Arbitrary Detention. [online] Available from: www.statelessness.eu/protecting-stateless-persons-from-detention [Accessed 2 February 2016].

Gibney, M. (2014) Statelessness and Citizenship in Ethical and Political Perspective. In: Edwards, A. and van Waas, L. (eds.) *Nationality and Statelessness under International Law*, pp. 44–63. Cambridge: Cambridge University Press.

Goris, I., Harrington, J. and Köhn, S. (2009) Statelessness: What It Is and Why It Matters. *Forced Migration Review*. [online] Available from: www.fmreview.org/FMRpdfs/FMR32/FMR32.pdf [Accessed 2 February 2016].

Hall, W. and Pearce Higgins, A. (1880) *A Treatise on International Law*. Oxford: Clarendon Press.

Hudson, M. (1952) Report on Nationality, Including Statelessness. Extract from the Yearbook of the International Law Commission vol. II, A/CN.4/50. [online] Available from: http://legal.un.org/ilc/documentation/english/a_cn4_50.pdf [Accessed 2 February 2016].

Inniss, L. (2007) A domestic right of return?: Race, rights, and residency in New Orleans in the aftermath of Hurricane Katrina. *Boston College Third World Law Journal*, 27(2), p. 325. [online] Available from: http://lawdigitalcommons.bc.edu/twlj/vol. 27/iss2/2/ [Accessed 2 February 2016].

Institute on Statelessness and Inclusion. (2014) The World's Stateless. Oisterwijk: Wolf Legal Publishers. [online] Available from: www.institutesi.org/worldsstateless.pdf [Accessed 2 February 2016].

International Covenant on Civil and Political Rights. (1976) UNTS, vol. 999, no. 14668. [online] Available from: www.ohchr.org/Documents/ProfessionalInterest/ccpr.pdf [Accessed 2 February 2016].

International Covenant on Economic, Social and Cultural Rights. (1976) UNTS, vol. 993, no. 14531. [online] Available from: www.ohchr.org/Documents/ProfessionalInterest/cescr.pdf [Accessed 2 February 2016].

Kingston, L. (2013) A forgotten human rights crisis: statelessness and issue (non)emergence. *Human Rights Review*, 14(2).

Kubben, R. (2014) To belong or not to belong. Historical reflections on foreigners, citizenship and law. *Tilburg Law Review*, 19(1–2), pp. 136–152.

League of Nations. (1930) *Convention on Certain Questions Relating to the Conflict of Nationality Laws*, 13 April, League of Nations, Treaty Series, vol. 179, p. 89, No. 4137.

Massey, H. (2010) UNHCR and De facto Statelessness. Geneva: UNHCR. [online] Available from: www.unhcr.org/4bc2ddeb9.pdf [Accessed 2 February 2016].

Milbrandt, J. (2011) Stateless. *Cardozo Journal of International and Comparative Law*, 20(1).

Office of the High Commissioner for Human Rights (OHCHR). (2006) The Rights of Non-Citizens. [online] Available from: www.ohchr.org/Documents/Publications/noncitizensen.pdf [Accessed 2 February 2016].

Oppenheim, L. (1912) *International Law. A Treatise*. Harlow: Longmans, Green.

Robinson, N. (1955) *Convention Relating to the Status of Stateless Persons – Its History and Interpretation*, pp. 11–13. Geneva: UNHCR.

UNGA. (1948) *Universal Declaration of Human Rights*. G. A. Res. 217A (III), UN Doc A/810, 10 December. United Nations General Assembly. [online] Available from: www.un.org/en/documents/udhr/ [Accessed 2 February 2016].

UNHCR. (2014) Handbook on Protection of Stateless Persons. Geneva: United Nations High Commissioner for Refugees. [online] Available from: www.unhcr.org/53b698ab9.html [Accessed 2 February 2016].

UNHCR. (1995) Note on UNHCR and Stateless Persons. United Nations High Commissioner for Refugees. [online] Available from: www.unhcr.org/3ae68cc014.html [Accessed 2 February 2016].

UNHCR. (1949) A Study of Statelessness. UN Doc E/1112. United Nations High Commissioner for Refugees. [online] Available from: www.unhcr.org/3ae68c2d0.pdf [Accessed 2 February 2016].

UNHCR/Asylum Aid. (2011) Mapping Statelessness. United Nations High Commissioner for Refugees/Asylum Aid. [online] Available from: www.unhcr.org.uk/fileadmin/user_upload/images/Updates/November_2011/UNHCR-Statelessness_in_UK-ENG-screen.pdf [Accessed 2 February 2016].

Van Waas, L. (2008) *Nationality Matters. Statelessness under International Law.* Antwerp: Intersentia.

Weissbrodt, D. and Collins, C. (2006) The human rights of stateless persons. *Human Rights Quarterly*, 28(1).

5 The state and the stateless

The legacy of Hannah Arendt reconsidered

Brad K. Blitz

Introduction

Since Hannah Arendt first discussed the condition of statelessness in *The Origins of Totalitarianism* in 1951, there have been few empirical investigations of the claims she advanced regarding the ways in which people may be stripped of their rights and the degree to which they may recover them.[1] Her writing has nonetheless inspired a new generation of researchers investigating contemporary forms of statelessness, often alongside the UNHCR which has set itself a goal of ending statelessness within ten years (see UNHCR 2014). This chapter re-examines Arendt's analysis of the mechanisms which gave rise to statelessness in the first part of the twentieth century and the forms of governance which she believed sustained such deprivation. I argue that Arendt's account, while inform-ative of some specific cases of statelessness, cannot explain how statelessness arises in many other situations and as a result fails to offer an insight into poten-tial remedies. Drawing upon two global investigations of stateless groups in Bangladesh, Estonia, Kenya, the Gulf States, Mauritania, Slovenia, Sri Lanka and Ukraine, I describe how some stateless groups have successfully militated for the restoration of their rights and suggest future avenues for research and humanitarian policy development.

Intellectual foundations

The concept of statelessness occupies a central place in Arendt's (1976) *The Origins of Totalitarianism*. According to her account, statelessness is a distinctly modern phenomenon which is noticeably broader than the definition as set out in the 1954 and 1961 UN Conventions.[2] One particularly controversial feature of her discussion of statelessness is her belief that statelessness is synonymous with a condition of rightlessness, a claim rejected by the UNHCR which has consist-ently maintained that stateless people enjoy human rights.

Arendt's writings now speak to a variety of distinct audiences and interest groups. The intellectual historian Martin Jay notes that Arendt is among a handful of thinkers whose name has been invoked both to legitimise and to dele-gitimise political and philosophical positions (see Jay 1986). This includes those who turn to Arendt in the name of protecting asylum seekers and non-citizens (see for example Fassin 2005; Krause 2008) as well as others who see in her writings food for revisionist accounts of the creation of Israel (Bernstein 1996). In the context of our reading of Arendt's writings similar silo effects – intellectual compartmentalisation – can be detected with the net result that the foundations of her arguments for the emergence of statelessness have not been actively explored. Neither has the problem of statelessness been examined alongside the lines of inquiry which run across Arendt's work and which her biographers suggest are logically connected. As a result, the theses developed and the conclusions she reaches in, for example, *Eichmann in Jerusalem*, and the intellectual debates they generated, have not informed a critical reading of the concept of rightlessness in *The Origins of Totalitarianism*, even though they address a common theme and raise critical questions about the state, the problem of intentionality, the role of political organisation, and membership as an antidote to arbitrary arrest, exclusion, and elimination. A central argument of this chapter then is that if scholars are to use Arendt as a basis for examining contemporary accounts of statelessness, then they should approach the themes she introduces with caution.

I have not mentioned the place of international law in the study of statelessness and will say little on the subject since it is amply covered by other authors in this volume (see De Chickera and van Waas; Vlieks; Swider). International law is sovereignty-affirming and does not recognise differences between states based on regime types, constitutional form, or historical development. While international law may exert some constitutive effects on states' preferences and the role of legal experts in clarifying international norms may certainly influence state behaviour, there is equally a need to explore endogenous political processes in order to understand how concrete problems that arise from state-designed deprivations may be mitigated and eventually resolved.

For social scientists interested in the problem of statelessness, Arendt remains the first port of call. For many years the topic was a minority interest recorded in some half dozen books. The UNHCR, which for decades had a mandate to work on statelessness alongside refugee protection, did little to advance an active agenda until a decade ago (for a comprehensive literature review see Blitz 2011). Now, by contrast, statelessness is a prominent area of policy which has been mainstreamed across UNHCR's operations in the form of an international advocacy campaign, #IBelong, and has attracted support from a growing number of NGOs, human rights activists, and academics.[3]

With some notable exceptions from a small group of area studies experts (see Manby 2016), the renewed interest in statelessness is situated in a noticeably different intellectual context from the one in which Arendt was writing, namely Nazism and to a lesser extent Stalinism. Contemporary studies now focus on issues which are emblematic of emergent twenty-first century problems such as the expansion of detention and the political rights of prisoners; the human rights challenges of removal, repatriation, and readmission of non-nationals in countries of origin; and the deprivation of citizenship of non-nationals.

The current fascination with Arendt and the renewed interest in what I will call the politics of deprivation have certainly refocused our attention but in so doing have also prompted us to take our eyes off the road. I will argue that in spite of its richness, a key limitation of Arendt's work is that it closes the door on restorative solutions to the problem of statelessness and on the practical recovery of rights. Much has already been said about the limited explanatory power of Arendt's model of totalitarianism for today's problems and I therefore wish to explore two other pathologies embedded in Arendt's work and which resonate with recent efforts to address the problem of statelessness: (1) her reliance on law as a source of protection; and (2) the effects on individuality.

Arendt's exposition of statelessness is chronicled in her chapter 'The Decline of the Nation State and the End of the Rights of Man', where she explains the condition of statelessness in the context of three losses: the loss of home, the loss of state protection, and the loss of a place in the world. These deprivations facilitate the unfolding tragedy of destruction and genocide. It is above all the absence of government – the only viable source of protection – which signals their doom. The presence of stateless people leads Arendt to claim that human rights, supposedly universal, have no meaning unless they can be anchored to an effective source of protection and for her the only option is the state.

How Jews and other victims of Nazism became stateless is a much more complicated tale. European states repeatedly stripped foreign-born individuals of their citizenship. We note that France introduced legislation to this end in 1915, three years before the new Soviet and Turkish governments denationalised Russian, Armenian, and Hungarian refugees. After the First World War Belgium and then Italy introduced laws to strip foreign-born individuals of their citizenship in 1922 and 1926 respectively; with Austria following in 1933. These actions predated the 1935 Nuremberg Laws which explicitly divided Germans into full citizens and citizens without political rights and thus created millions of stateless persons overnight.

Although many groups were affected by the above legislation, Arendt argues that Anti-Semitism was the catalyst for the development of totalitarianism which she claims was enabled by the union of multiple illiberal social processes. Specifically, she identifies Anti-Semitism, racism, imperialism, and the alliance between capital and the mob as the main ingredients in the witches' brew that is totalitarianism. All of these practices served to weaken the state, the legal guarantor of rights, and see it supplanted by the nation, an exclusive community (see also Tonkiss, this volume).

For Arendt, the confluence of the above developments hold greater explanatory power than ideological explanations for the development of Nazism and Stalinism. Ideology, she claims, was not a causal factor but simply a tool. Rather, Arendt argues that the ideologies of the late nineteenth and early twentieth centuries were cemented around a web of political interests which were institutionalised on ethno-national lines and represented, most notably in Austria-Hungary, an illiberal union of interests.

Elements of critique

Sixty years after Arendt first published her account of statelessness, several of the claims she made warrant revision. Moreover, many of her reflections do not lend themselves easily to an examination of other contexts in which statelessness is prevalent. While many stateless people live in non-democratic systems, with some notable exceptions, they are far from totalitarian. Rather we note that many stateless people live in particularly weak states (see Staples 2012; Mwangi, this volume,). Others who have written on totalitarianism also question the basis for Arendt's comparison of regime types and reformulation of Marxist notions where class conflict is replaced by racism and inter-ethnic/national contest (see Linz 2000).

Her discussion of the concepts of state and nation also introduces some important intellectual concerns. Arendt identifies qualified differences between states: the French Fourth Republic is, in her view, a collection of political parties; whereas Germany is a state where allegiance and obedience dominated all other forms of organisation. Yet, throughout, she treats questions of sovereignty and territoriality as fixed constructs. More importantly, she essentialises ethno-national groups, with the one exception being her discussion of Jews and the conflict between established communities in civic centres such as Berlin, Avignon and Bordeaux and new arrivals from Poland and Galicia. And yet, one might argue that she still essentialises these particular categories of Jew and creates another set of binary distinctions in her distinction between the urbane city dwellers and the poor village folk.

Related to this is Arendt's idealisation of the state. Central to her claim about the damaging effects of exclusion is a firm belief in state protection. Certainly, in her model, the loss of state protection logically connects the events surrounding denaturalisation and expulsion and the creation of new refugees with the end goal of Nazism. Denationalised people, and refugees, who are effectively stateless, are vulnerable and easier to deport and kill. However, the idea of the state as an effective guarantor of rights is deeply problematic, as informed by the vast population of 'people of concern', the de facto stateless – refugees and internally displaced people – who now number more than 63.5 million (see also De Chickera and van Waas, this volume). As Kelly Staples (2012) writes, citizenship in weak states like the Democratic Republic of Congo can hardly be considered rights-protecting. Further, in oppressive states like Myanmar, where the Rohingya have been brutally deprived of nationality and are the victims of atrocious crimes, the allure of citizenship may offer little protection since we note that in addition to the stateless Rohingya, over the past three years virtually all other non-Buddhist groups have been exposed to violence from internal security forces and outspoken racists. In both types of states, then, the ideas of citizenship, protection, and legitimacy must be seriously re-evaluated.

In this context, it is interesting to note some contemporary ironies, which further challenge Arendt's belief in the value of citizenship and state protection. First, the lines of political membership are more elastic than one might expect (see Isin and Nielsen 2008) and, moreover, just as quickly as citizenship may be removed it may also be granted. Today this is most evident in Russian spheres of influence. One only has to look at Russia's distribution of citizenship within Abkhazia or the Donbas region in Eastern Ukraine, clear attempts to undermine Georgian and Ukrainian sovereignty respectively, to understand how a state may rapidly increase its citizenry. Similarly, and even more spectacularly, we note that after decades of exclusion stateless Kurds in Syria were finally granted citizenship by the desperate Assad regime as it restocked its arsenal and took aim at the rebels in 2014.

Second, Arendt's belief in political organisation as an antidote to illiberal threats is challenged by both historical and contemporary accounts. In the context of the early twentieth century, Arendt's claims regarding the ennobling nature of political contest are at least partially contradicted by the rather mixed record from the Second World War and subsequent conflicts. Several of the groups identified by Arendt, for example those in the former Austro-Hungarian Empire, did organise and did mobilise but they also participated in the slaughter, often against each other. In this instance, there was a dark and instrumental aspect to the Nazi madness she describes in that it actually empowered independence movements that participated in simultaneous genocides against other national groups in parallel to the Nazi effort. Further, Arendt's belief in political mobilisation as a means of protection assumes that political processes are organised along common lines, irrespective of location, and ignores the relative power and centrality of *habitus* – the values, expectations and dispositions people bring with them as they enter political contest. Rather, Arendt's model presupposes that the various nationalities in the Austro-Hungarian lands that did militate entered a level field, which is not the case.

One final critique is of the destruction of individuality, which Arendt claims is an inevitable consequence of deprivation and the removal of rights. As she writes, 'the first essential step on the road to total domination is to kill the juridical person in man' (1976, p. 447). Arendt speaks of the stateless having been reduced to bare nature and describes a desperate people existing outside of the law. The macro-picture she presents is overwhelmingly accurate, but there are some counter-examples which shed light on alternative interpretations. For example, Kim Rygiel's recent work on migrant activism in the refugee camps in Calais presents a complex picture of contestation and personal assertiveness (2011). Others have found that the often quoted representation of 'bare life' by Giorgio Agamben (Agamben 1998) breaks down when one looks inside the refugee camp system more closely (Redclift 2013). Indeed, there are powerful contemporary accounts which are more nuanced and reveal potential cracks even in the totalitarianism of the Nazi system that Arendt described.

The writings of Primo Levi present a noticeably different picture from that which Arendt describes. Like Arendt, Levi was deprived of his rights under racial laws – Italian not German – and was deported to a concentration camp. Unlike Arendt, however, he was sent to the flagship Nazi camp, Auschwitz, where he spent 11 months. Shortly after his liberation, he began to record his experience of life in the camps, which is profoundly important. In contrast to Arendt, who discounts the possibility of individuality, Levi identifies ways in which it was retained and recovered in the most difficult of conditions. We see this in his memoir *If This Is a Man*, and indeed in his subsequent work *The Drowned and the Saved*, where Levi explores the idea of personal identity at its very limits and describes how individuals demonstrated 'the power to refuse our own consent' (see Levi 1959).

Levi distinguishes between the 'Musselmanner', the term used to describe those suffering from hunger and exhaustion who have consigned themselves to death and are prepared to sink (and hence become the drowned), and the adaptable, the strong and the astute. In Levi's account, the 'Musselmanner' are the backbone of the camp, the anonymous mass of non-men. Their experience and death contrasts with the paths to salvation which he claims are many and improbable and include doctors, tailors, shoemakers, musicians, cooks and the collaborators – Kapos – but also the organisers and the prominent, the hateful and selfish. Will-power, dignity and conscience are held in opposition to the way of beasts and evil: 'Many were the ways devised and put into effect by us in order not to die: as many as there are different human characters' (1959, p. 106).

But this is not a return to the state of nature. Not only do these people have numbers – tattoos – they also have names. Levi records many personalities including Alfred, Elias the insane dwarf who lives in spite of his defects, the cultivated Henri, Mendi the rabbi, and the Hungarian Bandi, alongside the simple bricklayer and non-captive worker, his friend Lorenzo. He writes:

> We do not believe in the most obvious and facile deduction that man is fundamentally brutal, egoistic, and stupid once every civilised institution is taken away. We believe rather that the only conclusion to be drawn is that in the face of driving necessity and physical disabilities many social habits and instincts are reduced to silence.
>
> (1959, p. 100)

Levi's opinions on the Nazi camp system have been echoed in other survivors' accounts and have been reaffirmed by researchers including the German sociologist Maja Suderland (2013), who argues that in spite of everything prisoners were still capable of acting and exerting a degree of control over aspects of their lives, for example over language. In this, Suderland agrees with Levi that control was grounded in the idea of *habitus*.

Contemporary forms of statelessness

The above discussion on adaptive responses and the role of agency casts a new light on the way in which contemporary forms of statelessness may be understood, as distinct from Arendt's model, and hints at ways in which this most basic deprivation may be confronted.

The ways in which statelessness is experienced today are varied and multiple; the deprivation of citizenship as highlighted by Arendt being one major cause among many others (see Blake, this volume), such as the loss of citizenship during the process of state succession (see Swider; Vlieks, this volume), gender-discriminatory laws (see Al Barazi and Tucker; Mulmi and Shneiderman, both this volume), and as a result of administrative obstacles the non-registration of births (see Blitz and Lynch 2011; see also Mwangi; Mulmi and Shneiderman, both this volume).

While the precise number of stateless people is unknown, there are concentrated groups of formerly stateless people which have been investigated. The ways in which they have experienced political and other deprivations is illustrative of the diversity and complexity of the phenomenon of statelessness. For example, in addition to the discussion in Oscar Gakuo Mwangi's chapter (this volume) on ethnic Somalis in Kenya, we note that the Nubians in Kenya have historically struggled to enjoy access to rights and have been discriminated against on account of their ethnic origin. Although the Nubians arrived with the British Army over 100 years ago they were never considered among the 42 recognised national groups, and have been denied documentation and associated political rights until recently. Many are still confined to the slums of Kibera on the edge of Nairobi. Similarly, the Estate Tamils in Sri Lanka, who arrived from Tamil Nadu over a century ago as plantation workers during British Colonial rule, were denied nationality and documentation and confined to plantations until 2003. Many still do not enjoy the same rights as citizens.

Two groups of stateless people which continue to garner international attention are the Rohingya of Burma and ethnic Haitians in the Dominican Republic. In the case of the Rohingya, hundreds of thousands were expelled from Burma in the 1960s by the military–socialist regime of General Ne Win during the Burmese Way to Socialism nationalisation programme. Subsequent expulsions include the murderous ethnic cleansing campaign Operation Dragon King (Naga Min), which drove more than 200,000 Rohingya into Bangladesh in 1978, where an estimated 10,000 died from starvation and disease.

The source of the latest tragedy lies in the disenfranchisement of the Rohingya in Burma by a 1982 Citizenship Law which legalised their exclusion. Denied citizenship inside Burma, further discriminatory policies and an increasingly brutal regime precipitated a series of refugee crises. In 1991, the Burmese army expelled more than 250,000 Rohingya, destroying villages and buildings on its way, and forcing them into towns in southern Bangladesh, primarily around Teknaf and Cox's Bazaar. Three decades later, the Bangladeshi response has hardened and the previous government has been accused of withholding food aid, frustrating NGO access to camps and, with the exception of a small minority of Rohingya, generally refusing to recognise their rights as refugees. Arendt would immediately identify with these people who are at great risk, especially in Burma where massacres are happening.

In the case of the Dominican Republic, as Jillian Blake records (Blake; Kingston, both in this volume), the plight of ethnic Haitians has been especially painful. Denied the right to register births, they have been subject to both individual and group expulsions. In September 2013, the long-running discrimination against Dominicans of Haitian descent took a turn for the worse when the country's Constitutional Court ruled that anyone born since 1929 to foreign parents who could not prove their regular migration status had been wrongly registered as Dominican. Human rights monitors estimate that the decision affects more than 250,000 people, who are liable to lose their Dominican nationality and become stateless and vulnerable to expulsion. This decision has attracted international condemnation and, in response, the government prepared special legislation which included other discriminatory requirements such as strict linguistic criteria, including competence in both written and spoken Spanish.

The benefits of citizenship

In order to examine Arendt's belief in the state's ability to guarantee rights, we conducted two studies. The first tested UNHCR's heralded reforms regarding the corrective power of legislation and the remedial power of the state. Our research included teams in a range of countries and regime types (democratic, quasi-democratic, non-democratic). In a qualitative study of Estonia, Slovenia, Ukraine, Mauritania, the Gulf States, Kenya, Sri Lanka and Bangladesh involving 120 participants, this project was structured about three main research questions:

1 Has the granting of citizenship enabled individuals to access rights and resources?
2 How has the granting of citizenship enabled individuals to enhance the quality of their lives?
3 What barriers prevent people who have been granted citizenship from the full enjoyment of their rights?

The findings were particularly illustrative of the diverse ways in which statelessness had been experienced and modified, in part through legal reform. For example, in the case of Kenya we found that hospital authorities refused to register the births of Nubian children; the state failed to issue certification of late registration of births; there was still a massive documentary challenge to meeting the requirements to prove citizenship, as well as inordinate delays. Citizenship had not improved access to housing rights, sanitation, water, or education for the participants interviewed.

By contrast, in Sri Lanka where reform has been publicly signalled by the change of nationality law in 2003, the research found that the use of a simplified procedure was a more effective proof of citizenship, whereby rather than applying to state authorities for citizenship, individuals could obtain a 'general declaration' countersigned by a justice of the peace. However, of the estimated 900,000 Estate Tamils, most still encountered practical problems as state administration bodies were not fully aware of the legal arrangements that followed the

2003 law. In practice, although the government granted the right to citizenship certificates for people of Indian origin, many of those interviewed were unable to obtain these documents and indeed there was widespread ignorance about the value of citizenship certificates. As a result, many individuals were denied the right to be included on voters' lists.

The comparative study identified a number of benefits that followed from reforms of nationality laws, but also highlighted existing discrepancies. While citizenship improved labour market access and property ownership, it did not remove substantial inequalities which were differentiated by age and location. The benefits of citizenship were not evenly distributed and there were noticeable cleavages within the populations affected. Fragmentation and division occurred before *and* after the granting of citizenship. And further systemic problems of poverty and corruption undermined the potential benefits that citizenship might bring (see also Kingston, this volume).

The research affirmed that documentation of all sorts, not just birth registration, proved to be essential to the realisation of human rights and that where there were a large number of stateless people relative to the overall population, as in Kenya, there was clear political interest in regularising their status. Hence demographic pressures revealed important cracks in Arendt's model of the hard nationalising state. Further this project found that populations with a recognised ethno-national identity were more easily integrated – a fact which undermines Arendt's assumption that ethno-national groups may enter political contest on equal terms. Rather, a shared understanding of the historical relationship of the state concerned to the respective populations appears to determine the degree to which formerly stateless groups have been integrated in all types of states, democratic and non-democratic. Most important, the research found that the ending of direct discrimination on the basis of nationality does not undo structural effects or other modes of discrimination which are often interwoven.

The costs of statelessness

To explore the system-wide, totalitarian aspect of statelessness, as described by Arendt, we conducted further empirical work which included a quantitative analysis of the impact of statelessness on 970 households, with a control group of natural-born citizens contrasted against those who had recently acquired citizenship. In order to examine the impact of deprivation of citizenship on livelihoods, the research used an adapted version of the Sustainable Livelihoods Framework which allows one to explore how livelihood strategies and choices may influence developmental outcomes. A central premise of this project is that statelessness is a vulnerability context that affects livelihoods, including the livelihood outcomes of an individual or a household as well as livelihood strategies. One of the advantages of using the Sustainable Livelihoods approach is that it not only takes into account the threats and challenges facing vulnerable people but also recognises the place of strategies, opportunities, and respective strengths of individuals, households, and /or communities in the struggle to secure livelihoods.

As such it provides a basis for exploring the potential for agency and hence creates a platform to discuss how to mitigate the effects of statelessness and compounded deprivation.

In our model, 'vulnerability' is contextualised by shocks and at the centre of the framework is a pentagon of assets which are defined in the Sustainable Livelihoods Framework in terms of five types of capital: Human Capital, which is defined in terms of people's health, knowledge and skills, all of which are needed for productive work; Natural Capital, which includes resources which can be converted into stock or energy flows, and materials from which we produce goods and services; Financial Capital, such as banknotes, shares and bonds, each of which enables the other types of capital to be traded; Physical or Manufactured Capital, which includes the factories, machines, and tools which enable the production process; and finally Social Capital, which is defined in terms of the institutions that help us maintain and develop the above forms of capital in partnership with others; e.g. families, communities, businesses, trade unions, schools, and voluntary organisations.

This methodology allowed the research team to examine the effect of loss of citizenship on five main asset types and to see how this affected individuals' livelihood strategies and the choices they made, and how this influenced their developmental outcomes. This was particularly important because while Arendt recognises a state of lawlessness in the Nazi system which created statelessness among people, unlike Redclift (2013) and Rygiel (2011), for example, she does not consider how individuals may develop defensive strategies beyond political contestation to assert claims to agency.

The project used mixed methods to evaluate the impact of citizenship and statelessness on livelihoods in Bangladesh, Kenya, Slovenia, and Sri Lanka. The central research instrument was a quantitative survey administered to 300 households in Kenya, Sri Lanka, and Bangladesh, while we used a smaller sample in Slovenia. In each of the four countries we used a control group and the survey was administered in the ratio of 50 per cent to stateless or formerly stateless people, and 50 per cent to long-standing citizens. In addition to the survey, in-depth interviews were conducted with 10–15 households in each country. Though selective, the information gathered from individual households over the course of the interviews offers important insights and draws attention to context-specific issues not adequately covered by the survey. Consultations were also made with UNHCR field and regional offices and literature reviews on issues confronting stateless people in all four countries were undertaken in order to inform the field research.

In-country research was undertaken by a partner organisation in each country: Al Falah in Bangladesh; Centre for Minority Rights and Development (CEMIR-IDE) in Kenya; Mirovni Institut (Peace Institute) in Slovenia; and the Department of Economics at the University of Colombo in Sri Lanka. These organisations had been selected because the local researchers had conducted previous studies with the communities concerned, were familiar with their needs, and were able to recruit local field researchers with the necessary cultural and language skills to conduct the surveys and interviews.

In designing the survey, the research team used a range of objective criteria and subjective rankings in order to explore the impact of deprivation of citizenship on livelihoods. In order to probe income, which is notoriously difficult with questionnaires, the research team used the proxy of expenditure and asked about spending on rent and lodging, food, transportation, education and health as well as savings. Further, participants ranked their health against a five-part scale, from extremely sick to very healthy (less than five days off sick in a year); and the rights investigated included exercising cultural and religious practices, physical security and the exercise of communal rights such as association in groups or members' clubs. The study also explored access to services including hospitals, the availability of safe drinking water, access to public transportation as well as primary and secondary schools; we also asked about access to police, courts, and legal assistance. Physical capital was investigated in the form of housing, shelter, the availability of toilets, vehicles and jewellery, while natural capital was examined in terms of land, livestock, access to rivers, lakes, and forests. Finally, financial capital was examined in terms of cash, savings, and mortgages as well as both formal and informal loans.

Using multivariate regression analysis to examine the survey data, the researchers identified the impact of statelessness on: 1. livelihood assets; 2. vulnerability; 3. livelihood strategies; and 4. gender parity. The survey and interview data brought up much information about the local context and it was revealed that in some cases the gap between citizens who had never been stateless and formerly stateless persons appeared to be narrowing. This prompted further questions about the role of social institutions, for example in Sri Lanka where labour unions were influential.

In addition the research team was able to develop some generalisable conclusions about the long-term effects of deprivation of citizenship and to quantify the harms resulting from the denial and deprivation of nationality and associated violations of human rights. Harms may be measured in the context of human development and specifically by the effect they have on the livelihoods of stateless and formerly stateless populations as compared to citizens. The results clearly point to the high human costs of statelessness in a way that has never been measured before. They also provide evidence of how hardship and harm can be reduced or, in situations where nationality is granted, of possible pathways to accelerate restoration of rights and development.

Even when citizenship reforms are introduced and discriminatory nationality laws amended, formerly stateless people endure continued hardships associated with the previous deprivation of nationality rights. Citizenship plays an important role in determining the livelihood outcomes of households, irrespective of their country of origin. The impact is seen through the money metric and more objective livelihood outcomes such as income and expenditure, as well as through more subjective measures of livelihood outcomes such as freedoms and happiness. The results showed that statelessness rendered households less able to access these assets. This was true for all assets and all countries examined, except for Sri Lanka where access to social and financial capital was not affected by citizenship.

One of the central findings of this project is that statelessness reduces household income by 33 per cent and decreases opportunities for spending. Further, we found that citizenship status is the most important explanatory variable for the five freedoms, which in turn affects happiness. Perhaps not surprisingly, the stateless and formerly stateless people were found to be overall less happy than the citizens. They enjoy less access to land and have limited opportunities for home ownership – a further important finding of this study is that statelessness reduces the odds of owning a house by 59.7 per cent.

Citizenship and gender are not significant in predicting livelihood outcomes, such as income and happiness, though gender is a leading indicator of education which in turn affects income and other livelihood outcomes. In all country cases, the findings demonstrate there is a male/female bias in individual income in both formerly stateless people and citizens. The lifting of citizenship barriers does not appear likely to improve these gender biases but that is not to say that the role of gender is unimportant for policy development. We note that having more females in the stateless household seems to increase the odds of having financial capital – irrespective of the country – with each additional female increasing the odds by 20.6 per cent. This suggests that while there may be significant societal discrimination against women, they are more likely to save and make income go further than men; reinforcing the need to consider further gender-inclusive poverty reduction strategies.

Applying Arendt to statelessness today

The above empirical studies are most telling about the nature of statelessness and open up several avenues for practical consideration. In the context of Arendt, we note that the antecedents of statelessness are more varied than she describes. Whereas Arendt explains how political interests coalesced in early twentieth century Germany, it is clear that today statelessness exists as the product of deliberate, accidental and circumstantial events and that these events do not necessarily entail the loss of rights in a totalising system. Rather, as other authors in this volume record, the fact that some groups such as the Nubians in Kenya and the Bihari in Bangladesh enjoyed access to courts highlights a major digression from Arendt's model, where the lack of citizenship provided no legal recourse. Further, extensive interview data records considerable evidence of daily contestation, a condition which runs counter to the negative account given by Arendt according to which the stateless are pitiful and unconnected individuals.

In support of Linz's argument, we also note that while we are able to distinguish between cases on the basis of which stateless people enjoy access to rights, this does not necessarily cut across regime type. Indeed, the totalitarian model as presented by Arendt appears insufficient. Rather, we can group together the democratic state of Slovenia with the non-democratic (until very recently) state of Myanmar and contrast these with two states with very different political traditions such as Sri Lanka and Ukraine, where there have been substantial attempts at reform but which were generated by different internal processes.

The research findings therefore highlight a much more ambiguous state and one which cannot necessarily act as a guarantor of rights even when committed to reform. Citizenship in several cases did not ameliorate the conditions of the formerly stateless and indeed, as noted above, in many states it is questionable just how valuable citizenship is in terms of practical protection. Statelessness is a structural problem, and while it frequently emanates from the conflict between state and nation, and the tussle for membership, as Arendt suggests, there are other modalities which need to be taken into account (see also Cole, this volume).

Conclusion

Arendt was, in many respects, an intellectual maverick to whom we owe considerable debt for her analysis of Nazism, Stalinism and for introducing the study of statelessness. However, her work is situated in a particular European context and therefore warrants a critical rereading when considering its application today. Statelessness in the twenty-first century is both more varied and more nuanced than we find in Arendt's writings but there may still be something to glean from them. The fact that the effects of statelessness endure over time suggests there is more mileage in Arendt's belief in international or interethnic conflict within the nationalising state and that this may continue to feed discriminatory forces. If that is so, then these conclusions have important ramifications for the design of humanitarian policy.

Nationality reform in and of itself does not necessarily provide much relief to the excluded. Rather, we should recognise the complexity that is statelessness and the challenges it poses, especially in the developing country contexts in which most stateless people are based. If one accepts that statelessness is a structural problem, then it is essential to identify ways of correcting the inequalities which continue to disempower and exclude. That also means including nationality criteria in development planning alongside other key indicators. The research suggests that by strengthening human capital – above all improving investment in health and education – the gap between the formerly stateless and natural born citizens can be reduced. Thus, just as we have pro-poor interventions which focus on specific categories, for example women, veterans or those living in river-basin conditions, we too should press for the inclusion of stateless people as a distinct category of beneficiary. Similarly, improving access to land and strengthening social institutions increases the odds of participation.

In our reassessment of Arendt's writings and their relevance to statelessness, this chapter has focused on the political constructs of power and the potential for contestation within systems and within states. I have argued that not only is Arendt's model of totalitarianism less applicable today but her reliance on law as a source of protection also runs counter to contemporary realities. Further, I have also argued that the absence of individuality in her discussion of statelessness is challenged by personal accounts both from the 1940s and from today. The participants in the studies discussed in this chapter enjoyed varying degrees of agency and in some cases were the drivers of change in systems, where they successfully laid claim to their rights. As with Levi's account, they too had names and were aware of their standing in the discriminatory order in which they lived. Such deep contextual information is missing from Arendt's account but is crucially important. By focusing the analysis within the state, and by analysing the context in which stateless people live, it is possible to identify interests, potential cleavages, and arenas for engagement. This includes working with development agencies and donor governments to treat the stateless as a specific category of beneficiary in the hope that in so doing, they remedy some of the effects of discrimination and disempowerment.

Notes

1 This chapter is based on an inaugural lecture delivered at Middlesex University London on 13 February 2014.
2 In both the 1954 Convention relating to the Status of Stateless Persons and the 1961 Convention on the Reduction of Statelessness, the concept of statelessness denotes the lack of a substantive relationship between an individual and a state.
3 See www.unhcr.org/ibelong/

References

Agamben, G. (1998) *Homo Sacer: Sovereign Power and Bare Life*. Stanford, CA: Stanford University Press.

Arendt, H. (1976) *The Origins of Totalitarianism*. New York: Harcourt Brace Jovanovich.

Bernstein, R. (1996) *Hannah Arendt and the Jewish Question*. Cambridge: Polity Press.

Blitz, B. K. (2011) Policy Responses and Global Discourses on the Rights of Non-Citizens and Stateless People. In Sawyer, C. A. and Blitz, B. K. *Statelessness in the European Union: Displaced, Undocumented, Unwanted*, pp. 108–138. Cambridge: Cambridge University Press.

Blitz, B. K. and Lynch, M. (eds) (2011) *Statelessness and Citizenship: A Comparative Study on the Benefits of Nationality*. Cheltenham: Edward Elgar.

Fassin, D. (2005) Compassion and repression: the moral economy of immigration policies in France. *Cultural Anthropology*, 20(3), pp. 362–387.

Isin, E. F. and Nielsen, G. M. (eds) (2008) *Acts of Citizenship*. London: Palgrave Macmillan.

Jay, M. (1986) *Permanent Exiles: Essays on the Intellectual Migration from Germany to America*. New York: Columbia University Press.

Krause, M. (2008) Undocumented migrants: an Arendtian perspective. *European Journal of Political Theory*, 7(3), pp. 331–348.

Levi, P. (2013) *The Drowned and the Saved*. London: Abacus.

Levi, P. (1959) *If This Is a Man*. New York: Orion Press.

Linz, J. J. (2000) *Totalitarian and Authoritarian Regimes*. Boulder, CO: Lynne Rienner.

Manby, B. (2016) *Citizenship Law in Africa: A Comparative Study* (third edition). New York: Open Society Foundations. [online] Available at www.refworld.org/docid/56a77ffe4.html [Accessed 31 January 2016].

Redclift, V. (2013) Abjects or agents? Camps, contests, and the creation of 'Political Space'. *Citizenship Studies*, 3(4), pp. 308–321.

Rygiel, K. (2011) Bordering solidarities: migrant activism and the politics of movement and camps at Calais. *Citizenship Studies*, 15(1), pp. 1–19.

Staples, K. (2012) *Retheorising Statelessness: A Background Theory of Membership in World Politics*. Edinburgh: Edinburgh University Press.

Suderland, M. (2013) *Inside Concentration Camps: Social Life at the Extremes*. Cambridge: Polity Press.

UNHCR. (2014) Concept Note – A Campaign to End Statelessness. [online] Available at: www.unhcr.org/53174df39.html [Accessed 31 January 2016].

Part II

Living statelessness

Photo 3 Camp near Anse a Pitre in Haiti.
Source: © Logan Abassi.

Camp for displaced persons from the Dominican Republic on the outskirts of a town called Anse a Pitre in the northeastern part of Haiti, 24 November 2015. As of 15 July 2015 149,000 Haitians have crossed back into Haiti from the Dominican Republic. Of those, 42,000 were deported from the DR and 2,100 risk becoming stateless. Camps have sprung up near the major border crossing points.

6 Challenging the disunity of statelessness in the Middle East and North Africa

Zahra Al Barazi and Jason Tucker

The right to a nationality is in and of itself a human right.[1] When an individual does not have a nationality, this right has been violated, regardless of the reasons behind the deprivation of nationality. There are many in the Middle East and North Africa (MENA) who have had this right violated. Accurate statistics on statelessness are hard to come by, and that is especially true in a region like the MENA, where State statistical reporting on populations is at best limited. Although UNHCR reports a total of 444,237 persons under its statelessness mandate, highlighting several countries that have particularly significant stateless populations, in reality the figure is much higher. This is for several reasons, predominantly that Palestinians are not counted in this figure, nor are stateless refugees, but mostly that as an invisible and ostracised group there often are no figures of those affected (See Institute on Statelessness and Inclusion 2014). Despite the substantial under-reporting, what is known is that the MENA region has some of the highest levels of statelessness worldwide (Van Waas 2010).

Statelessness in the MENA takes many forms and many profiles – a Bidoon from Kuwait, a non-ID Palestinian living in Jordan, a Maktoum in Lebanon, a Dom in Iraq and a child of a Syrian mother and unknown father born in Egypt. All these individuals, whose statelessness has resulted from discrimination,[2] are connected in that their right to a nationality has been violated and as a consequence they have to live with the often-similar consequences of living without a nationality.

This chapter seeks to explore, through an understanding of the history and development of the situation of statelessness across the region – a consequence of nation-state formation, state succession and/or discriminatory ethnic, religious and gender law and policy – the striking commonalities in both the causes and consequences of statelessness. It will go on to reflect on how the MENA region lacks a common language on statelessness which may have contributed to the fact that these groups are often discussed in isolation of one another, with a limited sense of having a shared cause. The chapter wishes to show how the current framework for understating statelessness in the region can obstruct opportunities to address the issue regionally and can even be used to perpetuate statelessness. By showing how the issue of statelessness is understood in the MENA, it could prove useful to others in understanding how the framework of understanding statelessness in other regions is having both positive and negative impacts upon work towards the goal of ending statelessness.

The commonalities in the causes and perpetuation of statelessness in the MENA

When trying to describe the causes of statelessness in the MENA, it quickly becomes apparent that despite the local specificities (which occur everywhere) there are strong commonalities between states. Indeed, the causes are often so interlinked between states that it is hard to describe statelessness in the region in neat categories. However, an overview must be given in order to reflect on these commonalities, which are used as a foundation to question why the issue of statelessness in the MENA is often divided into the specific population groups or even the individuals it affects. The following sections detail, in brief, the three major causes of statelessness across the MENA. These are: statelessness which arose at the time of nation-state formation, gender discrimination in nationality laws and ethnic, religious and political discrimination. The descriptions of often very complicated causes of statelessness provided here give only a brief summary. More detailed analysis and reflection has been referenced throughout.

Statelessness which arose during nation-state formation or succession

Statelessness in the MENA can be seen to have initially arisen following the creation of the modern nation-states in the region. As Laura van Waas has observed:

> [The] MENA has seen its share of political upheaval with the region swept first by the dissolution of the Ottoman Empire and later by a wave of decolonisation. Processes of state formation were therefore evident across the region over the course of the twentieth century and as each state sought to develop its own identity it faced the question of who to include as citizens. The nationality acts that were adopted following the establishment of the MENA countries as we know them today, largely in the 1950s to early 1970s, answered this need to delineate the terms of membership of the state.
>
> (Van Waas 2010, p. 6)

The MENA was divided up into independent nation-states, based largely on previous colonial divisions. In so doing many people were rendered stateless for a variety of reasons and across a range of states in the region. Inclusion in the new states was normally based on being recorded in a census or some other form of registration, or having resided in the state on a specific date. Those who did not or could not register/prove their residence were often excluded. As the following examples reflect, this often lead to large-scale and protracted situations of statelessness.

Kuwait is host to around 100,000 people who were not included in the initial body of its citizenry and/or their descendants (Immigration and Refugee Board of Canada 2005). In the 1959 Nationality Law, the newly formed nation-state of Kuwait considered only those who had been living on the territory since 1920 as citizens (Kuwait Nationality Law 1959). The Kuwaiti authorities' failure to register all inhabitants before Kuwait gained independence in 1961 meant that many thousands of people were rendered stateless. This arose due to some Bedouin being inaccessible to registration teams, and the lack of awareness of the importance of registration among some of the population, as well as issues such as illiteracy (Al Barazi and Tucker 2014, pp. 13–19). There is a similar story in Saudi Arabia and the United Arab Emirates (UAE). Often those who were excluded in these states were nomadic and difficult to reach, sometimes living across the new nation-state borders, so the need to register was unclear to them and some feared it could potentially lead to double taxation. In all three states, once the initial body of citizenry had been established and these people were excluded, they came to be framed by external actors as a distinct group *based* on their statelessness, and were often persecuted as a consequence.

While the discrimination against the population rendered stateless in Saudi Arabia, the UAE and Kuwait at the time of state formation arose later on, in Lebanon discrimination in access to initial registration played a significant part from the outset (Tucker 2013, pp. 23–31). Lebanese citizenship was legally formulated in 1924, though the country gained its independence in 1946. Citizenship was initially granted based on a person's inclusion in the 1932 census. During this census parts of the population were overlooked and others were actively encouraged to register, while some were not aware of the importance of registering at all. Since then, this exclusion from the initial body of citizenry has only been partially and insufficiently addressed (Van Waas 2010).

The Palestinians remain the best known and most numerous stateless population which arose out of state succession in the region.[3] The Arab–Israel conflict which followed the British mandate withdrawal from Palestine and the establishment of the State of Israel led to mass statelessness among the Palestinians. There are reportedly 5.5 million Palestinians living in the West Bank, Gaza, Lebanon, Jordan and Syria alone, the majority of whom are stateless (Institute on Statelessness and Inclusion 2014, pp. 128–129). Many more Palestinian refugees and diaspora reside in these aforementioned countries without registering or can be found in other countries in the region. The reasons that the Palestinians remain stateless in Jordan, Lebanon or Syria, despite many being born and raised in the country, is a combination of legal exclusion, policy and practice, which seeks to restrict access to nationality, as well as the active choice of some Palestinians to remain stateless so as not to relinquish their claim to the right to return to Palestine (see Akram 2002; Khalil 2009).

Apart from the Palestinians there is another large and protracted stateless refugee population in the region, the Sahrawi, from Western Sahara. While Morocco and Mauritania had both claimed control over Western Sahara for several decades before the Spanish withdrawal of administrative control over the territory in 1975, following this conflict erupted. Morocco came out on top and assumed control over most of the territory. Due to conflict, or the desire not to live under Moroccan control, many fled to neighbouring states. It is reported that well over 100,000 Sahrawi refugees currently live in Algeria and Mauritania (UNHCR 2016a; UNHCR 2016b). As those who fled have not been granted Moroccan nationality, and the majority have not managed to secure Algerian or Mauritanian nationality, this population is believed to be stateless (Institute on Statelessness and Inclusion 2014, p. 122).

The aforementioned instances of statelessness arising as a consequence of state formation or state succession are by no means the only ones to be found in the MENA. However, they are the best documented and largest currently identified. What this section shows is that the largest cause of statelessness in the region is a consequence of state formation or succession. Discriminatory access to citizenship and/or insufficient policies, or implementation thereof, in ensuring that all people on the territory could acquire a nationality meant that many states in the region began life by excluding some of their previous members. Other cases of exclusion were clearly targeted at certain populations, such as the Palestinians and the Sahrawi. Despite these instances of statelessness arising many decades ago, the situation of these people and their descendants continues to this day. One way this has been perpetuated is the result of gender discrimination in nationality laws in the region.

Gender discrimination in nationality laws in the MENA

Discrimination against women in nationality laws can be found in legislation around the world. Yet in the MENA this problem is more concentrated than anywhere else. The Women's Refugee Commission succinctly summarises the complex and multi-faceted nature of this form of discrimination and its ability to cause childhood statelessness:

> Gender discrimination in nationality laws occurs when women cannot acquire, change, retain or pass on their nationality to their children and/or non-national spouses on an equal basis as men. Gender discrimination in nationality laws can result in statelessness where children are born to a mother who is a national, reside in their mother's country and cannot obtain any other nationality for many reasons which include:
>
> • The father died before the birth of the child
> • The father is unknown
> • The father is stateless and has no nationality himself
> • The father is unable to confer his nationality
> • The father is unwilling or unable to take the necessary steps to acquire a nationality for his child.
>
> (Women's Refugee Commission 2013, p. 1)

Of the 27 countries where discrimination against women can be found in nationality laws, nearly half of these are in the MENA (Institute on Statelessness and Inclusion 2014, p. 106). In the region there are several forms of gender discrimination in the nationality laws, all of which have an impact in terms of creating and perpetuating statelessness.

First, there are the states where women cannot pass their nationality to their children on an equal footing to men. Bahrain, Iran, Iraq, Jordan, Kuwait, Lebanon, Libya, Oman, Qatar, Saudi Arabia, Syria and the United Arab Emirates all deny women the right to pass their nationality on to their children either in all circumstances or only under specific exceptions (Global Campaign for Equal Nationality Rights 2016). As mentioned above, in cases where the father does not have a nationality, is unable or unwilling to confirm his parentage, or the father is missing or unknown, the child, not being able to acquire the mother's nationality, will be stateless.

Another form of gender discrimination in nationality laws is women not being able to pass their nationality on to their non-national spouses, or change, acquire or retain their nationality on a par with men. While these specific issues are not significant contributors to statelessness in the region, they can in some situations lead to statelessness, such as where a woman automatically loses her nationality if she marries a foreigner. In addition to the countries in the previous paragraph, this form of discrimination also exists in the legislation in Iraq, Egypt, Mauritania, Morocco, Tunisia and Yemen (Global Campaign for Equal Nationality Rights 2016).

This situation is not static, however, with some states in the region seeking to neutralise the gender discrimination in their nationality law. Reforms in the nationality law of Egypt in 2004 and Morocco in 2007 mean that women are now able to pass their nationality on to their children. New regional and international coalitions have been established to challenge gender discrimination in the nationality laws, and MENA states have been the subject of research into the causes and consequences of this form of discrimination.[4]

On the other hand, the war in Syria and the massive displacement it has caused has meant that this form of discrimination is having more of an impact in terms of creating new cases of statelessness. This is because, when combined with factors such as fathers who are missing or not able to confirm their parentage, marriages that cannot be formalised due to refugees' lack of legal status, lack of birth registration, limited access to documents and the destruction of civil documentation, there is a real danger of a new generation of stateless children being born inside Syria as well as in exile (Institute on Statelessness and Inclusion and The Global Campaign for Equal Nationality Rights 2016, para. 19).

Ethnic, religious and political discrimination

Statelessness has also resulted from the 'Arabisation' movement that took hold of the region in the 1960s and 1970s. As a result of this movement to 'Arabise' the region, and the desire to weaken any other potential ethno-cultural opposition, a census was conducted in 1962 in the Al-Hasake region of northeast Syria, where a large number of Kurds lived. A Refugees International report observed that:

> An estimated 120,000 people or about 20 percent of Syrian Kurds lost their citizenship, a number which has since more than doubled to approximately 300,000 at present.... The census reflected a political agenda to Arabize the northeast, an area rich in natural resources, and to identify recent illegal migrants from Turkey. To retain their citizenship, Kurds had to prove residence in Syria dating from 1945 or before. Implementation of this order went awry. Even Kurds with proof of residence lost their nationality; others were compelled to pay large bribes to retain it.
>
> (Refugees International 2006, p. 1)

The census was largely exclusionary and arbitrarily imposed on the Kurds, which led to a situation where two groups of stateless Kurds were created, those who were registered as *ajanib* (foreign) and others who were not registered at all, the *maktoumeen* (hidden) (Human Rights Watch 1996; KurdWatch 2010). The number of stateless Kurds in Syria had fallen to 160,000 in 2013, in part due to a 2011 naturalisation decree allowing some *ajanib* to naturalise, but also due to the high number of people fleeing the country during the ongoing conflict (Institute on Statelessness and Inclusion 2014, p. 111).

Some Kurds in Iraq have also suffered as a result of Arab nationalism. In 1980, a decree was passed in Iraq that saw the denationalisation of as many as 300,000 Faili Kurds, with the justification that they were of 'foreign origin' and not loyal to the country (Institute on Statelessness and Inclusion 2014). This denationalisation and subsequent forced deportation to Iran arose out of a suspicion that the Faili Kurds, as a largely Shi'a Muslim community, who lived in and across the border area between Iraq and Iran, were loyal to Iran (Campbell 2010). While some managed to acquire another nationality, many remained stateless. With the fall of Saddam Hussein, a law in 2006 repealed the 1980 decree and allowed the Faili Kurds to reacquire their citizenship and return to Iraq if they so wished. However, due to certain documentary requirements to reacquire nationality, an unknown number have not been able to benefit from this decree and remain stateless in both Iraq and Iran (Institute on Statelessness and Inclusion 2014).

With regard to Libya, it is believed that statelessness affects various ethnic minority populations as a consequence of the 'Arabisation' of the country under the leadership of Moammar Gadhafi. The three groups who are believed to be most affected by restricted access to citizenship, or have faced denationalisations, are the Berber (Amazigh), Tuareg and Tebu (Institute on Statelessness and Inclusion 2014). While there is no information on the total number of people affected by statelessness in the country, it is estimated that up to 50,000 Tebu alone may be stateless (Institute on Statelessness and Inclusion 2014, p. 109).

In Mauritania in 1989, amidst social and political turmoil, the predominantly Arab government arbitrarily denaturalised over 60,000 'Black Mauritanians', and expelled the stateless population from the country (Köhn 2011). Expulsions of these people into Senegal and Mali continued into 1990 and the Black Mauritanians remained in exile until the regime that caused their statelessness came to an end in 2005. Since then some have been allowed to return, though restricted access to identity cards, a new exclusionary census in 2010–2011 and the end of repatriation has meant that their situation is far from resolved (Köhn 2011). This is summarised by the Institute on Statelessness and Inclusion:

> There remain 13,703 refugees from Mauritania in Senegal and 12,897 in Mali, as well as just over 5,000 in France. It is therefore unlikely that they are currently recognised as nationals by Mauritania – nor have they yet acquired a new nationality in their state of refuge. This means that the remaining 30,000 or so Black Mauritanians living in exile are likely to be stateless refugees.
>
> (2014, pp. 115–116)

Denaturalisation of those believed to threaten the narrative of the nation, or the distribution of power, does not only affect groups. Individuals across the region have also been rendered stateless. Two prominent recent examples of this include the denaturalisation of seven Emirati activists (who did not have another nationality and thus were rendered stateless) by the UAE in 2011. The denationalisation was appealed in court but the appeal was rejected, with the authorities justifying the denationalisation based on the threat they posed to state security (Al Barazi and Tucker 2014). Similarly, in Bahrain in November 2012 the government withdrew the citizenship of 35 of its citizens who played a role in the opposition movement (all of whom were reportedly Shi'a Muslims), with only six of these people believed to hold another nationality; therefore 29 were rendered stateless (Al Barazi and Tucker 2014).

Summarising the commonalities

The above three major causes of statelessness in the region cannot in actuality be divided in any meaningful way. They are heavily and often inextricably intertwined with regard to creating new cases of statelessness and perpetuating statelessness in the region. Take for example stateless persons in Kuwait. Statelessness in the country arose due to the initial exclusion from the citizenry of certain people from the newly-formed nation-state. While they were initially excluded accidentally, the stateless of Kuwait have become a group bound by their shared statelessness and the increasing discrimination they face by the government authorities, especially after the withdrawal of Iraqi troops from Kuwait in 1990. This group discrimination was not the cause of their statelessness, rather the group, commonly referred to as the 'Bidoon':

> is best described as a construction of the Kuwaiti Government, members of this group are not part of it voluntarily. On the contrary, membership of the

Bidoon is unintentional and unwanted. Over time, it has developed into a classification forced upon its members. Today, this construction by the Kuwaiti Government is used to marginalise and oppress the Bidoon.

(Affleck 2012)

The gender discrimination in the nationality law can be seen as part of the colonial legal legacy and is linked with state formation as well. Indeed, 'Many of these [MENA nationality] laws are rooted in colonial legacies, reflecting the discrimination against women embedded in colonial powers' legal systems, which included other forms of discrimination' (Global Campaign for Equal Nationality Rights 2016). Children in families in which both parents are stateless cannot obtain citizenship, but also children of stateless fathers, even where the mother is a Kuwaiti citizen, have no access to citizenship. Consequently, the stateless population continues to grow.

Kuwait has also received a number of stateless refugees and migrants, some of whom have been rendered stateless by state formation or succession in other states in the region. Currently there are believed to be as many as 70,000 Palestinians in Kuwait, though in the past this number could have been as high as 400,000 (O'Toole 2015). An unknown number of these Palestinians may have citizenship of other states; however it is likely that the majority are stateless. Kuwait has also become host to a number of Syrian refugees. The Institute on Statelessness and Inclusion explains how gender discrimination in Syria's nationality laws, combined with the large numbers of Syrians fleeing their country and the ongoing conflict, is causing an ever-expanding stateless problem for the region:

Significantly, gender discrimination in nationality laws can perpetuate statelessness across generations, as male children who are rendered stateless through this provision will go on to have their own stateless children who cannot access nationality even if their mother is a citizen. The danger of intergenerational statelessness is further exacerbated by the existence of other stateless populations in Syria as well as challenges related to registration, documentation and proof of identity.

(Institute on Statelessness and Inclusion and The Global Campaign for Equal Nationality Rights 2016, para.17)

Syria is only one out of 12 states in the region with gender discrimination in their nationality law, meaning that women cannot pass their nationality to their children on a par with men. Kuwait is only one of many states whose formation led to large swathes of the population being rendered stateless. Ethnic, religious and political discrimination in access to nationality can also be seen across the region. Other states host considerably larger numbers of stateless Syrian, Sahrawi and Palestinian refugees. Rather than targeting Kuwait as specifically problematic, it has been chosen here as an example to reflect upon the interlinked nature of statelessness in the region. A holistic understanding of statelessness in Kuwait has to draw on an understanding of issues arising from state formation and the initial identification of the state's citizenry, gender discrimination in the nationality law, the colonial legacy in terms of delineating states and their legal legacy, ethnic and religious discrimination and the presence of stateless refugees and migrants. All these factors have an impact on statelessness in Kuwait, as in other states in the region where there are multiple, though largely similar, factors that create and perpetuate statelessness. The division of specific statelessness issues, groups or even individuals is therefore artificial.

Challenges to unification

Despite the above-mentioned commonalities in the creation, perpetuation and consequences of statelessness, the framework for understanding statelessness in the MENA is characterised by disunity and the isolation of specific groups of stateless people from each other. There are significant challenges in terms of overcoming disunity. However, the possibilities that a unified approach provides may prove advantageous when working towards tackling statelessness in the MENA. To better comprehend the current framework for understanding statelessness in the region, we should consider some of the key interlinked discourses that have led to this current disunity: the 'self' labelling of the stateless, the official discourse and the civil society and international organisation discourse.

'Self'-labelling[5]

One of the main struggles in creating this unification is that the communities themselves often do not see the similarities between themselves and other stateless groups in their community, country or the region. The following examples, which draw on the lived experiences of stateless individuals in the MENA, reflects how this disunity between individuals affected by statelessness exists at an individual level.

A young woman in her mid-20s, Lina is very aware of the potential consequences that may arise from gender discrimination in the Kuwaiti nationality law.[6] Her mother married an Iranian without registering the marriage, and just after Lina was born her father left with no trace as to where he had gone. Kuwaiti nationality law does not allow her to become a national on the basis of her mother's nationality, unless she registers that her father is unknown,[7] something she is not prepared to do. Not having been able to obtain a nationality, she believes, is keeping away potential suitors – not having a secure legal status, and the uncertainty of what the future may hold because of that, scares men from committing.

Meanwhile, across the city a teenager in her final year of school is very aware of what the consequences of living as a Bidoon could be. She sees her brothers suffering, trying to get a job or finish their education, and senses the tense frustration in her family when anyone discusses future ambitions or dreams. She knows that her only way out of this cycle of living as a stigmatised Bidoon girl is to marry out of it, to marry a Kuwaiti citizen and to rely on him to acquire a nationality.

Not far off in the Kurdistan region of Iraq, another girl in her mid-20s recently fled the Afreen region of Syria with her family and is now living in Sulimaniya. She was born a stateless Kurd, like her parents before her. Her grandparents were made stateless in the 1960s, and she and all her siblings and cousins have known no other status. Their statelessness has hampered her ability to complete her education back in Syria, and her brothers struggled to get jobs. Now in Sulimaniya, she hopes that they may be able to make a fresh start. Further north in Dohuk, a young 15-year-old sits with her five-month-old baby on her lap. Due to her displacement she entered an early marriage, which was never registered, and now her husband has left and she has not registered the birth of her son. She recognises the importance of having her child registered – she has been told that a certificate is needed to enter school, but has no idea how to make this happen. The nationality law of her country does not allow her to transfer her nationality to her child, so if the father is never legally acknowledged her child will be stateless.

Four young women live not far from one other, all very aware of the politics and challenges that face their families and communities. They are all aware of the importance of having a nationality, and of the consequences of not having one. Despite the interlinked nature of the cause and consequences of their statelessness, these women do not know of their shared goal. They had little understanding of how their statelessness was situated within the wider framework for understanding or addressing the stateless in their country or the wider region. The 'form' of statelessness which impacts them is often an external label which obscures the wider issue as well as obscuring shared goals between stateless persons often living in the same communities. The external labelling is the result of the official, civil society and international organisation discourses on statelessness.

Official discourse

One of the major reasons why stateless persons might not see the similarities between the causes and consequences of their situation is the way in which the government authorities have framed the issue across the region.

Even when we only look at the way the issue is phrased, with the different terminologies used, the problem begins.[8] In Arabic there is no specific word for 'statelessness' (Gyulai 2012). The terminology found in the United Nations statelessness conventions is *adim aljinsiya*,[9] which translates to 'lacking nationality' and is a literal description of what statelessness is. When looking more at domestic legislation, this internationally used term is in fact not commonly found.[10] Instead, each country has phrased the issue in its own way. For example, one term, such as in Article 3(4) of the Jordanian nationality law, or Article 3(c) of the Syrian nationality law,[11] is *la jinsiya laho*, which literally means 'does not have a nationality'. Other terms that describe the status, such as *maktoum al kayd* or *maktoumeen* (found in Lebanon and Syria), are literally another way of expressing 'without' in Arabic.

Most importantly though is that terms that are used to describe communities are now the common terms used to describe the phenomenon. So, instead of describing a person as stateless, it is more common practice to describe them as the community they have come from. The most obvious example is the term *Bidoon* – an abbreviated form of *bidoon jinsiya*, which translates to 'without nationality' to describe those who are stateless in the Gulf for historical reasons as described above.

Additionally, not having a coherent and consistent legal terminology of statelessness allows governments the space to bestow their own terms on the stateless in order to hide their failure to ensure everyone has a right to a nationality behind a group and also issue specific discourses. For example, in Kuwait the Bidoon are often described as 'illegal residents'[12] and some stateless Kurds in Syria are known as *ajanib* – literally meaning 'foreigner'.

Civil society and international organisation discourse

At an international level, while statelessness has only recently gained momentum as an important issue,[13] many key international civil society players have been working with different stateless groups for several decades. However, too often they have focused on the issue only in relation to certain groups or communities – for example, looking specifically at the Bidoon (Human Rights Watch 2011) or the Kurds of Syria (Refugees International 2006) or the denaturalised Palestinians in Jordan (Human Rights Watch 2010). This is also true for the causes of statelessness. A significant amount of research and advocacy on gender discrimination in nationality laws, or the arbitrary deprivation of nationality, has been undertaken, but rarely are these firmly situated within the wider causes of statelessness in the region (see Women's Refugee Commission 2013). National civil society organisations also often work on the issue from the perspective of the community affected, and not from that of statelessness and the right to nationality. For example, those advocating an end to gender discrimination in nationality law often approach it from a women's rights perspective, ignoring the reality that the consequence of not having a nationality is most severe on the male children of these women (see Women's Refugee Commission 2013).

This compartmentalisation of the discrimination that causes statelessness, as reflected in the work of national and international civil society organisations, can also be seen in how international organisations and human rights mechanisms are addressing the issue. For example, an analysis of the Committee on the Rights of the Child recommendations on the right of a child to gain a nationality at birth shows that the recommendations are often related to preventing statelessness among children of certain groups and are not looking to ensure this right for all children in the country in question.[14] Further to this, international organisations can be seen as reinforcing the differentiation of groups and issues, for example by adopting the terminology developed by states, who seek to hide the statelessness of populations by using various legal statuses or terms to describe them.

Conclusion

Put simply, whether you are a *maktoum*, a *bidoon* or *adim aljinsiya*, you are equally stateless. The discussion in this chapter has documented the common causes of statelessness in the MENA as well as why these individuals and groups are often isolated from one another in the framework of understanding stateless-ness in the region. The exploration of similarities that can form a foundation for unity, as documented in this chapter, provides a means to challenge the current disunity in tackling statelessness in the region. Obviously there is no one-size-fits-all approach to addressing the issue of statelessness, and local specificities will be important. However, by critically reflecting on our framework for understanding statelessness in the MENA, some of these local specificities can be seen in a new light. Some of these are constructed differences that are reinforced through the dis-course of a range of actors, whether this is intentional or unintentional. When we strip away the constructed difference, then we can appreciate the striking similar-ities in the causes and consequences of statelessness in the MENA.

In seeing the similarities and the need for unification, new opportunities arise. For example in many regions of the world there are now regional networks and initiatives on statelessness.[15] These organisations collaborate on research, share skills and resources and use their collective strength to advocate for change. Such a regional network would be a great asset in working towards ending state-lessness in the MENA.[16] Given the massive challenges that those seeking to address statelessness in the region face, and the multi-generational nature of statelessness in the MENA, such an asset should not be overlooked. However, for such opportunities to reach fruition powerful discourses on statelessness will need to be challenged and decades of disunity overcome. This in itself will be no easy feat.

Notes

1 See as one example Article 15 of the Universal Declaration of Human Rights.
2 For a broader discussion of how discrimination plays a part in the causes and con-sequences of statelessness, see Kingston, this volume.
3 It is important here to note that in referring to the Palestinians, we are only referring to those who meet the definition of a stateless person under international law regard-less of whose international protection mandate the individual falls under. See Article 1, UN General Assembly, *Convention Relating to the Status of Stateless Persons*, 28 September 1954, United Nations, Treaty Series, vol. 360, p. 117. Available at: www. refworld.org/docid/3ae6b3840.html [Accessed 26 September 2016].
4 See the Campaign for Equal Nationality Rights, launched in 2014 by the Women's Refugee Commission, Equality Now, the Equal Rights Trust, the Institute on State-lessness and Inclusion, UN Women and UNHCR. For research on the consequences of being born stateless in certain MENA states see Women's Refugee Commission (2013).

5 These stories come from varying interviews carried out by the authors in the MENA between 2013 and 2015.

6 Article 4 of the Kuwaiti nationality law 1959 does not allow women similar rights to men on transferral of nationality.

7 Article 4 of Kuwaiti nationality law 1959.

8 For a broader discourse on terminologies and conflating 'nationality' and 'citizenship', see Tonkiss, this volume.

9 See, for example, article 7(2) of the Covenant on the Rights of the Child in Islam, as well as the Arabic versions of UNHCR and Inter-Parliamentary Union (2005); UN Committee on the Rights of the Child (2013), *List of issues in response to the second periodic report of Kuwait*, CRC/C/KWT/Q/2, 10 May 2013. Available at: www2. ohchr.org/english/bodies/crc/docs/AdvanceVersions/CRC-C-KWT-Q-2_ar.doc; UN (2007), *The Excluded*. Available at: www.un.org/arabic/events/tenstories/2007/the excluded.shtml; Frontiers Ruwad (2009).

10 One main example is the Tunisian nationality law – as Tunisia is one of the few state parties from the MENA region to the UN statelessness conventions, this may have influenced the terminology used in its national legal framework.

11 Law No. 6 of 1954 on Jordanian Nationality and Legislative Decree 276 on Syrian Nationality Law.

12 For more discussion on using this phrase in describing the stateless, see Blake, this volume.

13 We now have, for example, regional networks on statelessness in many regions across the world, and the UNHCR have established an iBelong campaign galvanising momentum to eradicate statelessness by 2024.

14 See the Institute on Statelessness and Inclusion civil society toolkit on the CRC www. institutesi.org/ourwork/children.php

15 For example the European Network on Statelessness, the American Network on Nationality and Statelessness, the Statelessness Network Asia Pacific and African Citizenship Rights in Africa.

16 There is however some current effort to create one to fulfil this exact gap.

References

Affleck, D. (2012) *Being 'Without' – Who are the Bidoon of Kuwait?* Right Now: Human Rights in Australia. [online] Available at: http://rightnow.org.au/opinion-3/being-"without"---who-are-the-bidoon-of-kuwait/ [Accessed 12 March 2013].

Akram, S. (2002) Palestinian refugees and their legal status: rights, politics, and implications for a yust solution. *Journal of Palestine Studies*, 31(3), pp. 36–51.

Al Barazi, Z. and Tucker, J. (2014) Citizenship as a Political Tool: The Recent Turmoil in the MENA and the Creation and Resolution of Statelessness. In Kruiniger, P. (ed.) *Nationality and Statelessness in the Middle East and the Dutch Legal Practice*, pp. 73–79. The Hague: Boom Legal Publishers.

Campbell, E. (2010) *The Faili Kurds of Iraq: Thirty years without nationality*. Refugees International. [online] Available at: http://reliefweb.int/report/iraq/faili-kurds-iraq-thirty-years-without-nationality [Accessed 3 June 2014].

Frontiers Ruwad. (2009) Invisible citizens. A legal study of statelessness in Lebanon. [online] Available at: www.frontiersruwad.org/pdf/FR_Stateless_BOOK_Arabic_2010. pdf [Accessed 5 February 2016].

Global Campaign for Equal Nationality Rights. (2016) Middle East and North Africa. [online] Available at: http://equalnationalityrights.org/countries/global-overview/8-middle-east-north-africa [Accessed 5 February 2016].

Gyulai, G. (2012) *Statelessness in the Tower of Babel – How Do You Say Stateless in your Language?* European Network on Statelessness, 20 June. [online] Available at: www.statelessness.eu/blog/statelessness-tower-babel-%E2%80%93-how-do-you-say-stateless-your-language [Accessed 5 February 2016].

Human Rights Watch. (2011) Prisoners of the Past. [online] Available at: www.hrw.org/sites/default/files/reports/kuwait0611WebInside.pdf [Accessed 23 June 2014].

Human Rights Watch. (2010) Stateless Again: Palestinian-Origin Jordanians Deprived of their Nationality. [online] Available at: www.refworld.org/docid/4b6ae5702.html [Accessed 23 June 2014].

Human Rights Watch. (1996) Syria: The Silenced Kurds. [online] Available at: www.hrw.org/sites/default/files/reports/SYRIA96.pdf [Accessed 23 June 2014).

Immigration and Refugee Board of Canada. (2005) Kuwait: Treatment of Bidoon by the Kuwaiti authorities (January 2003 – October 2005), 21 October, KWT100681.E. [online] Available at: www.refworld.org/docid/440ed71912.html [Accessed 26 September 2016].

Institute on Statelessness and Inclusion. (2014) The World's Stateless. [online] Available at: www.institutesi.org/worldsstateless.pdf [Accessed 7 February 2016].

Institute on Statelessness and Inclusion and The Global Campaign for Equal Nationality Rights. (2016) Submission to the Human Rights Council at the 26th Session of the Universal Periodic Review Syrian Arab Republic. [online] Available at: www.institutesi.org/SyriaUPR2016.pdf [Accessed 7 February 2016].

Inter-Parliamentary Union. (2005) Nationality and Statelessness. A Handbook for Parliamentarians. [online] Available at: www.ipu.org/PDF/publications/nationality_ar.pdf [Accessed 6 February 2016].

Khalil, A. (2009) Palestinian Refugees in Arab States: A Rights-Based Approach. *Robert Schuman Centre for Advanced Studies CARIM Research Report No. 2009/08.* [online] Available at SSRN: https://ssrn.com/abstract=1523510 [Accessed 15 November 2015].

Köhn, S. (2011) *Fear and Statelessness in Mauritania*, Open Society Foundations. [online] Available at: www.opensocietyfoundations.org/voices/fear-and-statelessness-mauritania [Accessed 6 February 2016].

KurdWatch. (2010) Stateless Kurds in Syria: Illegal Invaders or Victims of a Nationalistic Policy? [online] Available at: www.kurdwatch.org/pdf/kurdwatch_staatenlose_en.pdf [Accessed 23 July 2014].

Kuwaiti Nationality Law. (1959) [online] Available at: www.refworld.org/docid/3ae6b4ef1c.html [Accessed 14 March 2014].

O'Toole, M. (2015) *Palestine–Kuwait relations: 'Ice has started to melt'.* Al Jazeera. [online] Available at: www.aljazeera.com/news/2015/08/palestine-kuwait-relations-ice-started-melt-150805072107680.html [Accessed 12 October 2016].

Refugees International. (2006) Buried Alive: Stateless Kurds in Syria. [online] Available at: www.refworld.org/docid/47a6eba80.html [Accessed 26 September 2016].

Tucker, J. (2013) *Challenging the tyranny of citizenship: Statelessness in Lebanon.* The University of Bath. [online] Available at: http://opus.bath.ac.uk/43313/ [Accessed 27 October 2015].

UN Committee on the Rights of the Child. (2013) *List of issues in response to the second periodic report of Kuwait*, CRC/C/KWT/Q/2, 10 May. [online] Available at: www2.ohchr.org/english/bodies/crc/docs/AdvanceVersions/CRC-C-KWT-Q-2_ar.doc [Accessed 12 October 2016].

UNHCR. (2016a) Algeria Global Focus. [online] Available at: http://reporting.unhcr.org/node/7039 [Accessed 12 October 2016].

UNHCR. (2016b) Mauritania Global Focus. [online] Available at: http://reporting.unhcr.org/mauritania [Accessed 12 October 2016].

United Nations. (2007) The Excluded. [online] Available at: www.un.org/arabic/events/tenstories/2007/theexcluded.shtml [Accessed 3 August 2015].

Van Waas, L. (2010) The Situation of Stateless Persons in the Middle East and North Africa, UNHCR. [online] Available at: www.unhcr.org/uk/protection/statelessness/4ce63e079/situation-stateless-persons-middle-east-north-africa-laura-van-waas.html [Accessed 12 October 2016].

Women's Refugee Commission. (2013) Our Motherland, Our Country: Gender Discrimination and Statelessness in the Middle East and North Africa. [online] Available at: www.wluml.org/sites/wluml.org/files/Our_Motherland,_Our_Country_final_for_web.pdf [Accessed 11 February 2015].

7 Race-based statelessness in the Dominican Republic

Jillian Blake

Introduction

This chapter analyses the phenomenon of statelessness in the Dominican Republic, with a focus on the racially and ethnically discriminatory laws and policies that create statelessness in the country. The case study of the Dominican Republic demonstrates that statelessness can be a result of national efforts to expel racial and ethnic minority groups deemed socially undesirable. The Dominican Republic is unique within the Americas, where statelessness has historically been rare due to widespread acceptance of a birthright citizenship standard. The vast majority of the stateless people in the Americas today are living in this small Caribbean country.

In 2013, the Constitutional Court of the Dominican Republic issued a ruling upholding a constitutional amendment to revoke the citizenship rights of persons born to undocumented immigrants in the Dominican Republic, creating a massive population of stateless persons who are predominately black and of Haitian origin. This statelessness crisis follows a long history of racial discrimination and disenfranchisement of dark-skinned Dominicans and persons of Haitian background in the Dominican Republic. Understanding the statelessness crisis in the Dominican Republic, and the relationship between irregular migration and statelessness, is especially important within the context of the Americas. The case study of the Dominican Republic serves as a warning to other American states that may consider abandoning birthright citizenship principles.

This chapter will first explore the norm of birthright citizenship in the Americas and present the history of national identity, race and migration in the Dominican Republic. Next, it will describe the evolution of immigration and nationality law and policy in the Dominican Republic and explain how the citizenship rights of black Dominicans and Dominicans of Haitian background were eroded over decades, culminating with the 2013 Constitutional Court decision (referred to as TC 168–13). It will then argue that the denial of citizenship rights in the Dominican Republic is a violation of international and inter-American law. Finally, the chapter will examine recent developments in the statelessness crisis in the Dominican Republic.

Jus soli citizenship and racial discrimination in the Americas

The 2013 Dominican Constitutional Court decision (TC 168–13) brought condemnation from international governments and organisations, while the government of the Dominican Republic maintained that the issue was only of domestic concern. The Caribbean Community (CARICOM), an international organisation made up of 15 Caribbean states, strongly denounced the ruling and suspended the Dominican Republic's application for membership in the organisation (Charles 2013).

'Birthright citizenship' in the Americas usually refers to citizenship determined by the territory of one's birth (also known as *jus soli* citizenship). *Jus soli* birthright citizenship is a norm almost universally accepted in the region, which has historically seen large migration movements, especially from Europe and Africa (OAS 2011, p. 17). Thirty states in the Americas grant automatic *jus soli* citizenship (Culliton-Gonzalez 2012, p. 133). The other major standard for granting citizenship, *jus sanguinis* – citizenship determined by blood relationship to a national of the state – is considered by Michael Lister to be 'likely to be incompatible with [a] liberal conception of citizenship' (Lister 2010, p. 200). According to Lister:

> [I]f citizenship is distributed on the basis of ethnic membership, then it is both overinclusive and underinclusive. It is underinclusive because it excludes some who are, or would be, fully contributing members of a political community for morally irrelevant reasons beyond their control. It is also overinclusive. Strong *jus sanguinis* extends citizenship … to some who are not, and who need not be, members of the political community in question.

Historically, the denial of birthright citizenship in the Americas has been tied to racial and ethnic prejudice and efforts to exclude or oppress minority groups. For example, in *Dred Scott* v. *Sandford* the US Supreme Court held that African-Americans, even those born free on US soil, were not citizens of the United States (*Dred Scott* v. *Sandford* 1857, p. 406). While the passage of the 14th amendment after the US Civil War in 1868 guaranteed citizenship to all persons born in US territory, attempts to limit the *jus soli* citizenship of Native Americans and persons of Chinese ancestry continued. In 1898, the Supreme Court held that persons of Chinese ancestry born on US soil were citizens, establishing the modern-day interpretation of *jus soli* citizenship under the 14th amendment in the United States (*United States v. Wong Kim Ark* 1898). More recently, campaigns to revoke *jus soli* citizenship in the United States have been targeted at the children of undocumented Hispanic/Latino immigrants (Culliton-Gonzalez 2012, p. 131). According to Richard T. Middleton, IV:

> [B]ecause citizenship affords its members various public goods that can only be denied to non-members, citizenship also maintains a discriminatory element. Thus, denial of citizenship is one method by which a state can

attempt to exclude individuals from feeling a sense of belonging and membership in the national community. This is particularly relevant when the lines are drawn in a manner to exclude racial and ethnic immigrant minorities, given that such individuals already typically face challenges being accepted as part of the in-group.

(Middleton 2011, p. 74)

A similar racial prejudice can be seen behind the Dominican Republic context discussed here.

National identity, race and migration in the Dominican Republic

Race and ethnicity have long impacted the national identity of the Dominican Republic, especially in relation to its eastern neighbour on the island of Hispaniola, Haiti. The Dominican Republic first gained independence in 1844 following a more than 20-year period of Haitian occupation, mainly under President Jean-Pierre Boyer (Lippmann Mazzaglia and Marcelino 2014, p. 164). The armed conflict between the two nations in the war for Dominican independence created distrust and animosity early on (ibid., p. 164). After gaining independence, many Dominican nationalists came to define themselves in terms of race, as white or Hispanic, as opposed to their Haitian neighbours whom they characterised as black (Sagas 2000, pp. 36–37; Middleton 2011, pp. 83–84). This racial distinction was rooted in a nationalist narrative that held Dominicans were descended from Spaniards, and Haitians were descended from African slaves. Apart from the arbitrariness of this categorisation, this narrative also ignored the fact that many Dominicans were of mixed racial and ethnic heritage (Sagas 2000, p. 37).

The view of white and Hispanic racial superiority was solidified under the dictatorship of Rafael Trujillo (1930–1961) who 'institutionaliz[ed] anti-blackness in Dominican society' where '*negro* [black] became synonymous with Haitian' and 'to call someone *negro* was the ultimate insult' (Middleton 2011, pp. 83–84). In 1937, the Trujillo government killed as many as 20,000 ethnic Haitians living in the Dominican Republic's border regions in a genocidal massacre known as the 'Parsley Massacre' (Davis 2012). According to Eduard Paulino:

After 1937 the Dominican culture became exclusive. On a local level people could work together and could accept that [they lived in a mixed] society, of which Dominicans of Haitian descent [were] a part. But at the state level there's still [today a] sense of rejection of dark-skinned Haitians.

(Ibid.)

Still, under the Trujillo regime many Haitians migrated to the Dominican Republic to provide the low-cost labour needed for the growing sugar industry, facilitated by bilateral agreements between the Dominican and Haitian governments (Ferguson

2003). During the Trujillo period the Dominican government was dependent on Haitian labour, and at the same time strongly racist and anti-Haitian (ibid.). The migration of Haitians to the Dominican Republic also displaced many Dominican agricultural and service workers, contributing to native-born resentment and xenophobia towards Haitian immigrants (SAIS 2015, p. 8). In the 1960s, migrant Haitian workers were placed in permanent settlements around agricultural centres called *bateyes*, decreasing the demand for continuing immigrant labour (Ferguson 2003, p. 11; SAIS 2015, p. 8). Living conditions in the *bateyes*, however, were deplorable. These communities often had no access to running water or educational and medical facilities, creating a large underclass of black Dominicans with Haitian heritage permanently living on the outskirts of society (SAIS 2015, p. 8).

Haitian migration to the Dominican Republic and other countries in the Americas, most notably the United States, increased dramatically in the 1970s (Coupeau 2008, p. 149). While migration earlier in the twentieth century was largely fuelled by demand in the Dominican agricultural industry, migration afterwards was increasingly due to political and economic instability and natural disasters in Haiti. Many fled Haiti for political and economic reasons during the dictatorships of François 'Papa Doc' and Jean-Claude 'Baby Doc' Duvalier, who ruled Haiti from 1957 until 1971 and from 1971 until 1986, respectively (Weinstein and Segal 1992). In 1991, the first democratically elected president of Haiti, Jean-Bertrand Aristide, was overthrown by the Haitian military in a *coup d'état* precipitating an international crisis as political refugees fled the country (Jones 1992, p. 84). Many Haitians fled on boats and rafts to the United States, and others crossed the land border to the Dominican Republic. By 1993, the Dominican Republic had between 2,500 and 3,000 Haitian political refugees and many Haitian economic migrants (Lippman Mazzaglia and Marcelino 2014, p. 164).

Another large wave of Haitian migrants fled their home country in 2010 after a 7.0-magnitude earthquake hit near the capital city, Port-au-Prince, killing more than 220,000 people and leaving more than one million homeless (Basu 2012). In the aftermath, the Dominican Republic 'launched a massive cross-border emergency assistance mission to Haiti, providing critical medical assistance, logistics support, and humanitarian aid' (Mendelson Forman and White 2011). Despite this commendable effort, soon after the earthquake the Dominican Republic resumed deportations of undocumented Haitians, including those impacted by the earthquake (Kristensen and Wooding 2013).

Immigration and nationality law and policy in the Dominican Republic: an erosion of fundamental rights

The 1929 Dominican Constitution granted citizenship to all persons born in the country regardless of their parents' race, ethnic origin or immigration status (Dominican Constitution, Article 8, 1929). The Constitution included minor exceptions to the birthright citizenship principle (based on birth on the territory) for children born to persons 'in transit' through the Dominican Republic or children of diplomats (Dominican Constitution, Article 8, 1929). According to a

1939 Dominican immigration law 'in transit' was defined as being in the country for ten days or fewer, for the purpose of reaching another destination (Dominican Migration Law 279, 1939). Despite this small 'in transit' exception, the 1929 Constitution recognised an almost absolute right to birthright citizenship; however, that right was slowly eroded in bureaucratic practice over the succeeding 75 years.

Dominican hospitals and civil registry offices routinely rejected identity documents or Dominican workplace identity cards taken by Haitian immigrants seeking birth certificates for, or seeking to register, their Dominican-born children (Open Society Institute 2010, p. 4). Officials often made the determination that Haitian immigrants were 'in transit' and that their children born in the Dominican Republic were therefore not legally entitled to citizenship (Open Society Institute 2010, pp. 4–5). In the 1980s and 1990s civil registry offices were no longer accepting workplace identification cards (which many Haitian immigrants possessed) and by the year 2000 many persons with valid forms of identification but considered 'Haitian' because of their skin colour or name were being turned away from civil registry offices for being 'in transit' through the Dominican Republic (Open Society Institute 2010, p. 5). As a result of decades of racial and ethnic discrimination against Haitian and dark-skinned parents of citizens born in the Dominican Republic, by the end of the twentieth century many Dominican citizens were living undocumented and were de facto stateless, unable to access basic state social services like healthcare and education.

In 2004 the Dominican Republic passed the General Migration Law No. 285–04 which established that 'non-residents' would be considered 'in transit' for purposes of determining the right to citizenship of their children born in the Dominican Republic (General Migration Law No. 285–04). This law effectively cancelled the previously almost absolute principle of birthright citizenship established in the 1929 Dominican Constitution, and legalised the previously de facto system of statelessness in the Dominican Republic. The law instructed hospitals to give non-residents different, non-official birth certificates for their children born in the Dominican Republic (Aber and Small 2013). The Dominican government began applying the 2004 migration law retroactively as well, taking away the fundamental rights of those previously recognised as citizens (Open Society Institute 2010, p. 9). One year later, the Dominican Secretary of Labour announced the country would 'dehaitianise' its population, and the country began a massive deportation campaign (Baluarte 2006, p. 25). This deportation 'campaign was carried out in brutal fashion; people were taken from their homes, families were separated, and large groups were pushed over the border at night with no food or money' (ibid., p. 26).

In 2007, the UN Special Rapporteur on contemporary forms of racism, racial discrimination, xenophobia and related intolerance visited the Dominican Republic and found that

> there is a profound and entrenched problem of racism and discrimination in Dominican society, generally affecting blacks, and particularly such groups

as black Dominicans, Dominicans of Haitian decent and Haitians. The dominant perception among most Dominicans is that mulatto skin tones distinguish them from darker-skinned Dominicans and Haitians.

(UN Special Rapporteur Report 2008)

Following the passage of the 2004 migration law additional regulations solidified its impact. A 2007 Dominican administrative order barred civil registry offices from giving official birth certificates to parents of children suspected of being non-citizens and a 2008 administrative memo instructed offices to confiscate 'irregular' national identification cards (Fordham Law 2013).

In 2010, the 2004 migration law was incorporated into the new Dominican Constitution. Soon after, Juliana Deguis Pierre, who was born to Haitian immigrants and registered as a Dominican citizen at birth, challenged the law after she was denied a national identification card and had her birth certificate confiscated at a civil registry office for having a Haitian-sounding surname (IACHR 2013). In its written decision in 2013, a majority of the Dominican Constitutional Court found that Ms. Deguis Pierre was never a Dominican citizen because her parents were undocumented at the time of her birth and therefore legally 'in transit' (*Dominican Court Decision* 2013, p. 66). In its decision, TC 168–13, the Court found that all 'non-residents' were 'in transit' and therefore their children born in the Dominican Republic were not entitled to birthright citizenship. The Court not only stripped Ms. Deguis Pierre of her previously recognised Dominican citizenship, but also ordered the Central Electoral Board to make an audit of the civil registry going back to 1929 to identify others who were born to undocumented parents and incorrectly registered as citizens (*Dominican Court Decision* 2013, pp. 99–100).

Two magistrates, Isabel Bonilla Hernández and Katia Miguelina Jiménez Martínez issued dissents in the case. Magistrate Bonilla Hernández argued that the Dominican Constitution guaranteed *jus soli* rights to all persons born in its territory, and even parents residing illegally were not 'in transit' as many had settled their families permanently in the country (*Dominican Court Decision* 2013, pp. 108–110). She also argued that applying the new migration law retroactively was in violation of the Dominican Civil Code (*Dominican Court Decision* 2013, p. 114). Magistrate Jiménez Martínez argued that the Inter-American Court of Human Rights had already held in 2005 that denial of citizenship rights to the children of Haitian migrants violated inter-American law, a decision with which the Dominican Republic had yet to comply (*Dominican Court Decision* 2013, pp. 130–134). In 2014, the United Nations High Commissioner for Refugees (UNCHR) estimated that the Constitutional Court ruling rendered as many as 200,000 persons born in the Dominican Republic stateless (Gaestal 2014).

The illegality of race-based statelessness under international law

The revocation of citizenship rights and the system of race-based statelessness in the Dominican Republic violate many established international conventions

including (but not limited to): the 1966 International Covenant on Civil and
Political Rights (ICCPR), the 1948 Universal Declaration of Human Rights
(UDHR), the 1969 International Convention on the Elimination of All Forms of
Racial Discrimination (Race Convention), the 1966 International Covenant on
Economic, Social and Cultural Rights (ICESCR), the 1954 Convention Related
to the Status of Stateless Persons (1954 Statelessness Convention), the 1961
Convention on the Reduction of Statelessness (1961 Statelessness Convention),
and the 1989 Convention on the Rights of the Child (CRC).

The Dominican Republic is party to the ICCPR and the Race Convention,
which prohibit racial discrimination (ICCPR, art. 2; Race Convention, art. 1).
The Race Convention defines racial discrimination as

> any distinction, exclusion, restriction or preference based on race, colour,
> descent, or national or ethnic origin which has the purpose or effect of nulli-
> fying or impairing the recognition, enjoyment or exercise, on an equal
> footing, of human rights and fundamental freedoms in the political, eco-
> nomic, social, cultural or any other field of public life.
>
> (Race Convention, art. 1)

The Race Convention also establishes the Committee on the Elimination of
Racial Discrimination (CERD), which monitors state compliance with the Convention (Race Convention, art. 9). The CERD has found that 'deprivation of citizenship based on race, colour, descent, or national or ethnic origin is a breach of
State parties' obligations' (CERD 2004, p. 14).

In 2001 the CERD denounced the discriminatory citizenship practices of the
Dominican Republic, expressing concern that:

> the large number of Haitians living in the country, the majority of them ille-
> gally ... are often unable to enjoy the most basic economic and social rights,
> such as housing, education, and health services.... The Committee [also
> expressed concern] about racial prejudices [that] exist not only against Hai-
> tians but also against the darker-skinned Dominicans.
>
> (CERD 2001, pp. 6–7)

In 2008, the CERD specifically addressed the 2004 Dominican migration law
(General Migration Law No. 285–04) that was later incorporated into the 2010
Dominican Constitution and upheld by the Constitutional Court in its ruling TC
168–13. The CERD found that the law 'considerably limits access to citizenship
for children of migrants of Haitian origin born in the Dominican Republic, and
may lead to situations of statelessness' (CERD 2008, p. 16).

The International Covenant on Economic, Social, and Cultural Rights
(ICESCR), to which the Dominican Republic is party, also prohibits discriminatory practices with regard to the rights in the treaty based on 'race, colour, sex,
language, religion, political or other opinion, national or social origin, property,
birth or other status' (ICESCR, art. 2(2)).

In addition to international conventions that prohibit racial and ethnic discrimination, the UDHR and ICCPR recognise a human right to nationality (UDHR, art. 15; ICCPR, art. 24(3)). Furthermore, the 1954 and 1961 Statelessness Conventions define and seek to prevent the condition of statelessness internationally. The Dominican Republic is not party to either convention but has signed (and not ratified) the 1961 Statelessness Convention. Because it has not ratified the treaty, it is not bound to its provisions; however as a signatory it is 'obliged to refrain from acts which would defeat the object and purpose of the treaty' (Vienna Convention on the Law of Treaties, art. 18). Under the 1961 Convention states agree to grant citizenship to persons born in their territory if those persons would otherwise be stateless. The 2004 migration law, the 2010 Constitution and the 2013 Constitutional Court decision contravened the object and purpose of the 1961 Statelessness Convention by rendering hundreds and thousands of people stateless, violating the Dominican Republic's obligations as a 1961 Statelessness Convention signatory.

Finally, the Dominican Republic's system of race-based statelessness violates its obligations as a party to the Convention on the Rights of the Child, which specifically addresses the right to nationality for children, requiring that children 'be registered immediately after birth and shall have the right to a name, the right to acquire nationality, and, as far as possible, the right to know and be cared for by his or her parents' (CRC, art. 7(1)).

In 2008, the Committee on the Rights of the Child condemned the Dominican Republic's practice of issuing different birth documents to children on the basis of the immigration status of the child's parents, which they found 'often disregards the long ranging residence [of the parents] in the Dominican Republic and prevents the acquisition of any nationality by the child' (CRC 2008, p. 39). The Committee also found that 'the children of Haitian immigrants and Haitian descendants [in the Dominican Republic] have restricted access to education, health and social services' (ibid., p. 27).

The illegality of race-based statelessness under inter-American law

Race-based statelessness in the Dominican Republic also violates inter-American law, including the 1948 American Declaration of the Rights and Duties of Man (American Declaration) and the 1969 American Convention on Human Rights (American Convention). The Dominican Republic is party to both conventions and both conventions establish a right to nationality and prohibit racial discrimination (American Declaration, art. II, XIX; American Convention, art. 20.1–3, 22.8).

The Inter-American Court of Human Rights (Inter-American Court) and the Inter-American Commission on Human Rights (Inter-American Commission), which are organs of the Organization of American States (OAS), interpret these legal instruments. Both bodies have specifically addressed the issue of racially and ethnically discriminatory statelessness in the Dominican Republic.

The Inter-American Commission has long held that the right to nationality is of unique and fundamental importance. The Commission held:

> [Nationality] is one of the most important rights of man after the right to life itself, because all other prerogative guarantees and benefits man derives from his membership in a political and social community – the States – stem from or are supported by this right (IACHR 1977, p. 10). In 2003, in an advisory opinion, the Inter-American Court of Human Rights took up the issue of statelessness in the Dominican Republic and found:
>
> The children of Haitians, who are born in the Dominican Republic, are not considered citizens, because Haitians are classified as aliens in transit. This situation has meant that Haitians are subject to deportation at any time and mass expulsions have been carried out in violation of due process. For decades the Dominican Republic has benefited from the cheap labour of Haitians and that State has developed a system that maintains the flow of migrant workers without taking the minimum measures to ensure their fundamental rights.
>
> (IACtHR 2003, p. 44)

In 2005, the Inter-American Court issued a landmark decision in *Case of Yean and Bosico Children* v. *Dominican Republic* finding that the Dominican Republic violated the right to nationality, a name and education of two girls of Haitian descent by denying them birth certificates, even though they, and their mothers, were born in the Dominican Republic (*Case of Yean and Bosico Children* v. *Dominican Republic* 2005). *Yean and Bosico* was the first judgment against the Dominican Republic since it had accepted the Inter-American Court's jurisdiction in 1999 (Baluarte 2006, p. 25). In its decision, the Inter-American Court found that in denying the two young girls' birth certificates the Dominican Republic violated their rights under article 3 (the right to be recognised before the law), article 5 (the right to humane treatment), article 18 (the right to a name), article 19 (the right to protection for children), article 20 (the right to nationality) and article 24 (the right to equal protection) of the American Convention (*Case of Yean and Bosico Children* v. *Dominican Republic* 2005, pp. 174–206).

Based on these findings the Court ordered the Dominican Republic to acknowledge responsibility for human rights abuses within six months, create procedures to ensure all children were issued birth certificates and pay monetary damages to the children in the case, among other requirements (Kosinski 2009, p. 387). The Dominican Republic did not comply with the Court's order, and instead the Dominican Senate issued a resolution rejecting the decision (ibid., p. 389). The Inter-American Court continued to condemn the Dominican Republic's practices towards migrants, finding in 2012 that Dominican military officers used excessive force in pursuing a group of Haitian migrants, resulting in seven fatalities and other injuries (*Case of Nadege Dorzema* et al. v. *Dominican Republic* 2012).

The Inter-American Commission expressed serious concern over the Dominican Constitutional Court's TC 168–13 decision and conducted an on-site visit to the Dominican Republic in the same year. The Commission found

> grave violations of the right to nationality, to identity, and to equal protection without discrimination ... [which] disproportionately affects persons of Haitian descent, who are also Afro-descendants and are often identified based on the color of their skin, which constitutes a violation of the right to equal protection without discrimination.
>
> (OAS 2013)

Most recently, in 2014, the Inter-American Court condemned the nationality and expulsion practices of the Dominican government in *Case of Expelled Dominican and Haitian People* v. *Dominican Republic*. The case involved 26 persons who were deported from the Dominican Republic from 1999–2000, only six of whom were Haitian nationals, and the systemic practice of collective expulsions based on skin colour from the Dominican Republic (Quintana 2014). The decision by the Inter-American Court touched on the broader issue of race-based statelessness in the Dominican Republic and found that the 2013 Constitutional Court ruling retroactively deprived persons of their citizenship in a discriminatory manner (*Case of Expelled Dominican and Haitian People* v. *Dominican Republic* 2014, pp. 313, 318). The Court also declared that the Dominican Republic has an obligation to prevent statelessness in its territory by granting nationality based on territory of birth if any other citizenship would not be immediately effective (ibid., pp. 250–261).

Recent developments in race-based statelessness in the Dominican Republic

In 2014, in response to a widespread international backlash against the 2013 Constitutional Court decision the National Congress passed, and President Danilo Medina signed, a new naturalisation law – Law 169–4. The law was aimed at restoring the citizenship rights of some of those left stateless from the 2013 Constitutional Court decision; however, according to the non-governmental organisation Human Rights Watch it 'has been riddled with design and implementation flaws that have thwarted the re-naturalisation process, and which continue to prevent individuals from exercising their right to nationality' (Human Rights Watch 2015).

Law 169–4 seeks to regularise the status of two groups of persons born in the Dominican Republic to non-residents/citizens: those born between 1929 and 2007 who appear in the Civil Registry (Group A), and those born in the Dominican Republic between 1929 and 2007 who do not appear in the Civil Registry (Group B). Those born after 2007 in the Dominican Republic, estimated to be more than 20,000 individuals, do not qualify for relief under Law 169–4 because in 2007 the Dominican Republic began entering births to non-residents in the Registry of Foreigners, rather than the Civil Registry (Cita 2015, p. 261).

Under Law 169–4, the Central Electoral Board will recognise original entries as valid and issue citizenship documents to an estimated 24,000 people (Human Rights Watch 2015; SAIS 2015, p. 45). Those in Group B (by far the largest group), estimated to include more than 100,000 people, first have to prove they were born in the Dominican Republic through documentary evidence, and then register as foreigners for two years, after which they can apply for citizenship (Human Rights Watch 2015; SAIS 2015, p. 46). Persons in Group B were first given 90 days to register with the government, which was then extended until February 2015 (ibid.). According to the Dominican Ministry of Interior, only 8,775 individuals applied for registration by the end of the open period, leaving the vast majority of those affected by TC 168–13 stateless and subject to deportation (ibid.). According to a 2014 report by the Johns Hopkins School of Advanced International Studies, the 'timeline specified in the [naturalisation law] has proved far too short for government offices to create robust mechanisms for efficiently receiving and reviewing applications' (SAIS 2015, p. 39).

In its 2014 decision in *Case of Expelled Dominican and Haitian People* v. *Dominican Republic* the Inter-American Court addressed Law 169–4, finding it created an obstacle to enjoying nationality and was therefore 'per se contrary to the right to nationality in a country with a jus soli regime' (Quintana 2014). The Inter-American Court found that the Dominican Republic had violated Article 20 of the American Convention by arbitrarily depriving persons of their nationality (*Case of Expelled Dominican and Haitian People* v. *Dominican Republic* 2014, pp. 323, 325). Furthermore, the Court found that the Dominican Republic had an obligation to prevent statelessness in its territory and therefore must nullify TC 168–13 and Law 169–4 (ibid., pp. 259–261, p. 469).

Less than two weeks after the Inter-American Court's decision in *Case of Expelled Dominican and Haitian People* v. *Dominican Republic*, the Dominican Constitutional Court issued a ruling declaring that the legal instrument that recognised the Inter-American Court's jurisdiction was never approved by Congress, and therefore was null and void (Amnesty International 2014; TC 256–14). Under the interpretation by the Constitutional Court, the Dominican Republic does not have to withdraw from the Inter-American Court, because it claims that it never was a member of the Court and therefore is not bound by any of its decisions. While the illegality of race-based statelessness in the Dominican Republic has been firmly established by numerous international bodies, the country continues to isolate itself from the international human rights community on this issue and fails to comply with international law.

Conclusion

The troubling case study of the Dominican Republic demonstrates that entrenched racial and ethnic prejudices can lead to the ultimate disenfranchisement of minority groups – statelessness. Despite the widespread condemnation from numerous states and international bodies, the Dominican

Republic continues to deny fundamental human rights to some of those born in its territory, including many it previously legally recognised as citizens.

The recent rulings of the country's Constitutional Court not only display its blatant disregard for the most basic human rights, but also its willingness to ignore long-standing legal principles and snub international courts and commissions. Without a dramatic change in direction the Dominican Republic will only isolate itself further and the tragedy of statelessness on Hispaniola will continue.

References – general

Aber, S. and Small, M. (2013) Citizen or Subordinate: Permutations of Belonging in the United States and the Dominican Republic. *Journal on Migration and Human Security*, 1(3).

Amnesty International. (2014) Dominican Republic: Withdrawal from Top Regional Human Rights Court Would Put Rights at Risk, 6 November. [online] Available from: www.amnesty.org/en/latest/news/2014/11/dominican-republic-withdrawal-top-regional-human-rights-court-would-put-rights-risk/ [Accessed 27 February 2017].

Baluarte, D. (2006) Inter-American justice comes to the Dominican Republic: an island shakes as human rights and sovereignty clash. *Human Rights Brief*, 13(2).

Basu, M. (2012) Two years on, Haiti still reeling from quake. *CNN*, 13 January. [online] Available from: www.cnn.com/2012/01/12/world/americas/haiti-two-years-later/ [Accessed 3 March 2017].

CERD (Committee on the Elimination of Racial Discrimination). (2008) Concluding Observations of the Committee on the Elimination of Racial Discrimination: Dominican Republic, UN Doc. CERD/C/304/DOM/CO/12.

CERD (Committee on the Elimination of Racial Discrimination). (2008) General Recommendation 30, Discrimination against Non-Citizens, UN Doc. CERD/C/64/Misc.11/rev.3 p.14.

CERD (Committee on the Elimination of Racial Discrimination). (2001) Concluding Observations of the Committee on the Elimination of Racial Discrimination: Dominican Republic, UN Doc. CERD/C/304/Add.74.

Charles, J. (2013) Caribbean leaders defend Haiti, denounce Dominican decision. *Black Star News*, 13 November. [online] Available from: www.blackstarnews.com/global-politics/others/caribbean-leaders-defend-haiti-denounce-dominican-decision.html [Accessed 6 March 2017].

Cita, R. (2015) US asylum eligibility: citizenship in the Dominican Republic. *Harvard Civil Rights–Civil Liberties Law Review*, 50(1).

Coupeau, S. (2008) *The History of Haiti.* Westport, CT: Greenwood Press.

CRC (Committee on the Rights of the Child). (2008) Concluding Observations: Dominican Republic, Consideration of Reports Submitted by States Parties under Article 44 of the Convention, UN Doc. CRC/C/DOM/CO/2.

Culliton-Gonzalez, K. (2012). Born in the Americas: birthright citizenship and human rights. *Harvard Journal of Human Rights*, 25(1).

Davis, N. (2012) The massacre that marked Haiti–Dominican Republic ties. *BBC News*, 12 October. [online] Available from: www.bbc.com/news/world-latin-america-19880967 [Accessed 3 March 2017].

Ferguson, J. (2003) *Migration in the Caribbean: Haiti, the Dominican Republic and Beyond.* Minority Rights Group International Report. [online] Available from: http://

114   *J. Blake*

minorityrights.org/publications/migration-in-the-caribbean-haiti-the-dominican-republic-and-beyond/ [Accessed 28 February 2017].

Fordham Law. (2013) Statelessness in the Dominican Republic. *The Record at Fordham Law*, 31 March. [online] Available from: http://flsrecord.com/stateless-in-the-dominican-republic/ [Accessed 3 March 2017].

Gaestel, A. (2014) Stateless people in the Dominican Republic hope to regain citizenship. *Los Angeles Times*, 16 June. [online] Available from: www.unhcr.org/cgi-bin/texis/vtx/refdaily?pass=52fc6fbd5&date=2014–06–17&cat=Americas [Accessed 5 March 2017].

Human Rights Watch. (2015) Dominican Republic: Thousands at Risk of Expulsion to Haiti, 30 June. [online] Available from: www.hrw.org/news/2015/06/30/dominican-republic-thousands-risk-expulsion-haiti [Accessed 3 March 2017].

IACHR (Inter-American Commission on Human Rights). (2013) IACHR Expresses Deep Concern Over Ruling by the Constitutional Court of the Dominican Republic, 3 October. [online] Available from: http://www.oas.org/en/iachr/media_center/PReleases/2013/073.asp [Accessed 3 March 2017].

IACHR (Inter-American Commission on Human Rights). (1977) Third Report on the Situation of Human Rights in Chile: Chapter IX: Right to Nationality. [online] Available from: www.cidh.org/countryrep/chile77eng/chap.9.htm [Accessed 25 February 2017].

IACtHR (Inter-American Court of Human Rights). (2003) Juridical Condition and Rights of the Undocumented Migrants, Advisory Opinion OC-18/03. [online] Available from: www.corteidh.or.cr/docs/opiniones/seriea_18_ing.pdf [Accessed 3 March 2017].

Jones, T. D. (1992) *Sale* v. *Haitian Centers Council*, Inc. *American Journal of International Law*, 88(1).

Kosinksi, S. (2009) State of uncertainty: citizenship, statelessness and discrimination in the Dominican Republic. *Boston College International & Comparative Law Review*, 32(2).

Kristensen, K. and Wooding, B. (2013) *Dominican Republic: Upholding the Rights of Immigrants and Their Descendants*. NOREF Report. [online] Available from: http://noref.no/Regions/Latin-America-and-the-Caribbean/Publications/Haiti-Dominican-Republic-upholding-the-rights-of-immigrants-and-their-descendants [Accessed 3 March 2017].

Lippmann Mazzaglia, N. and Marcelino, P. (2014) Migratory policy as an exclusionary tool: the case of Haitians in the Dominican Republic. *Laws*, 3(1).

Lister, M. (2010) Citizenship, in the immigration context. *Maryland Law Review*, 70(1).

Mendelson Forman, J. and White, S. (2011) *The Dominican Response to the Haiti Earthquake*. Center for Strategic and International Studies Report. [online] Available from: www.csis.org/analysis/dominican-response-haiti-earthquake [Accessed 3 March 2017].

Middleton, R. (2011) Principle of jus soli and its effect on immigration inclusion into a national identity: a constitutional analysis of the United States and the Dominican Republic. *Rutgers Race and Law Review*, 13(1).

OAS (Organization of American States). (2013) IACHR Wraps Up Visit to the Dominican Republic, 6 December. [online] Available from: www.oas.org/en/iachr/media_center/preleases/2013/097.asp [Accessed 3 March 2017].

OAS (Organization of American States). (2011) International Migration in the Americas: First Report of the Continuing Reporting System on International Migration in the Americas. [online] Available from: www.oecd.org/migration/48423814.pdf [Accessed 6 March 2017].

Open Society Institute. (2010) Dominicans of Haitian Descent and the Compromised Right to Nationality, October. [online] Available from: www.opensocietyfoundations. org/reports/dominicans-haitian-descent-and-compromised-right-nationality [Accessed 6 March 2017].

Quintana, F. (2014) *Inter-American Court condemns unprecedented situation of stateless-ness in the Dominican Republic*, European Network on Statelessness 27 October. [online] Available from: www.statelessness.eu/blog/inter-American-court-condemns-unprecedented-situation-statelessness-dominican-republic [Accessed 3 March 2017].

Sagas, E. (2000) *Race and Politics in the Dominican Republic.* Gainesville: University Press of Florida.

SAIS (Johns Hopkins School of Advanced International Studies). (2015) *Justice Derailed: The Uncertain Fate of Haitian Migrants and Dominicans of Haitian Descent in the Dominican Republic*, Report of the International Human Rights Clinic. [online] Available from: www.sais-jhu.edu/sites/default/files/Final-Report-Justice-Derailed-The-Uncertain-Fate-2015-v1.pdf [Accessed 3 March 2017].

UN Special Rapporteur Report (Special Rapporteur on Contemporary Forms of Racism, Racial Discrimination, Xenophobia and Related Intolerance & The Independent Export on Minority Issues). (2008) Follow up to and Implementation of the Durban Declaration and Programme of Action, UN Doc. A/HRC/7/19/Add.5.

Weinstein, B. and Segal, A. (1992) *Haiti: The Failure of Politics.* Westport, CT: Praeger.

References – international law

American Convention on Human Rights (American Convention). (1969) [online] Available at: www.cidh.oas.org/basicos/english/basic3.American%20convention.htm [Accessed 28 February 2017].

American Declaration of the Rights and Duties of Man (American Declaration). (1948) [online] Available at: www.cidh.oas.org/Basicos/English/Basic2.American%20 Declaration.htm [Accessed 3 March 2017].

Convention on the Reduction of Statelessness (1961 Stateless Convention). (1961) [online] Available at: www.unhcr.org/uk/protection/statelessness/3bbb286d8/ convention-reduction-statelessness.html [Accessed 22 February 2017].

Convention Related to the Status of Stateless Persons (1954 Statelessness Convention). (1954) [online] Available at: www.unhcr.org/uk/protection/statelessness/3bbb25729/ convention-relating-status-stateless-persons.html [Accessed 3 March 2017].

Convention on the Rights of the Child (CRC). (1989) [online] Available at: www.ohchr. org/EN/ProfessionalInterest/Pages/CRC.aspx

International Covenant on Economic, Social and Cultural Rights (ICESCR). (1966) [online] Available at: www.ohchr.org/EN/ProfessionalInterest/Pages/CESCR.aspx [Accessed 1 March 2017].

International Convention on the Elimination of All Forms of Racial Discrimination (CERD). (1969). [online] Available at: www.ohchr.org/EN/ProfessionalInterest/Pages/ CERD.aspx [Accessed 6 March 2017].

International Covenant on Civil and Political Rights (ICCPR). (1966) [online] Available at: www.ohchr.org/EN/ProfessionalInterest/Pages/CCPR.aspx [Accessed 5 March 2017].

Universal Declaration of Human Rights (UDHR). (1948) [online] Available at: www. ohchr.org/EN/UDHR/Documents/UDHR_Translations/eng.pdf [Accessed 3 March 2017].

Vienna Convention on the Law of Treaties (VCLT). (1969) [online] Available at: https://treaties.un.org/doc/Publication/UNTS/Volume%201155/volume-1155-I-18232-English.pdf [Accessed 6 March 2017].

References – legal cases

Case of Expelled Dominican and Haitian People v. *Dominican Republic.* (2014) Inter-American Court of Human Rights.

Case of Nadege Dorzema et al. v. *Dominican Republic.* (2012) Inter-American Court of Human Rights.

Case of Yean and Bosico Children v. *Dominican Republic.* (2005) Inter-American Court of Human Rights, 8 September.

Dominican Court Decision. (2013) Tribunal Constitucional (Constitutional Court). Sentencia TC/0168/13 (Dominican Republic), 23 September.

Dred Scott v. *Sandford.* (1857) 60 U.S. 373.

United States v. *Wong Kim Ark.* (1898) 169 U.S. 649.

8 Statelessness, ungoverned spaces and security in Kenya

Oscar Gakuo Mwangi

Introduction

This chapter examines the relationship among ungoverned spaces, statelessness and security in Kenya. Statelessness is perceived as a political outcome of the relationship among politics, security and space. In other words, statelessness is a function of the intersection of politics, security and physical space. Statelessness is, therefore, examined not from a legal perspective but a spatial-political dimension. The arguments raised are that Kenyan Somalis and Somali refugees who live or reside in Kenya's ungoverned spaces are stateless persons given the adverse violent structural and physical conditions under which they live. Consequently, the stateless persons have, by political design and default, become political actors in the country. The structural and physical conditions have created the enabling environment and opportunities for some to participate in the activities of transnational armed non-state actors, particularly the Somali-based *Al-Shabaab* group. Alongside humanitarian concerns, then, the stateless constituency thereby constitutes a human and physical security threat in Kenya. Statelessness emanating from ungoverned spaces has a direct bearing on security governance, particularly the state's capacity to provide meaningful security to all those who reside in such spaces irrespective of citizen status.

The chapter is divided into four sections. The first section indicates the way in which statelessness is examined not from a legal perspective but a spatial-political dimension. The second examines the legal and administrative state of statelessness in Kenya. The aim is to provide essential information in order to understand how statelessness is examined in the context of ungoverned spaces. The third section outlines the structural and physical conditions of ungoverned spaces in Kenya. The fourth section examines the relationship among ungoverned spaces, statelessness and security in Kenya. By examining life experiences, this section demonstrates that the stateless constituency living in ungoverned spaces has become a significant political actor, hence a potential threat to security in Kenya. Qualitative research was adopted in this case study that focused on ungoverned spaces. The primary and secondary data used was derived from printed material. The conclusion offers recommendations on how states can address the reality of statelessness to transform its adverse implications, both for the State and for the individual stateless persons, into beneficial ones. This will include transforming individuals' adverse political actions into ones that are beneficial.

Statelessness and ungoverned spaces

A spatial-political examination of statelessness contributes to a much broader normative and empirical understanding of the concept in relation to politics, security and physical space, compared to the often-cited formal legal definitions. In relation to politics, security and space, the spatial-political dimension points out that geographical imaginations are significant to any analysis of terrorism, counterterrorism and evolving security landscapes. The perspective emphasises that the contemporary geopolitical landscape is established by multiple temporalities and multiple spatialities that exceed the states and security apparatuses in as much as these temporalities and spatialities are influenced by the latter institutions. Struggles over space and power are best analysed not only in terms of formal theories of international relations but also in terms of the ways in which geopolitics flows between formal theorising, applied statecraft and common spaces. Security practices themselves are best subjected to critical scrutiny as part of a wider study of sociopolitical spatial dynamics. Focusing entirely on threats and ignoring security as a fundamental factor in explaining political geographies is to render analysis partial. It is, therefore, important to demonstrate the ways in which security takes place and is played out across and through space. Hence the concern among security policymakers with 'ungoverned' spaces (Ingram and Dodds 2009, pp. 2–8). In the context of statelessness, the spatial-political dimension establishes the relationship between territory, the state and statelessness. The argument raised is that there is a fundamental relationship between space and statelessness emphasising that persons living or residing in ungoverned spaces can be referred to as stateless.

Ungoverned space is a physical or non-physical area characterised by the absence of functional state capacity or political will to exercise control. Physical space can include both land area and maritime areas. Non-physical space can, for example, involve financial space where low capacity or legal authority exists to prevent the financing of terrorist organisations to enable them to achieve their objectives. Terrorists thrive in ungoverned spaces (Whelan 2006, pp. 64–65). Ungoverned spaces describe a political condition along a continuum that includes weak and collapsed states (Menkhaus 2007, p. 3). Ungoverned spaces are also characterised by intrastate and interstate protracted social and political conflicts. They harbour criminal actors and networks posing a risk to national and regional security (Mkutu and Wandera 2013, pp. 14–15). Ungoverned spaces are spaces of insecurity. Spaces of insecurity are created by individuals and groups of individuals as they interact with each other. These regions of insecurity are inhabited and used by actors who sometimes act to change their situation of insecurity and might make it more insecure by using violence (Witsenburg and Zaal 2012, pp. 4–5). Ungoverned spaces are not necessarily anarchic. They have a variety of grassroots arrangements and systems of governance

(Menkhaus 2007, p. 4). There are several countries that experience problems associated with statelessness, ungoverned spaces and protracted situations of insecurity. These include among others, Afghanistan, Ethiopia, Eritrea, Iraq, Nigeria and Pakistan (Whelan 2006, pp. 69–70; Menkhaus 2007, pp. 5–12; Keister 2014, pp. 5–14). This chapter, however, pays attention to statelessness in Kenya in the context of the foregoing arguments. The following section examines the state of statelessness in Kenya.

The state of statelessness in Kenya

Kenya is not party to either the 1954 Convention relating to the Status of Stateless Persons or the 1961 Convention on the Reduction of Statelessness. It is, however, party to conventions aimed at promoting and protecting fundamental international human rights such as the 1990 African Charter on the Rights and Welfare of the Child, the 1989 UN Convention on the Rights of the Child, the 1966 International Covenant on Civil and Political Rights and the 1979 UN Convention on the Elimination of All Forms of Discrimination against Women (KNCHR/UNCHR 2010, p. 5). According to the United Nations High Commissioner for Refugees (UNHCR) statistics, statelessness is estimated to affect some 20,000 persons in Kenya. These are mainly members of minority groups. The number is, however, unscientific. A large but undocumented number of members of ethnic minority groups in Kenya are stateless. These include Kenyan Nubians, the Coastal Arabs and Kenyan Somalis. These minority groups all struggle with statelessness and discriminatory citizenship laws and practices. Consequently, a large percentage of such groups are unable to participate fully in the economic, social and political life of the country. In Kenya, some stateless people are included among refugees, compounding the problems of citizenship in the country (Blitz 2009, p. 41; Open Society Justice Initiative 2009, p. 2; KNCHR/UNHCR 2010, p. 5; Institute on Statelessness and Inclusion 2014, p. 64; Mandby 2014).

The official causes of statelessness in Kenya can be grouped into two broad categories: legal and administrative. The national laws of Kenya concerning the acquisition, restoration, retention and loss of citizenship have shortcomings that allow or fail to prevent statelessness (KNCHR/UNHCR 2010, p. 5). Kenya adopted a new constitution by referendum in 2010. The new constitution removed gender discrimination in nationality law, while permitting dual nationality for the first time. A new citizenship act in 2011 also created a temporary procedure for stateless persons who, having lived in Kenya since its independence, could trace their ancestry in the country and apply for Kenyan nationality (Institute on Statelessness and Inclusion 2014, p. 64). The recognition of stateless persons is now contained in Section 15 of *The Kenya Citizenship and Immigration Act*, No. 12 of 2011. Section 15 (1) states that:

> A person who does not have an enforceable claim to the citizenship of any recognized state and has been living in Kenya for a continuous period since

12th December, 1963, shall be deemed to have been lawfully resident and may, on application, in the prescribed manner be eligible to be registered as a citizen of Kenya if that person (*a*) has adequate knowledge of Kiswahili or a local dialect; (*b*) has not been convicted of an offence and sentenced to imprisonment for a term of three years or longer; (*c*) intends upon registration as a citizen to continue to permanently reside in Kenya or to maintain a close and continuing association with Kenya; and (*d*) the person understands the rights and duties of a citizen.

(Kenya 2011, pp. 15–16)

No regulations, however, have yet been adopted to implement the law. Likewise, no cases of recognition of Kenyan citizenship have been reported based on these provisions. There are groups currently under threat of non-recognition of Kenyan nationality. These include those of Somali descent and Muslims in the coastal and north-eastern regions of the country, whose applications for nationality documentation are subject to additional and highly time-consuming screening measures since these groups are associated with terrorism (Institute on Statelessness and Inclusion 2014, p. 64). Kenya's laws remain overpoweringly discriminatory and ineffective in addressing issues of statelessness and citizenship discrimination (Open Society Justice Initiative 2009, p. 2). The administrative causes of statelessness in Kenya reveal that there is a difference between law and actual practice. Persons may be at risk of becoming stateless due to the defective operation or under-regulated nature of Kenya's administrative practices regarding citizenship. For example, there are not sufficient regulations that guide the vetting process to which certain ethnic groups in Kenya are subjected (KNCHR/ UNHCR, 2010, p. 6).

In Kenya, it is rather difficult to make a clear distinction between *de jure* and de facto stateless persons (for an explanation of these terms, see de Chickera and van Waas, this volume). Some of Kenya's stateless can be classified as being *de jure* stateless. There is a particularly relevant connection between lack of documentation on the one hand, and statelessness on the other. In Kenya, three minority groups in particular – the Kenyan Nubians, Somalis and the Coastal Arabs – have long been on the fringes of Kenyan citizenship. Due to discrimination, bureaucracy and lack of documentation, these groups have been struggling for a long time, with limited success, to be recognised as Kenyan citizens. While some members of such groups have acquired Kenyan citizenship, many have not. They all suffer varying degrees of 'ineffective nationality'. Moreover, the nationality status of persons within these minority groups is fluid. Hence it becomes difficult to make a clear distinction between the *de jure* and the de facto stateless among them (Equal Rights Trust 2010, p. 74). The Kenyan state, for instance, imposes strict registration processes on Kenyan Somalis. This is not only a function of the presence of thousands of Somali refugees in Kenya, but it is also due to a combination of decades of Somali separatism and the nature of the transboundary movements of Somali pastoralists. The registration process is characterised by suspicion, harassment and corruption. Some of the poorest

Kenyan Somalis register themselves as refugees so as to receive basic necessities, at the risk of losing their Kenyan nationality (Equal Rights Trust 2010, p. 77). The Equal Rights Trust (ERT) points out that:

> These vulnerable Kenyan communities include persons who are *de jure* stateless, others who have received citizenship but do not enjoy effective nationality, and still others who have never received personal documents, and therefore are not easily identifiable as either *de jure* or de facto stateless. In such cases, a long investigative process would be necessary on a case-by-case basis to determine whether individuals are *de jure* stateless (and consequently eligible for protection under the 1954 Convention) or not.
>
> (2010, p. 77)

In summary, although Kenya is party to a variety of conventions aimed at promoting and protecting fundamental international human rights, it is not party to either of the statelessness conventions. The country's official causes of statelessness are both legal and administrative. The laws concerning citizenship have shortcomings that fail to prevent statelessness while the country's administrative practices regarding citizenship are defective. In Kenya it therefore becomes difficult to make a clear distinction between *de jure* and de facto stateless persons. Having examined the state of statelessness in Kenya from a legal–political perspective it becomes much clearer to analyse statelessness in the context of ungoverned spaces. In order to do so, it is first and foremost important to briefly indicate the structural and physical conditions of ungoverned spaces in Kenya.

Ungoverned spaces in Kenya

Kenya's ungoverned spaces or forgotten 'badlands' cover 80 per cent of the country's geographical territory. The north-eastern region, which is the focus of this chapter, covers approximately 22 per cent of Kenya's geographical territory, and contains slightly over 5 per cent of the country's population (Mwangi 2006, p. 82). Kenya's north-eastern region that borders Somalia emerged as a distinct administrative entity dominated by ethnic Somalis after the country's independence in December 1963. It is the most marginalised region in the country. The region is characterised by a history of insurgency, misrule and repression, chronic poverty, massive youth unemployment, high population growth, insecurity, poor infrastructure and lack of basic services. The conflict in neighbouring Somalia has adversely impacted upon the region and Kenyan Somalis. The long and porous Kenya–Somalia border is impossible to police effectively. Small arms flow across the border unchecked. Somali clan-identity politics and conflicts frequently spill over into the region, often resulting in violent conflicts. The considerable stream of refugees into overflowing camps creates an additional strain on local residents and the country generating a strong official and public backlash against Somalis, both those who are themselves from Somalia and those who are from Kenya (International Crisis Group 2012a, p. 1). The biggest settlement in the region is Dadaab refugee camp, which currently hosts over 300,000 Somali refugees. It is one of the largest concentrations of Somalis any-where in the world (Bradbury and Kleinman 2010, p. 21; UNHCR 2015, p. 4).

Kenya's north-eastern region is considered a security threat by the Kenyan state (Bradbury and Kleinman 2010, p. 9). The threat is perceived to emanate from several sources. These sources include: *Al Qaeda*'s presence in East Africa and Somali-based *Al-Shabaab*'s attacks in Kenya; the existence of a permissive, 'ungoverned' environment that allows individuals involved in the terrorist attacks in Kenya to live and organise undetected in local communities; the high level of social and economic deprivation and grievances among Kenya's Muslim youth population, which makes them vulnerable to recruitment by extremist organisations; and the proximity to Somalia and its potential destabilising effect on Kenya. The argument that fragile states and ungoverned spaces are a threat to international security leads to the conclusion that the state weakness in a region like north-eastern Kenya is a driver of insecurity (ibid., pp. 25–28). I argue that the adverse structural and physical conditions of these ungoverned spaces render those who live in them stateless.

Ungoverned spaces, statelessness and security in Kenya

There is a fundamental relationship among ungoverned spaces, statelessness and security in Kenya. This relationship is examined in the context of marginalisa-tion, corruption, violation of human rights and radicalisation of Kenyan Somalis and Somali refugees in the north-eastern region of Kenya. The Kenyan Somali community residing in north-eastern Kenya is categorised as marginalised and other Kenyan communities perceive the Kenyan Somali community as respons-ible for the growing security risks in the country. Members of the Somali-Kenyan and Somali communities point out that they are profiled on the basis of ethnicity and religion, the consequences of which are dire on their human security (Kenya 2013, p. 61; Botha 2014, pp. 12–15). The primary and second-ary data used in the analysis of the relationship among ungoverned spaces, state-lessness and security was sourced from printed material.

The treatment of Kenyan Somalis by the state has been criticised for creating 'hierarchies in citizenship' (Lind *et al.* 2015, p. 25). Successive governments have launched various operations to scrutinise the identity and origins of Kenyan Somalis in order to distinguish Kenyans of Somali descent from 'foreign' Somalis, the latter of whom are often expelled from Kenya on security grounds (ibid., p. 25). According to Article 8 of the country's Constitution, Kenya is a secular state (Kenya 2010, p. 15). Kenyan Muslims, however, feel discriminated against when applying for national identity cards and passports. They are required to produce additional documentary evidence of citizenship, unlike Christian applicants who only need two birth certificates, that is, their own and that of one of their parents. Applicants with Islamic names are required to produce, in addition, the birth certificate of one of their grandparents (Botha 2014, p. 8). This extra requirement in the registration process is akin to identifying

Muslims and in particular Somalis (who are often Muslim) as stateless persons according to the definition of stateless persons outlined in *The Kenya Citizenship and Immigration Act* (Kenya 2011, pp. 15–16). State interventions alone do not, however, produce a 'marginalised identity'. Equality in citizenship is as much a function of state–society relations as it is a function of citizen–society relations. The dynamics of interaction between the Kenyan Somali community and other Kenyan communities also influence a sense of citizenship among Somalis (Lind *et al.* 2015, pp. 26–27).

Insecurity in north-eastern Kenya is institutionalised and it adversely affects the Somali population there. The impact is reflected in the 'othering' of Somalis in Kenyan society, irrespective of their nationality (Lind *et al.* 2015, p. 10). For Somalis in this region, insecurity has acquired value and stability and it has become an integral component of daily life. The 'othering' of Somalis by the Kenyan state and society also raises bigger questions about the extent of the integration of Kenya's Somali community into the country and inspires debates about the *Kenyanness* of the community and their fate (Atta-Asamoah 2015, p. 6). The construction of Somalis as an 'outside' threat to peace and stability is a distinct characteristic of Kenya's security thinking (Lind *et al.* 2015, p. 15). The neglect and marginalisation of Somali communities in the north-eastern region of Kenya provides fertile ground for radicalisation (Cilliers 2015, p. 23).

The relationship among corruption, human rights violations and ungoverned spaces in Kenya manifests itself in the way in which the human and physical security of stateless persons is affected in such spaces. The rights of Kenyan Somalis and Somali refugees in Kenya's ungoverned spaces are often violated as a result of corruption by security and security-related agencies. This heightens their grievances against the state. The politicisation and securitisation of Kenyan Somalis and the construction of the presence of Somali refugees as constituting a potential security threat in the country has increased a sense of fear in non-Somali communities, while also providing cover for measures that target Somalis (Lind *et al.* 2015, pp. 26–27). It has made them among the most vulnerable victims of Kenya's corrupt police and immigration services, which subject Kenyan Somalis and Somali refugees to both psychological and physical violence (Human Rights Watch 2010, p. 4). The Kenyan police have also been implicated in the torture, disappearance and unlawful killing of alleged terrorism suspects and individuals of Somali origin, and Somali refugees in Mombasa, Nairobi, the north-eastern region and other parts of Kenya (Human Rights Watch 2014, p. 131).

Kenya's Directorate of Immigration and Registration of Persons is responsible for population registration and the maintenance of an inclusive population register, migration management, border control and refugees' welfare supervision (MICG 2015). According to Article 14(1) of the Constitution of Kenya, a person is a citizen by birth if on the day of the person's birth, whether or not the person is born in Kenya, either the mother or father of the person is a Kenyan citizen (Kenya 2010, p. 17). Section 18 of *The Kenya Citizenship and Immigration Act* states that after having fulfilled certain conditions, a person who qualifies to be registered as a citizen of Kenya under this Act will be issued with a certificate of registration as a Kenyan citizen (Kenya 2011, p. 17). The registration of citizens is mandatory as specified in the country's *Registration of Persons Act*, Chapter 107. Section 6(1) of the Act states that every person who attains or has attained the age of 18 years and is unregistered is legally responsible to register under this Act within 90 days of attaining that age. The Act also specifies the penalties imposed for failing to do so (Kenya 2014, pp. 5–6). The country's Directorate of Immigration and Registration of Persons has, however, issued documents such as birth certificates and identity cards illegally to some foreigners. They have been registered faster than the local people because money changes hands for the service (Kenya 2013, pp. 60–63). A study of the issuance of national identity cards in Kenya conducted by the Kenya National Commission on Human Rights (KNCHR) in 2007 established that refugees had acquired Kenyan identity cards after bribing elders, registration officers and the provincial administration. Many of these refugees alleged that they had come to Kenya in the early 1990s, and had paid sums of about US$25 for the identity cards. Some received identity cards on the same day upon payment whereas others got theirs after a few months. They also alleged that unlike other Kenyans they did not attach any supporting documents to their applications (KNCHR 2007, p. 9). To this extent uncounted numbers of Somalis, including some *Al-Shabaab* members, have taken advantage of corruption in Kenya to secure Kenyan identity cards (Menkhaus 2012, pp. 1–2).

Kenya's counterterrorism measures aimed at *Al-Shabaab* involve coercive measures to identify and remove individuals who are in the country illegally. Most of those arrested are Somalis, fuelling allegations of ethnic profiling by such authorities as well as fuelling anti-Somali sentiment among ordinary Kenyans (International Crisis Group 2012a, p. 1; Lind *et al.* 2015, p. 25). The country's counterterrorism functions, which deal mainly with repressive measures, are divided between the three branches of the National Police Service: the Kenya Police (including the Antiterrorism Police Unit (ATPU) and the paramilitary General Service Unit (GSU)); the Directorate of Criminal Investigation (CID) and the Administration Police (AP); and non-police agencies such as the National Intelligence Service (NIS) and elements of the Kenya Defence Forces (KDF) (US 2014, p. 26). The ATPU has often been accused of violating the fundamental rights of Kenyan Somalis and Somali refugees in the country. Religious discrimination and ethnic discrimination are inextricably linked when it comes to the ATPU's operations. The ATPU has targeted ethnic Somali Kenyans and Somali refugees, most of whom are Muslims, in large-scale, abusive operations (Open Society Foundations 2013, p. 19; Margon 2014, p. 3). A case in point was the large-scale counterterrorism operation in Kenya known as Operation *Usalama* (peace and security) Watch. The Somali community in the country became scapegoats in the Operation. Thousands of Somalis were subjected to arbitrary arrest, harassment, extortion and ill-treatment when the Operation began in early April 2014. Over 1,000 individuals were forcibly relocated to overcrowded, insecure refugee camps in north-eastern Kenya, while hundreds of others were deported back to Somalia. Operation *Usalama* Watch was implemented following an attack in Mombasa on 23 March and explosions in the Somali-dominated Eastleigh suburb of Nairobi on 31 March 2014, which killed at least ten people and injured several others. Though the government of Kenya had legitimate security concerns, the counterterrorism operation was also an excuse for the blanket targeting of the Somali community in the country (Amnesty International 2014, p. 4; 2014/2015, p. 213). The collective punishment method that has been employed by the Kenyan authorities is neither legal nor appropriate. There are blurred lines between what constitutes someone as an irregular immigrant and what constitutes someone as a refugee (Rawlence 2014, p. 2).

As a result of political and economic marginalisation, corruption and human rights violations, Somalia's growing Islamist radicalism is spilling over into Kenya. *Al-Shabaab* has built a cross-border presence and a clandestine support network among Somali Muslim populations in the north-eastern region of Kenya and is radicalising and recruiting the youth from these communities by exploiting long-standing grievances against the central state. Radicalisation is now a grave threat to Kenya's security and stability (International Crisis Group 2012a, p. 1; Mann 2013, p. 1). *Al-Shabaab* is radicalising Kenyan Somali youth as well as Somali refugees in an attempt to fight in Somalia and conduct terrorist attacks in their own country. The sociopolitical conditions under which Somali refugees live in the ungoverned spaces makes them vulnerable to the advances of *Al-Shabaab*, enabling the group to strengthen its foothold in Kenya. The country's inability to address growing radicalisation has not only enabled *Al-Shabaab* to recruit fighters in Kenya, but has also facilitated the spread of the group in the country and the broader region (International Crisis Group 2012a, p. 13; Botha 2014, p. 4). As such, political and religious leaders from the region claim that some of the youth have succumbed to the ideology of *Al-Shabaab* and have repeatedly said that they would play their role in preventing the establishment of radical schools and the teaching of extremist ideologies (Mukinda 2015).

Al-Shabaab recruits heavily in north-eastern Kenya, as is evident in the many cases of missing young men in the region, who later admit in telephone calls to their parents that they have joined the group and are in training camps in Somalia. However, no appropriate action is taken since parents whose children have joined *Al-Shabaab* do not disclose it for fear of reprisals from the group as well as Kenyan security agencies (Allen 2015; Mohamed 2015). Suspects and supporters of the group live among the residents and political and religious leaders from the region acknowledge the need to 'purge from within ourselves' the threat of terrorism (Mukinda 2015). These leaders, while emphasising that the group has infiltrated the region, constantly appeal to the local residents to cooperate with the state in weeding out the group and its sympathisers among the local residents and Somali refugees (Mukinda 2015). The Supreme Council of Kenya Muslims (SUPKEM) chairman has said that as religious leaders they would support the state in an effort to flush out terrorists and terrorist groups hiding among the residents in the region (Hajir 2015). *Al-Shabaab* was recruiting and radicalising Somali Muslim youth in refugee camps and towns in the region long before the KDF intervened in Somalia in October 2011 (Kagwanja 2015). In its attempts to destabilise East Africa and beyond, *Al-Shabaab* has been recruiting as many members as it can. As such, it has been targeting the vulnerable marginalised Kenyan Somali youth and Somali refugees, pointing out that its activities are acts of legitimate self-defence carried out on East African Muslims' behalf against 'oppressive unbelievers' and their governments in the region (African Union 2015, p. 4). *Al-Shabaab*'s recruitment drives in Kenya have been greatly aided by the presence of both sympathisers, such as influential religious preachers, and allied organisations (Anzalone 2012, p. 10).

It is in the context of political marginalisation, corruption and human rights violations, radicalisation and recruitment that Kenyan Somalis and Somali refugees in Kenya's ungoverned spaces, as stateless persons, have become significant political actors in the country. North-eastern Kenya is very difficult to secure due to the vast geographical terrain, long border, isolated villages and the ability of *Al-Shabaab* to easily infiltrate the area (African Union 2015, p. 4). The group and its sympathisers occasionally launch deadly attacks against government and civilian targets in the region (International Crisis Group 2012a, p. 1). The north-eastern region is now a conflict zone in the war against *Al-Shabaab*. The group's aim is to destabilise the region and part of its strategy is to outmanoeuvre the KDF and wage a low-intensity asymmetrical war not only in the region but elsewhere in Kenya (International Crisis Group 2012b, p. i). Some sections of the local residents are *Al-Shabaab* sympathisers who leak vital information to the group. This crucial information assists the group in carrying out its attacks effectively. The local residents also do not cooperate with the police in exposing its sympathisers and activities, hence making it difficult to contain the group (Kenya 2013, p. 59).

The politicisation of the Somali refugees' plight by both the Kenyan state and *Al-Shabaab*, to the extent that they have become significant political actors in security matters, is also due to the fact that they are large in numbers. The Somalis are by far the largest refugee community in Kenya (Lind *et al.* 2015, p. 29). As of December 2015, the UNHCR in Kenya assists 420,711 registered refugees from Somalia. They currently reside in the Dadaab and Kakuma refugee camps as well as urban areas. The Dadaab refugee camps host 332,455 people, the Kakuma refugee camp 55,092 people and urban areas 33,164 people. Female refugees represent half of the total population and 58 per cent of the population is made up of children. The majority of Somali refugees in Dadaab originate from the South Central regions of Somalia, particularly Bakool, Shabelle-Hoose, Gedo, Middle Juba, Luuq, Lower Juba, Bay and Benadir. These regions are predominantly *Al-Shabaab* strongholds (UNHCR 2015, p. 4). The Dadaab refugee camp is composed of five sub-camps. These are Dagahaley, Hagadera, Ifo, Kambios and Ifo 2. The Dadaab camp is the largest refugee camp complex in the world (MSF 2014). Suspicions by state officials in Kenya and the wider society that Somali refugees are involved in terrorism and are used by *Al-Shabaab* as recruitment agents have deepened. Consequently, Somali refugees and Somalis who are Kenyan nationals have been the targets of xenophobic, criminalising discourse by society and government actors alike, more than the other refugee communities in the country (Lind *et al.* 2015, p. 29). The state in Kenya is deeply concerned about the fast-growing refugee population and the fact that refugee camps are now quasi-permanent settlements. The state is also uneasy about the security threat posed by Islamist militants, the growth of the native ethnic Somali population and the increasing economic clout of Somalis. It is also aware of growing anti-Somali sentiments in the country (International Crisis Group 2012a, p. 8; 2015, pp. 5–7).

Somali refugees in Kenya are associated with terrorist activities aimed at causing psychological and physical damage to the country (Kiunga 2015). The depiction of the refugees as significant political actors, hence a threat to national security, is evident in the political rhetoric and actions of Kenya's political leaders and senior state officials. More often than not, the political rhetoric or discourse translates into political action. For example, in March 2014 the then-Cabinet Secretary (CS) for Interior, Joseph Ole-Lenku, issued a directive to all refugees in towns and cities to relocate to the Kakuma and Dadaab refugee camps. According to Ole-Lenku, the directive was necessitated by the nature of the emerging security threats and the need to regularise the activities of refugees. However, the directive was not implemented, following fervent resistance from human rights and civil society groups, who pointed out that it was inconsistent with the national discourse on counterterrorism and would have an adverse impact on the country's commitment to its international obligations to refugees, asylum seekers and people seeking protection (Atta-Asamoah 2015, p. 6).

The role of Somali refugees in the activities of *Al-Shabaab* is documented in various governmental and intergovernmental reports. Kenya intelligence reports indicate that all refugee camps in north-eastern Kenya have been infiltrated by the group. The reports also indicate that refugees living in and out of camps host *Al-Shabaab* militants. The group has recruited a big number of refugees in Kenya to provide cover for its operations. The refugees help coordinate attacks in the region and are also used to recruit young members into *Al-Shabaab* (Mukinda 2015). The reports further point out that *Al-Shabaab* is taking advantage of international laws that govern refugee status. The group has deep connections within legally established medicine and food networks, hence international aid to refugees easily ends up with the group. Medical supplies are diverted to *Al-Shabaab*, providing its injured militia with medical treatment (Mukinda 2015). *Al-Shabaab* sympathisers move freely as they are duly registered as refugees. The nature of refugee camps also provides a perfect cover for the group's agents and the illegal arms trade is rampant in these camps. Informal settlements in the camps provide good storage for weapons and security operations in the camps are often perceived as violating the fundamental rights of refugees (Mukinda 2015).

Located 100 kilometres from the long and porous border between Kenya and Somalia, Dadaab's primarily Somali population is viewed by Kenya authorities as a source of *Al-Shabaab*'s attacks in the country. The consequences are violent crackdowns in the camp and thousands of detentions in Nairobi. The treatment of Somali refugees in Kenya remains at the forefront of the debate on security, immigration and the Kenyan state's relationship with its Somali population (Rawlence 2014, p. 2). The Kenyan state emphasises that Dadaab is a breeding ground for terrorism. The police have occasionally seized weapons among refugees in the camps. Local residents facilitate the movement of new recruits and weapons within the Dadaab refugee camp (Mukinda 2015; Mutambo 2015b).

There has been a concerted effort by politicians to link major terrorist attacks in Kenya, such as those at the Westgate Mall and at Garissa University – attacks conducted by *Al-Shabaab* in September 2013 and April 2015 respectively – to Somali refugees (Kiunga 2015). In the Westgate Mall attack 67 people of different nationalities were killed and 200 injured (Kenya 2013, p. 29). The 2 April 2015 Garissa University attack left 142 students, three police officers and three soldiers dead, while 78 civilians were injured (African Union 2015, pp. 1–22). Following these attacks, the government of Kenya sought to close the Dadaab refugee camp and repatriate its occupants, saying it served as a 'nursery' for *Al-Shabaab* (Laing 2015). Kenya's Deputy President (DP) William Ruto gave the United Nations (UN) three months to close the Dadaab refugee camp, failing which Kenya would forcefully return the refugees to Somalia. The DP's comments came days after leaders from north-eastern Kenya called for the closure of refugee camps in the region, arguing that *Al-Shabaab* planned its attacks in these camps (Daily Nation 2015). The political leaders argued it was time to do away with the camp, as a way of denying terrorists a place to hide. According to the Leader of Majority in Kenya's National Assembly, who is also a Member of Parliament (MP) from the region, the camps are centres for the provision of training, coordinating and assembly of terrorism networks, hence the need to relocate refugees back to Somalia so as to contain the national security threat (Mutambo 2015a). The UNHCR, which is also responsible for the plight of refugees, has been accused of facilitating terrorism in the country. Kenya's CS for Interior Joseph Nkaissery linked some employees at the UNHCR to terrorism in the country. He also revealed that refugee camps in the country, particularly in the Dadaab complex, had become a haven for terrorists and their agents and called for the repatriation of Somali refugees to Somalia. The CS pointed out that the final planning and logistical supports for nearly all terrorist activities in Kenya are executed under the cover of refugee camps (Angira 2015).

The threat to close down and repatriate Somali refugees forcefully under the guise of security is, however, a violation of Kenya's obligations towards promoting and protecting fundamental international human rights. It is in this regard that the UN warned Kenyan authorities that closing the world's largest refugee camp complex would have extra humanitarian and practical consequences and would violate international law (AFP 2015). Kenya has faced considerable pressure from the West not to close down the camps –including from United States (US) President Barack Obama and his Secretary of State John Kerry, who both visited Kenya in 2015 to offer US financial and security support (Laing 2015). Refugees themselves have refuted claims that they support terrorists and the

UNHCR has several times denied being lacklustre in allowing in sympathisers, saying it adheres to existing legal frameworks when handling refugees in the country (Mutambo 2015a). For many of the refugees, life is a daily struggle for their dignity. While there may be some that are recruited into violent extremism, and while most of the suspects in terrorist attacks have been Muslim and Somali, it does not mean that the whole refugee community should be punished (Kiunga 2015).

Living in ungoverned spaces is living in limbo. Given the absence of functional state authorities that can provide meaningful economic and political goods, particularly basic security, persons living under such conditions can become easily vulnerable to other individuals, groups of individuals or organisations that provide alternative means of basic survival. Such vulnerable persons can in the long run become adverse political actors if they participate in the activities of violent non-state armed actors such as terrorist organisations. This is the scenario that is unfolding in Kenya's ungoverned spaces whereby the stateless constituency has become a significant political actor and threat to national security.

Conclusion

Statelessness emanating from ungoverned spaces has a direct bearing on security governance, particularly on the state's capacity to provide meaningful security to all those who reside in such spaces. The Kenyan Somalis and Somali refugees residing in Kenya's ungoverned spaces are, in the spatial-political sense, stateless. Their lives can be defined as lives in limbo. The structural and physical conditions under which they live renders them vulnerable to recruitment by extreme political groups. Not only do these conditions adversely affect their human security, both psychologically and physically, but they also risk rendering them a security threat to other communities and the state in general. The stateless constituency residing in ungoverned spaces in Kenya is increasingly becoming an active participant in the activities of *Al-Shabaab*, a transnational armed non-state actor. States that have a stateless constituency, particularly residing in ungoverned spaces, need to take remedial measures that mitigate the security threat.

To respond to the realities of politically active stateless persons residing in ungoverned spaces, states need to rethink their local-level security governance approaches in such spaces. The tendency for many states is to rely on formal, fear-based, goal-oriented approaches rather than informal, people-friendly, process-oriented approaches. The informal process approach takes into account the needs and desires of the local-level people, rather than results. The needs and desires are based on traditional institutions, be they norms or customs of the communities living in ungoverned spaces, so as to mitigate the detrimental effects of insecurity. These can include customary or traditional legal institutions or conflict management institutions. These informal-oriented processes tend to produce positive outcomes. This includes the mitigation of all forms of intolerance, enhancing reconciliation, reduction of petty corruption and building both social and political trust at the local level, leading to the peaceful coexistence of communities in such spaces. Formal, fear-based, goal-oriented approaches that use formal justice systems are not appropriate at the local level as they tend to exacerbate rather than mitigate corruption, human rights violations and insecurity, thereby enhancing social exclusion and political intolerance. Adopting informal, process-oriented techniques may not deal with the problems associated with this statelessness at the legal level, but it may address them at a spatial-political level so that the lives of stateless persons will not be lives in limbo.

References

AFP. (2015) UN warns Kenya over closing world's biggest refugee camp. Agence France-Presse. *Daily Nation*, 14 April. [online] Available at: www.nation.co.ke/news/Kenya-warned-over-closing-worlds-biggest-refugee-camp/-/1056/2685768/-/3xg978z/-/index.html [Accessed 15 April 2015].

African Union. (2015) Terrorist Attack, Garissa University, Kenya, 2 April. Incident Analysis, ACSRT/Incident Analysis-009–2015, African Union, Algiers, 6 April.

Allen, K. (2015) Al-Shabaab recruiting in Kenyan towns. *BBC News*, 16 April. [online] Available at: www.bbc.com/news/world-africa-32329518 [Accessed 16 April 2015].

Amnesty International. (2014/2015) *The State of the World's Human Rights. Amnesty International Report 2014/2015*. London: Amnesty International.

Amnesty International. (2014) *Somalis are Scapegoats in Kenya's Counter-terror Crackdown*. London: Amnesty International.

Angira, Z. (2015) UN agency staff linked to terror. *Daily Nation*, 5 October. [online] Available at: www.nation.co.ke/news/UN-agency-staff-linked-to-terror/-/1056/2900374/-/h0g00sz/-/index.html [Accessed 7 October 2015].

Anzalone, C. (2012) Kenya's Muslim youth center and Al-Shabaab's East African recruitment. *CTC Sentinel*, 5(1), pp. 9–13.

Atta-Asamoah, A. (2015) Responses to insecurity in Kenya: Too much, too little, too late? *Institute for Security Studies (ISS) East Africa Report*, 3(April 2015).

Blitz, B. K. (2009) Statelessness, protection and equality. *Forced Migration Policy Briefing 3*. Refugees Studies Centre, Oxford Department of International Studies, University of Oxford.

Botha, A. (2014) Radicalisation in Kenya: Recruitment to al-Shabaab and the Mombasa Republican Council. *Institute for Security Studies (ISS) Paper 265*, September.

Bradbury, M. and Kleinman, M. (2010) *Winning Hearts and Minds? Examining the Relationship Between Aid and Security in Kenya*. Medford, MA.: Feinstein International Center, Tufts University.

Cilliers, J. (2015) Violent Islamist extremism and terror in Africa. *Institute for Security Studies (ISS) Paper 286*, October.

Daily Nation. (2015) DP Ruto orders UN to close Dadaab refugee camp in 3 months. *Daily Nation*, 11 April. [online] Available at: www.nation.co.ke/news/-/1056/2682630/-/155cjanz/-/index.html [Accessed 12 April 2015].

Equal Rights Trust. (2010) *Unravelling Anomaly: Detention, Discrimination and the Protection Needs of Stateless Persons*. London: Equal Rights Trust.

Hajir, A. (2015) Supkem to form body to monitor Islamic institutions in fight on radicalization. *Daily Nation*, 7 April. [online] Available at: www.nation.co.ke/counties/Supkem-Garissa-fight-radicalism/-/1107872/2678204/-/pn8rkxz/-/index.html [Accessed 9 April 2015].

Human Rights Watch. (2014) *World Report 2015: Events of 2014.* New York: Human Rights Watch.

Human Rights Watch. (2010) *'Welcome to Kenya': Police Abuse of Somali Refugees.* New York: Human Rights Watch Report, June.

Ingram, A. and Dodds, K. (2009) Spaces of Security and Insecurities: Geographies of the War on Terror. In Ingram, A. and Dodds, K. (eds) *Spaces of Security and Insecurities: Geographies of the War on Terror.* Surrey: Ashgate.

Institute on Statelessness and Inclusion. (2014) *The World's Stateless. Institute on Statelessness and Inclusion,* December. The Netherlands: Wolf Legal Publishers.

International Crisis Group. (2015) Kenya's Somali north east; devolution and security. *Africa Briefing No. 114,* 17 November. International Crisis Group, Nairobi/Brussels.

International Crisis Group. (2012a) Kenyan Somali Islamist radicalisation. Policy Briefing, *Africa Briefing No. 85,* 25 January. International Crisis Group, Nairobi/Brussels.

International Crisis Group. (2012b) The Kenyan military intervention in Somalia. *Africa Report No. 184,* 15 February. International Crisis Group, Nairobi/Brussels.

Kagwanja, P. (2015) Garissa has amplified seven myths on terror in Kenya. *Daily Nation,* 11 April. [online] Available at: www.nation.co.ke/oped/Opinion/Garissa-has-amplified-seven-myths-on-terrorism-in-Kenya/-/440808/2682818/-/7x8ixvz/-/index.html [Accessed 12 April 2015].

Keister, J. (2014) The illusion of chaos: why ungoverned spaces aren't ungoverned, and why that matters. *CATO Institute Policy Analysis No. 766,* 9 December.

Kenya. (2014) *Registration of Persons Act,* Chapter 107, Revised Edition 2014 (2012). Nairobi: National Council for Law Reporting.

Kenya. (2013) *Report of the Joint Committee on Administration and National Security and Defence and Foreign Relations on the Inquiry into the Westgate Terrorist Attack, and other Terror Attacks in Mandera in North-Eastern and Kilifi in the Coastal Region.* Eleventh Parliament – First Session – 2013. Nairobi: Kenya National Assembly.

Kenya. (2011) *The Kenya Citizenship and Immigration Act, 2011, No. 12 of 2011.* Kenya Law Reports. Nairobi: National Council for Law Reporting.

Kenya. (2010) *The Proposed Constitution of Kenya,* 6 May 2010. Nairobi: Government Printer.

Kiunga, M. (2015) Refugees are victims of violence too, so they need our protection, not rejection. *Daily Nation,* 13 April. [online] Available at: www.nation.co.ke/oped/Opinion/Dadaab-Refugees-Repatriation-Terrorism/-/440808/2684570/-/oe31jj/-/index.html [Accessed 14 April 2015].

KNCHR. (2007) *An Identity Crisis? A Study on the Issuance of National Identity Cards in Kenya.* Nairobi: Kenya National Commission on Human Rights.

KNCHR/UNHCR. (2010) *Out of the Shadows: Towards Ensuring the Rights of Stateless Persons and Persons at Risk of Statelessness in Kenya.* Nairobi: Kenya National Commission on Human Rights in Partnership with the United Nations High Commissioner for Refugees, July.

Laing, A. (2015) Kenya accuses UN staff in Dadaab refugee camp of aiding terrorists. *Telegraph,* 6 October. [online] Available at: www.telegraph.co.uk/news/worldnews/africaandindianocean/kenya/11915592/Kenya-accuses-UN-staff-in-Dadaab-refugee-camp-of-aiding-terrorists.html [Accessed 7 October 2015].

Lind J., Mutahi P. and Oosterom, M. (2015) Tangled Ties: Al-Shabaab and Political Volatility in Kenya. Institute of Development Studies (IDS), *Addressing and Mitigating Violence Evidence Report No. 130.*

Mandby, B. (2014) How will the UNHCR's statelessness campaign affect Africa? *African Arguments*, 12 November. [online] Available at: http://africanarguments.org/2014/11/12/how-will-the-unhcrs-statelessness-campaign-affect-africa-by-bronwen-manby/ [Accessed 6 August 2015].

Mann, S. (2013) Tit-for-tat: Kenya, Somalia, and the resurgence of al-Shabaab. *Small Wars Journal*, 29 November. [online] Available at: http://smallwarsjournal.com/printpdf/14989 [Accessed 6 August 2015].

Margon, S. (2014) Human Rights Vetting: Nigeria and Beyond. Testimony of Sarah Margon, Washington Director, Human Rights Watch, The House Foreign Affairs Sub-committee on Africa, Global Health, Global Human Rights, and International Organizations, July.

Menkhaus, K. (2012) After the Kenyan Intervention in Somalia. Enough project, January. [online] Available at: www.enoughproject.org [Accessed 15 July 2015].

Menkhaus, K. (2007) Terrorist Activities in Ungoverned Spaces: Evidence and Observations from the Horn of Africa. Paper prepared for 'Southern Africa and International Terrorism' workshop, 25–27 January, South Africa.

MICG. (2015) Directorate of Immigration and Registration of Persons, Ministry of Interior and Coordination of Government. [online] Available at: www.immigration.go.ke/ [Accessed 15 July 2015].

Mkutu, K. and Wandera, G. (2013) Policing the Periphery: Opportunities and Challenges for Kenya Police Reserves, Small Arms Survey Working Paper 15, *Small Arms Survey*, Graduate Institute of International and Development Studies, Geneva.

Mohamed, A. (2015) Al-Shabaab now recruiting from soccer clubs, says Northeastern. *The Star Newspaper*, 16 April. [online] Available at: www.the-star.co.ke/news/al-shabaab-now-recruiting-soccer-clubs-says-northeastern#sthash.Ohw5yBEj.dpbs [Accessed 17 April 2015].

MSF. (2014) *Dadaab refugees: An uncertain tomorrow*. Geneva: Médecins San Frontières.

Mukinda, F. (2015) Refugee hosted Yumbis attackers: Report. *Daily Nation*, 30 May. [online] Available at: www.nation.co.ke/news/Yumbis-Garissa-Attackers-Al-Shabaab-Intelligence-Report/-/1056/2734882/-/46oj4nz/-/index.html [Accessed 1 June 2015].

Mutambo, A. (2015a) In wake of Garissa attack, Kenya frustrated by Dadaab issue. *Daily Nation*, 14 April. [online] Available at: www.nation.co.ke/news/Dadaab-Refugee-Camp-Terrorism-Somalia-Repatriation/-/1056/2686320/-/4as3n9/-/index.html [Accessed: 15 April 2015].

Mutambo, A. (2015b) Why Dadaab refugee camp is still a long way from closure, 24 years on. *Daily Nation*, 5 May. [online] Available at: www.nation.co.ke/news/Dadaab-refugee-camp-closure-still-a-long-way/-/1056/2706804/-/iq6d95z/-/index.html [Accessed 6 May 2015].

Mwangi, O. (2006) Kenya: conflict in the 'Badlands': the Turbi massacre in Marsabit District. *Review of African Political Economy*, 33(107), pp. 81–91.

Open Society Foundations. (2013) *Counterterrorism and Human Rights Abuses in Kenya and Uganda: The World Cup Bombing and Beyond*. New York: Open Society Foundations.

Open Society Justice Initiative. (2009) Citizen Discrimination and the Right to Nationality in Kenya. Statement Submitted by the Open Society Justice Initiative for Consideration by the United Nations Human Rights Council at its Eighth Session, on the occasion of its Universal Periodic Review of Kenya, October.

Rawlence, B. (2014) Somali Refugees in Kenya: The Case of the Dadaab Camp. Africa Programme Summary, Chatham House, London, The Royal Institute of International Affairs, 8 May.

UNHCR. (2015) Government of Kenya and Government of Somalia. Voluntary Repatriation of Somali Refugees from Kenya: Operations Strategy, 2015–2019.

US. (United States) (2014) *Country Reports on Terrorism, 2013*. Washington: US Department of State Publication, Bureau of Counterterrorism.

Whelan, T. (2006) Africa's ungoverned space. *Naçäo & Defesa*, 114(3), pp. 61–73.

Witsenburg, K. and Zaal, F. (2012) Spaces of Insecurity. In Witsenburg, K. and Zaal, F. (eds) *Spaces of Insecurity: Human Agency in Violent Conflicts in Kenya*, African Studies Collection, 45. Leiden: African Studies Centre.

Photo 4 Three Stateless Dalit in Nepal.
Source: © Greg Constantine.

For decades some 4 million people in the Terai region of southern Nepal could not acquire Nepali citizenship certificates, as the government claimed the people were from India, not Nepal. While citizenship was extended to millions of people in 2007, it is estimated that several hundred thousand in the region are still excluded from Nepali citizenship, primarily those from lower castes, specifically the Dalit, or untouchables. Walking several hours from their remote village, three Dalit carry bundles of firewood to sell in the dusty markets of Lahan.

9 Citizenship, gender and statelessness in Nepal

Before and after the 2015 Constitution

Subin Mulmi and Sara Shneiderman

Introduction[1]

Nepal's limited definition of citizenship has the potential to exacerbate existing problems of statelessness, and has been one of the most hotly debated issues in recent years. Nepal has experienced ongoing sociopolitical transformation since the 1950s. Most recently, a decade-long civil conflict between Maoist and state forces ended in 2006 with a Comprehensive Peace Agreement. Thus began a period of what is often called 'post-conflict' state restructuring. After two Constituent Assembly elections in 2008 and 2013, the second Constituent Assembly promulgated a new constitution in September 2015 (for more information on Nepal's recent history see Adhikari and Gellner 2016; Einsiedel *et al*. 2012; Hutt 2004; Shneiderman *et al*. 2016; Thapa with Sijapati 2003; Whelpton 2005). This contentious document sparked months of protest and violence (on the part of both state actors and protestors), in which over 50 people lost their lives. Central to the constitutional debate were the constraints placed on the conferral of citizenship by women and by naturalised citizens of all genders to their offspring. These constitutional ambiguities, along with difficulties often experienced in obtaining citizenship certificates even in cases where the legal framework should grant such a certificate, have the potential to render significant numbers of people stateless. This chapter explores the history and current context surrounding these issues of citizenship, gender and statelessness in Nepal.

The country's formal legal framework for designating citizenship was introduced through the enactment of the Nepal Citizenship Act in 1952. Pursuant to this Act, distribution of citizenship certificates began to those aged 16 and above. Absence of the citizenship certificate results in the person being unable to exercise basic rights inherent to the citizens of Nepal. Currently, the document serves as the foundation of legal identity and often as the prerequisite for obtaining other identity documents such as passports, driving licences, voter ID cards, birth registration certificates, children's minor ID cards, land ownership certificates and Permanent Account Number certificates. People without such certification cannot open bank accounts, pursue higher education, register to vote (*Sarojnath Pyakurel* v. *Office of the Prime Minister and Council of Ministers et al. 2011*), obtain social security allowances, file for a change of address or even get a mobile phone card. Indeed, the Equal Rights Trust has concluded that such persons cannot live a decent life (Equal Rights Trust 2015). Additionally, these documents serve as the basis for social inclusion and a common national identity.

Article 10 of the *Constitution of Nepal* states that 'No citizen shall be denied the right to citizenship'. This may seem like a circular statement, but what it means is that no one who is entitled to citizenship shall be denied access to his or her citizenship rights due to the lack of documentation. However, there have been consistent attempts by the state since its unification in 1769 to limit accession into the category of 'Nepali citizen', for reasons that will be described in the next section. The citizenship certificate, or *nagarikta pramanpatra* in Nepali, is the primary document that confers citizenship to an individual in Nepal. However, while the Supreme Court of Nepal in the case of *Ashok Kumar Shah* v. *Ministry of Home Affairs et al.* (2010) stated, '[t]he mere absence of a citizenship certificate of Nepal does not mean that the person concerned is not a citizen of Nepal', many persons in Nepal in fact find themselves unable to access citizenship rights because they lack the citizenship certificate. Where such persons do not have another state upon which to call for citizenship, this renders them effectively stateless. According to a survey conducted by Forum for Women, Law and Development (hereafter FWLD) (2015), there are currently 4.6 million people without citizenship certificates in the country. Since the reasons for non-acquisition of citizenship certificates are not explained, it is difficult to prove that those people are stateless in the strict legal sense. Consequently, the government of Nepal has repeatedly expressed its explicit dissatisfaction when this number is linked with the issue of statelessness.

Interestingly, the Supreme Court of Nepal in the case of *Raju Ahmed* v. *Government of Nepal* (2013) held that citizenship by descent is a right, whereas citizenship by naturalisation depends on the discretion of the state. Considering the fact that children born to Nepali mothers and foreign fathers are only eligible to acquire naturalised citizenship, and as of now none of them have been able to do so, their nationality status is also questionable, thereby raising the issue of statelessness yet again. Additionally, patriarchal bureaucratic practices that ignore existing legal provisions result in the non-acquisition of citizenship certificates for the children of single mothers. This is another significant reason behind the massive number of people without citizenship certificates in Nepal. The case of orphans without legal guardians and those raised without proper documentation is no different, as the regulations deprive them from even applying for citizenship certificates, despite the constitution clearly recognising them as citizens.

History of the citizenship law of Nepal

To understand the current context of statelessness in Nepal, we must understand the history of the country's citizenship law. As a country of nearly 30 million, geographically sandwiched between India and China, two of the most populous countries in the world, Nepal has always faced challenges in recognising and defining its own citizens. This is in part due to the country's ethnolinguistic diversity: Nepal is home to over 100 languages and over 60 indigenous nationalities (*adivasi janajati*), in addition to a large number of Hindu caste groups. Given this complexity, many erstwhile citizens of Nepal share cultural and linguistic practices with those across borders, both southwards in India and northwards in China's Tibetan Autonomous Region. While this diversity is sometimes positively highlighted in nationalist visions of Nepal's unique identity vis-à-vis its two neighbours, it can also be seen as a negative attribute that challenges a homogenous vision of the Nepali nation-state unified around the concepts of the Hindu religion, the Nepali language and the cultural practices of hill communities, rather than plains or mountain communities (for more on the dynamics of national identity and nation-state formation in Nepal, see Burghart 1984; Lecomte-Tilouine 2009; Pigg 1992; Rupakheti 2016; for discussion of the notion of 'nation State' itself see Tonkiss, this volume). The fact that Nepal and India have shared one of the longest open borders in the world since the 1950 Indo-Nepalese Friendship Treaty means that mobility between the two countries is widespread, creating at once great openness and a constant concern about differentiating Nepali and Indian citizens. While the border between Nepal and China's Tibetan Autonomous Region is subject to greater regulation, there is still regularised cross-border mobility for residents of border areas, as mandated by treaty between China and Nepal (for more on cross-border mobility between Nepal and its neighbouring countries, and its impact on citizenship, see Middleton 2013; Richardson *et al.* 2009; Shneiderman 2013, 2015 Ch. 4).

Nepal's 1854 Muluki Ain (Country Code), as promulgated by the Rana oligarchy, first distinguished between citizens and non-citizens, mainly for the purpose of registering land and other fixed assets. Koirala (2014) points out that rules for issuing passports were made even before the adoption of substantive provisions on citizenship certificates. However, there is no evidence that formal legal provisions regulating citizenship existed before 1950. At that time, the more fluid understanding of how people enter and leave citizenship, and the narrower understanding of which rights should be associated with citizenship, meant that the forms of statelessness, both de facto and *de jure*, that we currently see in Nepal were not yet evident.

Citizenship law from 1951 to 1990

The first Citizenship Act was drafted on 8 May 1952, laying down formally for the first time the qualifications for becoming a Nepali citizen. The Act specified that the following persons whose domicile was within Nepal could acquire the citizenship of Nepal:

* persons born in Nepal;
* persons whose father or mother is born in Nepal; and
* persons with permanent residence in Nepal living with their families.

Naturalised citizenship could be acquired by the following persons, though their country of domicile was not Nepal:

- persons born in another country to a Nepali father or mother born in Nepal, who could not acquire the citizenship of the foreign country;
- women born to Nepali parents and married to foreign men in the following cases:
  - death of the husband;
  - separation of the couple;
  - failure of the husband to take proper care of the wife; and
  - divorce.

The Citizenship Act of 1952 remained effective even after the promulgation of the Constitution of 1959. With the dissolution of the multi-party system and the introduction of the Panchayat regime in 1963, another constitution was promulgated in the same year. Under the new constitution, the law on citizenship came in the form of the Nepal Citizenship Ordinance, 1963 which was enacted on 15 December 1963, repealing the previous Act of 1952. The same Ordinance was adopted in 28 February 1964 as the Citizenship Act, 1964.

This Act made some drastic changes to the citizenship law of Nepal. Citizenship by descent could only be acquired by persons whose fathers were Nepali citizens at the time of the child's birth. With regard to naturalised citizenship, the residency requirement was increased from five to 15 years and the mandatory requirement of being able to speak the national language was also added. Foreign women married to Nepali men could acquire Nepali citizenship if they provided evidence that they had initiated the process of rescinding citizenship of the foreign country. This was an indication of the more restrictive understanding of citizenship that was to come and paved the way for the current context of statelessness.

Citizenship law from 1990 to 2006

Despite the restoration of multi-party democracy in 1990, after 30 years of authoritarian monarchical rule under the Panchayat system the Citizenship Act of 1964 was retained. The Second People's Movement of 2006 led to the adoption of an interim constitution in 2007. This constitution had the same provisions regarding naturalised citizenship, but regarding citizenship by descent, it allowed citizenship to persons born to a father *or* mother who were Nepali citizens at the time of the child's birth. However, a prohibitory clause superseded this provision stating that persons born to Nepali mothers and foreign fathers could only acquire a naturalised citizenship certificate. This provision resulted in preventing children of single mothers and those whose fathers refused to acknowledge their paternity from obtaining citizenship certificates. The prerequisites for today's situation of statelessness were therefore created in 2006.

Citizenship provisions in the new constitution

After the 2012 failure of the first Constituent Assembly to promulgate the consti-tution, the second Constituent Assembly promulgated the constitution on 20 September 2015. Though not significantly progressive compared to the previous constitution, the final provisions removed the restrictive requirement that both a person's 'father *and* mother' be Nepali citizens at the time of citizenship acquisi-tion, which was included in the draft constitution.[2] If it had been allowed to proceed, this provision would have rendered a huge population stateless due to the large numbers of individuals who either do not have information about their father's identity, or were born to a foreign father but also do not have access to citizenship in the father's country.

Widespread protests and pervasive expressions of public opinion that women should be able to confer full citizenship broke out during the consultation process on the draft constitution. As a result, the citizenship by descent provision was amended to the more liberal 'father *or* mother' (this issue was covered widely in both national and international media at the time, e.g. see Rajbhandary 2015; Sharma 2015; Thapa 2015). However, the provisions still discriminate between men and women, thereby continuing the frailties of the previous consti-tution. Specifically, Articles 11(5)[3] and 11(7)[4] of the constitution outline special conditions for children to acquire citizenship through mothers, despite Article 11(2)(b)[5] providing equal rights to women to confer citizenship. Considering that there are 898,800 (Central Bureau of Statistics 2012) children below the age of 16 living with single mothers, their nationality status is made uncertain by these provisions and they are at risk of statelessness. Indeed, as the provisions dis-cussed below indicate, it is in fact persons who are already the most vulnerable in society that may find themselves unable to assert their Nepali citizenship.

Citizenship through mothers only if the father is unidentified

Article 38(1) of Part 3 of the constitution has ensured: 'Every woman shall have equal right to lineage without any gender discrimination.' However, the right of women to confer citizenship only when the father is unidentified not only under-mines the independent identity of women but also denies their unquestionable biological role in birthing children. The law also requires that children must be born in Nepal and reside in the country as well. This requirement restricts chil-dren born to Nepalis working or resident in other countries and children born to rescued trafficked women from acquiring the citizenship of Nepal. Furthermore, the phrase 'if the father is unidentified' is ambiguous. There are many cases in Nepal where the children have been abandoned by the father and have not been able to acquire the citizenship of Nepal or any other country. In the absence of a clarification in the constitution and the related laws, it cannot be unquestionably asserted that the aforementioned cases fall under this provision. In fact, it is entirely unclear as to what kinds of cases fall under this category. In the mean-time, this lack of clarity leaves individuals effectively stateless.

Naturalised citizenship

According to Article 11(7), the children of Nepali women and foreign men can acquire Nepal's naturalised citizenship if they have resided in Nepal and have not acquired the citizenship of their fathers. However, according to several civil society organisations of Nepal, the practice of distributing these naturalised citizenship certificates has been limited.[6] Since 2006, no one has been able to acquire citizenship through this process. Such citizenship certificates are issued by the Ministry of Home Affairs after receiving a recommendation from the District Administration Office. However, the Ministry has not decided upon the case of a single applicant. A writ petition was filed in the Supreme Court of Nepal by Raju Ahmed in 2010 against the Ministry, demanding that a decision be made on his application for naturalised citizenship. Accordingly, the Supreme Court issued a directive order on 10 July 2013 to the Ministry to fulfil the petitioner's demand. The Ministry is yet to comply with the order. It is unknown how many such applications have been submitted to the Ministry. In any case, the law and the subsequent practice of law makes such applicants incapable of acquiring the citizenship certificate of Nepal, again rendering them stateless.

Citizenship of orphans

Article 11(4) of the constitution addresses the citizenship of persons whose parents (both father and mother) are unidentified, stating that such persons must be accorded citizenship by descent until their father or mother is identified. However, the Nepal Citizenship Regulation, 2006 includes additional conditions that must be fulfilled to acquire the citizenship certificate. Only those children who have been legally adopted or who have been raised in government-approved Child Care Centres are allowed to apply for such citizenship certificates. Street children and children who have grown up working as domestic helpers, or have been raised in school hostels, are deprived from even applying for such citizenship certificates and may find themselves stateless.

Case studies of individuals unable to acquire Nepali citizenship

The following case studies represent real-life situations where citizenship certificates could not be acquired despite legal provisions stating otherwise, due to the legal and constitutional problems mentioned above. Names have been changed to protect anonymity. The information was collected through face-to-face interviews with these individuals conducted by co-author Subin Mulmi and other members of FWLD, at the FWLD office premises in Kathmandu. All details are presented with permission of the interviewees. The case studies presented below were selected to represent the diverse cases of statelessness that FWLD is currently pursuing before the Supreme Court of Nepal.

Sharmila Rai and Shabnam Rai

Sharmila Rai and Shabnam Rai were born to a Nepali mother and a Nepali father. Their father abandoned them when they were two and six years old, respectively. Shabnam always wanted to become a doctor but in order to enrol for the entrance examinations, the concerned office required her citizenship certificate. Thus, she applied for a recommendation letter from the Ward Office in order to get her citizenship certificate in the year 2014. Their mother Shanti Rai was humiliated by officials in the District Administration Office who rejected her application, yet asked personal questions about Shabnam's biological father. She took her case to the Home Minister, the Prime Minister and the President, but her case was not heard. In the absence of the father's citizenship documents, it could not be verified if the father was a citizen of Nepal or a foreigner. All the concerned offices refused to process her application, and she could not apply for the medical entrance examination.

The younger daughter Sharmila was in Grade 9 when her birth registration certificate was requested by the Examination Board in order to complete the registration form for the School Leaving Certificate (government exams at the Grade 10 level). The Ward Office rejected the application to register her birth without her father's documentation. A writ petition was filed in the Supreme Court seeking an interim order to grant Sharmila the permission to complete the application form without the birth registration certificate. The plea was heard by the Court and the Court also issued a directive order to the concerned Ward Office to issue Sharmila's birth registration certificate. After acquiring birth registration certificates which specifically mentioned that their father is 'unidentified', they applied for their citizenship certificates invoking Article 11(5) of the new constitution in October 2015. However, their application was rejected, stating that the new law would not apply to earlier cases such as theirs.

Reshma Thapa

Reshma's mother Sita Thapa married Keshav Thapa at the age of 15 in May 1995. Reshma was born in the same year. A few months after the birth of Reshma, her father left the family to live separately. Sita acquired her citizenship certificate in 2004 via her father (rather than her husband). After almost ten years of separation, Keshav and Sita both agreed to divorce, with Sita securing legal guardianship of Reshma. Reshma was raised by Sita without any assistance from the father or his family. Reshma applied for the citizenship certificate in the Ward Office where Sita's citizenship was issued on 24 February 2012. The Ward Office rejected her application, stating that citizenship certificates can only be acquired in the location of the father's residence, and also sought the citizenship of the father. The father refused to support Reshma's application. Reshma is now 21 years old, without a citizenship certificate, and is unable to apply for entry to higher education.

Hari Bista and Gorakh Bista

Hari and Gorakh's father died when Hari was five and Gorakh was only one year old in 1980. Their father Diwas Bista died without having acquired a citizenship certificate. Their mother Sharmila Bista married Fadanand Kumar six years after the death of their father. Since then both Hari and Gorakh were raised by their stepfather and mother. Hari and Gorakh went to the concerned office to apply for their citizenship certificates with all the necessary documents including the death certificate of their father, the marriage registration of their parents and the citizenship certificates of their stepfather and mother, but their applications were rejected. Sharmila was even humiliated by the government officials. The reason for denying their application was stated as the mother's decision to get married to another man. The citizenship certificate of the dead father was requested. Hari is now 40 and Gorakh is 36. Both of them work in places where a citizenship certificate is not required. Hari has worked all his life as a teacher, frequently shifting schools when asked for a citizenship certificate. Gorakh is a designer who works for an IT company but is not recognised as a formal staff member of the company and thus gets paid off the record.

Ram Krishna Yadav

Ram Krishna Yadav's mother is a Nepali citizen and his father, Dhiraj Krishna Yadav, though having resided in Nepal all his life, has not acquired citizenship of Nepal. Dhiraj's father and his grandfather also both resided in Nepal all their lives without acquiring the citizenship of Nepal. In accordance with the law, Ram could only apply for naturalised citizenship, which he did in 2007. In order to initiate the process, the Ward Office asked for a document certifying that Ram had not acquired citizenship of India. For years Ram struggled to obtain this piece of evidence. Without a Nepali citizenship certificate, Ram could not even travel to India in order to inquire about the document. Though Nepal shares an open border with India and requires no visa or passport to travel, officials on both sides may still legally request to see a legal identity document that certifies the nationality of the person before allowing cross-border travel. After three years of struggle, Ram was able to procure a letter from the Indian Embassy certifying that he was not a citizen of India. As naturalised citizenship certificates are only provided by the Home Ministry, his application was sent to the Ministry. His case has remained undecided for five years. Ram has been offered several working positions but has not been able to accept employment without a citizenship certificate. At the age of 32 with two children, he is still economically dependent on his mother.

Hitesh Pradhan

Hitesh was born in western Nepal. At eight years old, he left his home town and went to Kathmandu, where he worked as a domestic helper in an ethnic Newar household (the indigenous community of the Kathmandu Valley, with relatively high socio-economic status). The homeowners allowed him to adopt their last name. When he came of age, he applied for a citizenship certificate in order to obtain a driving licence. He had learnt to drive and had been offered a job as a taxi driver. In the District Administration Office, he stated that he had no idea where his parents were and tried to apply as an orphan. But he was not even allowed to file an application, as he needed to furnish evidence of having grown up in a government-certified child care centre, or the citizenship certificate of his legal guardian. Without either document, his claim was not heard. He is still working as a domestic helper in another household.

These individuals share a genuine claim to citizenship of Nepal. Indeed, in every case Nepal is the primary and only appropriate state upon which they can call for citizenship. They are trapped by the gender-based discrimination in Nepali citizenship law and by the implausible requirements of proof needed to demonstrate that they in fact fall into appropriate categories of persons eligible for Nepali citizenship. While each case is different, taken together the denial of citizenship in these cases demonstrates the denial of citizenship to precisely those most vulnerable members of society for whom citizenship protections are primarily intended. These individuals are rendered effectively stateless, though it is contentious to argue this due to their self-identification with the state of Nepal.

Statelessness in Nepal

Article 1(1) of the 1954 Convention Relating to the Status of Stateless Persons sets out the definition of a stateless person as follows:

> For the purpose of this Convention, the term 'stateless person' means a person who is not considered as a national by any State under the operation of its law

The International Law Commission (2014) has concluded that the definition in Article 1(1) is part of customary international law (UNHCR 2014a, p. 9), thus making it binding even for non-parties to the treaty like Nepal. Since Article 1(1) is to be interpreted in line with the ordinary meaning of the text, read in context and bearing in mind the treaty's object and purpose, pursuant to Article 31(1) of the Vienna Convention on the Law of Treaties (1969) (United Nations 1969), also indicated in the preamble and in the *Travaux Préparatoires*, the object and purpose of the 1954 Convention is to ensure that stateless persons enjoy the widest possible exercise of their human rights (see also de Chickera and van Waas, this volume).[7]

Establishing whether persons like Sharmila and Shabnam Rai, Reshma Thapa, Hari and Gorakh Bista, Ram Krishna Yadav and Hitesh Pradhan are 'considered as a national under the operation of its law' is a mixed question of fact and law (UNHCR 2014a, p. 12). The reference to 'law' in Article 1(1) of the Convention encompasses not just the legislation, but also regulations, orders, judicial case law and customary practice (UNHCR 2014a, p. 12). It requires a careful analysis of how a State applies its nationality laws in an individual's case in practice along with any review/appeal mechanisms that may impact the individual's status.[8] Since a state may not practise the law in its entirety, as evidenced in the cases of Reshma Thapa and Hari Bista, even going so far as to ignore the provisions, applying this approach in practice may lead to a different conclusion than one deduced from a purely legal analysis of the nationality laws. Hence, the analysis of the legal provisions in the constitution and the relevant Acts, Regulations and Directives will not suffice. Their implementation must also be studied in order to determine whether the laws have resulted in the creation of stateless persons.

Role of the competent authority

The competent authority to confer, distribute or withdraw nationality documents must thus be identified in order to determine the nationality status of the individual. Competence in this context also refers to the authority responsible for clarifying the nationality status where nationality is acquired or withdrawn automatically (Hague Convention 1930). District Administrative Offices, Municipalities, Village Development Committees, Ward Offices and the Ministry of Home Affairs are the competent authorities to provide citizenship certificates in Nepal.

Where the competent authorities treat an individual as a non-citizen even though he or she would appear to meet the criteria for automatic acquisition of citizenship under the operation of a country's laws, it is their position rather than the letter of the law that is determinative in concluding that a State does not consider such an individual as a national (Hague Convention 1930, p. 16) or citizen (hereafter used interchangeably, though for a problematisation of this approach, see Tonkiss, this volume). This scenario frequently arises where discrimination against particular groups is widespread in government departments or where, in practice, the law governing automatic acquisition at birth is systematically ignored and individuals are required instead to prove additional ties to the State (Hague Convention 1930).[9]

In addition to the cases mentioned in this chapter, there are ample further cases in Nepal where citizenship certificates by descent have been denied to applicants applying through their mothers without the details of their fathers (the list of cases can be found in National Women Commission and Forum for Women, Law and Development 2014, pp. 4–19; Equal Rights Trust 2015, pp. 12–14; IWRAW 2011, p. 7), despite the law specifically addressing their rights to acquire citizenship.

According to a study by FWLD (2015), the number of persons without citizenship in Nepal is expected to rise to a staggering 6.7 million by 2021 (out of 25 million eligible population[10]) from the already appalling figure of 4.6 million (out of 20.4 million eligible population) (FWLD 2015, p. 2). Another study, however, found that about 95 percent of those without citizenship certificates in the surveyed districts had not applied for such documentation with the concerned

authorities (FWLD 2014, p. 8). Without having applied to the competent authority for the citizenship certificate, it cannot be deduced that such people are not
nationals of Nepal. Conversely, however, without the citizenship certificate, they
cannot be *formally* recognised as nationals of Nepal.

Cases of non-application for acquiring nationality

In all the cases mentioned above, applications for nationality were made to the
competent authorities. However, in Nepal there are also cases where individuals
have never come into contact with the State's competent authorities for various
reasons, including geographical inaccessibility or lack of awareness. We must
therefore analyse the State's general attitude towards the nationality status of
persons in such cases. If the State has a good practice of recognising, in a non-
discriminatory manner, the nationality status of all those who appear to come
within the scope of the relevant law, this indicates that the person concerned is
considered as a national by the State (UNHCR 2014a, p. 16). However, if the
individual belongs to a group that is generally denied identification documents
issued only to nationals, this indicates that he or she is not considered a national
by the State and is thus stateless (UNHCR 2014a).

Despite the overwhelming list of international obligations that Nepal holds
with regard to citizenship, as mentioned in the next section, the provisions are
still discriminatory, certifying the intent of the state to deny citizenship to children of single mothers, children born to Nepali mothers and foreign fathers, and
orphans. It is uncertain whether the nearly 900,000 children of single mothers
will be able to acquire citizenship when they attain the age of 16. Though these
groups of people have been addressed by the Constitution in Articles 11(4), (5)
and (7), respectively, the general practice has been to refuse their applications
for citizenship certificates and thus it can be said that these groups of people in
Nepal are in fact stateless.

Review or repeal proceedings

In cases where an individual's nationality status has been the subject of review
or appeal proceedings, whether by a judicial or other body, its decision must be
taken into account (UNHCR 2014a). However, a different approach is justified
in countries where the executive ignores the positions of judicial or other review
bodies (even though these are binding as a matter of law) with impunity
(UNHCR 2014a). In such cases, the declaration by State authorities that such
groups are not nationals would be decisive rather than the decision of the judicial bodies that disagree with the statement (UNHCR 2014a, p. 20).

The previous constitution as well as the current constitution have allowed the
filing of public interest litigation in the Appellate and Supreme Court of Nepal in
cases where the competent authority has denied citizenship certificates to those
who are deemed citizens by the constitution of Nepal. Sabina Damai, a resident
of Dolakha district whose father abandoned her and was thus raised by her

mother, filed a writ petition in the Supreme Court in 2010 seeking citizenship through her mother. The Court decided in Damai's favour (*Sabina Damai and FWLD* v. *Government of Nepal* 2011), ordering the District Administration Office to provide a citizenship certificate to her. The precedent held that children of single mothers whose fathers are unidentified must be provided with a citizenship certificate through the mother in all similar cases. The Ministry of Home Affairs even issued a circular[11] dated 23 January 2013 to all the Regional Administrative Offices and the District Administrative Offices to distribute citizenship through mothers when the father of the child is untraceable or unidentified. Even then, applicants with similar cases were not provided with citizenship certificates through their mothers as evidenced in two more cases (*Shanti Nagarkoti and Bhola Nagarkoti* v. *Government of Nepal* 2014; *Barsha Sharma* v. *District Administration Office Banke* 2014) where such applications were made after the circular mentioned above was issued. Sharmila Rai and Shabnam Rai also applied for their citizenship certificates after the circular was issued, but their applications were rejected. Thus, the position of the competent authorities that deny citizenship certificates without proof of the father's citizenship is decisive and so these groups are deemed stateless.

Role of the international community in addressing statelessness in Nepal

During the 2006–2015 constitution writing process, Nepal was repeatedly reminded by the international community to adhere to the international human rights standards on nationality. Though not a party to either of the Statelessness Conventions, Nepal has ratified other treaties that protect the right to nationality. Specifically, Nepal has the obligation to comply with Article 15 of the Universal Declaration of Human Rights (UDHR), 1948 which states that, 'every individual has the right to nationality and nobody shall be arbitrarily deprived of nationality' (UNGA 1948). The International Covenant on Civil and Political Rights, 1966, to which Nepal is a party, also states that nobody shall be arbitrarily deprived of nationality (UNGA 1966). Nepal has also ratified the Convention on the Elimination of All forms of Discrimination against Women (CEDAW), 1979 which in Article 9 states that women have equal rights to men to confer citizenship on their spouse as well as their children. In addition to these two treaties, Nepal has ratified the International Covenant on Economic, Social and Cultural Rights (ICESCR), 1966 and the Convention on the Rights of Children (CRC), 1989.

The CEDAW Committee, in the Concluding Observations on 29 July 2011, strongly urged Nepal to 'ensure that the new Constitution provides for equal and full citizenship rights for women, including by exerting their right to transfer citizenship to their children and foreign husband'.[12] The Concluding Observations of the Human Rights Committee in March 2014 recommended Nepal to 'ensure that citizenship provisions of the new Constitution guarantee the equal right of women to acquire, transfer and retain citizenship'. Even the Committee on

Economic, Social and Cultural Rights raised concerns regarding the provision in the constitution that restricted 'transmission of nationality by a Nepalese woman to her child'.[13] The CRC Committee, in its Concluding Observations of 9 June 2016, recommended that Nepal amend its legislation on transmission of nationality by '[m]aking citizenship by descent accessible through proof of citizenship of one of the parents, regardless of parent's sex'.[14]

Nepal also received recommendations from five states (Canada, Hungary, Sierra Leone, Spain and New Zealand) during the 23rd Session of the Universal Periodic Review (UPR) regarding the need to amend existing citizenship law to ensure equal nationality rights between men and women.[15] All of these recommendations were accepted by Nepal as already implemented or in the process of implementation. Despite these international obligations, the laws of Nepal are still discriminatory towards women and also restrict certain groups of people from obtaining citizenship, in many cases due to their perceived ethnic identification with either populations to the south in India or populations to the north in China's Tibetan Autonomous Region. The issue of statelessness is hardly discussed by policy makers in Nepal, even though, as this chapter has demonstrated, there are certain groups who are indeed stateless.

Role of UNHCR in Nepal

Though the concerned Committees of the various Human Rights Treaties have addressed the problems related to nationality, the issue of statelessness has not been adequately tackled by any international body. Quantitative data on the stateless population of Nepal is not available as necessary efforts to identify stateless persons have not been carried out. UNHCR has been involved in statelessness issues and with stateless persons since its inception in 1950. The organisation's mandate is to protect refugees and to help them find solutions to their plight. Since 1995, the mandate of the Office has been expanded by the UN General Assembly to include responsibilities relating to non-refugee stateless persons and prevention and reduction of statelessness more broadly. According to the Handbook for Parliamentarians (2014), these resolutions do not affect UNHCR's activities in those states that are party to the statelessness conventions (for more on UNHCR's role relating to statelessness see Staples, this volume).

According to the *Conclusion on Identification, Prevention and Reduction of Statelessness and Protection of Stateless Persons* (UNHCR 2006), UNHCR clearly has the mandate to identify populations with undetermined nationality residing within designated territories, in cooperation with other UN agencies. In November 2014 UNHCR launched the #IBelong Global Campaign that aims to end statelessness globally by 2024. The High Commissioner stated in his 2014 End of Year Message that this

> was just the first step in what will have to be a sustained effort, working closely with governments and civil society across the globe, to bring about

the necessary legislative changes to prevent new cases of statelessness and resolve existing situations by 2024.

The *Global Action Plan to End Statelessness 2014–24 (GAP)* (UNHCR 2014b) was published at the time of the 2014 campaign launch. It sets out ten key actions to achieve the goal of ending statelessness by 2024, alongside global milestones for assessing interim progress. The GAP primarily focuses on persons of concern under UNHCR's statelessness mandate who are not refugees.

Consequently, the 4.6 million people who do not have citizenship certificates in Nepal fall under this statelessness mandate. Nepal also has the international obligation to comply with the ten actions to end statelessness, and similarly UNCHR is obligated to assist the State. Even though Nepal does not recognise any population as stateless, Actions Two (Ensure that no child is born stateless), Three (Remove gender discrimination from nationality laws), Seven (Ensure birth registration for the prevention of statelessness), Eight (Issue nationality documentation to those with entitlement to it), Nine (Accede to the UN Statelessness Conventions) and Ten (Improve quantitative and qualitative data on stateless populations) are applicable to Nepal irrespective of the non-recognition. UNHCR Nepal has currently prepared the Strategy for Implementing GAP, addressing Actions Three, Eight and Ten, which is a welcome change to their approach in tackling the problems related to statelessness in Nepal.

Conclusion

The term 'stateless' is seldom used in public discourse in Nepal. Since the constitutional and legal provisions have embodied a wide group of people under the category of citizens, it is generally presumed that there are no 'stateless' persons in the country. However, a proper comparative analysis of the international standards of statelessness with the situation of Nepal proves that there are certain groups of people who are effectively stateless. Citizenship certificates distinguish Nepali citizens from non-citizens of Nepal, and the refusal to provide citizenship certificates according to the laws of Nepal thus deems a person stateless. A study of the historical development of the country's citizenship laws shows that they have been constructed to discriminate against women. As a result of this, children of Nepali mothers and unidentified/foreign fathers have not been able to acquire citizenship certificates. The new constitution contains similar provisions, and continues to leave orphans, children of single mothers and other vulnerable individuals at risk of statelessness.

The open border with India and widely prevalent tradition of cross-border marriage has been cited by the government as the rationale for these restrictive citizenship provisions. Patriarchal assumptions embedded in the legal code have deprived women of the right to confer citizenship to their children independently. This has resulted in clear discrimination in the legal provisions and the practice of denying citizenship certificates to certain groups of people by the competent authorities, despite orders of the supreme judicial body. Such groups of people have thus become stateless, and thus command the protection of international law pursuant to the provisions of the 1954 Convention Relating to the Status of Stateless Persons and the Convention on the Reduction of Statelessness (UNGA 1961). The role of UNHCR is subject to much scrutiny in a context in which efforts to identify stateless populations in Nepal are not yet adequate. However, statelessness in Nepal has garnered wider attention as a result of the Global Campaign to end statelessness, which has led to efforts to improve quantitative and qualitative data on stateless populations by 2024. However, the efforts to bring this discussion into the public realm, and into policy discussion at the state level, remain insufficient. Statelessness has existed in Nepal for more than half a century, but national and international attention to this problem has been largely absent. The first step would be to identify the number of stateless people in the country and maintain a strong database of such people. This would strengthen advocacy efforts and demonstrate the severity of the problem.

The problem of statelessness in Nepal is primarily of non-migratory nature, which means that persons become and remain stateless within their 'own country' (see also Vlieks, this volume). Thus, a key remedy will be swift and accessible nationality verification efforts. Since the existing number of people without citizenship is huge, and many are impaired in accessing citizenship because they live in geographically inaccessible areas, special programmes to provide citizenship certificates to people living across the country's varied terrain must be conducted. In the past, integrated mobile camps were organised before national elections in order to ensure nobody was deprived of voting. Such efforts should be initiated regularly. Vital information such as birth registration, death registration, marriage registration and migration status, which serve as necessary evidence for citizenship applications, are poorly recorded in Nepal. Thus, vital registration systems must also be strengthened.

Finally, it is time for a deeper questioning of the exclusionary vision of Nepali nationalism based on patriarchal frameworks for understanding lineage and descent. Nepal's ethnic and linguistic diversity should be understood as an asset, and citizenship granted through the appropriate procedures to all those who qualify regardless of their parentage or ethnolinguistic, cultural or regional heritage. In this way, Nepal's particular context of statelessness could be addressed.

Notes

1 The authors are grateful for support from the Wenner-Gren Foundation, the UBC Hampton Faculty Fellowship, and the Forum for Women, Law and Development. We are indebted to the stateless people of Nepal whose situation we seek to document here. We also thank the editors of this volume for their helpful suggestions along the way.
2 The first draft of the constitution prepared by the Constitution Drafting Committee of the Constituent Assembly in July 2015, Article 12(1)(b) included: 'Any person whose either father or mother was a citizen of Nepal at his or her birth and both father and mother are citizens of Nepal at the time of receiving citizenship.'

3 A person born to a Nepali citizen mother and having his/her domicile in Nepal but whose father is not traced shall be conferred the Nepali citizenship by descent. Provided that in case his/her father is found to be a foreigner, the citizenship of such a person shall be converted to naturalised citizenship according to the Federal law.

4 Notwithstanding anything contained elsewhere in this Article, in case of a person born to a Nepali woman citizen married to a foreign citizen, he/she may acquire naturalised citizenship of Nepal as provided for by a Federal law if he/she has permanent domicile in Nepal and he/she has not acquired citizenship of the foreign country.

5 Any person whose father or mother was a citizen of Nepal at the time of the child's birth.

6 Nepal Civil Society Network of Citizenship Rights, the Global Campaign for Equal Nationality Rights and the Institute on Statelessness and Inclusion 2015, *Joint Submission to the Human Rights Council at the 23rd Session of the Universal Periodic Review: Nepal*, p. 6. This report states that 'research conducted by FWLD reveals that in the first six years of the implementation of these provisions, not a single naturalisation application was successful'.

7 See the second and fourth paragraphs of the Preamble of the 1954 Convention Relating to the Status of Stateless Persons United Nations, Treaty Series, vol. 360.

8 This approach reflects the general principle of law set out in Articles 1 and 2 of the 1930 Hague Convention on Certain Questions Relating to the Conflict of Nationality Laws.

9 Ibid.

10 Eligible population means people 16 and older, since the citizenship certificate can only be acquired after reaching that age.

11 Circular of the Department of Citizenship and Weapons issued on 23 January 2013, Ref. No. 180/2069/70, p. 1.

12 Recommendation of the CEDAW Committee to Nepal in 2011, para. 25, 26 and 49 (CEDAW/C/NPL/CO/4–5); *See also* Concluding Observation of the CEDAW Committee to Nepal, para. 198, A/59/38 (2004).

13 Recommendation of the Committee on Economic, Social and Cultural Rights on the Third Periodic Report of Nepal in 2014, para. 12 (E/C.12/NPL/3).

14 Recommendation of the Committee on the Rights of Children on the third to fifth periodic reports of Nepal in 2016, para 27 (CRC/C/NPL/3–5).

15 UN Human Rights Council, Report of the Working Group on the Universal Periodic Review: Nepal, 8 July 2013, A/HRC/25/9. Available at www.upr-info.org/sites/default/files/document/nepal/session_23_-_november_2015/recommendations_and_pledges_nepal_2015.pdf [Accessed 7 October 2016].

References

Adhikari, K. and Gellner, D. N. (2016) New Identity Politics and the 2012 Collapse of Nepal's Constituent Assembly: When the Dominant Becomes Other. *Modern Asian Studies*, 50(6), pp. 2009–2040. [Accessed 17 February 2016].

Ashok Kumar Shah v. *Ministry of Home Affairs et al.* (2010) Case No. 2064-0622. Decided on 2 March 2010.

Barsha Sharma v. *District Administration Office Banke.* (2014) Writ No. 070-WO-0153. Decided on 24 December 2014.

Burghart, R. (1984) The formation of the concept of nation-state in Nepal. *The Journal of Asian Studies*, 44(1), pp. 101–125.

Central Bureau of Statistics. (2012) *National Population and Housing Census, 2011*, vol. 1, *Constitution of Nepal*. Kathmandu: Government of Nepal, Central Bureau of Statistics.

Einsiedel, S. von, Malone, D. M. and Pradhan, S. (eds) (2012) *Nepal in Transition: From People's War to Fragile Peace*. New York: Cambridge University Press.

Equal Rights Trust. (2015) My Children's Future: Ending Gender Discrimination in Nationality Laws. [online] Available at: www.equalrightstrust.org/ertdocumentbank/ My%20Children's%20Future%20Ending%20Gender%20Discrimination%20in%20 Nationality%20Laws.pdf [Accessed 12 February 2016].

FWLD (Forum for Women, Law and Development). (2015) Acquisition of Citizenship Certificates in Nepal: Estimation and Projection. [online] Available at: http://fwld.org/ publications/acquisition-citizenship-certificate-nepal-estimation-projection/ [Accessed 18 January 2016].

FWLD (Forum for Women, Law and Development). (2014) Acquisition of Citizenship Certificate in Nepal: Understanding Trends, Barriers and Impacts. [online] Available at: http://fwld.org/publications/acquisition-citizenship-certificate-nepal-understanding-trends-barriers-impacts/ [Accessed 24 January 2016].

Hague Convention on Certain Questions Relating to the Conflict of Nationality Laws. (1930) [online] Available at: http://eudo-citizenship.eu/InternationalDB/docs/ Convention%20on%20certain%20questions%20relating%20to%20the%20conflict%20 of%20nationality%20laws%20FULL%20TEXT.pdf [Accessed 12 January 2016].

Hutt, M. (ed.) (2004) *Himalayan People's War: Nepal's Maoist Rebellion*. London: Hurst and Company.

IWRAW. (2011) Asia Pacific Occasional Papers Series. *Women's Right to Nationality and Citizenship*, No. 9. Kuala Lumpur, Malaysia: International Women's Rights Action Watch Asia Pacific.

Koirala, Y. (2014) *State and Citizenship*. Dillibazar, Kathmandu: Makalu Publishing House.

Lecomte-Tilouine, M. (2009) *Hindu Kingship, Ethnic Revival, and Maoist Rebellion in Nepal*. New Delhi: Oxford University Press.

Middleton, T. (2013) Anxious belongings: anxiety and the politics of belonging in sub-nationalist Darjeeling. *American Anthropologist* 115(4), pp. 608–621.

National Women Commission and Forum for Women, Law and Development. (2014) Analysis of Nepalese Citizenship Laws from a Gender Perspective. [online] Available at: http://fwld.org/wp-content/uploads/2016/06/Analysis-of-Nepalese-Citizenship-Laws-from-a-Gender-Perspective.pdf [Accessed 12 January 2016].

Pigg, S. L. (1992) Inventing social categories through place: social representations and development in Nepal. *Comparative Studies in Society and History*, 34(3), pp. 491–513.

Rajbhandary, A. (2015) 'Being Nepali or becoming Nepali?' *Nepali Times*, 12 March. [online] Available at: http://nepalitimes.com/article/nation/citizenship-in-the-name-of-the-mother,2076 [Accessed 12 December 2015].

Raju Ahmed v. Government of Nepal. (2013) Writ No. 067-WO-1249. Decided on 10 July 2013.

Richardson, D., Poudel, M. and Laurie, N. (2009) Sexual trafficking in Nepal: constructing citizenship and livelihoods. *Gender, Place and Culture*, 16(3), pp. 259–278.

Rupakheti, S. (2016) Reconsidering state–society relations in south Asia: a Himalayan case study. *Himalaya, the Journal of the Association for Nepal and Himalayan Studies*, 35(2), pp. 73–86.

Sabina Damai and FWLD v. Government of Nepal. (2011) Writ no 06/0703. Decided on 27 February 2011.

Sarojnath Pyakurel v. Office of the Prime Minister and Council of Ministers et al. (2011) Writ no. 2067-WS-0017. Decided on 7 February 2011.

Shanti Nagarkoti and Bhola Nagarkoti v. Government of Nepal. (2014) Writ No. 0880. Decided on 24 March, 2014.

Sharma, G. (2015) Nepali single mothers say law change would make children stateless. *Reuters*, 8 January. [online] Available at: www.reuters.com/article/us-nepal-citizenship-idUSKBN0KH19620150108 [Accessed: 14 December 2015].

Shneiderman, S. (2015) *Rituals of Ethnicity: Thangmi Identities Between Nepal and India*. Philadelphia: University of Pennsylvania Press.

Shneiderman, S. (2013) Himalayan border citizens: sovereignty and mobility in the Nepal–Tibetan autonomous region (TAR) of China border zone. *Political Geography*, 35(July 2013), pp. 25–36.

Shneiderman, S., Wagner, L., Rinck, J., Johnson, A. and Lord, A. (2016) Nepal's ongoing political transformation: a review of post-2006 literature on conflict, the state, identities and environments. *Modern Asian Studies*, 50(6), pp. 2041–2114.

Thapa, M. (2015) Women have no nationality: why I burned my country's new constitution. *The Record*, 21 September. [online] Available at: http://recordnepal.com/perspective/women-have-no-nationality [Accessed 14 December 2015].

Thapa, D. and Sijapati, B. (2003) *A Kingdom Under Siege: Nepal's Maoist Insurgency 1996–2004*. Kathmandu: Martin Chautari.

UNHCR. (2014a) Handbook on Protection of Stateless Persons, Under the 1954 Convention Relating to the Status of Stateless Persons. [online] Available at: www.unhcr.org/uk/protection/statelessness/53b698ab9/handbook-protection-stateless-persons.html [Accessed 28 January 2016].

UNHCR. (2014b) Global Action Plan to End Statelessness. [online] Available at: www.refworld.org/docid/545b47d64.html [Accessed 28 January 2016].

UNHCR. (2006) Conclusion on Identification, Prevention and Reduction of Statelessness and Protection of Stateless Persons, No. 106 (LVII). [online] Available at: www.refworld.org/docid/453497302.html [Accessed 29 January 2016].

UNGA. (1966) International Covenant on Civil and Political Rights. United Nations, Treaty Series, vol. 999, p. 171. [online] Available at: www.refworld.org/docid/3ae6b3aa0.html [Accessed 6 December 2015].

UNGA. (1961) Convention on the Reduction of Statelessness, United Nations, Treaty Series, vol. 989. [online] Available at: www.refworld.org/docid/3ae6b39620.html [Accessed 6 December 2015].

UNGA. (1948) Universal Declaration of Human Rights, 217 A (III). [online] Available at: www.refworld.org/docid/3ae6b3712c.html [Accessed 6 December 2015].

United Nations. (1969) Vienna Convention on the Law of Treaties, 23 May. United Nations, Treaty Series, vol. 1155, Article 31(1). [online] Available at: www.refworld.org/docid/3ae6b3a10.html [Accessed 6 December 2015].

Whelpton, J. (2005) *A History of Nepal*. Cambridge: Cambridge University Press.

10 Members of colonised groups, statelessness and the right to have rights

Tendayi Bloom

Now, we had no choice. We did not request this citizenship, did not want it, and opposed it.

How can a citizen have a treaty with his own government?
Chief Clinton Rickard (Rickard 1973, p. 126 and p. 56 respectively)

Introduction[1]

Indigenous political theory offers an important critical resource in developing more nuanced broader understandings of citizenship and thereby also nuanced practice in the area of statelessness. Citizenship of a recognised State is often seen uncritically as the first and most important step in addressing the deprivations experienced as a result of statelessness. However, considering analyses offered by those contesting aspects of their citizenship can help to demonstrate problems with this approach. Nothing in this chapter should be seen as denying the obligation of a State to offer citizenship or as suggesting any individuals *should* reject it. Indeed, in the contemporary world such citizenship is in fact often needed both to pursue human rights claims and to be heard through standard political and legal spaces. Instead, this chapter argues that alongside supporting individuals to access their rights in whichever way necessary, there needs to be a significant re-examination of the liberal theoretical understanding of the State system itself in the light of the claims *both* of stateless persons *and* of members of Indigenous Nations. While acknowledging potential problems in this terminology, this chapter adopts the word 'Indigenous' here because it is one of the terms used in theorising in this area.[2]

Contexts of colonisation vary widely, as do individual responses to them (e.g. see Bruyneel 2004). Sometimes citizenship of a dominant society has been sought by members of colonised groups as a means of accessing rights. Sometimes it has been opposed as a colonising tool that reinforces inequalities and weakens rights obtained in other ways. Then there is the role of the memberships of the colonised groups themselves, whether they are conceived as citizenships or otherwise, which are recognised to different extents within the system of

States. Given the inequality of power between a State and an individual and also between recognised States and Indigenous governments, citizenship of settler States is withheld, offered or imposed according to the interests of that State. This challenges the notion of citizenship as related to individual self-rule. For the most part, liberal theorists of noncitizenship and statelessness have shied away from engaging with the challenges posed by colonisation, with notable exceptions (e.g. Nyers 2011; Kingston 2014; Tully 1993; Carens 1992; Young 1989), and, overall, this body of theorists has engaged insufficiently directly with Indigenous political theory (e.g. Simpson 2000; Turner 2006; Wilkins 2003; Wilkins and Stark 2011; Wilkins and Lomawaima 2001). The chapter does not hold that members of Indigenous groups are stateless – for the most part they are not – but examines their contestations of existing citizenship regimes, as well as their navigations of them, to move towards a more complex understanding of the role of citizenship in rights protection. Through its analysis of these tensions this chapter problematises a structure that assumes that the problems associated with statelessness can be addressed uncomplicatedly through citizenship of currently recognised States alone.

With a focus primarily on North American contexts, though also touching upon debates generated elsewhere, this chapter, then, problematises the remedies currently offered for the problems associated with statelessness which are rooted in an assumption of citizenship of a member of the existing community of States as the only way in which people can or should relate politically within a State's territory and internationally (something contested in the context of the former USSR by Swider, this volume). Discourse around statelessness often constructs citizenship of a recognised State as the core or even sole allocator of rights, personhood and political existence, and as unambiguously desirable. Examining the roles of citizenship in contexts of colonisation provides another set of perspectives. It shows how a fixation on conferring citizenship without examining why a lack of citizenship in fact brings such vulnerabilities risks reinforcing precisely the unjust structures that create the problems in the first place.

In this chapter, various cases are briefly presented. I do not pretend to offer a deep analysis of them, but instead use them to explore the meaning of State citizenship and rejection of State citizenship, including the resultant denial of the freedom to move, for example, and the role of unrecognised citizenships. It argues that, given the messy reality of contemporary States, the attachment to binary forms of individual–State engagement (e.g. citizen/not citizen), and the common assumption that these be mutually exclusive, is problematic. Looking beyond the members of colonised groups, this helps to illuminate wider inconsistencies within liberal frameworks and advocates a rethink of appropriate remedies for the problems that result. This chapter is written from the perspective of liberal political theory, tentatively suggesting lessons that can be learnt within this field by taking seriously the developments in Indigenous studies and Indigenous political theory.

Challenging citizenship

The situations for individual members of Indigenous National groups within settler States do not fit neatly into liberal political theoretic discourses that assume the existing State system as a starting point, even those which challenge existing structures by highlighting the rights of those written out of theory. Citizenship theorist Peter Nyers made a similar claim in 2011, lamenting the absence of consideration of Indigenous populations in key books on citizenship and noncitizenship (Nyers 2011; Bosniak 2006; Shachar 2009). For Nyers, this omission may be because their situation just cannot be addressed within existing liberal political theory structures, while Audra Simpson suggests that the demands of Indigenous nations may just be 'unintelligible to the western and/or imperial ear' (Simpson 2000, p. 114).

Indeed, modern liberalism in its very creation defined members of certain groups outside the liberal nexus. Consider for example John Locke's discussion of how the failure of the 'Wild Indians' to use European farming techniques disqualifies individuals from ownership of their land (Locke 1823, p. 116), who come to be excluded altogether from recognition in the project of citizenship and State-making (e.g. Tully 1996; Bishop 1997; Goldie 2015). And so, just as new forms of equalising and empowering citizenship were being developed in England, France and America to replace subjecthood, new hierarchies were being constructed within those same political theoretical frameworks (e.g. see Hall 2002, developed in Bloom forthcoming). Contemporary liberalism, arising out of this tradition, will need to work hard if it is to hear the claims of those traditionally excluded from it, but hopefully that does not mean that it will be impossible for it to do so. An important start will be to acknowledge both the theoretical and the real-world effects of colonialism, including what this may mean for the legitimacy of existing States and the State system. Indeed, it will be necessary to address the failings in what Dale Turner refers to as 'White Paper liberalism' (Turner 2006 – see particularly p. 15).

The difficulty in accommodating Indigenous claims within liberal theoretical frameworks that do not do this may derive partly from a trope often found either implicitly or explicitly in liberal theorists' discussion of Indigenous rights claims. Those advocating for the rights of those who have traditionally been excluded from liberal theory often advocate new theorisations that are post-national or civic (e.g. Tonkiss 2013). If Indigenous claims are framed as primarily ethnic-based or first-comer claims, there is a risk that they appear to be symbolic of a form of social organisation that is supposed to have been surpassed by civic and post-ethnic nationalisms (e.g. see discussion in Kymlicka 2000, p. 230). As a result, their claims can seem to replicate the very tropes against which such contemporary liberal theorists set themselves – the ethnic-based presentations of entitlement based on an indigeneity that exclude new arrivals from accessing political spaces. On one level, this could be seen as irrelevant, since the primary claim within Indigenous political theory is not that Indigenous groups should be understood *within* existing States and their theoretical frameworks but that they are *prior to* those States, which took control illegitimately. That means that if their *raison d'être*, whatever it is, is problematic to liberal States, it can be seen as problematic in the same way as those of other States that are openly non-liberal.

The language of indigeneity is also contentious in liberal theoretic discussion of statelessness. This is because it is sometimes used by majority groups to assert a right to exclude minorities who are represented as non-Indigenous. For example, indigeneity discourse in the Dominican Republic has been used to exclude those identified as having Haitian heritage from full citizenship (e.g. Blake, this volume, see also Nooksack discussion below). However, the two uses of indigeneity claims are of different forms (though of course these may be blurred in some cases). Although it may seem trivial, let me briefly set this out. The indigeneity claim of a colonised group need not be based on race, or on 'we got here first'. Insofar as it is an 'Indigenous' claim, it refers to an illegitimate seizure of lands and properties that were previously owned, or non-consensual imposition of political structures upon pre-existing political systems, or the vital relationship of specific places with cultural practices, for example. While these claims may also be contested (e.g. by questioning whether this requires that people can inherit claims or obligations from previous generations), they are claims which can fit within progressive liberal thinking. The conflicts described in this chapter can also be usefully understood through the lens of consent, including whether State power is consensual; a claim to recognition of human dignity; and/or individual autonomy, the right to choose one's own life path. In addition, it will be necessary to put on the table also the poverty and social exclusion that in fact persists among Indigenous communities in the States concerned.

As Joseph Carens' wider corpus is largely focused on the rights of migrants and the unimportance of 'we got here first' claims, it is particularly interesting to see how he proceeds with his analysis of the complex constellation left by colonisation in Fiji (see Carens 1992). People were brought to Fiji from the Indian Subcontinent as indentured labourers when both regions were under British imperial rule. Carens explains that this was done because, to preserve 'Native Fijian' culture, the British administration had blocked the employment of Indigenous Fijians. This meant that labour needed to be sought from elsewhere (Carens 1992, p. 561). According to the most recent census data (from 2007), around half of the population on the Fijian islands is of Indigenous Fijian descent (56.8 per cent, referred to here as 'Native Fijians'), and about one-third of Subcontinent descent (37.5 per cent, referred to here as 'Indian Fijians').[3] And indigeneity is used as an argument for special protections for Native Fijians and Native Fijian culture. In his paper, Carens describes how controversial laws still restricted the land ownership rights of Indian Fijians and gave special political powers to the Fijian Council of Chiefs (for example Carens 1992, p. 596). Carens observes that the Fijian case is one full of 'moral complexities and ambiguities' with much wider implications, demonstrating both conflicting justice claims and conflicting intuitive sympathies (Carens 1992, p. 577). Liberalism was not designed to deal with the aftermath of colonisation, and indeed in its modern reinvention it was directly and explicitly part of the legitimation of the colonial projects (e.g. Losurdo 2014). This does not mean that it cannot be used in new ways, but to do so will require acknowledgement of the existing problems and much reframing work.

Interestingly, Carens supports a set of policies providing special protections to Native Fijians, protecting their way of life linked to the geography of Fiji. His argument does not rest in indigeneity per se, but rather in vulnerability, and that there is nowhere else where such persons could live out their cultural practices. Others contest this analysis because of the weight it puts on authenticity (e.g. Johnson 2002) and the ethnically-based restrictions it causes to those of Subcontinent heritage. Irrespective of whether one agrees or not with Carens on his appraisal of the Fijian case, this case is symbolic of the contentions that arise when considering Indigenous rights within a liberal framework. The Fijian case is particularly important to consider because the Indian Fijians and the Native Fijians, and their ancestors, have all been victims of the colonial regime. As such, the case allows us to consider whether there are Indigenous claims even without any recall to historic injustices between the groups directly involved.

Lindsey Kingston draws attention to the claims of members of Indigenous groups in her discussion of statelessness – and does so in the context of consent and vulnerability rather than indigeneity. She notes that:

> several groups – including many members of Europe's Roma community and some Indigenous nations – reject state citizenship. These marginalized communities are often ignored by scholars and advocates who only consider one type of inclusion: formal citizenship.
>
> (Kingston 2014, p. 134)

For her, it is key to the difficulty she describes that some groups, including some identifying as Indigenous peoples, do not 'conform to the state model' (Kingston 2014, p. 133). This chapter takes the worry further, to propose that citizenship regimes, in their assumption of binarity and mutual exclusivity, can in fact actively exclude, disenfranchise and subdue political claims of members of such groups through the giving and withholding of State membership, and the constructing and controlling of the structures of Indigenous groups themselves, including deciding on the status of their own citizenship regimes (e.g. see Turner 2003; Simpson 2008). That is, State citizenship can be experienced as stifling, rather than only emancipatory and empowering.

In some cases, the conflict may be based around a group's nonconformity to State-like structure as Kingston suggests above, but irrespective of a group's own structure, conflict may also be based upon an objection to colonisation that has created the currently existing State system in which some individuals do not have an internationally recognised State with which they consider it appropriate to affiliate, or with which to affiliate solely. Indeed, as Douglas George-Kanentiio puts it, 'Indigenous peoples were entirely isolated from [the process of European state formation] until very recently' (George-Kanentiio 2006). Seeing citizenship in this way also alters the implications of maintaining such a citizenship as the sole form of recognition within the international system and provides another way to understand the privations associated with a lack of a recognised citizenship.

Liberal political theory, like the political structures it theorises, tends to deny Indigenous rights and forces claims to be formulated within the legal framework of the formal State in question (Mörkenstam 2015, p. 9; see also Simpson 2000, p. 119; Turner 2003, p. 233; Turner 2006). In practice, Indigenous groups are constrained to use dominant liberal and other concepts in order to explain their political theoretical ideas (see also Tully 1995, 2000, p. 36) and to do so through institutions run, or at least created, by those working within these same dominant conceptual frameworks, both domestically and internationally. This chapter could itself be accused of forcing the claims of members of Indigenous groups to be framed within a liberal political framework. This is not the intention. The intention here is to use the discourses in Indigenous political theory to critique liberal citizenship assumptions from within that discourse. Members of Indigenous groups are not the only ones to have traditionally been excluded from liberal political thinking. In 2000, Phillip Cole warned that if liberal political theory fails to include the rights of migrants, we have come to the end of political theory (Cole 2000). In the same year, Audra Simpson made a related statement: 'how may a society operate in a just manner without considering the claims of native people and other cultural groups?' (Simpson 2000, p. 113). These worries are not unconnected (something also noted in Walia 2013, for example). Examining the political realities of the claims of members of Indigenous groups can help uncover deeper problems in the nature of dominant State citizenships. As such, it can also help to explain some of the difficulties in the standard theories as they are applied to the diverse and complex phenomenon of statelessness.

Stateless peoples and stateless people

My concern in this chapter is that individual members of groups colonised by existing States in fact suffer current vulnerability and impairment of individual autonomy because of both external beliefs about their membership and individual beliefs about the polity in which they want to participate. That is, I do not want to engage with the meaning of nationhood and the appropriate relationship between this, citizenship and statelessness – an important and challenging analysis of this is presented elsewhere in this book (Tonkiss, this volume). Instead, I am interested in examining the nature of the vulnerability and potential institutional silencing of such individuals within the recognised avenues for expression of the dominant system and what this may imply for the wider discussion of both citizenship and statelessness.

Some of the complexities in this case can be seen, for example, in the discussion surrounding both Nooksack 'disenrollment' – referring to individuals who are 'disenrolled' from tribal membership against their will – and 'disenrollment' more generally (e.g. see detailed analysis in Galanda and Dreveskracht 2015). The Nooksack Tribal Territory spans parts of both British Columbia in Canada and Washington in the US. Since 1998, the Tribe's governing body has made efforts to remove membership from some people (e.g. see Galanda and Dreveskracht 2015, the authors of which have provided legal representation for the disenrollees). This is reported to have been done in various ways: in direct racial terms relating to blood quantum (many of those threatened with disenrollment are reported to be of mixed Nooksack and Filipino heritage), in relation to historical discrepancies in the original grant of Tribal membership and connections with organised crime (e.g. Cabrera 2000). Those contesting the disenrollment are reported to see it as a way to remove political opposition from the electorate and as causing a serious harm to the individuals affected (e.g. Wilkins 2013). Commentators bemoan the current lack of an effective remedy for individuals threatened with disenrollment (e.g. Galanda and Dreveskracht 2015). This seems similar to the problem of denationalisations globally, including the loss of State citizenships, which have been notoriously difficult and slow to contest, even when they give rise to statelessness.

The discussions arising from this are useful in trying to understand the contemporary role of Tribal citizenships and their interaction with State citizenships. In a 2013 Nooksack Tribal Court judgment, the statement of the Judge, as quoted by scholar David Wilkins at the time, is particularly interesting in helping to identify problems in dominant perceptions of statelessness. He cites her as stating that the loss of tribal membership is 'a fundamentally different proceeding than a loss of United States' citizenship'. Wilkins reports that she goes on to explain that:

> A person who is disenrolled from her tribe loses access to the privileges of tribal membership, but she is not stateless. While she loses the right, for example, to apply for and obtain tribal housing through the Tribe, her ability to obtain housing in general is unaffected. Though she loses the right to vote in tribal elections, she does not lose the right to vote in federal, state, and local elections. While the impact on the disenrollee is serious and detrimental, it is not akin to becoming stateless.
>
> (Wilkins 2013)

Conversely, as several contributors to this current volume have argued, it is not possible to resolve the problems associated with statelessness by simply granting every person just any citizenship. This is because what is problematic about statelessness is not the absence of citizenship, but the loss of rights and political being that is associated with statelessness. In this case, then, the fact that US citizenship is recognised and dominates Nooksack membership does not mean that the problem of statelessness is absent when a person loses his or her principal political membership. For individuals wholly embracing US citizenship and seeing Nooksack status as a minority membership within that, the quoted statements of the judge are correct. Their loss of tribal membership is of much less importance than the loss of US citizenship would be. However, for individuals that consider Nooksack membership to be an important, primary, or even only, political identity, the privations associated with the loss of Nooksack membership look more serious.

The notions of 'stateless peoples' and 'stateless people' are closely interconnected. The key problematisation presented here derives from institutional set-ups that force individuals to choose between, on the one hand, statelessness or aspects of statelessness in the international system, and on the other, capitulation to what may be considered to be colonial citizenship, which in turn might be seen by some to detract from struggles for group autonomy, thus potentially forcing some people to act counter to their political convictions. This is not to suggest that all or even most members of Indigenous groups reject the citizenship of settler States – indeed members of Indigenous communities are active citizens of the US and for example serve in the US army in large numbers. In 2013 0.7 per cent of the entire veteran population was composed of individuals identified as American Indians or Alaskan Natives (United States Department of Veterans Affairs 2015, p. 5). And it is also not to ignore the many innovative ways in which members of Indigenous groups must negotiate their many political memberships, including both claiming and rejecting aspects of citizenships (e.g. consider the Dakota Access Pipeline protests at the time of writing: Hayes 2016; Meyer 2016; Sammon 2016). This chapter observes that such conflicts can and do arise.

Crucially, the discourse relating to the members of all such groups in some way shares problematics in terms of the mismatch between an individual's sense of belonging and the forms of externally *recognised* political memberships available to him or her. The questions these struggles raise (and the solutions that individuals have found) challenge the logic of existing State-based political groupings as the only forms of political enfranchisement and assumptions that memberships need to be mutually excluding. The early instruments relating to statelessness saw it as a problem of the same sort as dual citizenship. They aimed to allocate to every person one and only one citizenship to avoid the challenge to existing structures that would otherwise arise. The question of Indigenous people's citizenships and struggles must be understood within this context – and provides an important counterpoint to it.

Fending off citizenship

Initial engagements between European and Indigenous societies that led to today's liberal democratic settler States can be seen to have three conflicting underlying assumptions.[4] First, there has been the idea that colonised territories were uninhabited lands before European colonisation, nullifying the land claims of those who were already living there by simply ignoring their existence.[5] Second, those lands were acknowledged to be inhabited, but colonisation was seen as legitimised by the different moral worth of the persons living there, or of their cultures. Related, colonisation was presented as a civilising tool. Third, relations of European colonial powers with the colonised peoples were developed in the same way as they were with other foreign powers.[6] This latter gave rise to treaties and agreements that were seen as sitting within international rather than domestic law (for the American context, see detailed study in Deloria and Wilkins 1999). These three ways of characterising what was happening at the time of colonisation gave rise to different ways of trying to justify the violence that took place and takes place today. They also (even if implicitly) affect contemporary liberal discourses in this area in ways that need to be examined.

The US context is vast and experiences across the territories and over time are varied. However, the Federal move towards converting persons from subjects of foreign powers to citizens of the US took place particularly towards the end of the nineteenth century. The 1887 Dawes Act[7] introduced the infamous 'Allotment Policy', which gave Indigenous individuals land that had previously been held in common by national groups in exchange for US citizenship. This is often seen as part of an intentional policy both to break up national groups and to push individuals to adopt the ideology of individual ownership and citizenship of the United States. It is also seen as a key starting point in the efforts in the United States 'to impose citizenship on Indians', with one lawyer adding, '[i]n the process, it opened up 100 million acres of Indian land for expropriation' (Michaels 1998, p. 1576). The 1924 Indian Citizenship Act[8] then imposed US citizenship upon all remaining noncitizen Indigenous individuals who were born within the territory of the United States. The way in which this citizenship was imposed raises questions for the meanings of citizenship more broadly.

It can sometimes be difficult for theorists in the liberal tradition to examine citizenship divorced from the mythology of emancipation surrounding its development. Examining the Indigenous experience of citizenship in the examples given here is, therefore, illuminating since the history of modern citizenship for Indigenous people in settler States is different from its history for the settler communities in those States and in Europe. For the settlers in America, citizenship represented a breaking away from subjection to a monarch and a deeply hierarchical system of government and society. The new forms of political membership in France, for example, have been described as born of nationality, blood, family and land, and so in direct rejection of serfdom (Weil 2008, p. 25). The Indigenous peoples discussed here did not share this history.

That is, 'Native peoples saw no need to be emancipated from a feudal, medieval social order they had never experienced' (Witkin 1995, p. 355). To the settler population in America, citizenship represented freedom from the Crown and from a system in which wealth was directed upwards and the productive work was carried out by those least well remunerated for it. It represented a new form of equal ownership of society and self-rule through the *demos*. For the Indigenous population, citizenship was more complex. Initially largely excluded from it, even when it was allowed and then imposed, it formed part of a subjection to a colonial system within which had been developed a new system of racialised hierarchy and of imposition of power. Contemporary citizenship needs to be seen against this backdrop. It is vital for theorists to take Indigenous experiences and analyses of settler citizenship seriously, since without doing so not only are individual members of Indigenous groups forced to bear the burden of a system that struggles to acknowledge their claims, but the system itself is impoverished, and worse. This is not to suggest any idealised notion of the Indigenous societies in question either before or after colonisation, but only to recognise different experiences of the initial coming of modern State citizenship.

Not only was American citizenship itself experienced in some cases as a tool of political subjection, the forced granting of citizenship also had implications for systems of rights that had been negotiated between Indigenous peoples and settler States. As Chief Clinton Rickard emphasises in his autobiography, and in the quotation given at the head of this chapter, the worry was that it would not make sense for citizens to be in a treaty relationship with their State of citizenship. That is, he feared that rights that had been negotiated in treaties would be nullified. Before the 1924 Citizenship Act, one commentator observes of one group that '[t]he leaders knew it would be impossible for the Haudenosaunee to sustain a formal treaty with the United States if they accepted citizenship in what they saw as an alien nation' (George-Kannentiio 2006, p. 27). Eleanor Roosevelt, wife of US President Theodore Roosevelt, was a long-time campaigner for the rights of Indigenous people in the US, so it is interesting to follow a shift that Laurence Hauptman traces in her thinking (Hauptman 1999). He argues that while initially she saw citizenship as a means to accessing rights and empowerment, she later changed her mind, writing in her regular newspaper column: 'under the guise of giving them the right to citizenship, we are allowing predatory interests, sometimes state interests, sometimes groups or individuals to despoil their lands' (quoted in Hauptman 1999, p. 7).

The reality of Indigenous citizenship of settler States demonstrates, then, that in fact, '[c]itizenship is not as many other memberships voluntary' (Hammar 1986, p. 740). That is, in the cases discussed, decisions about citizenship are taken by a State and not by an individual. This is seen both in the campaigns of individuals to obtain citizenship and the attempts of others to reject it. And it provides an important perspective on statelessness. The fact of involuntary citizenship, and of citizenship as the only means to avoid substantial privation, risks undermining the voluntary notion of liberal citizenship more generally. It also suggests that if the imposition of citizenship is sometimes experienced as disenfranchising, perhaps claiming noncitizenship within the recognised system of States could be seen as an empowered political step, raising important weaknesses in the existing system.

Lacrosse and the challenge of borders

The Six Nations Iroquois Confederacy, also known as The Haudenosaunee Confederacy (e.g. Simpson 2000, p. 127; Marques 2011, p. 385), includes peoples located in what is now Southeastern Canada and the Northeastern United States (Cayuga, Mohawk, Oneida, Onondaga, Seneca and Tuscarora peoples). The Haudenosaunee Confederacy describes itself as a peaceful league of nations that has existed for generations, with its current elected governance structure adopted in 1924.[9] In response to the passing of the 1924

Indian Citizenship Act, the Haudenosaunee Confederacy sent a letter to the US government stating that they were not, had never been and did not intend to become, American citizens, a position still held by the organisation, and periodically reaffirmed (Witkin 1995, p. 380). The use of this case is not intended to denigrate the struggles of other groups, but to take advantage of the wealth of literature available around the Haudenosaunee case and the symbolism of the acts of their lacrosse team.

The Iroquois National team is recognised as a full member of the Federation of International Lacrosse.[10] In 2010, the Men's World Lacrosse Championship was held in Manchester, UK. The Iroquois team was predicted to do very well (indeed, in the championships since then in which they have been able to compete, both Men and Women Iroquois National teams have finished in the top three).[11] However, in 2010, the players did not make it to the tournament. They were prevented from travelling on Haudenosaunee travel documents and were not willing to take up Canadian or US passports, purportedly noting that as they would be competing against the US and Canadian national teams it did not make sense to travel on US or Canadian travel documents (Marques 2011, p. 385) and that they felt it important to ensure that their sovereign passports be recognised (Haygood 2010). In the same year, another set of travellers who had been able to leave Canada on Haudenosaunee travel documents in fact found themselves blocked from re-entry to Canada (see Horn 2010). Far from representing a lack of relationship with the system of States and the US and Canada, this challenging of the border can perhaps be seen as another dimension of the 'new ways of "being political"' found in the literature on 'the politics of movement', which contests existing State and State-citizenship frameworks (Nyers and Rygiel 2012; Isin 2002).

The Haudenosaunee passport was first used for travel to the League of Nations in 1923 and its modern form has been used since 1977, though the reaction of border forces to it has been inconsistent (e.g. Marques 2011, pp. 388, 390; see also Hill 2015). In the US, this has been further complicated since the 2004 Intelligence Reform and Terrorism Prevention Act[12] came into force (e.g. see Haygood 2010; Kingston 2011) which, in 2008, led to a rule changing the acceptable format for identity documents. In response, the Haudenosaunee Confederacy:

> expressed concern that the proposed rule would necessarily and unintentionally interfere with and undermine the ability of the Haudenosaunee to document the identity and citizenship of its people. They also expressed concern that the proposed rule would interfere with the aboriginal and treaty rights to freely pass the international border without burdensome costly documentation requirements.
>
> (Federal Register Publications 2007)

In fact, as Lindsey Kingston observed in 2011, Haudenosaunee passports *were* found not to meet the requirements (Kingston 2011), and although alterations have since been made (Hill 2015), as of November 2016 the Confederacy website states that it cannot guarantee that the documents will be accepted by US border guards.[13] Since 2010, Haudenosaunee lacrosse players' experiences have been mixed. In 2012 members of the male under-19 team travelled to Finland on Haudenosaunee passports,[14] while in 2015 members of the female under-19 team were again unable to travel to the UK on these documents,[15] though this received less coverage than the 2010 case.

At the time of the 2010 Championship the official UK position was that if the Haudenosaunee players were to travel on their own passports, they would need the US and Canada to vouch that they would be allowed to return home after the tournament (Kaplan 2010). No resolution could be reached in time and the team were unable to make it to the tournament (e.g. *The Economist* 2010; Kaplan 2010; see also Kingston 2011). Joe Heath, identified as General Counsel to the Onondaga, one of the nations that make up the Haudenosaunee, is quoted as describing the bureaucracy that would not let them travel as part of a 'racist colonial, assimilationist machine' (*The Economist* 2010). The discussion in this chapter suggests that this incident should indeed be seen within the context of an international system that enables and condones this form of reinforcement of the status quo through the control of citizenship regimes and so limits the potential for individual autonomy and freedom in problematic ways. In this case, the Haudenosaunee lacrosse players were forced either to use the citizenship of a recognised State that they rejected or be outside the system of States and so be unable to travel. This makes the coercion to conform to existing citizenship regimes seem inhibiting rather than empowering. Often the debates around noncitizenship and statelessness focus on contexts in which the individuals concerned are abject and have little choice and little ability to make known their views about the citizenships most likely to be available to them. This case provides a useful counterpoint.

At the same time, borders within the American continents can also be sites where rights *qua* members of Indigenous groups can be both enacted and challenged (Simpson 2014, p. 116). Audra Simpson has written widely about this zone of contestation, and describes how she personally is forced to define herself at borders (e.g. Simpson 2000). In one anecdote, she explains that on her way from Montreal to Brooklyn, and despite having shown her card which demonstrates her membership of a group with the right to cross freely at this border, she was asked many unnecessary questions. This included the comment that she should apply for a green card. Simpson retells the exchange (Simpson 2014, p. 119):

> 'Look, I was born down there; I don't need a green card; I'm not an immigrant; I am part of a *First Nation*, and this is the card that proves it!'
>
> Upon hearing this [the border guard's] posture completely changed, she pushed my card to me, and said, 'Well then, *you* are an American.'
>
> To which I said, '*No*, I am not, *I am a Mohawk*.'

Simpson goes on to describe how the border guard reacted aggressively to this exchange, and how Simpson herself felt drained by the contestation of her own citizenship that it symbolised. The assumption that there is only one real system of citizenship and rights operating (the one which includes Canada and the US) and the difficulty Simpson experiences in being heard within it reinforces the need to question the assumed centrality of State citizenship in rights-claiming in liberal political theory. And the literature is littered with similar examples (e.g. see Marques 2011, p. 392; Nyers 2011, p. 4).

The border also helps to illustrate the nature of the power relationships involved between political entities. The 2004 Act mentioned above requires that identity documents must pass certain US-imposed security standards in order to be accepted at border posts. On one hand, and based on certain understandings of sovereignty and duty to citizens, this is fair enough. It subjects everyone to the same checks at border posts. But the Haudenosaunee case helps to highlight something else that is in play (and which reaches beyond the experience of border-crossers and of Haudenosaunee). That is, no matter what members of the Haudenosaunee think of their passports and the security needs in their territories, in the end they must be recognised by States within the international system of States in order to have clout. In relation to law enforcement, Simpson observes a perpetuation of 'the notion that there are actually only *two* legitimate political regimes in play – Canada and the United States' (Simpson 2008, p. 196; sepa-rately, see the discussion of the US/Mexico border in Luna-Firebaugh 2002). The control of the use of State citizenship (and the difficulties put in place for those choosing not to use State citizenship) is an important part of this.

The border, then, is important in constructing the political relationships in ways that go beyond the border itself. The rejection of US citizenship, even if only in some spheres, and the affirmation of the political membership of an entity that is not recognised as a State within the State system, both chal-lenge the wider assumption that noncitizenship, and statelessness within that system, must necessarily be seen as forms of disenfranchisement. As in other cases discussed in this book, this case suggests that the problems associated with noncitizenship and statelessness, such as the inability to move, are not problems with statelessness or noncitizenship per se, but with the reaction to the challenge that being stateless makes to the existing system of States that relies upon its own ability completely to assign all people to one and only one recognised State.

Binarity and mutual exclusivity

As was argued above, the pervasive modern form of citizenship was developed particularly in Europe. It grew into its contemporary form in the period after the First World War, through the League of Nations (e.g. Anderson 1991; see also Hammar 1986, p. 735). Citizenship emerged as a means of dividing up the world's people, with membership of a State and of a nation largely, but not always, coinciding (Hammar 1986, pp. 741, 743). Once this mode of organising identities and rights is replicated worldwide as the only official global system, it becomes largely necessary for individuals to be members of a modern recognised State in order to be represented on the world stage and in order to claim access to the modern internationally recognised sets of rights and protections. As such, 'Nations and nationalities seem very much obligatory categories of modern space and modern political subjectivity, respectively' (Biolsi 2005, p. 239). Crucially, it is also largely membership of such a political entity that gives people and peoples 'a seat at the table of the community of nations' (Biolsi 2005, p. 240). That said, though, Indigenous groups have managed to establish alternative routes to recognition and voice, leading to the creation, for example, of the UN Working Group on Indigenous Populations and the 2007 Indigenous Declaration which aimed to alleviate this exclusion from international systems (e.g. see OHCHR 2013), as well as through resistance and protest.

Despite this, within this State-driven structure individuals' memberships and entitlements in a 'nation within' inside the borders of a State generally need to be constructed using frameworks acceptable to that dominant State's institutions. This is something highlighted by lawyers (e.g. Michaels 1998) and throughout the discourse relating to the definition of Indigenous membership (e.g. Turner 2003; Barcham 2000, p. 144). Indigeneity is forced then to be constructed either/both as sufficiently *within* settler culture to serve settler interests, or/and as sufficiently *other* to be recognised as Indigenous, using racial criteria including the 'blood quantum', and other ethnic criteria (e.g. see Simpson 2014, p. 138, 2008, p. 207, 2000; Osburn 2000; Barcham 2000). Eileen Luna-Firebaugh goes further, arguing that in constructing a border between two recognised States that goes through territories where Indigenous people live, and constructing the identities of those now living within those now distinct territories, settler States have even sometimes created new distinct membership groupings, including creating what has become two peoples where once there was only one (Luna-Firebaugh 2002, p. 161). Homi Bhabha's classic 1983 piece, 'The Other Question ...' presents this constructing of the 'other' in a fixed, non-evolving way, as an important feature of colonial discourse more generally. What Bhabha calls 'fixity' (Bhabha 1983, p. 18) is found throughout the work of theorists in this area; though differing from Bhabha in a complex constellation of ways, the core concern is that an 'other' non-State membership within the liberal framework of States ends up being defined in a fixed and simplistic way so that people are constrained in how they can live out their lives, making it more difficult, for example, for people to be recognised in their claiming of multiple and changing political and other identities. Binarity in questions of membership and citizenship is problematic because of the complicated range of ways in which individuals in fact relate with existing States, not least in navigating the effects of colonisation.

In the case of urban Maori, Manuhuia Barcham observes that 'definitions of Maori and other Fourth World peoples are, more often than not, derived from notions of indigeneity contingent upon the possession of "authentic" cultural norms and traditions.' (Barcham 2000, pp. 139, 140). The 'authenticity' comes to be defined as external and fixed rather than organic, as part of a lived and vital reality. And rights to self-determination are thereby required to be constructed as based on something inhering in ethnicity rather than in individual interests in it or in individual autonomy, liberty and/or equality. This has serious implications. It forces Indigenous cultures to appear 'backward' and inflexible, their rights-claiming to seem ethno-nationalist in a way that has been rejected by much contemporary liberal political theory.

Barcham goes on: 'Western metaphysics has a long history of structuring reality in terms of dichotomies and binary oppositions', with one of the pair defined positively and the other negatively, the second as 'the absence of the first' (citizen, non-citizen; authentic, inauthentic) (Barcham 2000, p. 147). This can be seen in the efforts to eradicate both statelessness and dual citizenship in the same breath. As such, urban Maoris, as presented by Barcham, for example, do not fit comfortably into the binaries available (Indigenous/not indigenous; modern/traditional) and so their rights both as Maoris and as New Zealanders are difficult to claim. Indigenous people wanting to claim rights within a majority State, *qua* members of an Indigenous group, must navigate a path between being at the same time sufficiently 'other' and operating within State political and legal systems. There is often pressure to be seen as a minority within a hegemonic State, inhibiting the recognised means by which to contest that State and the State system.

These complications are perhaps best seen in the statement of one lawyer in the US who notes that Indigenous persons seeking legal training in order to defend rights within the American system have to contend with much conflict. He writes: 'To some, becoming a member of the Bar and swearing to uphold the Constitution are unacceptable and tantamount to treason' (Michaels 1998, p. 1583). That is, the problem here is that within States as they are currently constructed, in order to claim rights one must reinforce the status quo. This is more entrenched than just the situation in one or another country alone. The international discourse relating to citizenship, noncitizenship and statelessness means that it is difficult to envisage more nuanced relationships with States. In reality, it seems that political engagement of Indigenous individuals within settler States is complex and multidimensional and that many individuals are comfortably citizens of settler States while also navigating their other memberships and contesting aspects of both. Apart from engagement with settler States and Indigenous National groups, individuals may relate to global, regional and provincial governmental and membership structures as well as urban political entities (Barcham 2000). They may also engage politically as members of other groups, such as women, disabled persons, or workers, for example. Studying the complexity of individuals' political engagement makes clear the bluntness of State citizenship alone as a tool of rights protection, both in this context and more broadly.

Conclusions

While it is vital that in our modern world everyone has access to some recognised State citizenship, it is also vital that people should be able to contest such citizenships without losing access to rights as a result. As the cases discussed here make clear, people have rational and political reasons to reject a particular citizenship, or to reject using it in some situations. If, however, this is the case and, as has been shown, people in fact reject the use of State citizenships in situations where their own capabilities are impaired as a result, it is essential to re-examine both the assumption that citizenship of a recognised State is unambiguously desirable and the coercion that the privations associated with statelessness impose upon individuals to take up citizenships. This reiterates the urgency of serious efforts, alongside those to ensure *access* to some State citizenship for everyone, to ensure rights irrespective of citizenship status or lack thereof, allowing people to take up or to reject citizenships consensually.

This chapter makes three recommendations for both theorists and policy makers in order to make both discourse and policy more just. First, citizenship in one of the internationally officially recognised States needs to be less crucial for rights protection and legal personhood. Today, rejecting a recognised State citizenship often carries with it a significant penalty, as can be seen in the case, for example, of the restrictions on movement of the members of the Iroquois National Lacrosse Team. Second, it needs to be easier legally both to acquire and to reject recognised citizenships so that citizenship can regain a democratic and emancipatory element, which can only make sense if it is grounded in the freedom of all either to accept or reject it. At root, though, this chapter calls, third, for a reconsideration of the meaning of citizenship through an acknowledgement of statelessness, and a reconceptualisation based on the acknowledgement of very different experiences of liberal democratic citizenship regimes.

Notes

1 Thank you (in alphabetical order) to Daniele Botti, Phillip Cole, Andrew Marsh, Janina Pescinski, Katherine Tonkiss, David Wilkins and Susan Williams for their careful reading of earlier versions of this chapter, and for their helpful comments. Thank you also to all those who participated in the animated discussion and probing questioning following the presentation of a version of this chapter at the 2015 ECPR General Conference held in August at Université de Montréal, Canada. The errors that remain are my own.

2 A useful discussion of the terminology here is provided in Wilkins and Stark 2011, p. xvii. They adopt 'Indigenous' for collectives but 'Indians' and 'American Indians' for individuals. In this short chapter I will stick with the one term, 'Indigenous', though acknowledging that it is problematic.

3 Fiji Bureau of Statistics online Population and Demography resource, www.statsfiji. gov.fj/index.php/social/9-social-statistics/social-general/113-population-and-demography (Accessed 7 March 2016).

4 This is quite simplistic. For a much deeper analysis see (Wilkins and Lomawaima 2001; Wilkins 2003).

5 It was only in 1992 that Australian courts saw a landmark decision that overturned the doctrine that Australia was *terra nullius* at the point of settlement by Europeans. This was a historically important decision in the context of the issues raised in this chapter, since it showed that Eddie Mabo, a Torres Strait Islander, maintained, with his group, proprietary rights over their land because they held such title before contact and it had never been passed to Australia by any treaty or recognised exchange.

6 For a list of treaties between the US government and Native American groups, see the Avalon Project of the Yale University Law School: http://avalon.law.yale.edu/subject_menus/ntreaty.asp (Accessed 5 April 2016).

7 Text of the 1887 Dawes Act (including facsimile of the original) is available here: www.ourdocuments.gov/doc.php?flash=true&doc=50 (Accessed 8 March 2016).

8 Text of the 1924 Indian Citizenship Act (including a facsimile of the original) is available here: www.archives.gov/global-pages/larger-image.html?i=/historical-docs/doc-content/images/indian-citizenship-act-1924-l.jpg&c=/historical-docs/doc-content/images/indian-citizenship-act-1924.caption.html (Accessed 8 March 2016).

9 Website of the Haudenosaunee Confederacy: www.haudenosauneeconfederacy.com (Accessed 8th November 2016).

10 List of Members of the Federation of International Lacrosse: http://filacrosse.com/members-by-type/ (Accessed 8 November 2016).

11 Official World Lacrosse Rankings: http://filacrosse.com/world-rankings/ (Accessed 8 November 2016).

12 www.nctc.gov/docs/irtpa.pdf (Accessed 8 November 2016).

13 www.haudenosauneeconfederacy.com/hdc.html (Accessed 8 November 2016).

14 http://indiancountrytodaymedianetwork.com/2012/07/07/iroquois-nationals-ready-world-lacrosse-championships-finland-121910 (Accessed 8 November 2016).

15 http://indiancountrytodaymedianetwork.com/2015/07/20/passports-rejected-haudeno saunee-womens-lax-withdraws-world-championships-161139 (Accessed 8 November 2016).

References

Anderson, B. (1991) *Imagined Communities.* London: Verso.

Barcham, M. (2000) (De)Constructing the Politics of Indigeneity. In Ivison, D., Patton, P. and Sanders, W. (eds) *Political Theory and the Rights of Indigenous Peoples*, pp. 137–151. Cambridge: Cambridge University Press.

Bhabha, H. K. (1983) The Other Question…. *Screen*, 24(6), pp. 18–36.

Biolsi, T. (2005) Imagined geographies: sovereignty, indigenous space and American Indian struggle. *American Ethnologist*, 32(2), pp. 239–259.

Bishop, J. D. (1997) Locke's theory of original appropriation and the right of settlement in Iroquois Territory. *Canadian Journal of Philosophy*, 27(3), pp. 311–337.

Bloom, T. (forthcoming) *Noncitizenism.* London: Routledge.

Bosniak, L. (2006) *The Citizen and the Alien: Dilemmas of Contemporary Membership.* Princeton: Princeton University Press.

Bruyneel, K. (2004) Challenging American boundaries: indigenous people and the 'gift' of US citizenship. *Studies in American Political Development*, 18(1), pp. 30–43.

Cabrera, L. (2000) Nooksacks allege Filipino family has conquered tribe from inside. *Los Angeles Times*, 15 October 2000.

Carens, J. (1992) Democracy and respect for difference: the case of Fiji. *University of Michigan Journal of Law Reform*, 25(3–4), pp. 547–632.

Cole, P. (2000) *Philosophies of Exclusion: Liberal Political Theory and Immigration.* Edinburgh: Edinburgh University Press.

Deloria, V. and Wilkins, D. E. (1999) *Tribes, Treaties, & Constitutional Tribulations.* Austin, TX: University of Texas Press.

Economist, The (2010) The Iroquois and their passports: unfair play. *The Economist*, 22 July 2010.

Federal Register Publications (2007) Card Format Passport; Changes to Passport Fee Schedule [72 FR 74169] [FR 74–07].

Galanda, G. S. and Dreveskracht, R. D. (2015) Curing the tribal disenrollment epidemic: in search of a remedy. *Arizona Law Review*, 57(2).

George-Kannentiio, D. M. (2006) *Iroquois on Fire: A Voice From the Mohawk Nation*. Westport: Praeger.

Goldie, M. (2015) Locke and America. In Stuart, M. (2015) *A Companion to Locke*. London: Blackwell.

Hall, C. (2002) *Civilising Subjects: Metropole and Colony in the English Imagination 1830–1867*. Cambridge: Polity.

Hammar, T. (1986) Citizenship: membership of a nation and of a state. *International Migration*, 24(4), pp. 735–748.

Hauptman, L. M. (1999) Eleanor Roosevelt and the American Indian: The Iroquois as a case study. *The Hudson Valley Regional Review*, 16(1).

Hayes, K. (2016) Why you should be talking about Standing Rock on the eve of the election. *Truthout*, Monday 7 November 2016.

Haygood, W. (2010) Iroquois Nationals lacrosse team asks White House to honor sovereign passports. *Washington Post*, 14 July 2010.

Hill, S. (2015) My six nation Haudenosaunee passport is not a 'fantasy document'. *Guardian*, 30 October 2016.

Horn, Greg (2010) Canada prevents Mohawks from returning home on Haudenosaunee passports. *Kahnawake News*, Tuesday 1 June 2010.

Isin, E. F. (2002) *Being Political: Genealogies of Citizenship*. Minneapolis: University of Minnesota Press.

Johnson, J. (2002) Liberalism and the politics of cultural authenticity. *Politics, Philosophy and Economics*, 1(2), pp. 213–236.

Kaplan, T. (2010) Iroquois defeated by passport dispute. *New York Times*, 16 July 2010.

Kingston, L. (2014) Statelessness as a lack of functioning citizenship. *Tilburg Law Review*, 19(1–2), pp. 127–135.

Kingston, L. (2011) Opting Out of Legal Nationality: Identity, Passports and the Iroquois Nationals Lacrosse Team. *Western Political Science Association*, 2011 Annual Meeting Paper [unpublished].

Kymlicka, W. (2000) American Multiculturalism and the 'Nations Within'. In Ivison, D., Patton, P. and Sanders, W. (eds) *Political Theory and the Rights of Indigenous Peoples*, pp. 216–236. Cambridge: Cambridge University Press.

Locke, J. (1823) *Two Treatises of Government*, Volume V from The Works of John Locke. [online] Available at: http://socserv2.socsci.mcmaster.ca/econ/ugcm/3ll3/locke/government.pdf [Accessed 5 March 2017].

Losurdo, D. (2014) *Liberalism: A Counter-History*, trans. G. Elliott. London: Verso.

Luna-Firebaugh, E. (2002) The border crossed us: border crossing issues of the indigenous peoples of the Americas. *Wicazo Sa Review*, 17(1), pp. 159–181.

Marques, N. T. C. (2011) Divided we stand: the Haudenosaunee, their passport and legal implications of their recognition in Canada and the United States. *San Diego International Law Journal*, 13 (November), pp. 383–426.

Meyer, R. (2016) The legal case for blocking the Dakota access pipeline. *The Atlantic*, 9 September 2016.

Michaels, M. A. (1998) Indigenous ethics and alien laws: native traditions and the United States legal system. *Fordham Law Review*, 66(4), pp. 1565–1584.

Mörkenstam, U. (2015) Recognition as if sovereigns? A procedural understanding of Indigenous self-determination. *Citizenship Studies*, 19(6–7).

Nyers, P. (2011) Alien equality. *Issues in Legal Scholarship*, 9(1), pp. 471–486.

Nyers, P. and Rygiel, K. (2012) *Citizenship, Migrant Activism and the Politics of Movement*. Abingdon: Routledge.

OHCHR (2013) *Indigenous Peoples and the United Nations Human Rights System*. New York and Geneva: United Nations.

Osburn, R. (2000) Problems and solutions regarding indigenous peoples split by international borders. *American Indian Law Review*, 24(2), pp. 471–486.

Rickard, C. (1973) *Fighting Tuscarora: The Autobiography of Chief Clinton Rickard*. Syracuse: Syracuse University Press.

Sammon, A. (2016) A History of Native Americans Protesting the Dakota Access Pipeline. *Mother Jones*, 9 September 2016.

Shachar, A. (2009) *The Birthright Lottery: Citizenship and Global Inequality*. Cambridge: Harvard University Press.

Simpson, A. (2014) *Mohawk Interruptus: Political Life Across the Borders of Settler States*. Durham; London: Duke University Press.

Simpson, A. (2008) Subjects of sovereignty: indigeneity, the revenue rule, and juridics of failed consent. *Law and Contemporary Problems*, 71(3), pp. 191–215.

Simpson, A. (2000) Paths Toward a Mohawk Nation: Narratives of Citizenship and Nationhood in Kahnawake. In Ivison, D., Patton, P. and Sanders, W. (eds) *Political Theory and the Rights of Indigenous Peoples*, pp. 113–136. Cambridge: Cambridge University Press.

Tonkiss, K. (2013) *Migration and Identity in a Post-National World*. Basingstoke: Palgrave Macmillan.

Tully, J. (2000) The Struggles of Indigenous Peoples for and of Freedom. In Ivison, D. Patton, P. and Sanders, W. (eds) *Political Theory and the Rights of Indigenous Peoples*, pp. 36–59. Cambridge: Cambridge University Press.

Tully, J. (1996) Rediscovering America: The Two Treatises and Aboriginal Rights. In Rogers, G. A. J. (ed.) (1996) *Locke's Philosophy: Content and Context*. Oxford: Clarendon Press.

Tully, J. (1995) *Strange Multiplicity: Constitutionalism in an Age of Diversity*. Cambridge: Cambridge University Press.

Tully, J. (1993) *An Approach to Political Philosophy: Locke in Contexts*. Cambridge: Cambridge University Press.

Turner, D. (2006) *This is Not a Peace Pipe: Towards a Critical Indigenous Philosophy*. Toronto: University of Toronto Press.

Turner, D. (2003) Oral Traditions and the Politics of (Mis)recognition. In Walters, A. (ed.) (2003) *American Indian Thought*, pp. 229–238. New York: Wiley.

United States Department of Veterans Affairs (2015) *American Indian and Alaska Native Veterans: 2013 American Community Survey*, May 2015.

Walia, H. (2013) *Undoing Border Imperialism*. Oakland: AK Press.

Weil, P. (2008) *How to be French: Nationality in the Making Since 1789*, trans. C. Porter. London: Duke University Press.

Wilkins, D. (2013) The Disenrollment Disaster: My Citizenship Is Better Than Yours! In *Indian Country Today Media Network*, 7 November 2013. [online] Available at: https:// indiancountrymedianetwork.com/news/opinions/the-disenrollment-disaster-my-citizenship-is-better-than-yours/ [Accessed 9 March 2017].

Wilkins, D. (2003) *The Navajo Political Experience*, Revised Edition. Lanham, MD: Rowman and Littlefield.

Wilkins, D. E. and Lomawaima, K. T. (2001) *Uneven Ground: American Indian Sovereignty and Federal Law*. Norman: University of Oklahoma Press.

Wilkins, D. and Stark, H. K. (2011) *American Indian Politics and the American Political System*, Third Edition. Lanham, MD: Rowman and Littlefield.

Witkin, A. (1995) To silence a drum: the imposition of United States citizenship on native peoples. *Historical Reflections/Réflexions Historiques*, 21(2), pp. 353–383.

Young, I. M. (1989) Polity and group difference: a critique of the ideal of universal citizenship. *Ethics*, 99(2), pp. 250–274.

11 Recognition, nationality, and statelessness

State-based challenges for UNHCR's plan to end statelessness[1]

Kelly Staples

Introduction

This chapter offers a theoretically informed approach to UNHCR's action on statelessness. It aims to assess the plausibility of UNHCR's claim that 'with adequate leadership and effective implementation, statelessness can be ended' (UNHCR 2014a, p. 4). The chapter focuses in particular on the agency's approach to birth registration, documentation, and discrimination, reflecting in each case on the politics of recognition. It considers in particular the situation of some of the states where UNHCR is aware of statelessness and 'risk of statelessness' but lacks reliable data, examining some of their common features and the challenges these pose for eliminating statelessness. The chapter argues in conclusion that understanding statelessness and the potential for limiting it will require us to acknowledge and challenge the myth that the state system can provide for even a basic universality of human status. Statelessness, I argue, is unlikely to be ended in the short or even medium term. State 'fragility' and competition between ethnic and social groups for resources of all kinds continue to be contributory factors to statelessness. Moreover, the proposed solutions, which include reform of nationality laws, ensuring birth registration, and issuing documentation carry their own risks in such contexts. This means not only that efforts to understand and recognise statelessness must continue, but also that those of us concerned with it must think more critically about the 'state' part of statelessness. While some of Arendt's twentieth-century insights are now anachronistic (see Blitz, this volume), the model of statehood which underpins many contemporary accounts of nationality and statelessness is still at odds with the reality in much of the world.

Recognition, nationality, and statelessness

As is well-known by this point in the book, statelessness is defined as the condition of those persons not considered as a national by any state. In this section, I address statelessness, as well as what it can tell us about being considered as a national. In doing so, I draw on the concept of recognition, which has recently been reintroduced to the theory of international politics as a way of articulating the relationship between the individual, state, and state system. Being considered as a national by a state implies a particular type of recognition of the individual by the state. It also entails a specific relationship between the individual and the state, even though the character of this relationship varies enormously between (and often within) states. What has often been seen as so valuable about the state's recognition of individual persons as nationals is the basis of nationality in equality. Hannah Arendt contrasted this with the unpredictability of other forms of recognition based on our more idiosyncratic traits (Arendt 1973, p. 301). More recently, Mervyn Frost has argued that the international society of sovereign states builds on these virtues, providing for global norms and interstate relationships which 'remedy some of the deficiencies' of the state system (Frost 1996, p. 158) in keeping with UNHCR's hopes for 'adequate leadership and effective implantation'.

Statelessness has often been characterised as a major failing of the state system, but it is a failing that is arguably the result of that very system; in particular, of the way that recognition of individuals has come to be organised (see Staples 2012a). The assumption that nationality is a non-discriminatory mode of recognising individual persons, founded in the objectivity of law, is hard to reconcile with the existence of statelessness (see Staples 2012b). One of the first experts on statelessness expressed concern that a strictly formal conception of nationality which ignored its political dimensions would result in 'legal fiction' (Weis 1979, p. 241). A view from international relations instead demonstrates the function of nationality as a tool for discriminating between, and sometimes within, national populations. The ideal of nationality as an objective, equal status under law which provides for the basic protection of all is undermined in practice by the reality that the majority of stateless persons are members of *in situ* stateless populations, and 'consider themselves to be in their own country' (Institute on Statelessness and Inclusion 2014, p. 8). While sovereignty is not an absolute characteristic of the state, it can, in certain circumstances, lead to a situation in which people with an apparently objective claim to be considered nationals of a given state go unrecognised as such. *Recognition* of nationality, then, is a vital aspect of state power. In terms of responding to statelessness, the importance of state recognition makes it difficult for third parties (other states, or international agencies like UNHCR) to determine nationality status, or even to influence states in their nationality law and policy.

Even so, and as Frost and UNHCR assert, there have long been criticisms of states' failures to consider long-established populations as nationals. In some cases, international pressure has been a factor in the acquisition or confirmation by stateless populations of nationality in what they consider to be their own country. In 2008, a solution was found for the formerly stateless Urdu speakers in Bangladesh. After nearly 40 years of exclusion, the disjuncture between nationality law (formally non-discriminatory) and widespread policy discrimination was bridged, resulting in the documentation of approximately a quarter of a million people (UNHCR 2014a, p. 9). UNHCR credits this success to 'sustained community based advocacy, a successful litigation strategy and lobbying for the implementation of court decisions' as well as 'increasing pressure from the international community' and UNHCR liaison (UNHCR 2014a, p. 9). The change was also 'achieved at a time of political transition' and hence 'an opportune moment' (UNHCR 2014a, p. 11). Key in this case were the facts that nationality law in Bangladesh was not itself discriminatory, and that domestic legal institutions were effective.

Where nationality law is itself discriminatory, advocates for the reduction of statelessness should be warier of intervention in the name of the apparently objective entitlement of a stateless minority to that nationality. As already mentioned, considerations of nationality are a matter of (still substantively sovereign) nationality law. And as statelessness has always demonstrated, nationality laws can be limited in their consideration even of populations with strong and exclusive connections to that state. A brief example is illustrative of the sovereign and effective character of even explicitly discriminatory nationality laws. In the Democratic Republic of Congo (DRC), the nationality status of the Banyamulenge (Congolese Tutsis) has been contested since at least 1981, when a previous citizenship law affording nationality to certain categories of person was rescinded. There have also been several waves of exile from the DRC, with Banyamulenge persons fleeing to Rwanda at times of heightened tension. In February 2010, a tripartite agreement between UNHCR and the governments of Rwanda and DRC set out provisions for the return from Rwanda of tens of thousands of Congolese Tutsi refugees.

However, UNHCR intervention into the highly politicised question of where these people belonged did not settle the matter. Suspicions in DRC abounded that the agreement was a cover for the mass migration of Rwandans into the disputed and conflicted Kivu border regions. At the time, International Refugee Rights Initiative made the important point that:

> At the heart of this story is the question of the 'true' citizenship of [...] Congolese refugees [...]. There is no 'true' answer to this question, and certainly not one that can be answered only at a legal level, or that can be imposed from outside.
>
> (2011, p. 28)

This case is not unique. The belief that it is possible to objectively determine a person or group's nationality and proper place, independent of their recognition as nationals by the state, has had devastating consequences in other cases, for example the repatriation by UNHCR of stateless Rohingya refugees to Myanmar between 1992 and 1995, now widely held to have been problematic (Human Rights Watch 1996). When a regime shows unambiguously that it does not consider members of a minority group to be its own nationals, it seems dangerous (as Human Rights Watch noted back in 1996) for UNHCR or anyone else to expect 'the government to assume "ultimate responsibility"' for their safety (Human Rights Watch 1996, no page).

As Katja Swider's chapter in this volume notes, statelessness and the protection of human rights are not (in principle or in specific cases) necessarily in tension. Indeed, human rights are in principle universal, rather than contingent on nationality status, and as she astutely notes, it may be counter-productive to reassert the fundamental importance of nationality. The reality remains, however, that in much of the world, nationality is – as a matter of fact – a condition for the protection of fundamental rights. Furthermore, the vulnerabilities of many (though not all) stateless groups demonstrate the extent to which the protection of human rights remains contingent on recognition. Swider's account does clearly demonstrate the moral hazards of forcing particular stateless persons to acquire a nationality against their will, in particular where their rights would be less protected after acquisition. Certainly, in some instances, remaining stateless will be preferable to acquiring a nationality. Indeed, the cases briefly discussed above demonstrate that the demands of order can be at odds with the demands of justice when it comes to the allocation of individuals to states. It has sadly not been uncommon for third parties to encourage states to grant or confirm nationality to populations in respect of whose members the relevant authorities are unwilling to confer even a basic respect.[2] It is hard in such cases not to see the grant or confirmation of nationality as the kind of 'legal fiction' Weis warned against.

This section of the chapter has briefly sketched the central and constitutive role of recognition on nationality, and the particularist (and hence limited) ordering logic of the practice of nationality. It has also tried to argue that attempts to formalise the ties of specific individuals and groups to particular states can be at odds with the interests of the affected persons, or – perhaps more troublingly – even at odds with the willingness or ability of relevant authorities to recognise them as a national. The search for truth and finality in confirming the nationality of individuals and groups that are stateless or whose nationality status is unclear can reflect an ordering logic (knowing for sure who, in the final analysis, belongs where) that created and aggravates statelessness (cf. Tonkiss, this volume). Ambiguities and complexities in nationality are a reality of the world as it is currently organised, and cannot easily be eliminated. It is with this awareness that we must consider approaches to statelessness.

The concept of statelessness

In 2014, UNHCR unveiled its new Global Action Plan on Statelessness. The Plan outlines ten actions to end statelessness, and makes the claim that with 'adequate leadership and effective implementation', statelessness can be ended within a decade' (UNHCR 2014b, p. 4). Action 1 aims at the resolution of 'existing major situations of statelessness'. Action 2 aims to 'ensure that no child is born stateless'. Action 3 is directed at removing 'gender discrimination from nationality laws'. Action 4's objective is to prevent 'denial, loss or deprivation of nationality on discriminatory grounds'. Action 5 aims to prevent statelessness in cases of state succession. Action 6 seeks to 'grant protection status to stateless migrants and facilitate their naturalization'. Action 7 is aimed at ensuring 'birth registration for the prevention of statelessness'. Action 8 is concerned with issuing 'nationality documentation to those with entitlement to it'. Action 9 promotes accession to the UN Statelessness Conventions (the 1954 Convention on the Status of Stateless Persons and the 1961 Convention on the Reduction of Statelessness). The final action, action 10, aims to 'improve quantitative and qualitative data on stateless populations'.

Before exploring a few selected aspects of the Plan, it is worth addressing the background context. In 2010, an expert meeting convened by UNHCR adopted what are now commonly called the Prato conclusions. The Conclusions addressed the concept of stateless persons, paying close attention to the importance of law in constituting nationality. Of particular interest was the acknowledgement that nationality is not always conferred *ex lege* (by operation of law). The Conclusions state that 'in the case of non-automatic modes of acquisition, a person should not be treated as a "national" where the mechanism of acquisition has not been completed' (UNHCR 2010, p. 4). It is also noted that when it comes to the determination by a third party of whether a person is stateless, 'the test is whether a person is considered as a national at the time the case is examined and not whether he or she might be able to acquire the nationality in the future' (UNHCR 2010, p. 3). This has the benefit of acknowledging both the importance and complexity and ambiguity of legal recognition as a source of nationality and of protection against statelessness. Nationality law, like all law, is an exercise in interpretation (Dworkin 1982, p. 179) on the part of relevant authorities.

Perhaps more importantly, the Conclusions record the necessity of identifying *which* authorities in a given state are 'competent to establish/confirm nationality' (UNHCR 2010, p. 3). In subsequent guidelines, UNHCR has further clarified that:

> Some States have a single, centralized body that governs nationality issues that would constitute the competent authority for the purposes of an analysis of nationality status. Other States, however, have several authorities that can determine nationality, any one of which might be considered a competent authority depending on the circumstances. Thus, it is not necessary that a competent authority be a central State body. A local or regional administrative body can be a competent authority as can a consular official and in many cases low-level local government officials will constitute the competent authority. The mere possibility that the decision of such an official can later be overridden by a senior official does not in itself exclude the former from being treated as a competent authority.
>
> (UNHCR 2012, paragraph 21)

This is a further welcome development insofar as it directly acknowledges the importance of local juridico-political contexts in seeking confirmation of nationality when it is unclear and where statelessness is a possibility.

These developments in UNHCR's approach to nationality and statelessness have gone a considerable way to acknowledging the role of, and limits to, nationality law, in providing for nationality. The Global Action Plan, launched with much fanfare in 2014, identifies several risk factors for statelessness. It notes that 'individuals can be *at risk of* statelessness if they have difficulties proving that they have links to a state' (my emphasis), and that 'lack of birth registration can create such a risk' (UNHCR 2014b, p. 18), particularly 'where it is likely in the specific context that nationality may be questioned' (UNHCR 2014b, p. 20). The term 'at risk of statelessness' might be seen as a logical development of the outcomes of the Prato expert meeting, including the 2012 guidelines. It has the advantage of acknowledging the ambiguities of nationality and statelessness, which can't always be determined in the abstract. The concept of being at risk of statelessness also allows for early interventions aimed at *making the claim* to nationality and securing meaningful identification with the state. However, in other ways, the Plan reflects a more simplistic relationship between legal reform, non-discrimination, and the reduction of statelessness. Going forward, I outline some reasons for scepticism about UNHCR's claims about ending statelessness, particularly in relation to states facing other challenges. I narrow the focus to the provisions of the Global Action Plan for preventing discrimination, and ensuring birth registration and the provision of nationality documentation, as well as making some observations about the relationship between these. The primary emphasis, then, is on actions 4, 7, and 8.

Registration and documentation

Action 7 of the Plan seeks to 'ensure birth registration for the prevention of statelessness' and Action 8 seeks to ensure that nationality documentation is issued 'to those with entitlement to it' (UNHCR 2014b). This Action notes that:

> Individuals can be at risk of statelessness if they have difficulties proving that they have links to a State. Lack of birth registration can create such a risk. This is because birth registration documents where a person was born and who their parents are – key pieces of information needed to establish which country's nationality a child can acquire.
>
> (UNHCR 2014b, p. 18)

The situation concerning the relationship between birth registration and avoidance of statelessness is complex. As the Plan acknowledges, 'lack of birth registration on its own does not usually make people stateless' (UNHCR 2014b, p. 19). However, the importance of the encounter between individual and state means that they are often vital attributes of nationality. Birth confers no 'inherent' status; it must be registered, documented, and made legible (Scott 1999) to the appropriate authority, which must recognise the claim implicit in the documents. Indeed, the 2030 UN Sustainable Development Goals acknowledge that birth registration is an aspect of legal identity, and, by implication, not its equivalent (United Nations General Assembly 2015, Goal 16.9). Plan International, who have done extensive work on birth registration, clearly acknowledge that the provision of a certificate is an essential component of birth registration (Plan International 2016a, no page), although no specific mention of birth certificates is made in the Global Action Plan. Birth certificates provide a mechanism for individuals to assert their legal identity to relevant authorities, and an opportunity for those authorities to authenticate or verify that official identity against an official record in a database (Gelb and Clark 2013, p. 6) or other civil registration system.

These registration systems, especially when – as is now encouraged – digitised, can carry risks. Plan International notes that:

> There are many issues to think about, such as identity theft, privacy violations, targeted oppression based on personal characteristics, exploitation by registration agents, and exclusion from the benefits of birth registration if systems aren't designed to meet the needs of already marginalised groups.
>
> (Plan International 2016b)

Plan points in particular to several risks of direct interest to an assessment of the risk of statelessness. One risk arises in the potential for targeting of various kinds, including exploitation, based on personal characteristics. The risks anticipated extend to risk of 'personal security violation or exploitation', especially where birth registration happens 'outside [of] a controlled institutional environment' (Plan International 2015, p. 7).

A further reason for caution resonates with Arendt's observation in the 1950s that 'only with a completely organized humanity could the loss of home and political status become identical with expulsion from humanity altogether' (Arendt 1973, p. 297). The more organised inclusion is, the higher the stakes are in being excluded. This remains an important consideration when thinking about the move to universalise registration and documentation, which will logically entail that in some circumstances at least, remaining unregistered and undocumented will be situations of greater vulnerability than before. The tendency to uphold a binary distinction between nationality and statelessness is clear in the current approach to registration. However, recent work on statelessness has begun to destabilise this binary. For her part, Arendt overstated the starkness of the divide (Blitz this volume; Staples 2012b). Stateless persons are not always in the position of abjection suggested by her account of 'the scum of the earth' (Arendt 1973, p. 269). Furthermore, in practice, the line between statelessness and nationality is often unclear, as UNHCR's use of the phrase 'at risk of statelessness' suggests but then obscures.

The Global Action Plan also notes that the inability to acquire documents proving nationality can occur 'due to discrimination against particular groups' (UNHCR 2014b, p. 21). In Myanmar, the births of Rohingya children have often been unregistered, leading to significant problems in the encounters of these children and their families with the state (Lee 2015, paragraph 54). In such cases, nationality verification and confirmation exercises can sometimes regularise the relationship between the individual or minority and the state. Again though, the importance of recognition, and the 'valid but unlawful' (Weis 1979, p. 242) character of even discriminatory nationality law can undermine even well-meaning external support for these campaigns.

The recent pilot citizenship verification exercise in Myanmar, for example, seems, on the basis of the United Nations Special Rapporteur's 2015 report, to have been undertaken inconsistently and in bad faith. She notes in her report that 'even for those who have received their citizenship cards, life has not changed' (Lee 2015, paragraph 42). Documentation can also always be unrecognised or rescinded. In February 2015, the president of Myanmar announced that all Temporary Registration Certificates had to be returned to the authorities by the end of May of that year (Burmese Rohingya Organisation UK 2015). In pointing to the limitations of documentation in either confirming or constituting an objective status, I do not mean to dispute the general importance of documentation as an attribute of nationality. Even so, the means by which identification is operationalised cannot be separated out from their deliberate and unintended ends, nor from the underlying social and political context. Forst's distinction between a respect concept and a permission concept of toleration (Forst 2007, p. 219) are of interest here. His account of edicts of religious toleration demonstrates clearly the risks of a legal position which fixes one's position in 'a situation of being "merely" tolerated'. He makes the argument that permissive toleration, even when made juridical, often leads to 'cultural and social stigmatization, political powerlessness, and dependency' (Forst 2007, p. 218). On the same lines, Lindsey Kingston notes that:

> statelessness is both a *cause* of marginalisation, as well as a *symptom* of it. That is, most stateless populations lack legal nationality because they are part of a marginalised group that faces systematic discrimination and oppression from the start (Kingston this volume).

Brad K. Blitz's research has also shown that '[f]ragmentation and division occurred before *and* after the granting of citizenship' (Blitz this volume).

The Global Action Plan's account of being at risk of statelessness has the advantage of recognising the contingency of statelessness. Furthermore, its acknowledgements that 'lack of nationality documentation alone does not usually mean that a person is stateless' (UNHCR 2014b, p. 21) and that 'lack of birth registration on its own does not usually make people stateless' (UNHCR 2014b, p. 19) are welcome insofar as they open up a space between registration and documentation, nationality, and statelessness. The more political account of statelessness reflects the fact that official identities must often be authenticated, and that it can be at the moments of identification or authentication that one's statelessness becomes apparent. Seen in this light, the emphasis on birth registration and documentation as adequate responses to statelessness is problematic. Particularly in states where discrimination is entrenched and even legalised, they may in fact risk exacerbating discrimination.

Discrimination and risk of statelessness

Action 4 of the plan (prevent denial, loss or deprivation of nationality on discriminatory grounds) is a response to the fact that 'the majority of the world's known stateless populations belong to minority groups' (UNHCR 2014b, p. 14). As the Action Plan states, 'discrimination against marginalized ethnic and social groups may create particular risks of statelessness' (UNHCR 2014b, p. 15). In spite of an impressive international legal framework on non-discrimination, there is still no part of the world without at least one state that 'has not yet learned to live with or tolerate its minorities' (UNHCR 1995, p. 67). Ethnic conflict and ethnic discrimination are vital determinants of statelessness and of being 'at risk of statelessness', though they are not necessarily insurmountable, as recent successes reveal. Under Action 4, UNHCR's stated goal is a situation where 'no states have nationality laws which permit denial, loss or deprivation of nationality on discriminatory grounds' (UNHCR 2014b, p. 13). However, as we have already seen, external influence over nationality law is limited, and even campaigns to confirm stateless people's legal status can risk stigmatisation in the absence of the right social and political conditions. It is doubtful that a strong norm against denial, loss or deprivation of citizenship will emerge in the short term, even if UNHCR meets its target of 103 states parties to the 1961 Convention, which 'sets rules for the conferral and non-withdrawal of citizenship to prevent cases of statelessness from arising' (UNHCR 2014c). Furthermore, as UNHCR acknowledges in its approach to statelessness determination since the 2010 Prato Conclusions, the role of a variety of 'competent authorities' in interpreting and implementing nationality law suggests that legal reform will not always change realities on the ground.

The conditions for meaningful legal reform are also almost certainly unevenly spread, and a lack of access to relevant officials by UNHCR is likely to pose significant challenges to the agency's strategy in several states. Several of the states where UNHCR is aware of statelessness (UNHCR 2016) are not party to any of the conventions under UNHCR's mandate (for example Myanmar, Thailand, Syria, and Brunei). Each of these states also ranks highly on at least one indicator in the most recent Fragile States Index (Myanmar on group grievance; Thailand on factionalised elites and group grievance; Syria with a score of nine or above on seven of ten indicators[3]; Brunei on legitimacy of the state) (Fund for Peace 2016a). In each case, non-ratification of UNHCR conventions and aspects of state fragility suggest that the prospects for reform of nationality law and policy in accordance with international standards may be particularly problematic.

In spite of considerable pressure on Myanmar, for example, resolution to the situation of the stateless Rohingya seems unlikely in the short term. In spite of unprecedented legal reform since the regime change of 2011, the UN Special Rapporteur remained concerned in 2015 by discrimination against ethnic and religious minorities (Lee 2015, paragraph 27). She notes in this report the proposal of new laws with the 'potential to fuel existing tensions between ethnic and religious minorities in the country' (Lee 2015, p. 27), for example the Law for Health Care Relating to Control of Population Growth of 23 May 2015. This law:

> permits the government to control population growth in certain areas by limiting how often women may have children. It has been widely condemned both for violating women's rights and for its potential to be used as a tool for ethnic and religious discrimination against communities like the Rohingya.
>
> (Equal Rights Trust 2015)

Discriminatory laws remain an important root cause of statelessness, as a 2014 report by the Institute of Statelessness and Inclusion (ISI) clearly shows (Institute on Statelessness and Inclusion 2014). Some states, for example Myanmar, are likely to remain resistant to bringing nationality law and other relevant laws into line with international standards. In other cases, such as Bangladesh prior to the reforms discussed, it is the implementation, rather than the letter of the law that is the problem. There is also a good handful of states with situations of statelessness that are 'un- or underreported' (Institute on Statelessness and Inclusion 2014, p. 59) in which statelessness is likely to be the result, in part, of weak states. The ISI report notes that:

> Many millions of people are undocumented as nationals for a variety of reasons (including discrimination against ethnic minorities and the rural poor and the general weakness of state institutions and identification systems in some countries).
>
> (Institute on Statelessness and Inclusion 2014, p. 15)

In Afghanistan, Syria, Iraq, Democratic Republic of Congo, the existence of sizeable stateless populations is either known or strongly suspected (Institute on Statelessness and Inclusion 2014). Each also features prominently in a range of datasets on the character of their statehood. In each case, high levels of state violence (Gibney *et al.* 2016), societal violence (Gibney *et al.* 2014), fragility (Fund for Peace 2016a), political instability (Marshall *et al.* 2016), ethnic conflict and ethnic discrimination (Giradin *et al.* 2015) overlap.[4] In these states, laws may lack legitimacy, or else exert little influence on policy in practice. In Afghanistan, for example, it is noted that the risk of statelessness arises as it is a country 'with many ethnic minority groups, poor infrastructure and weak institutions, as well as a long history of conflict and displacement' (Institute on Statelessness and Inclusion 2014, p. 79). The report also notes that in the conflict-scarred Eastern Democratic Republic of Congo, 'state institutions are mostly not effective' (Institute on Statelessness and Inclusion 2014, p. 64), and the report points also to the impact of manipulations of policy (Institute on Statelessness and Inclusion 2014, p. 25). However, the ISI report, like the Global Action Plan, focuses primarily on the relationship between nationality law and statelessness. Indeed, the relationship between discrimination, weak institutions, poor infrastructure, conflict, and statelessness is not well understood, and there is a need for further research into this nexus (though see Al Barazi and van Waas 2015).

Recognition of statelessness

As I hope the chapter has shown, the prospects of eliminating *in situ* statelessness are contingent on legal and political factors relating to the state in question. I have also pointed to some of the limits of strictly legal responses to *in situ* and migration-related statelessness in the light of state resistance to legal reform, discrimination, or other political factors (for example institutional weakness, conflict, or political instability). Arguably, then, there is a sound case for providing instead for the protection of stateless migrants and refugees. UNHCR's goal for 2024 is for there to be 50 states with determination procedures 'which lead to a legal status that permits residence and guarantees the enjoyment of basic human rights, and facilitate naturalization for stateless migrants' (UNHCR 2014b, p. 16). In this last part of the chapter, I will offer some quite brief thoughts about the implications for stateless persons of being identified through such state determination procedures, taking seriously the acknowledgement of UNHCR that stateless persons 'are often unwilling to be identified because they lack a secure legal status' (UNHCR 2014b, p. 25).

For various reasons, not least of which is the persistent unwillingness of state authorities to play host to stateless persons, taking 'refuge' in statelessness as a means for people to remain 'where they are and avoid being deported' (Arendt 1973, p. 278) is often not an option today. At the time of writing, no state that is host to a significant number of stateless migrants has made a pledge to implement a determination procedure leading to legal status, residence, and the enjoyment of basic rights (UNHCR 2011, p. 37). The view from international relations theory makes it clear how exceptional it is for an individual to be recognised as stateless: individuals are recognised 'by international law only in exceptional circumstances' (Brown refers us to pirates and diplomats) (Brown 2002, p. 115). This is the reality of recognition and identification in world politics: 'People are not governed in relation to their individuality or identity but as members of populations' (Ruppert 2009, p. 4).

Given its weakness (relative to nationality) as a form of status, it can be argued that determinations of statelessness should generally be a last resort (see Institute on Statelessness and Inclusion 2014, p. 143). However, while it is often to be preferred that a nationality could be *properly* established in most cases, there often comes a point at which 'it is better to acknowledge that the person is stateless' (Institute on Statelessness and Inclusion in UNHCR 2013, p. 43). There are also ethical implications in determining that someone is stateless. Many stateless Palestinians, for example, resist the label 'stateless', which they think risks weakening their claim to what they themselves consider to be their country (Fiddian-Qasmiyeh 2016). Many existing determination procedures also risk stigmatising stateless persons, and there are good reasons to think that poor procedures unconnected to a secure legal status might be more dangerous than being invisible. In many countries, stateless persons are subject to indefinite detention, and in 'fortress Europe' a raft of Readmission Agreements setting the stage for the removal of stateless persons to third countries have been agreed. The continuing hostility to asylum seekers and unwillingness to offer resettlement places to UNHCR are also important considerations in thinking about the added value of statelessness determination procedures. In the UK, for example, there has been a 'deportation turn' (Gibney 2008, p. 146), and extended use of unlimited immigration detention in recent years, which will give us cause to look closely at the protection conferred by the country's new statelessness determination procedure.

There are related reasons for a degree of caution in UNHCR'S drive for better identification of statelessness and better data on it (UNHCR 2014b, actions 6 & 10). Although UNHCR has been clear that 'having comprehensive and accurate information about who is affected by statelessness, and where, is a means to an end, not an end in itself' (UNHCR 2013, p. 47), this entails that it may have other, unintended outcomes. The risks of aggravating discrimination and oppression are important considerations, especially in the light of a critical literature on biometrics which details its role in deciding between permissible and impermissible persons (Wortman 2009, p. 6). The use of biometrics in asylum management has seen clear 'function creep' (Ajana 2013, p. 576). In Europe, the Eurodac database (the European fingerprint database for identifying asylum seekers and irregular border-crossers) has been much criticised from the standpoint of the right to privacy and 'informational self-determination' (Aus 2003, p. 37). The enthusiasm for technological solutions to birth registration, which may produce databases which give the appearance of an objective source for determination of nationality, may also create risks. It is not necessarily too cynical to wonder whether birth registration databases might be accessed by third countries during statelessness determination procedures, and used to deny statelessness, even if the competent authorities of the state in which the birth was registered do not consider the person as a national. State power over recognition of individuals is such that determination of statelessness carries its own risks.

Conclusion

I have pointed in this chapter to some gaps – which can lead to recognition or non-recognition – between nationality, law, registration, and documentation. In discriminatory or divided social and political contexts, these gaps raise the risk of statelessness. The gaps also reflect an underlying paradox of identity and identification in the state system. While the myth of certainty and ultimate belonging – according to which everyone has their own state – continues to manifest in all kinds of ways, it is clear that the grant of nationality is often arbitrary and sometimes capricious. In Krause's words, stateless persons 'induce us to grow fully aware [...] of the fact that, in the modern nation state, it is the state that constitutes the citizenry, and not the other way round' (Krause 2008, p. 338). The additional gap between nationality law and its interpretation and implementation makes statelessness difficult to resolve.

I hope to have demonstrated in this chapter that there is, in spite of the obvious importance of having an official identity as safeguard against statelessness, a real need to think critically about the politics of recognition. Political theory can be useful in reminding us that practices of identification only make sense in the context of much deeper frameworks of acknowledgement, recognition, and non-recognition, which are constitutive in important ways of states, individual persons, and international relations (see Staples 2012a). The centrality of recognition, registration, and documentation to the state and wider state system means that it will always be worth thinking carefully about the implications of these practices on marginalised and excluded people. Registration alone can mean little in the absence of documents, the value of which is in turn contingent on the interpretation of competent authorities. Documents have often been used as tools for targeted stigmatisation, and can limit the possibilities for hiding from the state.

There are also a number of states in which high levels of violence, fragility, and instability overlap with ethnic discrimination and ethnic conflict. The myth of a completed state system in which the global population is allocated neatly to sovereign states is both utopian and potentially dangerous. Social, economic, and political challenges to the vision of statehood which underpins the current international approach abound in today's world. These cannot be resolved by campaigns for legal reform given the general importance of recognition, and the specific issues that arise in contexts of deep discrimination and state weakness. Acknowledging this reality need not lead us into pessimism about the prospects for addressing the present state of statelessness. As Katherine Tonkiss argues, 'there is a space between the universalism of human rights and the reification of national group membership, which can offer us a useful way of thinking about how to realise normative claims for the rights of stateless persons' (Tonkiss this volume). There is growing scholarly interest, reflected in this volume as a whole, in the *politics* of statelessness. In this discussion, belonging is better understood 'as a negotiated and dynamic institution' (Isin and Nyers 2014, p. 2), with the effect that 'statelessness, rather than being a form of radical exclusion, becomes a mode of differential and precarious inclusion' (Sigona 2016, p. 275). These approaches are better able to acknowledge 'the tension, ambiguity and conceptual limitations of "statelessness" and citizenship' (Redclift 2013, p. 308).

This chapter has attempted to sketch some of the complexity and plurality of political and legal forms of recognition and non-recognition, in particular in states where law is not the primary constituent of personal status. Recent ethnographic research into stateless populations can also help us to understand the complexities of status and recognition in relation to stateless communities (for example Balaton-Chrimes 2014; Reddy 2015; Flaim 2017). These more pluralistic, complex, and ambiguous spaces may be more useful avenues for research in thinking about the recognition of people than the current one-size-fits-all approach reflected in the Global Action Plan.

Notes

1 An early draft of this chapter was circulated as part of The Duke Human Rights Center at The Kenan Institute for Ethics spring symposium on 30 May 2015, entitled '*UNHCR's Global Action Plan to End Statelessness: A Critical Examination of Identification Infrastructures*',

2 While Swider's argument rests on an expansive account of human rights, this would perhaps be too demanding at present. For that reason, my focus here is on the more basic equality of status which recognition as a national implies.

3 The full list of indicators can be found at Fund for Peace (2016b).

4 We could look also at the Central African Republic, Libya, Somalia, Sudan, South Sudan, and Yemen.

References

Ajana, B. (2013) Asylum, identity management, and biometric control. *Journal of Refugee Studies*, 26(4), pp. 576–595. Available at: https://doi.org/10.1093/jrs/fet030 (Accessed 8 November 2016).

Al Barazi, Z. and van Waas, L. E. (2015) *Statelessness and Displacement.* Tilburg University/Norwegian Refugee Council. Available at: www.institutesi.org/stateless_displacement.pdf (Accessed 8 November 2016).

Arendt, H. (1973) *Origins of Totalitarianism.* 5th edition. New York: Harcourt Brace Jovanovich.

Aus, J. P. (2003) Supranational Governance in an 'Area of Freedom, Security, and Justice': Eurodac and the Politics of Biometric Control. *SEI Working Papers*, (72). Available at: www.sussex.ac.uk/webteam/gateway/file.php?name=sei-working-paper-no-72.pdf&site=266 (Accessed 8 November 2016).

Balaton-Chrimes, S. (2014) Statelessness, identity cards, and citizenship as status in the case of the Nubians of Kenya. *Citizenship Studies*, 18(1).

Brown, C. (2002) *Sovereignty, Rights, and Justice: International Political Theory Today.* Cambridge: Polity.

Burmese Rohingya Organisation UK. (2015) *The Rohingya, the Citizenship Law, Temporary Registration, and Implementation of the Rakhine State Action Plan.* Available at: http://burmacampaign.org.uk/media/BROUK-White-Card-Briefing.pdf (Accessed 8 November 2016).

Dworkin, R. (1982) Law as Interpretation. *Critical Inquiry*, 9(1), pp. 179–200.

Equal Rights Trust. (2015) *Myanmar Enacts Disriminatory Population Control Law, Further Threatening the Rohingya.* Available at: www.equalrightstrust.org/news/myanmar-enacts-discriminatory-population-control-law-further-threatening-rohingya (Accessed 8 November 2016).

Fiddian-Qasmiyeh, E. (2016) On the threshold of statelessness: Palestinian narratives of loss and erasure. *Ethnic and Racial Studies*, 39(2), pp. 301–321.

Flaim, A. (2017) Problems of Evidence, Evidence of Problems: Expanding Citizenship and Reproducing Statelessness Among Highlanders in Northern Thailand. In Lawrance, B. N. and Stevens, J. (eds) *Citizenship in Question: Evidentiary Birthright and Statelessness.* Durham, NC: Duke University Press.

Forst, R. (2007) To Tolerate Means to Insult: Toleration, Recognition, and Emancipation. In van den Brink, B. and Owen, D. (eds) *Recognition and Power: Axel Honneth and the Tradition of Social Critical Theory*, pp. 215–237. Cambridge: Cambridge University Press.

Frost, M. (1996) *Ethics in International Relations: A Constitutive Theory.* Cambridge: Cambridge University Press.

Fund for Peace. (2016a) *Fragile States Index 2016.* Available at: http://fsi.fundforpeace.org (Accessed 8 November 2016).

Fund for Peace. (2016b) *Indicators.* Available at: http://fsi.fundforpeace.org/indicators (Accessed 8 November 2016).

Gelb, A. and Clark, J. (2013) Identification for Development: The Biometrics Revolution. *Center for Global Development Working Paper 315*, 1–81. Available at: https://doi.org/10.2139/ssrn.2226594 (Accessed 8 November 2016).

Gibney, M. (2008) Asylum and the expansion of deportation in the United Kingdom. *Government and Opposition*, 43(2), pp. 146–167.

Gibney, M., Cornett, Linda, Wood, Reed, Haschke, Peter, and Arnon, Daniel. (2014)

Societal Violence Scale. Available at: www.politicalterrorscale.org/Data/Download. html (Accessed 8 November 2016).

Gibney, M., Wood, R., Cornett, L., Haschke, P., and Arnon, D. (2016) *Political Terror Scale*. Available at: www.politicalterrorscale.org/Data/Download.html (Accessed 8 November 2016).

Giradin, L., Hunziker, P., Cederman, L., Bormann, N., and Vogt, M. (2015) *Geographical Research on War*. Available at: https://growup.ethz.ch/ (Accessed 8 November 2016).

Human Rights Watch. (1996) *Burma: The Rohingya Muslims: Ending a Cycle of Exodus?* Washington, DC: Human Rights Watch. Available at: www.hrw.org/legacy/ summaries/s.burma969.html (Accessed 8 November 2016).

Institute on Statelessness and Inclusion. (2014) *The World's Stateless*. Oesterwijk: Wolf Legal Press.

International Refugee Rights Initiative. (2011) *Shadows of Return: The Dilemmas of Congolese Refugees in Rwanda*. Available at: www.refworld.org/publisher,IRRI,,, 53b3dc834,0.html (Accessed 8 November 2016).

Isin, E. F. and Nyers, P. (2014) Introduction: Globalizing Citizenship Studies. In Isin, E. F. and Nyers, P. (eds) *Routledge Handbook of Global Citizenship Studies*, pp. 1–11. Abingdon; New York: Routledge.

Krause, M. (2008) Undocumented migrants: an Arendtian perspective. *European Journal of Political Theory*, 7(3), pp. 331–348.

Lee, Y. (2015) Report of the Special Rapporteur on the situation of human rights in Myanmar. *Human Rights Council*, (A/HRC/28/72). Available at: https://documents-dds-ny.un.org/doc/UNDOC/GEN/G15/060/75/PDF/G1506075.pdf?OpenElement (Accessed 8 November 2016).

Marshall, M., Gurr, T. F., and Harff, B. (2016) *Political Instability Task Force*. Available at: www.systemicpeace.org/inscr/PITFProbSetCodebook2015.pdf (Accessed 8 November 2016).

Plan International. (2016a) *Birth Registration*. Available at: https://plan-international.org/ birth-registration/digital-birth-registration (Accessed 8 November 2016).

Plan International. (2016b) *Doing Digital Birth Registration the Right Way*. Available at: https://plan-international.org/blog/2015/06/doing-digital-birth-registration-right-way# (Accessed 8 November 2016).

Plan International. (2015) *Identifying and Addressing Risks to Children in Digitised Birth Registration Systems: A Step-by-Step Guide*. Available at: https://plan-international. org/publications/identifying-and-addressing-risks-children-dbr-systems#download-options (Accessed 8 November 2016).

Redclift, V. (2013) Abjects or agents? Camps, contests, and the creation of 'political space'. *Citizenship Studies*, 17(3–4), pp. 308–321.

Reddy, M. (2015) Identity paper/work/s and the unmaking of legal status in Mae Sot, Thailand. *Asian Journal of Law and Society*, 2(2), pp. 251–266.

Ruppert, E. (2009) Numbers Regimes: From Censuses to Metrics. *CRESC Working Paper Series*, 44(68). Available at: www.cresc.ac.uk/medialibrary/workingpapers/wp68.pdf (Accessed 8 November 2016).

Scott, J. C. (1999) *Seeing Like A State: How Certain Schemes to Improve the Human Condition Have Failed*. New Haven: Yale University Press.

Sigona, N. (2016) Everyday statelessness in Italy: Status, rights, and camps. *Ethnic and Racial Studies*, 39(2), pp. 263–279.

Staples, K. (2012a) *Retheorising Statelessness: Towards a background theory of membership in world politics*. Edinburgh: Edinburgh University Press.

Staples, K. (2012b) Statelessness and the politics of misrecognition. *Res Publica*, 18(1), pp. 93–106.

UNHCR. (2016) *Global Trends 2015*. Available at: www.unhcr.org/uk/statistics/unhcrstats/576408cd7/unhcr-global-trends-2015.html (Accessed 8 November 2011).

UNHCR. (2014a) *Resolving Existing Major Situations of Statelessness*. Available at: www.refworld.org/pdfid/54e75a244.pdf (Accessed 8 November 2016).

UNHCR. (2014b) *Global Action Plan to Prevent Statelessness*. Available at: www.unhcr.org/uk/protection/statelessness/54621bf49/global-action-plan-end-statelessness-2014–2024.html (Accessed 8 November 2016).

UNHCR. (2014c) *1961 Convention on the Reduction of Statelessness: Introductory Note*. Available at: www.unhcr.org/uk/protection/statelessness/3bbb286d8/convention-reduction-statelessness.html (Accessed 8 November 2016).

UNHCR. (2013) *UNHCR Statistical Yearbook 2013*. Available at: www.unhcr.org/uk/statistics/country/54cf9bd69/unhcr-statistical-yearbook-2013–13th-edition.html (Accessed 8 November 2016).

UNHCR. (2012) Guidelines on Statelessness No. 1: The definition of 'Stateless Person' in Article 1(1) of the 1954 Convention relating to the Status of Stateless Persons, *HCR/GS/11/*. Available at: www.refworld.org/pdfid/4f4371b82.pdf (Accessed 8 November 2016).

UNHCR. (2011) Pledges 2011: Ministerial Intergovernmental Event on Refugees and Stateless Persons. Available at: www.refworld.org/docid/50aca6112.html (Accessed 8 November 2016).

UNHCR. (2010) The Concept of Stateless Persons under International Law: Summary Conclusions. Available at: www.refworld.org/docid/4ca1ae002.html (Accessed 8 November 2016).

UNHCR. (1995) *Note on UNHCR and Stateless Persons*, Geneva: UNHCR. Available at: www.unhcr.org/uk/excom/scip/3ae68cc014/note-unhcr-stateless-persons.html (Accessed 27 February 2017).

Weis, P. (1979) *Nationality and Statelessness in International Law*. 2nd edition. Alphen aan denj Rijn: Sijthoof and Noordhoff.

Wortman, R. A. (2009) The problems with identity: distribution, agency, and identification. *The Humanities Review* 8(1), pp. 5–12.

Part III

Theorising statelessness

Photo 5 Photographer's father in Boudhanath, Nepal.
Source: © Lodoe Laura. Pala and my Camera, Boudha, 2016.

My father, born in Tibet, fled his homeland in 1959 fearing persecution from the People's Liberation Army. The occupation of Tibet has led many Tibetans to emigrate from the Chinese-controlled state. Today around 150,000 Tibetans live in exile, mostly in neighbouring India, Nepal and Bhutan, many unable or unwilling to claim citizenship of another nation. This photograph was taken in Boudhanath in the capital city of Nepal, where my father has a room in a Tibetan Buddhist monastery he helped build in the 1980s. As a first-generation Canadian living in Canada, my work explores my often complicated relationship with place-based identity. Throughout the years my father and I have had many barriers in connecting, including language, culture, and geography. Through photography, he and I try to form a more meaningful relationship, and a deeper understanding of one another.

Part III

Theorising statelessness

Photo 3. [illegible] my father in Dhalhousie, [illegible]

Source: [illegible]

My father, born in Tibet, fled his homeland in 1959 during invasion from the People's Liberation Army. The occupation of Tibet has led many Tibetans to [illegible] from the Chinese-controlled state. Today around 150,000 Tibetans live in exile, mostly in neighbouring India, Nepal and Bhutan, many unable or unwilling to obtain citizenship or exercise rights. This photograph was taken in Dhalhousie, India, [illegible] where my father [illegible] in a Tibetan Buddhist [illegible] he helped build in the 1960s. As a first-generation Canadian [illegible] in Canada, my work explores my often-complicated relationship with [illegible]. Throughout the years my father and I have had many [illegible] in [illegible], including language, culture, and geography. Through photography, we find a way to form a more meaningful relationship, and a deeper understanding of one another.

12 Why end statelessness?

Katja Swider

Introduction

The UNHCR refers to statelessness as a 'curse', and prioritises tackling it through its eradication (UNHCR 2014a, pp. 2, 9), rather than through ensuring access to legal rights by stateless persons. Jean Asselborn, Minister of Immigration and Asylum for Luxembourg, described the EU's support for the eradication of state-lessness as an act 'on behalf of stateless persons'.[1] Yet, the case studies described in this chapter illustrate that emphasis on replacing statelessness by a nationality[2] is not always in the interest of stateless persons. Nationality status can be more problematic than statelessness in specific circumstances due to, for example, a peculiar historical context of a stateless population, political convictions of the individuals concerned, or the risk of human rights violations associated with acquiring a particular nationality. Pursuing the elimination of statelessness as a policy goal per se, without regard to preferences and the human rights situation of the affected persons, cannot be justified by reference to the interests of those persons.[3] This chapter argues that a statelessness policy informed by the interests of stateless persons should prioritise the identification and protection of stateless persons over the elimination of statelessness. In many cases the two policy goals of protecting stateless persons and eliminating statelessness will not be in tension with each other when access to a wider range of rights can best be achieved through the acquisition of an appropriate nationality (Hirsh Ballin 2014). However, when this is not the case, priority should be given to wider protection of the human rights of affected persons over the goal of eradicating statelessness.

The chapter is structured as follows. The first part briefly describes three main sets of statelessness policy goals pursued within the UN legal system: The pro-tection of stateless persons, the reduction of statelessness, and the identification of stateless persons. A hierarchy among these goals is identified, where the reduction of statelessness is seen by the UNHCR as the primary goal, and the identification and protection of stateless persons as secondary goals, for cases where the reduction efforts fail.

The second part discusses three case studies in which goals on statelessness are in tension with each other. It illustrates that prioritising the reduction of state-lessness over the protection and identification of stateless persons can cause normative problems with regard to upholding the interests and the access to human rights of affected individuals.

The third part evaluates the UN policy goals on statelessness in light of human rights, and suggests reconsidering the current hierarchy of policy goals on statelessness so as to ensure that the interests of affected individuals are at the heart of any policy on statelessness.

Defining goals on statelessness

Protection

The 1954 UN Convention relating to the Status of Stateless Persons (1954 Convention) is the main international legal instrument guaranteeing rights specifically for stateless persons. Curiously, the 1954 Convention does not use the word 'protection' when formulating its own objectives, but instead speaks of assuring 'stateless persons the widest possible exercise of [...] fundamental rights and freedoms' (1954 Convention, Preamble). The language of protection was extended to discussions of statelessness by the UNHCR, presumably appropriated from the agency's work on the protection of refugees. The term 'protection' has a number of meanings and connotations, which are useful to clarify in the context of statelessness. Unlike with the case of refugees, the definition of statelessness does not refer to harm or persecution (1954 Convention, art. 1).[4] Even though statelessness often leads to practical hardships, a stateless person, unlike a refugee, is not by definition in danger. The protection of stateless persons therefore does not necessarily refer to shielding from danger.[5] Since the 1954 Convention is the main international legal instrument on the protection of stateless persons, 'protection' in the context of statelessness is best understood in light of the preamble to this Convention, according to which the Convention aims to 'assure stateless persons the widest possible exercise of [...] fundamental rights and freedoms' (1954 Convention, Preamble). For the purposes of this chapter, the goal of protecting stateless persons is defined as assuring the widest possible exercise of fundamental rights and freedoms.

The content of those rights and freedoms is described in the 1954 Convention, and subsequently interpreted and supplemented by UNHCR policy documents, such as the UNHCR *Handbook on the Protection of Stateless Persons* of 2014. Some of these rights are accessible to any stateless person who is present on the territory of a State Party, such as the right to identity documents, the right of access to courts, and the right to primary education (1954 Convention, arts. 27, 16, 22). The enjoyment of other rights is dependent on whether the person enjoys legal residence or whether the State Party is his or her place of habitual residence (UNHCR 2014c, paras 132–139). These concern inter alia the right to work, the right to social security benefits, and the right to obtain travel documents. Accessing some rights may be made conditional on the same requirements that apply to foreigners generally,[6] for example the right to move freely within the territory of the state, while other rights need to be provided on the same basis as for nationals, such as the freedom of religion.

It is important to remember that the human rights legal frameworks have developed since 1954 at the UN, regional and national levels. Subsequent human rights instruments also apply to stateless persons and may offer in some cases a higher level of protection than the 1954 Convention. But some 1954 Convention rights are still of great importance nowadays to stateless persons in light of contemporary migration challenges. These are the right to identity documents for stateless persons who do not have residence rights in the host state,[7] the right to travel documents for stateless persons with a residence permit,[8] and the protection against expulsion of legally residing stateless persons.[9] An important principle enshrined in the 1954 Convention which also carries great value today is that when accessing the Convention rights no requirements can be imposed on stateless persons which they cannot comply with due to being stateless.[10]

Stateless persons do not enjoy a default right to reside anywhere in the world based on their nationality status, and therefore the right to legal residence is of particular importance to them, especially since in most states it is a gateway to accessing all the other rights listed in the 1954 Convention. Legalising the residence of stateless persons (unless specific exceptions apply)[11] forms part of the contemporary understanding of a protection regime for stateless persons.

Reduction

Reduction of statelessness refers here to the broad set of mechanisms which aim at ensuring that statelessness occurs as little as possible. Some of these mechanisms target existing cases of statelessness, and others prevent new instances of statelessness from arising. International norms on both types of mechanisms are described below.

Prevention

Attempts to prevent statelessness through international law predate the UN era. States have been trying to coordinate their nationality laws so as to avoid statelessness and multiple nationalities as much as possible without compromising their sovereign rights to decide who their nationals are (Donner 1994, p. 202; League of Nations 1930). Nowadays, the most influential and widely ratified treaty on preventing statelessness is the 1961 UN Convention on the Reduction of Statelessness (1961 Convention).[12] It obliges State Parties to attribute nationality at birth and to prevent any loss of nationality that results in statelessness later in life. These measures are not airtight,[13] as State Parties are allowed to make the acquisition of nationality at birth subject to a number of exhaustively listed conditions, and as a result of those acquisition can be delayed in time or not happen at all, possibly resulting in temporary or lifelong statelessness. For example, a child who does not reside in either the state of his or her birth or in the state of nationality of his or her parents may not be able to enforce his or her right to a nationality against any state, even if we assume that all states involved are parties to the 1961 Convention (1961 Convention,

arts. 1, 4). As to the prevention of loss of nationality that results in statelessness, the Convention also allows for a wide range of exceptions. For example,
a naturalised national who resides abroad for more than seven years and does
not register with the appropriate state authorities may lose the nationality of a
State Party and thereby become stateless. Interestingly, the 1961 Convention
prohibits the voluntary renunciation of nationality that results in statelessness,
unless this prohibition hampers the right to seek asylum or leave one's own
country. Thus, a person is not allowed, under the 1961 Convention, to
renounce his or her nationality due to, for example, political or religious
beliefs that are incompatible with membership in that state.

The 1961 Convention is a widely ratified, powerful mechanism for reducing
statelessness through prevention, but cannot on its own eliminate statelessness
completely even if it *were* universally ratified and perfectly implemented, which
is far from being the case at the moment (Vonk *et al.* 2013).[14]

In addition to the 1961 Convention, other international treaties contain legal
provisions that aim at preventing statelessness among specific groups. For
example, the International Covenant on Civil and Political Rights guarantees
every child 'the right to acquire a nationality', and so does the Convention on
the Rights of the Child, the latter also emphasising specifically the undesirability
of statelessness among children. The Convention on the Elimination of All
Forms of Discrimination against Women ensures that women do not become
stateless as a result of marrying a foreigner or of the husband changing his
nationality. These provisions illustrate that the goal of preventing statelessness
also manifests itself in other human right treaties.[15]

Remedying existing cases of statelessness

While norms on the prevention of statelessness are well developed in international law, few legal solutions to the existing cases of statelessness have
been agreed on in treaties. The 1961 Convention, for example, contains no
such solutions. Granting nationality to adults automatically without their
consent, whether they are stateless or nationals of another state, is generally
not acceptable under international law (Donner 1994, pp. 128–150, 160–165).
The will of an individual, and also of a state, is seen as crucial for the acquisition of nationality during adulthood.[16] Therefore, norms on granting nationality
to stateless adults are often of an optional rather than strictly compulsory
nature, or are formulated as an obligation of effort rather than an obligation of
result. The 1954 Convention contains an obligation to 'facilitate' the naturalisation of stateless persons 'as far as possible', and to 'reduce as far as possible
the charges and costs' of naturalisation proceedings for stateless persons (1951
Convention, art. 32). The European Convention on Nationality, a regional convention within the Council of Europe, obliges its State Parties to facilitate the
access to nationality of a number of groups, including stateless persons (ECN,
art. 6(4g)).

Eradication

Complete eradication of statelessness has been considered a goal by the UNHCR in recent years. Since international treaties leave gaps through which stateless-ness can still be created and offer no effective mechanisms for eliminating exist-ing cases of statelessness, the complete eradication of statelessness is not possible solely on the basis of the existing relevant international norms. Argu-ably it would require not only supplementary norms, but a fundamental rethink-ing of the concept of state sovereignty, which is rooted in the states' discretion to determine the composition of their populations (Swider and Heijer 2016, forthcoming).

The idea of ending statelessness, however, features in the policy documents of the UNHCR as an ideal to strive towards, or as an overarching project for various activities addressing statelessness, in particular within the UNHCR campaign to 'End Statelessness in 10 Years' (UNHCR 2014b; UNHCR 2014a). It is doubtful, however, whether the UNHCR's goal to 'end stateless-ness' should be understood literally as trying to ensure that no single person is stateless by 2024. Various activities brought under the umbrella of 'ending statelessness', such as the elimination of gender discrimination in nationality laws, are useful for reducing statelessness, but do not cumulatively ensure that all existing cases will be resolved, and no new ones will ever occur. It is also rather contradictory that under the 'End Statelessness' campaign the UNHCR urges states to invest in long-term structural legal mechanisms for the protec-tion of stateless persons, such as statelessness determination procedures (UNHCR 2014b, action 6), which would not be necessary if statelessness was indeed to disappear by 2024. Nonetheless, it is important, in light of this chap-ter's discussion, to note that the overarching slogan of the main statelessness policy for the coming decade focuses on ending statelessness rather than on protecting stateless persons.

The goal to reduce statelessness in international law can thus be summarised as aiming at as few instances of statelessness as possible. Strong, but not air-tight, legal mechanisms for preventing statelessness have been developed, but equally strong norms on addressing existing instances of statelessness are lacking.

Identification

In 1995, the UN General Assembly mandated the UNHCR 'to identify, prevent and reduce statelessness and protect stateless persons' (UNGA 1996; UNHCR 2006), mentioning identification as a distinct goal within statelessness policy. No UN treaty contains an explicit obligation to undertake any identification efforts with regard to statelessness. However, it is impossible to protect stateless persons and, in some cases, to reduce statelessness without knowing who the stateless persons are. The UNHCR has therefore concluded that the duty to identify state-less persons is implicit in the 1954 Convention (UNHCR 2014c, p. 6, para. 8).[17]

Identification in the context of statelessness can refer to different things. Recognising that a specific individual is stateless and supplying him or her with documents that prove the statelessness status is a form of identifying statelessness. Identification can also refer to various qualitative or quantitative mapping efforts with regard to the stateless, such as creating a demographic profile of a specific population, identifying legislative gaps that lead to statelessness, and collecting statistical information. Even though the UNHCR sees its identification mandate on statelessness broadly, and includes various information-gathering activities under it, for the purposes of this chapter identification will refer solely to the status determination of affected individuals.

Identification of stateless persons is not an end goal, but rather a tool to achieve the other goals relating to statelessness that are described above.

Prioritising reduction over protection

According to the UNHCR policy documents on statelessness, ensuring that individuals have a nationality is preferable to identifying and protecting them as stateless. This is sometimes stated explicitly, but is more often implied in the language and logic of policy documents on statelessness. The UNHCR *Handbook on the Protection of Stateless Persons* declares that 'as a general rule, possession of a nationality is preferable to recognition and protection as a stateless person' (UNHCR 2014c, p. 10, para 14). In a similar spirit, the 1954 Convention's 'Introductory Note by the UNHCR' of 2014 states that 'protection as a stateless person is not a substitute for possession of a nationality' and that 'the Convention requires that States facilitate the assimilation and naturalisation of stateless persons'. It also emphasises that the 1954 Convention is only useful for assisting stateless persons 'until their situation *can be* resolved' [emphasis added], implying that once a *mere prospect* for obtaining a nationality, and not the accomplished fact of acquisition of nationality, arises, the Convention should not be relied on, and the acquisition of nationality should be preferred.

Statelessness is routinely referred to as a problem per se, and not as a legal status which is associated with problems where the appropriate legal mechanisms for protection of stateless persons are lacking (UNHCR 2014a). The fact that a status or a condition leads to problems does not mean that this status or condition is a problem per se and needs to be eliminated. Sometimes the (legal) environment needs to be changed instead, so that affected persons no longer experience problems associated with their status without the phenomenon itself needing to be eradicated. For example, the policy of eradication is not pursued with regard to religious minorities that are being discriminated against, even though belonging to such group can also be associated with serious problems if appropriate legal mechanisms ensuring protection are lacking. With statelessness, however, the phenomenon itself is seen as a target of eradication, and not the legal framework that results in the rightlessness of stateless persons.

Applying goals on statelessness to case studies

This part discusses three case studies which illustrate how tensions among the goals on statelessness can take shape in practice and what normative issues arise from the discourse that prioritises reduction of statelessness over the protection of stateless persons.

Protected statelessness: the case of Latvian non-citizens

'Non-citizen' is a special legal status in Latvia given to former USSR citizens who reside in Latvia but are not nationals of Latvia or of any other state. There is a large stateless population of non-citizens in Latvia,[18] which was created as a result of a chain of historical events. During the Latvian occupation by the USSR, Soviet-sponsored mass immigration into the territory of Latvia from other SSRs took place. Upon the restoration of its independence half a century later, Latvia chose not to include the Soviet immigrants and their descendants in its citizenry. The Soviet immigrants were expected to either leave Latvia and become nationals elsewhere or go through a regular naturalisation procedure to obtain Latvian nationality. However, several years after independence, the large settled population of stateless ex-Soviet citizens was still in Latvia, and their legal status had to be formalised somehow. The Latvian state therefore created a transitional status of 'non-citizen', allowing its beneficiaries to live and work in Latvia until a more permanent solution involving a nationality could be achieved for them. It was (and still is) a strong matter of principle for the Latvian state not to automatically include the 'non-citizens' in its citizenry, for fear of implicitly recognising the legality of the Soviet occupation (Krūma 2014, pp. 325–328).

In the early years of Latvian independence there was also a concern that too many non-citizens would naturalise and that the growth in voting rights among this population would undermine Latvian independence from within. To prevent that, various barriers in the form of quotas and stringent naturalisation exams were introduced. It soon became apparent, however, that naturalisations were not happening at a high pace at all. Even after the state policy towards naturalisation and integration of non-citizens shifted from restrictive to welcoming, the naturalisation rates remain low (Krūma 2014, pp. 333–337, 342–351, 401–405).

Attempting to integrate non-citizens into the Latvian society, the Latvian government has not only relaxed naturalisation requirements, but in the past two decades has also significantly strengthened the legal position of non-citizens (Krūma 2014, pp. 377–398). The set of rights which one is entitled to through the status of a non-citizen goes well beyond the minimum requirements of the 1954 Convention, and includes the right to reside permanently in Latvia, to access most state welfare services related to housing, healthcare, education, and unemployment benefits, engage in most economic activities and so on. That is not to say that the rights of non-citizens are equivalent to those of Latvian citizens; the political participation rights of non-citizens are still limited, as is their access to certain types of jobs in the public sector and some property rights concerning the purchase of land. There is thus indisputable differentiated treatment between citizens and non-citizens, but the human rights situation of the latter can hardly be described as 'a life without dignity and security' (UNHCR 2014c, p. 1), the image which dominates the policy discourse on statelessness.

Latvian non-citizens present an interesting case of a stateless population which is well-protected in light of the standards of the 1954 Convention, yet is very sizeable, and thus stands firmly in the way of the goal to reduce statelessness. If the policy priorities of the UNHCR, placing the reduction of statelessness above the protection of stateless persons, are to be applied here, turning non-citizens into citizens is an important goal within the statelessness policy. That raises three normative questions.

First, the question of whether an international policy that does not merely focus on rights but on inclusion into the citizenry is justified and helpful in the sensitive context of Latvian statehood. The situation of non-citizens is indisputably problematic and probably undesirable for all the parties involved. There are disadvantages to both the state and the affected persons in the non-citizens' disenfranchised situation with their inability to participate in the political process of the country where they are settled. However, problematic as it is, it is important to consider whether the UNHCR should deal with the composition of Latvian citizenry. The status of non-citizens is highly politicised; it involves a state with a fragile sense of sovereignty and a group of individuals with a complex history within that state, who may or may not feel connected to it as its nationals. While the demand from the international community to provide protection, which perhaps includes facilitation of naturalisation 'as far as possible', to the non-citizens is justifiable from the perspective of human rights, insisting that non-citizens become citizens may unduly interfere with a sensitive national political process.

Second, the question of whether the goal to eliminate a status such as that of non-citizens has its ground in international legal norms. Safeguards offered by the 1961 Convention to prevent statelessness at birth could be effective in ensuring that children born to non-citizens in Latvia acquire Latvian citizenship. [19] However, the 1961 Convention does not insist that such acquisition of nationality happens automatically and allows the state to make it conditional on the will of the parents, and after the child reaches adulthood on his or her own will. Thus, the norms of the 1961 Convention allow the Latvian state to simply offer nationality to, as opposed to imposing it upon, Latvian-born non-citizens. If the community of non-citizens is solidified politically, and its members identify strongly with it across generations, norms of the 1961 Convention allow for the perpetuation of this status. They do not *require* it, as Latvia can opt for automatic imposition of nationality at birth, but they do *allow* it.

Another approach could be to apply the norms on the avoidance of statelessness after state succession to Latvia. If Latvia had followed those norms, non-citizens would have become citizens of Latvia regardless of their will at the moment of independence, unless they acquired another nationality (ILC 1999, Arts. 7, 8 (comment No. 5) and 11 (comment No. 6)). However, the Latvian state does not see its independence in 1990 as a case of state succession from the Soviet Union, but as a case of restoration of independence after an occupation by the Soviet Union, which changes the perspective on its potential responsibility to avoid statelessness among non-citizens. Moreover, applying norms on the avoidance of statelessness in the context of state succession to Latvia retroactively would be highly problematic. The past 15 years have seen turbulent legal and political developments during which the non-citizens have been excluded from the polity and discriminated against. Automatic conferral of citizenship on adults would at this stage be highly problematic from the perspective of international norms and considering the specific context of Latvian non-citizens. Existing reduction mechanisms for adults depend on the willingness of the state *and* of the non-citizen, and for children born in Latvia at least on the willingness of *either* the state *or* the non-citizen. The answer to the second question thus is that the existing legal norms on the reduction of statelessness offer some opportunities to reduce noncitizenship in Latvia in the long term, provided either the state or the individuals are willing to part with this status, but offer no guarantees of eradicating noncitizenship in Latvia if neither the state nor the individuals concerned want to do so.

Third, a controversial question arises of whether a high level of protection of non-citizens can be sacrificed to expedite their naturalisation. The wide range of rights Latvian non-citizens enjoy in Latvia is sometimes seen as a factor contributing to the perceived lack of interest among non-citizens to naturalise (Krūma 2014, p. 408). Indeed, if non-citizens would be unable to work, own any property or access basic human rights in Latvia without becoming citizens, perhaps their motivation to obtain citizenship would be higher. The UNHCR policy discourse that prioritises the reduction of statelessness over the protection of stateless persons confronts us with a normative question of whether it could be justifiable to lower the level of protection of non-citizens, or at least not encourage further strengthening of their legal status in Latvia, in order to make them more dependent on being nationals and thus more motivated to become citizens. This question applies to any other stateless population: Any efforts towards achieving the highest possible enjoyment of human rights by stateless persons will demotivate stateless persons from becoming citizens purely in order to access human rights. If the perfect protection of stateless persons worldwide could be achieved, the policy to reduce statelessness would have to rely on the appeal of states as political associations.

Dangerous nationality – the case of Samvel[20]

Samvel was born in Germany in 1995 to parents from the former Soviet Union, of Armenian ethnic origin. His parents resided on the territories of Russia, Moldova and Armenia while those were still part of the Soviet Union. They left the Soviet Union before its dissolution and were not within the territories of any of the successor states when the latter were formed. They never went back and never received any nationality from the successor states of the Soviet Union.

When Samvel was two years old, his family came to the Netherlands and applied for asylum. Samvel was registered in the Dutch population registry as Armenian, presumably based on the erroneous interpretation of the Armenian nationality legislation at the time. In 2005, the family's lengthy asylum procedure was still pending. Exhausted by the instability of their legal situation, the parents decided to accept a residence arrangement offered under an amnesty regulation. This regulation provided numerous asylum seekers in prolonged procedures the right to reside legally in the Netherlands, but with a lower level of protection than normally available for recognised refugees. One of the conditions for this residence permit was that any asylum claims would immediately and irrevocably be dropped.

When Samvel turned 18, he applied for a Dutch passport. He found out that he first needed to go through a naturalisation procedure. He complied with all the substantive requirements for naturalisation, such as high level of integration in the Dutch society, sufficient number of years of legal residence, no criminal record and so on. However, he encountered a problem at the administrative level when he was unable to show his foreign passport to the Dutch authorities. The requirement to identify oneself with a foreign passport in the naturalisation procedure applies to all candidates, and only refugees and stateless persons are exempted. Since Samvel's residence permit was not a refugee permit, and since the Dutch authorities have registered him as an Armenian national, he could not make use of either exception. He attempted to argue that he was in fact stateless, but since the Netherlands lacked an adequate statelessness determination procedure (Swider 2014)[21] he was not able to establish the fact of his statelessness in the eyes of the Dutch authorities. Without a passport from Armenia, his naturalisation was denied by the naturalisation agency, as well as upon appeal in court.

Even though based on Armenian nationality legislation Samvel is not an Armenian citizen,[22] he asked the Armenian embassy whether his situation could be resolved by easily obtaining Armenian nationality and an Armenian passport. He did not receive a formal response, but was told informally that if he would be willing to join the Armenian army, he would immediately be granted a nationality and a passport.[23]

Armenia is at war with a neighbouring state, and while a ceasefire has been formally established it is routinely violated. Serving in the Armenian army thus entails a high risk of actual danger in combat. In addition, and perhaps more importantly, the human rights situation within the army is so poor that instances of non-combat deaths and injuries are not uncommon (Council of Europe 2015, pp. 22–23). All this makes acquisition of Armenian nationality by serving in the Armenian army a dangerous option.

Samvel is stateless, but has a nationality within reach. It is not the nationality he aspires to have and which is appropriate to his life circumstances (Hirsch Ballin 2014) but it would nevertheless terminate his statelessness. His human rights situation, however, would suffer significantly if he becomes an Armenian national compared to his current human rights situation as a permanent stateless resident of the Netherlands.

His facilitated naturalisation is impeded by the Netherlands' failure to identify him as stateless, which is a gap that the Netherlands should doubtlessly address to comply with its international obligations. However, none of the international standards accepted by the Netherlands impose a strict obligation on the Netherlands to ensure Samvel becomes a Dutch national; there is merely an obligation to *facilitate* his *access* to nationality. Germany also does not have a strict obligation under the 1961 Convention to grant citizenship to Samvel, and neither does Armenia. As the relevant nationality laws and practices stand right now, Armenian citizenship is the only one accessible to him, and this fact does not violate relevant international legal norms. The norms on the reduction of statelessness do not impose standards on the type of nationality which needs to replace statelessness: There is no requirement of genuine links with the state, or that the state is prepared to protect the human rights of the person in question.

It is interesting to consider whether eliminating Samvel's statelessness through obtaining Armenian nationality would be seen as an achievement by a statelessness policy that prioritises reduction of statelessness. Since there are no standards on the content of the nationality that replaces statelessness and protection of stateless persons is a goal that is subordinate to the reduction of statelessness, it appears that supplying Armenian nationality to Samvel would be an acceptable solution to his statelessness. He does have a strong connection to another state, the Netherlands, the nationality of which comes with a higher level of protection. However, favouring solutions that ultimately lead to better protection is not an explicit policy priority in the discourse on statelessness. The discourse also does not insist that the human rights situation of the affected individuals should improve upon the acquisition of nationality, and Samvel's example illustrates how that can be problematic. His situation as an unrecognised stateless person in the Netherlands is significantly better in terms of protection of his rights than the situation he would face as a result of obtaining Armenian nationality.

Ignored statelessness: case of the Dutch municipal civil registry

This case follows up on one aspect of the previous case and considers the Dutch administrative practice of registering statelessness. It illustrates how not only the protection but also the mere recognition of statelessness can be in tension with the aim to reduce statelessness. In theory such tension should not exist, as long as the identification of an individual as stateless is understood as a declaratory and not a constitutive act (UNHCR 2014c, p. 10, para 16). In practice, however, the differences between constitutive and declaratory findings may get blurred, and the determination of statelessness may be perceived as indirectly creating statelessness, for example by validating practices that lead to the creation of statelessness.

Dutch state authorities are required to derive information about the nationality status of Dutch residents from the municipal records of personal data (*Basisregistratie Personen*) maintained by municipalities. Below, the Instructions on maintaining municipal records (*Handleiding Uitvoeringsprocedures*, hereafter 'the Instructions') issued by the Ministry of Interior are analysed (Dutch Ministry of Security and Justice 2015). This document is not legally binding, but is influential in implementing relevant laws, in particular the Law on Records of Personal Data (*Wet Basisregistratie Personen* 2013), and seems to reflect the way in which civil servants in fact operate with regard to registering statelessness (Dutch Committee for Migration Affairs 2013, p. 30; UNHCR 2011, pp. 17–19). Neither the Law nor the Instructions provide clear rules on how statelessness can be detected, and on the basis of what evidence a decision can be reached to register a person as stateless.

In addition to not establishing clear rules on registering statelessness, the Instructions are formulated in a way that discourages civil servants from recognising actual instances of statelessness (Swider 2014, pp. 10–21). For example, whenever the technical possibility of registering an individual as stateless is mentioned it is followed by a disclaimer that statelessness 'hardly ever occurs in practice' (Instructions, pp. 88, 151), which is strange considering the available statistics about the scope of statelessness worldwide, and in Europe in particular. According to the Instructions, the only two possible outcomes of loss of a nationality are the acquisition of a different nationality or the nationality status becoming 'unknown'[24]; no possibility of the individual becoming stateless as a result of having lost a nationality is mentioned (Instructions, pp. 332–334). In a section on state succession, the Instructions insist that individuals who have lost the nationality of the predecessor state are never stateless: not if the acquisition of the nationality of the successor state is delayed in time and not even when there is no clear prospect of acquiring any nationality of any of the successor states (Instructions, pp. 333–334). This is difficult to reconcile with the fact that state succession is one of the most widely known causes of statelessness. Another example is when the Instructions discuss the nationality status of children born to foreign parents in the Netherlands. If the acquisition of the parents' nationality is conditional upon a formal request to the relevant consular authorities and is conferred on the child retroactively from the moment of birth, the child cannot be registered as stateless, even if the necessary formalities at the foreign consulate did not take place (Instructions, pp. 139–140). This contradicts the definition of a stateless person established in the 1954 Convention, and accepted in the Dutch law, as the prospect of acquisition of nationality in the future is not relevant for determining whether a person is stateless at present.[25] Thus, a child who may acquire a nationality retroactively from birth after the parents register the birth with a relevant consular authority is stateless until such registration takes place, for as long as the acquisition of nationality is contingent upon future administrative processes.

While the Instructions' discouragement of the registration of statelessness makes little sense in light of the definition of a stateless person, known causes of statelessness, and norms on the protection of stateless persons, it does closely mirror international norms on the prevention and reduction of statelessness. These norms aim to prevent statelessness at birth and in the context of state succession and generally try to ensure that statelessness does not occur in practice. Even though the Instructions do not explicitly state that registration of statelessness should somehow be understood as creating statelessness, and thus should be avoided on the basis of norms on the reduction of statelessness, the language used suggests that such considerations may arise in practice. In combination with the lack of clear and explicit instructions on how to detect and approach statelessness, the Instructions may mislead the responsible civil servants into thinking that avoiding the recognition of statelessness helps to avoid statelessness.

In the case of Alina, a former Yugoslav national of Roma origin living in the Netherlands since the age of three, the denial of recognition of statelessness was substantiated in light of the international norms on the avoidance on statelessness, when the civil servant stated in relation to her case that:

> The nationality laws of most countries aim to avoid statelessness. This also holds for nationality laws of Bosnia and Herzegovina.[26]

Alina's request to change her nationality status from 'unknown' to 'stateless' was denied on the basis that she should have the right to a nationality of a Yugoslav successor state. This meant that she could not naturalise in the Netherlands, as she could not profit from the exemption on having to identify herself with a foreign passport.[27] Contrary to the intentions of the civil servant, the decision not to register Alina as stateless leads to the perpetuation of her statelessness potentially for life. If she has children in the Netherlands they may inherit her statelessness,[28] as the Netherlands does not apply statelessness safeguards to children whose nationality status is registered as 'unknown' in municipal records.

Nothing in the UNHCR policy documents can be interpreted as directly condoning the Dutch institutionalised practices of non-recognition of statelessness. In fact, the Handbook on the Protection of Stateless persons makes one helpful reference towards condemning such practices, namely that

> The illegality on the international level [of the act that leads to statelessness] is generally irrelevant for the purposes of [the definition of a stateless person]. The alternative would mean that an individual who has been stripped of his or her nationality in a manner inconsistent with international law would nevertheless be considered a 'national' [...]; a situation at variance with the object and purpose of the 1954 Convention.
> (UNHCR 2014c, p. 23, para 56)

However, the Dutch administrative practice does not discourage recognition of statelessness resulting from *illegal* acts, but discourages recognition of statelessness resulting from *almost any* acts. While the specific provisions of the two UN Statelessness Conventions and the UNHCR documents on statelessness cannot be held directly responsible for practices described in this case, the policy discourse that overemphasises and prioritises the reduction of statelessness over the importance of identification and protection of stateless persons may indirectly encourage such practices.

Evaluating goals on statelessness in light of human rights

The three case studies illustrate that applying UN statelessness policy goals in practice can lead to a number of normative problems related to the protection of the human rights and interests of those affected. The concluding section takes a step back and briefly examines the theoretical relationship between human rights discourse and the two goals on statelessness: protection of stateless persons and the reduction of statelessness. Identification of stateless persons is left out of this analysis, as it is not an end goal, but rather a means to achieve the other two. Is the prioritisation of the reduction of statelessness over the protection of stateless persons defensible in light of human rights?

First of all, it is important to point out that policies on statelessness are often framed in the human rights rhetoric. This also applies to justifying the reduction of statelessness (UNHCR 2012, p. 2, para 1). The protection of stateless persons is defined in terms of maximising their rights, in line with the preamble to the 1954 Convention discussed in the first section above. The link between the reduction of statelessness and human rights is less obvious. There are two ways to create this link. First, one can argue for the human right to a nationality and that statelessness per se is a violation of that right and thus needs to be eradicated. The second way to link reduction of statelessness to human rights is to maintain that possessing a nationality is the sole or better way of accessing human rights. Both are briefly discussed below, leading to the conclusion that neither forms a particularly solid human rights justification for a statelessness policy that prioritises reduction of statelessness over the protection of stateless persons.

Right to a nationality

The human right to a nationality features in the Universal Declaration on Human Rights (UDHR, Art. 15a; UNGA 1948) and in a number of subsequent international legal documents.[29] Although commentators have questioned whether the right to a nationality is a genuine human right and whether it is phrased in a useful manner in the Declaration (Hirsch Ballin 2014; Hanjian 2003; de Groot 1988, pp. 15–17), it seems to have become accepted as part of the human rights discourse on statelessness. To the extent that the mechanisms on the reduction of statelessness ensure that everyone can indeed exercise their right to a nationality, reduction of statelessness can be justified in light of the human right to a nationality. However, the norms on the reduction of statelessness go beyond providing a mere right to a nationality; they aim to ensure that as many people as possible *are in fact* nationals, and not just *have a right to be* nationals. The difference between the two is apparent in the context of voluntary statelessness, which is prohibited under the norms on reduction of statelessness (1961 Convention,

Art. 7(1); ECN, Art. 8(1)).[30] The limitation on the ability to become or remain stateless cannot be justified by nationality being a human right, but requires additional justification for constructing nationality also as *a duty*. A statelessness policy that prohibits voluntary statelessness thus cannot frame this prohibition in the discourse of human rights or refer to the interests of affected persons in this context.

Nationality as a gateway to human rights

The other argument for justifying the reduction of statelessness in light of human rights is based on the premise that being a national provides people with better chances of accessing human rights than being stateless. Based on available empirical evidence about the human rights situation of stateless persons worldwide, it indeed appears that statelessness is linked to numerous systematic, and sometimes massive, human rights violations. However, it is important to remember that first, the human rights situation of stateless persons differs significantly depending on the specific context of individual cases, and second, the human rights situation of nationals is very problematic as well in many contexts.[31] States are not equally willing and able to provide access to human rights for their nationals. According to the UN statistics, 96.8 per cent of the world's population lives in the country of their nationality, and human rights violations are not exclusively experienced by the remaining 3.2 per cent who are not within the jurisdiction of their state. A state is equally able to protect the human rights of nationals and of stateless persons, and in fact should protect the human rights of both categories equally, as both are equally human.

Nationality as the gateway to access rights, or as a 'right to have rights', is a description of a situation in which human rights fail; it is not an ideal to strive towards, as it goes deeply against what is commonly understood to be a human right (Griffin 2008). A primary goal of any statelessness policy based on human rights should be to ensure the protection of the human rights of stateless persons. The possession of nationality should not be the ultimate goal of a policy discourse on statelessness, but only a possible means to achieve the best possible protection of stateless persons. In cases where the acquisition of nationality does not offer the best possible protection or is not in line with the interests of the affected persons, other means should be given priority, such as protection under the statelessness regime.

Acquisition of a nationality by a stateless person can lead to the improvement of his or her human rights situation, but there is neither a theoretical nor an empirical guarantee that this will necessarily be the case. Moreover, insisting that stateless persons access human rights through the 'gateway of nationality' normalises the situation where the nationality status can be required for accessing human rights, which is contradictory to the ideal of human rights as accessible to any human being. In this context, the reduction of statelessness cannot be justified in light of human rights as an independent or superior goal, but merely as one of the possible ways of achieving the protection of currently stateless persons when the circumstances of a specific case warrant such a solution.

Conclusion

Tensions between the reduction of statelessness and the protection of stateless persons are structural, and not incidental. They are rooted in the fact that the status of a nationality does not necessarily offer protection and that the status of statelessness, if the 1954 Convention is complied with, may offer a decent level of protection. Resolving this tension by always prioritising the acquisition of a nationality may not be in the best interests of the individuals whose rights are supposedly protected.

If the interests and the human rights of the stateless are the guiding normative principle of the UNHCR's statelessness policies, the overemphasis on the elimination of statelessness needs to be reconsidered. Instead of insisting that every person is a national of a state, the focus should be on maximising access to rights by affected individuals.

Notes

1 Council of the EU, Press Release 893/15 of 4 December 2015: 'Council adopts conclusions on statelessness.'
2 In this chapter the terms 'nationality' and 'citizenship' are used interchangeably, and refer to the legal bond between a state and an individual who is considered as a national by that state. See for the discussion of the two terms, Tonkiss this volume.
3 See more on 'representing interests' in Goodin 2007; and Goodin 2003, pp. 208–210.
4 See also de Chickera and van Waas, this volume
5 Unless a stateless person also happens to be a refugee, in which case the refugee protection should take priority to ensure safety from persecution (see UNHCR 2014c, pp. 31–32).
6 Such a requirement should not be impossible to comply with for stateless persons because of their statelessness (see Art. 6 of the 1954 Convention).
7 Art. 27, 1954 Convention.
8 Art. 28, 1954 Convention.
9 Art. 31, 1954 Convention.
10 Art. 6, 1954 Convention.
11 See UNHCR *Handbook on the Protection of Stateless Persons*, Geneva (UNHCR 2014c, pp. 54–57).
12 Sixty-four States have ratified this Convention as of 6 November 2015.
13 Cf. Volker Türk, Foreword to the UNHCR *Handbook on the Protection of Stateless Persons*, Geneva (UNHCR 2014c, p. 1), where the author claims that the 1961 Convention 'provides a comprehensive set of tools for eradicating statelessness'.
14 The 1961 Convention has been ratified by 64 States. Various implementation problems with the 1961 Conventions have been highlighted in Vonk *et al.* 2013.
15 See also UNHCR Guidelines on Statelessness No. 4, para. 8 (UNHCR 2012).
16 The context of state succession constitutes an exception to this rule; international law accepts imposing a new nationality of a successor state on adults if they would otherwise become stateless as a result of state succession. See International Law Commission 'Draft Articles on Nationality of Natural Persons in relation to the Succession of States with commentaries' of 1999, in particular Arts. 7, 8 (comment No. 5) and 11 (comment No. 6). Another exception used to be the position of a married woman whose nationality changed automatically into the nationality of her husband, regardless of her will. Nowadays most states have abandoned this practice, and discrimination

against women in nationality law has been condemned in international legal instruments, such as the CEDAW.

17 The UNHCR draws a parallel with the Refugee Convention, which also does not contain an obligation to have refugee status determination procedures, but the implicit duty to do so under the Refugee Convention has been widely recognised.

18 Around 280,000 according to the governmental statistical data, see Baltic Institute of Social Sciences 'ANALYSIS OF INTEGRATION OF LATVIAN NON-CITIZENS' (Riga, 2014), p. 18; and K. Krūma 'COUNTRY REPORT: LATVIA' EUDO Citizenship Observatory, Country Report RSCAS/EUDO-CIT-CR 2013/13, last updated in February 2014, accessible here: http://eudo-citizenship.eu/docs/CountryReports/Latvia.pdf. The Latvian government does not consider non-citizens to be stateless persons, but the UNHCR does, and the requirements for accessing the status of a non-citizen leave no doubt that all non-citizens fall under the UN definition of a stateless person, and are thus considered as such for the purposes of this chapter.

19 Right now Latvian legislation on non-citizen status and on Latvian nationality is not fully in line with those standards, partially because Latvia does not consider non-citizens to be stateless, and does not apply the safeguards of the 1961 Convention to their situation.

20 Based on two similar cases of stateless persons in the Netherlands; anonymised case documentation is on file with the author. Names and some facts that are not essential to this chapter have been altered for privacy reasons.

21 A proposal for a statelessness determination procedure was published by the Dutch government on 26 September 2016, but has not been adopted at the time of writing.

22 The initial determination of citizenry in Armenia relied mostly on the Soviet residence registration system, and on residence in Armenia at the time of the adoption of the Armenian constitution (see Article 10 of the Law on Citizenship of the Republic of Armenia of 6 November 1995). Since Samvel was neither resident in Armenia at the time the Constitution was adopted, nor possessed the citizenship of the Soviet Republic of Armenia, he is not an Armenian citizen according to the law in force.

23 The acquisition of nationality could presumably happen on the basis of the wide discretionary powers of the state to naturalise individuals of Armenian origin without the latter having to comply with formal requirements for naturalisation (see Article 13 of the Law on Citizenship of the Republic of Armenia of 6 November 1995).

24 It is also specifically stated that 'unknown nationality' or the lack of a registration of nationality cannot lead to the conclusion that a person is stateless (see *Handleiding Uitvoeringsprocedures* (Handbook Implementing Procedure), version 2.2 of 31 August 2015, p. 161).

25 For the UNHCR definition, see Art. 1 of the 1954 Convention. This definition was implemented in Dutch legislation (see art. 1(1f) of the Dutch Nationality Law (*Rijkswet op het Nederlanderschap*)).

26 Email exchange with a civil servant handling the case from 7 to 28 July 2014, on file with the author.

27 Same obstacle that Samvel encountered in the previous case.

28 Unless they are able to obtain a nationality from the father.

29 In relation to children, for example, in the ICCPR, art. 24(3), and CRC, art. 7; regionally in Europe in the ECN, art. 4(a).

30 The UNHCR Handbook on the Protection of Stateless Persons allows the State Parties to the 1954 Convention to offer lower protection to persons who voluntarily renounce their nationality in order to be stateless, see the UNHCR *Handbook on the Protection of Stateless Persons*, Geneva (UNHCR 2014c, p. 56, paras. 161–162).

31 See also de Chickera and van Waas, this volume.

References

Council of Europe. (2015) *Report of the Commissioner for Human Rights 'Following his visit to Armenia from 5 to 9 October 2014'* (10 March 2015). [Online] Available from: https://wcd.coe.int/ViewDoc.jsp?id=2295815/ [Accessed 3 February 2016].

Donner, R. (1994) *The Regulation of Nationality in International Law*. 2nd edn. Irvington-on-Hudson, NY: Transnational.

Dutch Committee for Migration Affairs. (*Adviescommissie Vreemdelingenzaken*). (2013) *'Geen land te bekennen'* ('No country of one's own') (December 2013). [Online] Available from: http://acvz.org/pubs/geen-land-te-bekennen/ [Accessed 3 February 2016].

Dutch Ministry of Security and Justice. (2015) *Handleiding Uitvoeringsprocedures*. (Instructions on Implementing Procedures), version 2.2 of 31 August 2015. [Online] Available from: www.rvig.nl/documenten/richtlijnen/2015/08/31/handleiding-uitvoeringsprocedures-hup-2-2 [Accessed 3 February 2016].

Goodin, R. E. (2007) Enfranchising all affected interests, and its alternatives. *Philosophy & Public Affairs*, 35(1), pp. 40–68.

Goodin, R. E. (2003) *Reflective Democracy*. Oxford: Oxford University Press.

Griffin, J. (2008) *On Human Rights*. Oxford: Oxford University Press.

de Groot, G.-R. (1988) *Staatsangehörigkeitsrecht im Wandel: eine rechtsvergleichende Studie über Erwerbs- und Verlustgründe der Staatsangehörigkeit*. The Hague: Asser Press.

Hanjian, C. (2003) *The Sovrien: An Exploration of the Right to Be Stateless*. Vineyard Haven, MA: Polyspire.

Hirsch Ballin, E. (2014) *Citizens' Rights and the Right to be a Citizen*. Leiden: Brill Nijhoff.

ILC (International Law Commission). (1999) *Draft Articles on Nationality of Natural Persons in relation to the Succession of States with commentaries*. [Online] Available from: www.unhcr.org/5465e1ca9.pdf [Accessed 3 February 2016].

Krūma, K. (2014) *EU Citizenship, Nationality, and Migrant Status: An Ongoing Challenge*. Leiden: Martinus Nijhoff.

League of Nations. (1930) *Convention on Certain Questions Relating to the Conflict of Nationality Law*, 13 April 1930, League of Nations, Treaty Series, vol. 179, p. 89, No. 4137. [Online] Available at: www.refworld.org/docid/3ae6b3b00.html [Accessed 3 February 2016].

Swider, K. (2014) Statelessness Determination in the Netherlands, *Amsterdam Centre for European Law and Governance Research Paper Series*, Paper No. 2014–04, 8 May 2014. [Online] Available from: http://ssrn.com/abstract=2434573. [Accessed 3 February 2016].

Swider, K. and den Heijer, M. (2016, forthcoming) *Why Union Law Can and Should Protect Stateless Persons*.

UNGA. (1996) *Resolution 50/152* (9 February 1996), A/RES/50/152. New York: United Nations General Assembly. [Online] Available from: www.un.org/documents/ga/res/50/ares50–152.htm [Accessed 3 February 2016].

UNGA. (1948) The Universal Declaration of Human Rights. New York: United Nations General Assembly [Online] Available from: www.un.org/en/documents/udhr/ [Accessed 3 February 2016].

UNHCR. (2014a) *A Special Report: Ending Statelessness within 10 Years*. United Nations High Commissioner for Refugees. [Online] Available from: www.unhcr.org/546217229.html [Accessed 3 February 2016].

UNHCR. (2014b) *Global Action Plan to End Statelessness*. United Nations High Commissioner for Refugees. [Online] Available from: www.unhcr.org/54621bf49.html [Accessed 3 February 2016].

UNHCR. (2014c) *Handbook on the Protection of Stateless Persons*. United Nations High Commissioner for Refugees. [Online] Available from: www.unhcr.org/53b698ab9.html [Accessed 3 February 2016].

UNHCR. (2012) *Guidelines on Statelessness No. 4 'Ensuring Every Child's Right to Acquire a Nationality through Articles 1–4 of the 1961 Convention on the Reduction of Statelessness'* (21 December 2012). United Nations High Commissioner for Refugees. [Online] Available from: www.refworld.org/docid/50d460c72.html [Accessed 3 February 2016].

UNHCR. (2011) *Mapping Statelessness in the Netherlands*. United Nations High Commissioner for Refugees. [Online] Available from: www.refworld.org/docid/4eef65da2.html [Accessed 3 February 2016].

UNHCR. (2006) *Conclusion on Identification, Prevention and Reduction of Statelessness and Protection of Stateless Persons*. United Nations High Commissioner for Refugees. [Online] Available from: www.unhcr.org/453497302.html [Accessed 3 February 2016].

Vonk, O., Vink, M. and de Groot, G. R. (2013) Protection against Statelessness: Trends and Regulations in Europe, *EUDO-Citizenship Comparative Report Series*, May 2013. [Online] Available from: http://eudo-citizenship.eu/images/docs/eudocit_vink_degroot_statelessness_final.pdf [Accessed 3 February 2016].

Wet Basisregistratie Personen (The Law on Records of Personal Data) (2013). [Online] Available from: http://wetten.overheid.nl/BWBR0033715 [Accessed 3 February 2016].

13 Realising the rights of stateless persons

The doctrine of fiduciary duty and the role of municipal government

David Passarelli

Introduction

Many have commented on the lack of theoretical scholarship focused specifically on the question of statelessness (Belton 2011; Staples 2012) – it is a lacuna that this book and several other recent publications seek to address explicitly.

William Conklin, in his 2014 work, Statelessness: The Enigma of an International Community, asks 'why would a state be legally obligated to protect a stateless person if the state has determined the person stateless?' (2014, p. 21). His work is predicated on the idea that there exists a paradox in the international system: it provides international safeguards for all, but allows states to exist that deny these safeguards to some communities in practice. His work, like this one, inquires into the nature of the obligation to protect stateless persons. The two projects share a common goal in their search for ways to allocate responsibility for addressing the vulnerability of stateless persons that is independent of the sovereign will of states.

The argument taken up in this chapter is that insufficient attention has been paid to explaining the responsibilities that accrue to sub-state actors in addressing the vulnerabilities of stateless persons. What is the nature of this responsibility? What account of obligation can public authorities at the sub-state level draw on to interpret their obligations towards stateless persons? Are municipal authorities obliged to act in particular ways towards persons that the state does not recognise as members of the political community? This chapter charts a path towards an answer to these questions, without promising a solution to the global problem of statelessness.

Fieldwork undertaken by the author in Toronto (Canada) and London (United Kingdom) will inform discussion of these issues. This fieldwork revealed that local service providers experienced a tension between their responsibilities to discharge services impartially at the municipal level and national immigration imperatives. These concerns were echoed at a 2014 round-table seminar in Barcelona, Spain, to discuss city responses to irregular migration, during which the speaker for the Council of the London Borough of Islington noted that local authorities can 'find themselves with no guidelines or standards on how to interpret their own responsibilities' (Ajuntament de Barcelona 2014). The ambiguity that exists regarding the responsibilities of municipal authorities for stateless persons and irregular migrants more generally can lead to significant differences in service provision or, worse, a reluctance to accept responsibility for the protection of stateless persons. There is therefore a clear and urgent need to inquire into the nature of municipal authority and the scope of its associated responsibilities. Furthermore, by reflecting on the relationship stateless persons have with local authorities, one takes an important step towards a post-national conception of membership rights, disentangling the rights of stateless persons from their membership in a nation-state (see Katherine Tonkiss in this volume for problematisation of this term).

In the process of laying out a new way of thinking about the responsibilities of municipal authorities, this work is responding to calls for new, inward-looking theoretical frameworks focused on statelessness and the rights of stateless persons (Belton 2011). The claim advanced in the pages that follow is that there exists an obligation for local governments to respond to the needs of stateless persons and that this obligation arises from unique features of their relationship with this population, which can be conceptualised as a 'fiduciary relationship'.[1] One upshot of this framing is that duties of a fiduciary nature may be imposed unilaterally on municipal authorities simply by virtue of stateless persons inhabiting the space of the city. Being inhabitants as well, the needs of vulnerable *citizens* also fall within the scope of fiduciary concern. However, a fiduciary conception of municipal authority foregrounds the importance of equity in dealing with vulnerable parties, requiring of the fiduciary a duty of loyalty to the vulnerable party's best interests; and here, the degree of need and the limited options available to stateless persons to claim rights will come to matter greatly.

The challenges of statelessness

Statelessness is often the product of changes to the geopolitical environment or the deliberate, sometimes discriminatory, policies of government. This is the case for over 20,000 people who have been made stateless in the successor states that sprang up after the break-up of the former Yugoslavia and for the over 170,000 individuals who identify as stateless in Russia subsequent to the collapse of the Soviet Union (this case is developed in Swider, this volume). It is also so for the over 200,000 Rohingya people who had their citizenship cancelled with the passing of national legislation in Myanmar over 30 years ago. Contributing to our understanding of statelessness 'status', Lindsey N. Kingston helpfully points out that statelessness is 'both a cause of marginalisation, as well as a symptom of it' (Kingston, this volume). In Kenya, discriminatory citizenship laws affect the Nubian, Kenyan Somali, and Coastal Arab communities who have either been arbitrarily denied citizenship or have had their documentation taken from them, rendering them stateless. Oscar Mwangi suggests that there may in fact be many more stateless persons than even this description allows, owing to insecurity in ungoverned spaces within Kenya (Mwangi, this volume).

Caroline Sawyer and Brad K. Blitz observe that stateless persons lack basic protections that citizens enjoy by way of normal links with a government, as well as the means to access many basic rights (Sawyer and Blitz 2011). Where stateless persons lack an effective link to a government, it might simply be impossible for them to re-establish any such ties owing to administrative barriers, discrimination, the absence of proper identification, a combination of these factors or any number of others. Absent the possibility of regularising their status in their host country, stateless persons are at serious risk of falling into destitution (ENS 2014).

The stateless persons' tenuous link to their host state can make access to social goods quite challenging. In this, stateless persons share many of the challenges and frustrations of other persons living with precarious status. Jean Lambert, Member of the European Parliament, writing for the European Network on Statelessness, recently remarked:

> For stateless persons the fundamental rights that most people take for granted like education and healthcare, become impossible to access. Those who are stateless describe a feeling of not belonging, of their identity being 'rubbed out'.
>
> (Lambert 2015)

Persons with precarious status often fear contact with the state, believing that it might lead to reprisals and even deportation. This apprehension towards public authorities can be indiscriminate: lumping public officials and procedures that carry the promise of relief and protection together with those that lead to punishment and reprisals. This adds to the general insecurity of the community and undermines everyone's practical interests if, as a matter of routine, crimes and violence are left unreported for fear of contact with public officialdom. The Institute on Statelessness and Inclusion (ISI) observe in their 2014 report, *The World's Stateless*:

> Where a stateless person wants to assert their rights, or where they have become a victim of crime or exploitation, their statelessness can also stand in the way of getting help from the authorities or finding their way to a court. Their complaint may be readily dismissed or ignored, and they are powerless to take a stand against this due to their status of disenfranchisement.
>
> (2014, p. 30)

Some of the simplest solutions crafted to address statelessness become very difficult to implement when stateless persons fear contact with public authorities. Birth registration is impossible if one fears contact with health care professionals. Where status determination procedures are available (still woefully lacking in many places), stateless persons must first reveal themselves to public authorities with no guarantee that they will be able to retreat from a refused claim (moreover, appeals are often not possible in cases where an application for statelessness status has been rejected).

It is also not uncommon to find the threat of destitution actively promoted as a policy response to irregular migration, in an effort to strengthen immigration control and ensure that the 'benefits' bestowed on citizens are not appropriated by migrants that do not have residence permission (Da Lomba 2004, p. 365; Sigona and Hughes 2012; UNHCR 2014). The administrative powers of the state are such that barriers are easily erected that can prevent the effective realisation of rights even when these are guaranteed by law. The UK Home Office's 2007 policy entitled *Enforcing the Rules – A Strategy to Ensure and Enforce Compliance with our Immigration Laws* serves as a particularly stark example of at least one instance when the UK Home Office sponsored outright a policy of destitution in the service of immigration control. The policy states that 'those not prioritised for removal [...] should be denied the benefits and privileges of life in the UK and experience an increasingly uncomfortable environment so that they elect to leave' (UK Government 2007, p. 17).

Controlling access to social services is only one way, though an important way, governments have sought to monitor and deter unwanted migration (Morris 2003; Spencer and Pobjoy 2011; Sawyer and Blitz 2011). The exclusion of stateless persons and those with precarious status from the regime of social goods available to citizens within the state is increasingly seen as an extension of the state's sovereign power to exclude at the border. Such policy responses are a product of a 'chain of reasoning', whereby state authorities link (a) the state's authority to decide who may enter or exit the territory, with (b) the state's responsibility to secure the welfare of all residents (CoE 2007). The latter are often made conditional on the migrant having met the conditions of membership set by the state.

Such policies affect *irregular stateless migrants* disproportionally, i.e. migrants who are both stateless and do not have a regularised migration status (Nonnenmacher and Cholewinski 2014). The logic that underwrites policies such as the 2007 *Enforcing the Rules* policy presumes that those present in the state without permission may exercise an option to return 'home'. More likely, it confines the irregular stateless migrant to conditions of compound deprivation and severely curtails any hope of a more secure future (see Kingston, this volume). The environment that confronts these persons has aptly been described as one that entails 'a most severe and dramatic deprivation of the power of the individual' (McDougal *et al.* 1974, p. 960).

Hannah Arendt called attention to the problem of statelessness over fifty years ago, perhaps most poignantly when she observed that a nationality is effectively the 'right to have rights' (Arendt 1958). Concepts and norms of protection have evolved since; today, there is well-documented and widespread recognition in the domain of human rights law that the lack of citizenship in any state is a pernicious harm, but even in the absence of citizenship individuals do not instantly lose all rights. Instead, the challenge today seems to be moving beyond a point at which the rights of the stateless are held hostage to the caprice of governments.

The challenge posed by national sovereignty to the universal application of human rights law has eroded the enjoyment of rights of peripheral groups such as the stateless.

(The Equal Rights Trust 2010, p. XIV)

The issue of statelessness is not confined by debates about borders and membership. As Belton writes, any theoretical project should not be limited to determining who should be let in, but also be 'examining who has always been on the inside and to whom we need to justify their continued exclusion' (2011, p. 59). The account of responsibility put forward in this chapter resonates with the work of Engin Isin (2008), Arash Abizadeh (2008), and Peter Nyers (2010), among others, who argue that the boundaries of the political community should be rethought to better reflect its constituent subjects, audiences, and spaces. The following pages present an argument for expanding the municipal authority's sphere of responsibility, so as to better address the local effects of statelessness and the peculiar vulnerability of stateless persons.

The (amorphous) nature of fiduciary relationships

A fiduciary relationship is one that is built around notions of trust, loyalty, power, and vulnerability – it is purpose-built to safeguard the vulnerable in situations of power imbalance. This chapter argues that this is the best way of conceiving of the authority exercised by municipal authorities over the *inhabitants* of their cities. On this view, the authority of the municipal government is a form of public trust exercised on behalf of all *inhabitants*, but which must be discharged fairly and reasonably and with particular regard for the care of the most vulnerable. This section will explore the basic tenets of the concept, which is borrowed from the private and (more recently) public law contexts, to illuminate the relationship between municipal authorities and stateless persons.

The doctrine of fiduciary duty has a long history in legal theory. Its origins have been traced back to English common law, and more specifically the law of trusts. Scholars and jurists have only recently begun applying the concept to other types of social relations, for example, thinking of friendship as a fiduciary relationship (Leib 2009), parents as fiduciaries (Bryan 1995) or politicians as fiduciaries (Rave 2013). Tamar Frankel (1983, p. 793) has argued that a general societal shift is underway, one that will see the growth of 'a separate body of fiduciary law', adding, 'society is evolving into one based predominantly on fiduciary relations'. Indeed, over the last 50 years, a number of legal decisions have contributed to the expansion of the application of fiduciary duties outside of the private law context (e.g. *Authorson* v. *Canada* 2003).

Despite the growing scholarship on the subject, it remains challenging to capture a single, clear meaning of fiduciary obligations in a general definition. 'Fiduciary duty is complicated [...] in respect of its ambit, its scope, its termination, and the remedies for its breach', writes Rafael Chodos (2010, p. 838). He argues that the conclusion one must arrive at is that 'the notion is fuzzy' (2010, p. 846).

The difficulty arises from the multiplicity of ways fiduciary obligations may arise – the principle is stubbornly context-dependent. Yet, it is this focus on context that is also one of its most useful features, since it opens the possibility of escaping from the straightjacket of consent that is part and parcel of contracts and other self-assumed obligations. The latter are typically preferred for their ability to limit risk, since each party is aware at the outset of the limits of their responsibility. By contrast, relationships with a fiduciary component to them can arise in a number of scenarios where one party exercises almost exclusive discretionary control over the interests of a second, vulnerable party. This is exemplified, according to Sossin, in the 'case of administrative decision makers and vulnerable groups affected by their decisions' (2003, p. 129).

In brief, the principle states that fiduciary obligations arise between two parties (a fiduciary and a beneficiary) that are separated by a relationship of *power* and *vulnerability*. The key condition that signals a fiduciary relationship and thus triggers fiduciary obligations is that the beneficiary is *dependent* on the actions of the fiduciary and is vulnerable to the fiduciary's discretionary authority. Moreover, the fiduciary has a positive obligation to track the beneficiary's interests and act in such a way that is respectful of the power imbalance that inheres in their relationship. This is often expressed as the duty of loyalty to the interests of the beneficiary. Fiduciaries are bound to consider the interests of beneficiaries in a manner proportionate to the discretionary authority they hold over those same interests (Fox-Decent 2005, p. 267). So, the parent must act in consideration of the child's best interests, as do doctors with patients, lawyers with their clients, and it will be shown, municipal authorities with respect to the inhabitants of a city.

In Box 13.1, the conditions that give rise to fiduciary obligations according to the most prominent accounts in law are presented. Canadian Supreme Court Justices writing in the 1987 case *Frame* v. *Smith* suggest that these criteria constitute a 'rough and ready guide' for detecting the existence of a fiduciary relationship between two parties (see also *Lac Minerals Ltd.* v. *International Corona Resources Ltd* 1989). The reason for calling attention to Canadian jurisprudence in such an overt way is because the principle of fiduciary duty has known a somewhat unique trajectory in Canadian law and legal theory. Canadian courts are described by Lorne Sossin as having been 'at the forefront of exploring the many incarnations of fiduciary obligations', and more specifically, they 'have been instrumental in the recognition of public law fiduciary obligations' (2003, p. 130).

Box 13.1 Conditions establishing a fiduciary relationship

- The fiduciary has scope for the exercise of some discretion or power;
- The fiduciary can unilaterally exercise that power or discretion so as to affect the beneficiary's legal or practical interests; and,
- The beneficiary is peculiarly vulnerable to or at the mercy of the fiduciary holding the discretion or power.

(*Frame* v. *Smith*)

One may grant at this point that there exists a juridical concept that may be harnessed to constrain the abuse of power in *relationships* where one party exercises a degree of dominance over the interests of a second, vulnerable party. But when considering the plight of stateless persons and the challenges they face in accessing protections and basic human rights, one does not simply feel that there may be a transgression of law; rather, the intuition commonly evoked is that there is a shortcoming of justice.

It should be immediately apparent to those familiar with the work of Robert E. Goodin (1985a) that the legal formula above (Box 13.1) bears a strong resemblance to Goodin's *vulnerability principle* (Box 13.2). In developing the idea of a *vulnerability principle*, Goodin's aim was to take forward a discussion about social responsibility and provide a normative argument why obligations are owed to persons distant from us, as well as to those close to us. He proceeds with the aim of answering a single question, 'why should *we* assist the vulnerable?' Goodin argues that the intuition to favour particular attachments over moral obligations to those with whom one stands in more distant relationships deflects one badly from one's moral course (1985a, p. 24).

Box 13.2 Goodin's vulnerability principle

The relationship embodies an asymmetrical balance of power.

The subordinate party needs the resources provided by the relationship in order to protect his vital interests.

For the subordinate party, the relationship is the only source of such resources.

The superordinate party in the relationship exercises discretionary control over those resources.

Protecting the Vulnerable (Goodin 1985a, p. 195)

The discussion Goodin takes forward is concerned with the reallocation of the finite resources within a community to those most needful. This reallocation is not considered a matter of beneficence or charity, but a matter of justice. For Goodin, the criteria in Box 13.2 provide a basis for detecting relationships that hold the greatest potential for the exploitation of vulnerable persons. Ultimately, the decision to aid one individual over another should be a function of the relative vulnerability of the person in need.

Like Goodin, scholars and jurists writing about the principle of fiduciary duty fix on the notion of vulnerability and dependence to orient moral concern. Both Goodin's vulnerability principle and the fiduciary principle accomplish something arguably more valuable: they help identify what party bears responsibility to meet the claims of a person in need. 'Saying merely that "A is in need" leaves unspecified who should be responsible for meeting those needs. Saying that "A is vulnerable to B" provides a ready answer to that question' (Goodin 1985b, p. 779). For at least a few legal scholars, recent applications of the fiduciary principle in public law and the prospect of its future development are a sign that it is not merely a formalistic legal approach to relations between individuals and those in authority, but holds the potential to cast these relations in a new light (Sossin 2003; Fox-Decent and Criddle 2009).

Before concluding this section, one further dimension of fiduciary relationships needs to be addressed. It was suggested earlier that one of the great advantages of the fiduciary principle is that it is context-dependent and thus not reliant on prior consent or self-assumed obligation to ground responsibility. In Goodin's account, self-assumed obligations do not play an important role in assigning responsibility to aid a person in need. In this, Goodin is allied with scholars of feminist political theory who have long been critical of the notion of self-assumed obligations being the only basis for establishing a duty to aid others (Robinson 1999). In the case of fiduciary relationships, it is more contested ground. Some point to the need for a form of prior acknowledgement of the circumstances which may give rise to a fiduciary relationship; only then would it be reasonable to hold *the expectation* of fiduciary loyalty, e.g. a piece of legislation, or legal precedent, that acknowledges that specific circumstances give rise to a fiduciary relationship (Purkey 2013, p. 696). But Ethan Leib (2009, p. 672) points out that this is only one *formal* juridical view of the way fiduciary relationships arise. A facts-based analysis can also be used to reveal the existence of *informal* fiduciary relationships. These relationships spring up from the roles individuals fill. 'Particular relationships are recognised as fiduciary on a case-by-case basis by virtue of their possession of characteristics of fiduciary relationships,' writes Paul Miller (2013, p. 50). Further, Evan Fox-Decent (2005, p. 294) has argued that a fiduciary has to act in a manner respectful of the beneficiary's trust 'even where the beneficiary has done nothing evident to repose trust, and the alleged fiduciary denies the existence of any kind of trust relationship'.

The next section builds upon this discussion of fiduciary relationships. Owing to specific features of the stateless person's relationship with municipal authorities, the section argues that stateless persons may be considered beneficiaries of a fiduciary relationship with municipal authorities.

The nature of the municipality's duty to protect stateless persons

Parts of the discussion in this section draw on legal precedent and argumentation from the Canadian and British contexts, bearing in mind both the fieldwork undertaken by the author in the cities of Toronto and London and the degree to which the concept of fiduciary duty has been debated and enlarged in the Canadian context. The section begins by reviewing the relationship between municipal authorities and the inhabitants of the City of Toronto to illustrate that even where *citizens* are concerned the doctrine of fiduciary duty is contested. The ongoing juridical debate notwithstanding, the section proceeds to demonstrate (a) that as a concept, the fiduciary doctrine has normative and explanatory potential when considering the rights of stateless persons, and (b) that stateless persons should be considered beneficiaries of a fiduciary relationship with municipal authorities.

Who are fiduciaries and who are beneficiaries?

A landmark decision of the Supreme Court of Canada in 1984 ruled that the Government of Canada stands in a fiduciary relationship to its aboriginal peoples (*Guerin* v. *The Queen* 1984). Recently, numerous cases have been argued before Canadian courts that have helped determine whether municipal authorities also owe fiduciary duties, and if so to whom. It is beyond the scope of this chapter to discuss the numerous cases that have arisen that centre on a claim of redress for breach of a fiduciary duty in the municipal context, as the volume of case law is considerable. It is nevertheless important to draw attention to the fact that the definition of a beneficiary has varied over time. In some cases the beneficiary has been defined as the taxpayer (*MacIlReith* v. *Hart* 1908), while in others the description is applied to the electorate (*Toronto Party for a Better City* v. *Toronto* 2013) or the inhabitants of a city (*Bowes* v. *City of Toronto* 1858). It is not uncommon to find that one court has made a determination with regard to the standing of a claimant as a beneficiary of a fiduciary duty, only to have the determination reversed by a higher court (*Hawrelak* v. *City of Edmonton* 1976).

In the case of the City of Toronto, the interpretation of the courts and city officials can also be at odds. Here, an example from field research undertaken in the City of Toronto helps to illustrate the point.

In recent years, the City Council of Toronto has chosen to draw attention to and stress specific aspects of the City of Toronto Act in order to foreground a particular interpretation of its relationship with the inhabitants of the City. Specifically, paragraph 125 (1) of the City of Toronto Act states that 'The City of Toronto is hereby continued as a body corporate that is composed of the inhabitants of its geographic area' (2006). The emphasis on the inhabitants of a jurisdiction (i.e. Torontonians), without reference to immigration status, was seized upon deliberately by the Social Development Finance and Administration arm of the City authority in an effort to underscore the responsibility of municipal authorities for persons with an irregular status. The City of Toronto has since adopted the term *undocumented Torontonians* in City Council motions, and puts forward the following rationale for having shifted to the use of this term:

> In recognition of its responsibility to serve all Torontonians, Council has taken a proactive policy position committing to ensuring that immigrants without full status or full status documents have access to City services without fear.
>
> (City of Toronto 2014, p. 4)

The language used to describe the responsibility of the City of Toronto for irregular migrants is noteworthy. The term 'undocumented Torontonians' became commonplace after its introduction in City Council motions beginning in 2013, signalling that the geographical space the undocumented inhabit qualifies to place them within the scope of the City's concern. By doing so, the City of Toronto exercised its discretion in framing the relationship between the City and those it is responsible to, broadening the scope of its responsibility to include migrants without a permission of residence. In sum, while the courts may rule that the scope of municipal government responsibility is limited to its statute of incorporation and the powers granted to it through this statute, city officials may nevertheless interpret the scope of their responsibilities differently.

To be clear, the claim in this chapter is that municipal governments and the public authorities in their employ have the capacity to mitigate at least some of the immediate, practical harms arising from statelessness and that the duty to do so might be conceived of as a *fiduciary duty*. This is not an entirely new obligation being imposed; rather, it is an extension of a duty that some have already recognised as accruing to municipal authorities in respect of the persons that inhabit their cities, including others without either citizenship or a recognised immigration status.[2] The question taken up next is whether it is reasonable to incorporate stateless people in the scope of fiduciary concern.

To establish that stateless persons fall within the scope of fiduciary duties of municipal authorities one would need to point to certain relevant features of the relationship of those authorities with stateless persons. The reference points for establishing this relationship are drawn from Boxes 13.1 and 13.2. It would appear that at least three things would need to be established: (a) an imbalance of power between municipal authorities and stateless persons inhabiting a municipality; (b) the dependency of stateless persons on municipal authorities for certain resources vital to their interests; and, (c) a high degree of vulnerability to the discretional authority of municipal government (which controls access to services vital to the stateless person's well-being) combined with a limited capacity to reduce their vulnerability to this discretionary authority. Below, each criterion is addressed in turn.

The fiduciary has scope for the exercise of some discretion or power. The relationship embodies an asymmetrical balance of power.

That municipal authorities can exercise discretion is not in dispute. Local government is empowered to enact legislation and policies in furtherance of the public good and this legislation applies to all inhabitants of the municipal space. By virtue of this power, and the simple fact that few others possess similar authority, they stand in an asymmetrical relationship of power with stateless persons. Moreover, where stateless persons are detained for breach of immigration rules, the scope of this discretion is intensified and the divide in the balance of power enlarged.

Furthermore, municipal authorities enter into this relationship of power asymmetry the moment a stateless individual enters the municipal space. To be sure, time will affect the degree of discretion that municipal authorities can exercise. As a stateless person builds networks of relationships and relations of solidarity with other inhabitants, they may find creative ways of shielding themselves from the total domination of municipal and state authority. Vicki Squire (2011) has argued that the interaction between migrants, refugees, and their host communities, especially in city spaces, often gives rise to 'mobile solidarities'. Her work highlights the importance of looking beyond the legal definition of political community, and sheds light on the meaningful bonds that are created through collective engagement in the political and social life of the community. By the same token, the longer a stateless person inhabits the municipal space under the prevailing condition of power asymmetry, the more they stand to lose should they be forcibly removed – they stand to lose friendships, lovers, and other valued bonds with and within the community.

Insofar as public authorities attached to the municipality leverage the authority of municipal government, they exercise a measure of discretion over the interests of stateless persons. This unilateral discretion is both a practical and symbolic reminder of the asymmetrical balance of power between stateless persons and municipal authorities.

The fiduciary can unilaterally exercise that power or discretion so as to affect the beneficiary's legal or practical interests. The subordinate party needs the resources provided by the relationship in order to protect his vital interests. The superordinate party in the relationship exercises discretionary control over those resources.

This set of criteria is also readily met, perhaps most clearly through the control of forms of identification. Municipal authorities regulate the forms of identification that one needs in order to access various services – this can affect everything from the ability of a person to legally operate a vehicle to borrowing a book from a local library. In this way, municipal authorities, and by extension local service providers, act as gatekeepers to information and services that are instrumental to the health, security, and well-being of stateless persons, along with access to the numerous social goods necessary to living a minimally decent life. Further, they are under no obligation to provide accounts to stateless persons as regards the types of services they will be offered or the manner in which they will access such services. In this way, they unilaterally set the terms of the relationship and limit the means by which stateless persons can advance their interests. For example, one might think of the school board administrator that insists on certain forms of identification prior to allowing children to be registered in schools, or police officers that rely on the same to register complaints, or courts that similarly refuse access.

Local authorities are charged with managing the services that are of most critical value to stateless persons: schooling, healthcare, policing, pathways to employment, housing, and so forth. In addition to unilaterally setting the conditions of access, they also determine the kind and extent of service one will enjoy, while there is little to no scope for formal consultation or input by stateless persons. Take, for example, the case of education for stateless children. Assuming a parent lacks permission to be resident, he or she will also be denied a say in the policies that govern the education provided to his or her child by being denied a vote in school council elections. The quality of and access to education determines in significant ways the future potential of children. Limiting access to education either directly (by denying access) or indirectly (by promulgating administrative barriers that have the effect of preventing access) undermines the proper development of the child now, but also of his or her future self, constraining significantly his or her possibilities later in life.

Equally noteworthy is the lack of political voice through elections or the ability to hold public office for many stateless persons. This effectively locks in the power of other legal residents and their representatives to unilaterally set policies that affect the interests of stateless persons, absent any consultation.

The beneficiary is peculiarly vulnerable to or at the mercy of the fiduciary holding the discretion or power. For the subordinate party, the relationship is the only source of such resources.

It is in relation to this third set of criteria that the vulnerability of stateless persons stands out most starkly. Over 30 years ago, it was observed that, 'The possible value deprivations to which such a [stateless] person may be subjected are severe and all-encompassing, far beyond those common to aliens' (McDougal *et al.* 1974, p. 902). Vulnerability per se is not objectionable. A child is vulnerable to a parent's authority. Spouses are vulnerable to one another and increasingly so over time. One does not decry these situations as unjust. However, what is of concern in the case of stateless persons is that they find themselves in situations where their social welfare needs cannot easily be met by another party, since they cannot easily (if at all) extract themselves from the relationship of dependency they have with the municipal authorities where they reside – since they lack the protection of any other government. As Onora O'Neil points out:

> Where there are vast differences of power and vulnerability, it is all too easy for the powerful to make the vulnerable 'an offer they cannot refuse.' Like the Mafia, they can use the civil language of commerce or politics or labor relations, while exerting a pressure that coerces.
>
> (1998, p. 108)

Municipal, like national, authorities wield tremendous discretion in determining the fate of stateless persons. Without proper identification and the means to travel freely stateless persons cannot easily seek protection elsewhere, meaning they are confined to make a life for themselves in sometimes inhospitable places. In such circumstances, it is not uncommon for stateless persons to slip into a life of destitution. In addition to the other authors in this volume, numerous recent studies have called attention to the existence of a 'cycle of destitution', where the stateless person is left without the means of supervening on the conditions that trap them. As if this were not plenty already, their fear of public authorities increases the likelihood that their numbers will go uncounted and their needs overlooked.

Synthesis

Municipal authorities and local service providers deliver vital social goods and are charged with a general public duty to serve the interests of their communities. This duty has been characterised here as a fiduciary duty. Up until now it has been unclear on what basis one might include stateless persons within the scope of such a duty. This chapter has sought to demonstrate that stateless persons not only qualify as beneficiaries of the more narrow fiduciary duty of loyalty owed by local authorities, but that they are in fact a paradigmatic case of a beneficiary. This is a result of the distinct features of their relationship with these authorities: municipal governments have both the power and discretion to affect the vital interests of stateless persons and it is a relationship that stateless persons cannot easily exit. A responsibility therefore accrues to municipal authorities to address the needs of stateless persons, whether they want to or not.

There are practical constraints that will naturally affect the ability of municipal authorities to deliver the sort of assistance alluded to in this chapter. While some forms of assistance come at little cost (e.g. access to libraries), in most other cases the cost of social services is not insignificant. One must acknowledge that resources are a key constraint in the ability of municipal authorities to delivery on the fiduciary responsibilities outlined above.

There are two points that should be made in this respect; the first is cause for optimism, the second, less so. A 2015 study on 'Practices and Approaches in EU Member States to Prevent and End Statelessness', prepared for the European Parliament, argues that because of the unique protection gaps faced by stateless persons they are in fact owed a higher level of protection as compared to other non-nationals (De Groot *et al.* 2015). Where a finite amount of resources is concerned, as well as multiple constituencies laying claim to these limited resources, the doctrine of fiduciary duty demands that equity and reasonableness guide the fiduciary in adjudicating between the 'best interests' of the various beneficiaries. The doctrine (not unlike Goodin's approach) would see the interests of the most vulnerable served as a matter of priority. Some municipalities have done precisely this.

Local authorities in the UK have struggled with recent changes to the provision of civic legal aid, which was curtailed in 2013 so that it would only be available to those 'lawfully resident' in the country. This prevents those who have had an asylum claim rejected, including children asylum seekers, from accessing support for legal services. Local authorities have struggled to determine what obligations they have to make up for regarding the shortcomings in national funding for civic legal aid. In several cases, local authorities determined that they had an obligation to make up for the shortfall and serve the needs of a vulnerable constituency (Hertfordshire 2015).

While the commitment to the needs of the most vulnerable in these local communities is laudable, the existence of local safeguards can lead to undesirable consequences as well. Local authorities have observed that such safeguards serve the larger goal of ensuring that the UK meets regional and international human rights norms, all the while allowing the central government a free hand to restrict funding for services that do not contribute to advancing immigration enforcement priorities. The result in the UK has been greater pressure on local budgets, as some local authorities attempt to live up to a higher standard of protection in a climate of diminishing financial support from central government (Ajuntament de Barcelona 2014).

Conclusion

It is in the myriad spaces within the state where the most perverse effects of statelessness are experienced. This chapter has sought to address the unjustifiable exclusion of vulnerable persons from the care and services of public authorities at the municipal level. Several arguments are advanced in the process. First, that greater attention must be paid to subnational spaces as municipal authorities have an underappreciated capacity to address the effects of statelessness. Second, it is argued that municipal authorities stand in a fiduciary relationship with the inhabitants of their respective cities. Finally, the chapter argued that stateless persons qualify as beneficiaries of a fiduciary relationship with municipal authorities, and represent a vulnerable constituency with unique claims.

The approach advocated here can benefit contemporary discussions about the rights of stateless persons by challenging the notion that the scope of responsibility for the protection of stateless persons is constrained by the sovereign will of the state or is in fact limited to state action. Both the state and municipal authorities may be required to assume a fiduciary responsibility for stateless persons simply by virtue of their presence in the spaces they govern. Moreover, this conception of municipal authority requires that duties be discharged with due regard to principles of fairness and equity. This opens new possibilities for challenging practices that keep stateless persons in a perpetual state of disenfranchisement and casts serious doubts on pernicious practices such as the detention of stateless persons.

Recalling the intervention of the member of the Council of the London Borough of Islington cited earlier, one remains mindful of the challenges facing local authorities in terms of advocacy and protection. On protection, it is hoped that the fiduciary account of responsibility advances the discussion of public duty in such a way that municipal authorities might coalesce around shared understandings of responsibility for the protection of stateless persons. Further, it is hoped that by clarifying the duty of municipal authorities towards *inhabitants* of their spaces, this framing will aid in lessening the fear stateless persons harbour with respect to contact with those most capable of advancing their personal well-being. On advocacy, this work responds to calls for new, compelling, arguments that concerned parties can leverage in discussions with local and national authorities to develop novel responses to statelessness. It is also hoped that this framing of responsibility will counter the tendency 'to adopt excluding arguments' in places where financial support for public services open to stateless persons is at risk (Ajuntament de Barcelona 2014). Finally, it is hoped that this work might also serve as a call to action where local government is initially hesitant to embrace measures aimed at protecting stateless persons.

Notes

1 Application of the doctrine of fiduciary duty to the challenge of statelessness is inspired by the work of Lorne Sossin (2003), Evan Fox-Decent (2005) and Fox-Decent and Criddle (2009), and more recently Anna Lise Purkey (2013). Fox-Decent and Criddle have argued that one might conceive of the duty of states to protect human rights as a fiduciary duty. Purkey, building on these prior approaches, has recast the refugee–host state relationship in the fiduciary model, where the responsibility of states for refugees in protracted refugee situations is one of a fiduciary to a beneficiary. Fox-Decent and Criddle leave open the possibility that the concept of fiduciaries may illuminate other relationships where power is exercised over a vulnerable party – they observe that 'the fiduciary theory does not necessarily abolish the traditional distinction between citizens and denizens', rather 'it casts the distinction in a new light' (2009, p. 382).

2 Lorne Sossin (2003, p. 141) arrives at a conclusion sympathetic to the argument developed in this chapter; he writes:

> Parliament confers wide discretionary powers on the government of the day, so that they can be used in the nation's and the public's interests. Local authorities have wide discretionary powers conferred upon them so that they can be used in the interest of the locality and those that reside there. (I would not accept that today any group such as the ratepayers can be singled out as the beneficiary of local government powers.) *The recipients of the powers, whether national or local, are very much in the same position as they would be if they had fiduciary powers conferred upon them.* The powers are entrusted to them so that they can exercise them on behalf of the public or a section of the public.

References

Abizadeh, A. (2008) Democratic theory and border coercion: no right to unilaterally control your own borders. *Political Theory*, 36(1), pp. 37–65.

Ajuntament de Barcelona. (2014) *City Responses to Irregular Migrants*. Spain: Ajuntament de Barcelona. [online] Available at: www.slideshare.net/nevenoe/report-on-barcelona-roundtable-on-city-responses-to-irregular-migrants [Accessed 7 April 2015].

Arendt, H. (1958 [1966]) *The Origins of Totalitarianism*. Tenth edition. Cleveland, OH: The World Publishing Company.

Authorson v. *Canada* (Attorney General). (2003) 2 S.C.R. 40, 2003 S.C.C. 39, City of Toronto Act, 2006. S.o. 2006.

Belton, K. (2011) The neglected non-citizen: statelessness and liberal political theory. *Journal of Global Ethics*, 7(1), pp. 59–71.

Bowes v. *City of Toronto*. [1858] XI Moo PC 463.

Bryan, M. (1995) Parents as fiduciaries: A special place in equity. *The International Journal of Children's Rights*, 3(2), pp. 227–261.

Chodos, R. (2010) The nature of fiduciary law and its relationship to other legal doctrines and categories. *Boston University Law Review*, 91(3).

City of Toronto. (2014) Access to City Services for Undocumented Torontonians. Staff Report, City of Toronto. [online] Available at: www.toronto.ca/legdocs/mmis/2014/cd/bgrd/backgroundfile-69193.pdf [Accessed 9 January 2013].

CoE. (2007) *Documents – Working Papers – 2006 Ordinary Session (third part)*. Strasbourg: Council of Europe.

Conklin, W. (2014) *Statelessness: The Enigma of an International Community*. Portland, OR: Hart Publishing.

Da Lomba, S. (2004) Fundamental Social Rights for Irregular Migrants: The Right to Health Care in France and England. In Bogusz, B. (ed.) *Irregular Migration and Human Rights: Theoretical, European and International Perspectives*, 1st edn. Oxford: Routledge.

De Groot, G., Swider, K. and Vonk, O. (2015) *Practices and Approaches in EU Member States to Prevent and End Statelessness*. Constitutional Affairs. Brussels: Directorate General for Internal Policies, European Parliament.

ENS. (2014) *Still Stateless, Still Suffering: Why Europe Must Act Now to Protect Stateless Persons*. London: European Network on Statelessness.

The Equal Rights Trust. (2010) *Unravelling Anomaly*. London: The Equal Rights Trust.

Fox-Decent, E. (2005) The fiduciary nature of state legal authority. *Queen's Law Journal*, 31(1).

Fox-Decent, E. and Criddle, E. (2009) The fiduciary constitution of human rights. *Legal Theory*, 15(4), p. 301.

Frame v. *Smith*. (1987) 2 S.C.R. 99.

Frankel, T. (1983) Fiduciary law. *California Law Review*, 71(3), p. 795.

Goodin, R. (1985a) *Protecting the Vulnerable*. Chicago: University of Chicago Press.

Goodin, R. (1985b) Vulnerabilities and responsibilities: an ethical defense of the Welfare State. *The American Political Science Review*, 79(3), p. 775.

Guerin v. *The Queen*. (1984) 2 S.C.R. 335.

Hawrelak v. *City of Edmonton*. (1976) 1 S.C.R. 387.

Hertfordshire. (2015) Unaccompanied Asylum Seeking Children. [online] Available at: http://hertschildcare.proceduresonline.com/chapters/p_uasc.html [Accessed 11 July 2015].

Institute on Statelessness and Inclusion. (2014) *The World's Stateless*. Oisterwijk: Wolf Legal Publishers (WLP).

Isin, E. (2008) Theorizing acts of citizenship. In Isin, E. F. and Nielsen, G. M. (eds) *Acts of Citizenship*. New York: Zed Books.

Lac Minerals Ltd. v. *International Corona Resources Ltd.* (1989) 2 S.C.R. 574.

Lambert, J. (2015) The emerging role of the EU in eradicating childhood statelessness. *European Network on Statelessness*. [online] Available at: www.statelessness.eu/blog/emerging-role-eu-eradicating-childhood-statelessness [Accessed 13 December 2015].

Leib, E. (2009) Friends as fiduciaries. *Washington University Law Review*, 86(3).

MacIlReith v. *Hart*. (1908) S.C.R. 657.

McDougal, M., Lasswell, H. and Chen, L. (1974) Nationality and human hights: the protection of the individual in external arenas. *The Yale Law Journal*, 83(5), p. 900.

Miller, P. (2013) Justifying fiduciary duties. *McGill Law Journal*, 58(4), p. 969.

Morris, L. (2003) Managing contradiction: civic stratification and migrants' rights. *International Migration Review*, 37(1), pp. 74–100.

Nonnenmacher, S. and Cholewinski, R. (2014) The Nexus Between Statelessness and Migration. In Edwards, A. and van Waas, L. (eds) *Nationality and Statelessness Under International Law*, 1st edn. Cambridge: Cambridge University Press.

Nyers, P. (2010) No one is illegal between city and nation. *Studies in Social Justice*, 4 (2), pp. 127–143.

O'Neil, O. (1998) Rights, Obligations, and Needs. In Brook, G. (ed.) *Necessary Goods*, 1st edn. Lanham: Rowman & Littlefield.

Purkey, A. (2013) Questioning governance in protracted refugee situations: the fiduciary nature of the state–refugee relationship. *International Journal of Refugee Law*, 25(4), pp. 693–716.

Rave, D. (2013) Politicians as fiduciaries. *Harvard Law Review*, 126(3).

Robinson, F. (1999) *Globalizing Care*. Boulder, CO: Westview Press.

Sawyer, C. and Blitz, B. K. (2011) Introduction – Statelessness in the European Union. In Sawyer, C. and Blitz, B. K. (eds) *Statelessness in the European Union*, 1st ed. Cambridge: Cambridge University Press.

Sigona, N. and Hughes, V. (2012) *No Way Out, No Way In*. Oxford: ESRC Centre on Migration, Policy and Society.

Sossin, L. (2003) Public fiduciary obligations, political trusts, and the equitable duty of reasonableness in administrative law. *Saskatchewan Law Review*, 66(1).

Spencer, S. and Pobjoy, J. (2011) *The Relationship between Immigration Status and Rights in the UK: Exploring the Rationale*. COMPAS Working Paper. Oxford: Centre on Migration, Policy and Society, University of Oxford.

Squire, V. (2011) From community cohesion to mobile solidarities. *Political Studies*, 59(2), pp. 290–307.

Staples, K. (2012) *Retheorising Statelessness*. Edinburgh: Edinburgh University Press.

Toronto Party for a Better City v. *Toronto (City)*. (2013) 11 M.P.L.R.

UK Government. (2007) *Enforcing the Rules: A Strategy to Ensure and Enforce Compliance with our Immigration Laws*. London: Home Office, UK Government.

UNHCR. (2014) *Europe/Migrants : 'Let Them Die, This Is a Good Deterrence'*. Geneva: Office of the High Commissioner for Human Rights.

14 The right to family

Protecting stateless children[1]

Patti Tamara Lenard

Introduction

Stateless children can pose difficult moral challenges for the states in which they reside. This chapter argues that stateless children, in virtue of their profound vulnerability, are entitled to rapid access to the regularisation of their status, in the form of easy access to citizenship. Perhaps more controversially, the chapter also proposes that among the rights stateless children possess is the right to be with their parents or closest living family.[2] As a near necessary consequence of this right to family unity, parents possess the right to regularised status; it is derivative of their children's right to citizenship. I therefore distinguish between the entitlement of children to citizenship and the entitlement of their parents to the regularisation of status, which may or may not require that they be granted citizenship along with their children, but will require that they be granted leave to stay in the territory in which their children are made citizens.[3]

I begin by specifying in more detail the group of children with which I am concerned in this chapter. I then offer an account, as articulated by political theorists, for why children ought to occupy a moral status that is distinct from the status occupied by adults and therefore that they are deserving of distinct treatment. I then notice that the Convention on the Rights of the Child (CRC)[4] has acknowledged the particularly vulnerable status of children, in light of which it has articulated a robust set of human rights that are particular to children. The CRC is an international document, signed by 140 countries (but not the United States), that requires signatories to adopt laws that protect the rights of children as they are articulated in the CRC. In the cases that I am exploring, however, the state responsible for protecting their rights may be unclear, or it may be more politically difficult to assert or demonstrate; the consequence, as I will show, is that children's rights often go unprotected. As I suggest in the second section of the chapter, the challenge emerges in part from the conventional understanding of states as possessing the right to control the borders to their citizenry and to their territory *and* having the duty to protect the rights of children; there is a tension here, which has proven difficult to resolve in practice, to the grave detriment of children.

This section therefore focuses on those children who are rendered stateless or effectively stateless as a result of a combination of immigration law and border enforcement policies. Some of the conclusions will be applicable beyond this group, but space constraints do not permit me to address this here. Over the course of this section, I observe that the political theory of migration takes for granted that migrants are autonomous agents, and that this may impact upon the rights of those who find themselves stateless or effectively stateless as a result, but that this assumption cannot be made in the case of children, many of whom travel across borders with their parents or unaccompanied, but at the request or insistence of their parents. As a result, even if one believes that adult irregular migrants are stateless or effectively stateless by choice, the same cannot be said of children.

Putting the first two sections together, I argue that we must understand the state in which a child resides as responsible for protecting the rights of that child, and that this will often entail formalising the relationship by extending citizenship to stateless children, including those who are migrants; this is particularly true where a reasonable case can be made that it is in the best position to protect the child's right to nationality. Among the additional rights that the state of residence is obligated to protect is the right to family unity, and this right (I shall continue) entails also that a child's parents are entitled to citizenship. In the final section, I discuss and dismiss three objections to the proposal that stateless children *and* their parents are entitled to citizenship or some related status on their territory of residence: one which argues that the rights of stateless children can be met by appointing a citizen legal guardian rather than by granting citizenship to their parents; another which argues that granting citizenship to children who are stateless or effectively stateless in a migratory context creates a moral hazard, i.e. it will encourage more parents to put their children into precarious circumstances in an effort to secure citizenship for themselves; and a final one that proposes that repatriation to the parents' state of citizenship (assuming they have such a citizenship) respects the rights of stateless children.

Stateless children in the context of migration

I focus here on children rendered stateless as a result of their own migration or the migration of their parents. It includes children of irregular migrants, whose citizenship may be ambiguous; for example, these children may be entitled to the citizenship of their parents, or to the citizenship of the territory on which they were born, or neither, or both. It includes children of refugees, born in flight or in exile, in states that deny *jus soli* birthright citizenship to them. Controversially, it also includes children whose citizenship is not ambiguous (in particular those who are citizens of the state in which they reside, usually by birth), and for whom the benefits of citizenship are restricted by the irregular status of their parents (as I shall articulate). It includes children who have been coerced into migration by their parents or by traffickers and who are now residing on a territory in which they are not citizens without their parents. I refer to all of these children as stateless, since as a result of their situation, the rights to which they are entitled are not protected. I argue that such a child is not recognised as a national by any state.

Children in particular depend on states to provide them basic and essential services, which are practically inaccessible to children who do not possess legal identity documents (Bhabha 2011, p. 9).[5] Bhabha writes,

> statelessness is a particularly important social and political child-rights issue because children are peculiarly dependent on states. There are two aspects to this dependency: all children depend on states for basic services, and many children depend on states when their families fail them.
>
> (Bhabha 2011, p. 14)

Furthermore, their statelessness and their immaturity combine to make stateless children particularly vulnerable: Just like all children, 'stateless children are vulnerable and dependent, but they have the added handicaps that come from legal and social disenfranchisement. Unlike citizen or otherwise legal children, their claim to protections as minors is in tension with their excludability as outsiders' (Bhabha 2011, p. 16). Their statelessness appears to grant permission to states to refuse responsibility for protecting their rights.

The specialness of children and the Convention on the Rights of the Child

According to international law, children are typically understood to be individuals who are younger than 18 years old, though access to some aspects of adulthood are made available earlier (for example, to marry, to have sex, to join the military, etc., which are made available in some states to 16-year-olds). There is much political theory that considers whether children are entitled to rights and on what grounds these rights should be extended. One plausible view proposes that, since children are not fully developed, the best strategy is to restrict some rights to adults only, but then also to assign children some rights to which adults are not entitled. Following Joel Feinberg (1980), we can say that some 'liberty' rights are restricted to adults – rights to choose employment, to be free to choose a religion, to be free to speak publicly, and to vote, for example. What Feinberg terms 'welfare' rights are extended to both children and adults. Although it may be that the content of these differs for children and adults, welfare rights are those that protect important interests that are shared by both children and adults, including for example rights to healthcare access, to bodily integrity, and so on. There are also two broad sets of rights that are reserved for children. One set accrues to children by virtue of their inability to secure a particular subset of goods on their own, including for example food and shelter, which are provided to children by the adults in their lives. They include protective rights to which children are entitled in virtue of their vulnerability to the adults around them, including the risk of abuse and neglect from which they are not necessarily able to protect themselves without outside intervention. For many scholars, these rights include the right to be loved, which is essential for the normal development of children (Liao 2006).

Feinberg terms a second set of rights – to which children (but not most adults) are entitled – 'rights-in-trust', which he also terms 'rights to an open future'. As David Archard describes, 'These are the rights given to the child in the person of the adult she will become. They are the rights whose protection ensures that, as an adult, she will be in a position to exercise her' full set of rights (Archard 2014). The protection of these rights acts to limit parental and state interference with children – parents or other adults are obligated to ensure that whatever environment they provide to children, it is one that ensures that, in the future, children will be able to exercise their full set of rights. One practical consequence of understanding children as possessors of rights-in-trust is that there will be instances where children's freedom rights (which may for example lead a child to prefer to eat junk food, run into traffic, and so on) can be restricted to preserve their future ability to take maximal advantage of their rights. There is considerable debate around what it means to say that a child's future is open with respect to these rights, but it is sufficient to observe that in very general terms children are entitled to the conditions under which, in the future, they will be able to make good use of their liberty and welfare rights. Although there will certainly be disagreements at the margins, many actions perpetrated against children – for example deliberately maiming children to increase their pan-handling profitability – will clearly be in violation of their rights-in-trust. As this chapter shall suggest, permitting children to remain de facto or *de jure* stateless is, in effect, a violation of their rights-in-trust.

This way of understanding the rights of children is underscored by the commitments made in the 1989 UN Convention on the Rights of the Child, which begins in its preamble by acknowledging that in virtue of their status as children and in particular their 'physical and mental immaturity', they are 'entitled to special care and assistance', in particular of a type that permits them to, in time, 'be fully prepared to live an individual life in society'. The CRC outlines the agents that possess the duties to protect the rights of children, namely, the states in which they live, and impresses upon states the requirement that they cooperate (for example, allow the right to reside and prevent trafficking) when necessary to protect these rights. Children, regardless of their nationality, are treated as the responsibility of all states, especially where intrastate cooperation is essential to protecting the rights of children. The rights ascribed to children are then listed and are expansive. They include rights to non-discrimination (article 2); to life (article 6); to freedom of expression (article 12); to religion and conscience (article 14); to adequate health care (article 24), and so on.

One particular article of the CRC, 7(1), is worth highlighting:

> The child shall be registered immediately after birth and shall have the right from birth to a name, the right to acquire a nationality and, as far as possible, the right to know and be cared for by his or her parents.

Whereas the UN Declaration on the Rights of the Child stated that a child should be 'entitled [to a nationality] from birth', the CRC (and International Covenant on Civil and Political Rights (ICCPR)) retreat from this position. One explanation for the retreat is this: 'the drafters of the ICCPR [from which the wording of the CRC is taken] felt that a State could not accept an unqualified obligation to accord its nationality to every child born on its territory regardless of circumstances' (Doek 2006, p. 26). However, as I will demonstrate, this retrenchment is normatively troubling: acknowledging the right of children to parental care (where possible), as well as the rights referred to in the other articles, makes the right of the state to withhold citizenship more tenuous.

One notable feature of the CRC is its repeated highlighting of the right of children to be with their families, which the Convention writers are keen to emphasise as essential to child development. The right to be with one's family, and in particular the obligation of states to create and nurture situations in which children can be with, or remain with, their families, is highlighted in multiple different articles. For example, the preamble identifies the family as the 'fundamental group of society' as well as the 'natural environment for the growth and well-being of all its members and particularly children'; in light of this, the family is entitled to 'protection and assistance'. The preamble continues by acknowledging that, at least in ordinary circumstances, the child's development is best secured in a 'family environment'. Article 5 recognises the rights of families to take responsibility for their own children. Article 8 acknowledges that the family is a key source of identity for children, and therefore that to the maximum extent possible states should not interfere with children's ability to form strong family relations. Article 9 imposes on states the obligation to refrain, as much as possible, from separating children from their parents, except where this separation 'is necessary for the best interests of the child'.

The right of children to be with their families is deemed to be of such significance that the CRC articulates and rearticulates that this right cannot and should not be abrogated by the existence of national borders (Aunos and Feldman 2008). Article 10 demands of states that where children and parents are separated by national borders states must cooperate for the purpose of ensuring speedy family reunification. Article 20 acknowledges that there are circumstances in which children are separated from their parents by borders and imposes on states the requirement that they afford children 'special protection and assistance'. Article 22 acknowledges that these obligations are in force with respect to children seeking refugee status, who are entitled to the rights of family reunification in a safe and secure environment. Fundamentally, the CRC identifies states as the primary guarantor of the rights of children, while also demanding that states ignore national boundaries where necessary to protect those rights. It can therefore be read as admonishing states to ignore national boundaries and instead to prioritise the rights of children over their rights to control their borders and membership; as least as articulated in the CRC, states are obligated to cooperate to protect the rights of children on their territory, or who have links to their territory, independently of the borders that divide them from one another. And it asks states to prioritise the rights of children who are present on their territory over their own rights to control their borders by excluding them, in cases where these are in tension. In so doing, the CRC acknowledges that sovereign states possess the right to control their borders and access to full membership, but asks states to prioritise the human rights of children in cases where exercising these controls threatens to violate them.[6]

Political theory of migration and borders, and the place of stateless children

Stateless children are often unable to move and where they are stateless in the context of migration, migration restrictions are centrally responsible for the construction of their statelessness in the first place. The political theory of migration is concerned with the justice of borders that divide states. For some political theorists, borders are necessarily coercive and thus are never or nearly never justified (Abizadeh 2008). On this view, borders operate to restrict the freedom of movement of individuals, and in particular they restrict the opportunities they have to pursue their goals. Borders are, then, particularly egregious in a global environment characterised by significant wealth inequalities, since they serve not only to restrict movement in general, but in particular are deployed by wealthy states to prevent the entry of poor migrants seeking to improve the conditions in which they live (Carens 1987). States nevertheless defend their right to control their borders, citing the importance of a variety of values that states provide to their members, including the right to freedom of association (and the associated right to choose who will join the state as full members), access to democratic institutions, cultural protection and continuity, and access to redistributive policies that depend on the existence of trust and solidarity among members (Miller 2005; Moore 2006; Wellman 2008). For those who believe that, in the ideal, borders would be fully open (Cole 2000; Kukathas 2005), there is some recognition that as the world is presently organised, borders are here to stay; the goal is thus to press towards more or 'fairly' open borders (Bader 1997). For those who believe that borders will persist even in an ideal world, there is nevertheless recognition that the widespread inequality that the protection of borders enables in the present is deeply problematic. It is thus fair to say that nearly all political theorists of migration acknowledge that global inequality poses a genuine problem of justice for the legitimacy of border control, that borders ought to be more open than they are, and that global inequality is a challenge that must urgently be confronted.

One key aspect of the debate among political theorists about the legitimacy of borders is the role that they supposedly play in restricting or supporting the autonomy of individuals. As Joseph Raz articulates it, autonomy (understood as giving an individual the tools she needs to be the 'maker or author of his own life') has three components, all of which 'admit of degree'. An individual must possess adequate mental abilities, including 'minimum rationality, the ability to comprehend the means to realise his goals, the mental faculties necessary to plan actions'; an individual must have 'adequate options available for him to choose from'; and an individual must make her choice 'free from coercion and manipulation by others, he must be independent' (Raz 1986, pp. 373–374). Thus, the claim is roughly that the existence of uncrossable borders effectively closes off choices to which an individual is entitled, and which must be made available in order to support her autonomy (Abizadeh 2008). For those who dispute the claim that borders are coercive, what autonomy demands is that an adequate set of choices be made available for all, and not that every choice is open to them (Miller 2010). Although they may do so in the present context, uncrossable borders do not *necessarily* restrict autonomy in objectionable ways; they are therefore not necessarily coercive. There is a subtlety here that is important to identify: While coercion necessarily violates autonomy, the autonomy violation can be mitigated by adequate justification. As a matter of practice, states coerce citizens to engage in various actions they might not otherwise choose to do – pay taxes is the most frequently cited example – but the justifications offered by the state – that taxes support important infrastructure on which we all rely, that they fund redistributive programmes that protect the basic needs of all citizens, and in particular that there are opportunities for citizens to debate the merits of these taxes in democratic environments – can render the coercion justifiable (Blake 2001).

However, children are not autonomous in the ways that Raz describes; their mental faculties are underdeveloped in ways that make this reasoning about the coercion imposed by borders inapplicable to the case of children. The CRC acknowledges this by in effect codifying Feinberg's proposal that while children are not fully autonomous they nevertheless possess rights-in-trust that they be able to live autonomous lives in the future, and that borders can sometimes restrict their abilities to access their rights-in-trust. Children rendered stateless or effectively stateless as a result of irregular migration are at particular risk of being victimised by the existence of borders and the ways in which states prioritise their right to control borders over the human rights of children. These children are at particular risk when states prioritise border control over the obligations they have accepted as a result of signing the CRC.

In some cases, state immigration law has the effect of making irregular migrant children de facto stateless as a matter of policy, and in others states' border enforcement policies conspire to make irregular child migrants effectively stateless, even in cases where they (but not their parents) are citizens. This latter effect is the result of states treating border enforcement as something that happens at the border, but also beyond the border. It is a well-established fact in scholarship on migration that border control efforts have expanded beyond the border (Gibney 2006). The clearest way in which border control has expanded concerns the provision of public services to individuals resident on a territory; these services are oftentimes dispensed only where individuals receiving them can prove their right to be on a territory. Such proof is often impossible for the children of irregular migrants to provide because irregular migrant parents are reluctant to provide this proof on behalf of their citizen children, for fear of alerting authorities of their own irregular status. The effect is that many children who are entitled to services in virtue of their citizenship – not simply in virtue of their status as children – are not able to access them and suffer as a result. The category of children included in the category of stateless or effectively stateless as a result of (irregular) migration is, then, wider than might initially be assumed.

One option is to do as Joseph Carens suggested in a more general argument about mechanisms by which to respect the basic human rights of irregular migrants. He observed that although irregular migrants may have committed breaches of immigration law, they do not as a result forfeit their basic human rights. The practice of demanding that all people who request access to public services in protection of their basic human rights provide proof of a legal right to reside produces, problematically, a situation in which irregular migrants choose against accessing these services for fear of alerting authorities to their irregular status.

Carens proposes adopting a 'firewall', i.e. explicitly requiring basic service providers to avoid asking for proof of legal residence in advance of providing their service (Carens 2008). The purpose is to encourage irregular migrants (including, as is the focus in this chapter, stateless or effectively stateless individuals) to permit their rights to be respected, without fearing that they will be deported and that their family will be broken up. For those who zealously defend the right of states to control their borders, this kind of proposal rewards people for breaking immigration laws. But, says Carens, we must understand that although these individuals have broken immigration laws (and regardless of our views on the legitimacy of border control and its enforcement), they are entitled to have their human rights protected by whatever agent can do so. Put differently, as I have argued elsewhere, even if we agree that states are permitted to control their borders as a matter of state sovereignty, it does not follow that states may act however they wish in pursuit of border control; they are always limited by the requirement that they respect human rights as they enforce their borders (Lenard 2015), including their internal borders. Even heinous criminals, by their actions, do not sacrifice their basic human rights.

Let me offer one example. Stateless children have difficulties accessing education, including primary education, across different contexts of statelessness. In the case of children who are stateless or effectively stateless as a result of migration, this is no less a problem.

Acknowledging that this kind of service denial is common, the CRC demands in particular that primary education be provided to all children, regardless of status; children attempting to access primary education, that is, should not be required to provide evidence of status in order to be admitted to schools. To return to Feinberg's language, in singling out education as a basic service that must be provided to children regardless of their status, the CRC is not simply noting that the welfare rights of children must be protected, but that children's rights-in-trust are at specific risk where they are not permitted to access the basic education that is essential to exercising responsible choices in the future. Many states and sub-state units have adopted legislation that recognises this demand in principle; and yet, there is evidence that education is nevertheless denied to children who are unable to prove their right to be present on a territory (Bhabha

2009, pp. 439–440). Evidence also suggests that the firewall strategy continues to be poorly deployed, so that children's rights continue to be violated in ways that inflict long-term damage on their life prospects. To take just one example, although the city of Toronto adopted a 'Don't Ask Don't Tell' policy to protect the access of children in Toronto to primary education, proof of status remains mandatory for enrolment in all Toronto schools (Villegas 2010, and Passerelli this volume).

Note that in the case of children who are lawfully present (e.g. as citizens), what stateless parents, and parents with irregular status, are attempting to protect is their ability to be with their children. The danger they foresee is being detained and, possibly, sent 'home' without their children (I consider objections to this claim in the next section). The way to protect against that, in their estimation, is to have their children forego the services to which they are entitled, either in virtue of their childhood or in virtue of their citizenship. On behalf of their sense that keeping a family together is important, parents sacrifice their children's access to much-needed services, services to which their children are entitled as a matter of legally recognised *right*. In other words, a confluence of policies produces a situation in which the rights of children are not respected: If stateless parents, or those in irregular migration situations, opt to access the services their children need, and to which they are entitled, they risk being detained (and possibly deported); if parents choose against opting for these services, to protect against separating their family, they deprive their children of services to which they are entitled as a matter of justice. The practice of border control, which stems from the right of states to control their borders, puts children as a matter of fact in a situation in which their basic rights cannot be respected in full. The exercise of a state's right to control its borders produces a situation in which the rights of children are violated.

The weight of evidence, and the demands of children's rights, together amount to a case for the following two-pronged view: First, where they do not possess citizenship (or are not on the path to citizenship) children are entitled to citizenship. Second, because among the rights that children possess is the right to family integrity, their parents are, by virtue of their children's rights, entitled to regularised status as well; this is to protect children from having to choose between accessing the basic rights to which they are entitled and being with their family (or having their family make this choice on their behalf). The proposal that children, and also their parents, are granted regularised status – including clear and fair pathways to citizenship – is based on the recognition that states are collectively responsible for protecting children's rights, and more particularly, that the state in which a child resides has the particular responsibility for that child.

Objections

There are many objections one might raise to the way I have proposed resolving the tension between protecting stateless children's rights and state's rights to control their borders. I will consider and respond to three of them here: First, children whose parents are irregular migrants can be cared for by non-parental legal guardians, and it is therefore legitimate to expel irregular migrant parents in the service of border enforcement. Second, offering citizenship also to parents, as a way of respecting children's rights, will simply encourage adults to put their children into dangerous situations. Third, the right to family unity can be protected by sending stateless or effectively stateless children to the country of original citizenship of their parents, where such a state can (allegedly) be identified.

One objection acknowledges that children need special care, but denies that there is a special reason to protect their access to their own parents. On this view, states might take charge of appointing legal guardians to children, while detaining and deporting irregular migrant parents. One reason to propose such a policy is that it seems to recognise that children have special needs, which states are obligated to meet when parents are unable to do so. Indeed, in general, the state offers a kind of protection to children in cases where their parents are unable to fulfil their fiduciary duties towards their children; this is an observation that is central to the political theory of parental autonomy literature (for a discussion of the fiduciary duty of cities towards stateless children, see Passarelli, this volume). Parents are permitted wide discretion in making essential decisions for their children, so long as in doing so they meet their children's basic needs and protect their basic human rights. In cases where parents fail to do so, children are removed from their parents' care and others are assigned the responsibility for caring for them. In this case, a state might say, parents who have opted to place their children in precarious situations, either by refusing to access state services on behalf of their children, for fear of deportation, or by crossing borders and therefore putting their children into situations of precariousness, have forfeited their rights to care for their children. Deporting parents and assigning a legal guardian to care for the left-behind children may thereby seem appropriate.

There are many reasons to be sceptical of a solution of this kind. One reason to reject such a solution is simply because the state has a bad record in caring for the needs and rights of children who do not have, or are separated from, parents or other family members. There is ample evidence that the mechanisms states have in place to appoint alternative guardians, and to monitor their care-giving capacities, are inadequate and that guardians assigned to children are often poor alternatives to parents. A second reason to reject such a solution has to do with the related observation that parents are often the best providers of care to their children, even in challenging circumstances. The political theoretic literature on parental autonomy acknowledges that parents and children should not be separated except in extreme circumstances; children suffer when they are not with their parents, even in cases where parents are not able to provide the best and widest range of opportunities for their children. A related fact is that parents who have 'put' their children in these difficult migratory situations which have resulted in their children being stateless or effectively stateless, often believe (rightly, in fact) that these decisions are in the best interests of their children.[7] They are doing, in their own minds, the best for their children given the limited options with which they are presented, which often involve travelling from states in the midst of civil war or dire poverty.

The recognition that children do best when given an opportunity to grow in their own families is among the driving concerns of the CRC. Fundamentally, appointing a guardian and deporting a parent when that parent is able to provide the care the child needs or when the tools that this parent needs to provide for their child can be provided to them (in this case, in the form of a right to reside and then attain citizenship in the state in which their child is a citizen or on the road to citizenship) is a violation of that child's right. In other words, detaining and deporting parents, while acknowledging the importance of assigning a competent legal guardian, acknowledges the special care that children need, while ignoring that their parents are best placed to provide it. It is important to pay close attention to the rights of children and the duty this imposes on states to protect them. One might propose that appointing a legal guardian does so, but the child's right is not simply to adequate care and attention, but to their family when this care and attention can be provided to them by their family. The CRC explicitly, and repeatedly, states the importance of acting in the best interests of children.

A second objection emphasises the moral hazards of adopting the policy I propose. On this view, the worry is that rewarding parents with citizenship, or even the regularisation of their status, in cases where their protection is required to secure the basic rights and needs of their children, creates an even greater incentive than previously existed to migrate irregularly. This worry is expressed by former US Senator Tom Trancredo, who observed that policies that permit and encourage the providing of social services to irregular migrants simply encourage irregular migration. Thus, he says,

> Denying social services to them is something you have to do to stop the magnet effect that all of these combined things have, the health care, free schooling. This is all a magnet that draws people into this country and I'm trying to demagnetize it.

> (Bhabha, 2009, p. 416)

Yet, empirical investigations suggest that specific policies do not attract or deter desperate individuals seeking a better life for themselves; strong economies and stability are adequate 'pull' factors, and policies that attempt to deter migrants by denying their access to services have been shown to have limited impact on migratory decisions made by individuals in desperate circumstances.[8] Even more worrying, however, is the pitting of consequentialist reasoning about the negative impacts of large-scale migration against the basic human rights of the most vulnerable of individuals, which arrives at the unacceptable conclusion that rights can be sacrificed. It is of course true that as policy makers we are forced to balance rights against each other, and also against the costs of sustaining and protecting those rights. But where the rights of the most vulnerable of individuals are at stake, this balancing (especially in the face of limited empirical evidence that the feared consequences are likely) is unwarranted.

A final objection suggests that children's rights are respected if the family is deported together, and only applies in cases where there is dispute regarding parents' status as stateless. In other words, according to some states, if it is so important that children remain with their parents, then sending them to the country of original citizenship of their parents, along with the rest of the family, could serve to protect the right of children to be with their parents (Rozzi 2011, p. 198). Notice, of course, this claim would deny the *statelessness* of the parents; it requires that a deporting state asserts (against the claim of the would-be-deportee) a citizenship for those it intends to deport.

This objection can be met with two responses, one of which focuses on the deportation of child citizens and one that focuses on the deportation of child non-citizens. In the case of deporting child *citizens* (along with their stateless parents), note that the deportation protects one right, the right of children to be with their families, in exchange for another, the right of citizens to remain on the territory of which they are a citizen. This response is problematic for its clear willingness to violate a citizen's basic human right (to remain on the territory of the state in which one is a citizen); the right is meant to be inviolable for all citizens, including children. In the case of child non-citizens, the reason to worry about repatriation of entire families hinges on the confidence a deporting state has that the child's full complement of basic human rights can be respected in the country to which she will be deported (assuming she would be admitted in the first place, which is not at all a given).

Furthermore, for children whose legal identity is connected to the state in which they are born or are a long-term resident, deportation may move them further from the state with which they have the closest connection, reinforcing a situation of statelessness and effective statelessness. The child would remain a citizen of the state from which they are deported, but be unable to make use of that citizenship to secure the services to which they are entitled as a matter of legally recognised right. In the case of repatriating whole families, where the children are non-citizens of the deporting country, the repatriation can be legitimate only where the legal identity and status of the children can be confirmed in the country to which they are deported, and where that state is able to meet the children's basic needs and protect their basic human rights. In the many cases where this is not reasonable to expect, the deporting state retains the obligation to protect the rights of the child, and in so doing to extend citizenship (or a pathway to citizenship) to the child and to the child's parents.

Conclusion

This chapter's objective has been to argue that the state of residence possesses strong duties towards all children on its soil, independent of their legal status. The importance that states place on their right to control the composition of their citizenries and their territorial borders too often ignores the duty they possess to respect the basic human rights of all children on their territory, including those who are stateless or effectively stateless. I have argued this particularly in the case of children who are in this situation as a result of irregular migration, either because they have migrated irregularly themselves, or because their parents have migrated irregularly. Children are among the most vulnerable of human beings, and as the Convention on the Rights of the Child articulates, it is the collective responsibility of all states to ensure that they are protected. In this chapter, I have argued that the basic human rights of stateless children demand that they be granted citizenship of the state in which they live, and furthermore and more controversially, that their right to be securely with their family demands that their parents (or other appropriate family members where parents are not available) be given citizenship of that state (or a path to citizenship) also. States' rights to control their borders and access to full membership stop when the rights of children are at risk of being sacrificed.

Notes

1 I would like to thank Sinead Sullivan-Paul for her valuable research assistance in preparing this chapter.
2 In most cases, it will be a child's parents who are entitled to regularisation, but in cases where a child's parents are known to be dead or incapable of providing care, this right transfers to her closest living and able family members.
3 In this distinction, I follow a decision made in Israel in 2006, in which (assuming certain criteria were met) children of foreign labour migrants born in Israel were permitted to become Israeli citizens following the successful completion of military service, and their parents were simultaneously granted permanent residency status. This decision is not perfect, but it is a model for prioritising the rights of stateless children to citizenship. For a discussion of the decision, see http://hotline.org.il/en/migrants-en/%E2%80%8Fchildren-of-migrant-workers-in-israel/
4 The full text of the Convention is here: www.ohchr.org/en/professionalinterest/pages/crc.aspx
5 Bhabha estimates that 36 per cent of births are not formally registered.
6 The CRC does not indicate whether protecting children's rights should legitimate the violation of state sovereignty, however, but international practice has been to avoid violating state sovereignty as much as possible, even where human rights abuses are known to take place.
7 This is evidently a more complicated assertion, since often parents make decisions that they believe are in the best interests of their children, but where they are clearly wrong.
8 For example, the expansion of detention of migrants is often justified with respect to its deterrent effect, but there exists little evidence that the possibility of detention deters potential migrants from crossing borders in irregular ways (see Silverman and Nethery 2015).

References

Abizadeh, A. (2008) Democratic theory and border coercion: no right to unilaterally control your own borders. *Political Theory*, 36(1), pp. 37–65.
Archard, D. W. (2014) Children's Rights. In Zalta, E. N. (ed.) *The Stanford Encyclopedia of Philosophy (Winter 2014 Edition)*. [online] Available at: https://plato.stanford.edu/entries/rights-children/ [Accessed 24 February 2017].
Aunos, M. and Feldman, M. (2008) There's No Place Like Home: The Child's Right to Family. In O'Neill, T. and Zinga, D. (eds) *Children's rights: multidisciplinary approaches to participation and protection*. Toronto: University of Toronto Press.

Bader, V. (1997) Fairly Open Borders. In Bader, V. (ed.) *Citizenship and Exclusion*, pp. 28–60. London: Macmillan.

Bhabha, J. (2011) From Citizen to Migrant: The Scope of Child Statelessness in the Twenty-First Century. In Bhabha, J. (ed.) *Children Without a State: A Human Rights Challenge*, pp. 1–39. Cambridge, MA: MIT Press.

Bhabha, J. (2009) Arendt's children: Do today's migrant children have a right to have rights? *Human Rights Quarterly*, 31(2), pp. 410–451.

Blake, M. (2001) Distributive justice, state coercion, and autonomy. *Philosophy & Public Affairs*, 30(3), pp. 257–296.

Carens, J. (2008) The rights of irregular migrants. *Ethics and International Affairs*, 22(2), pp. 163–188.

Carens, J. (1987) Aliens and citizens: The case for open borders. *Review of Politics*, 49(2), pp. 251–273.

Cole, P. (2000) *Philosophies of Exclusion: Liberal Political Theory and Immigration*. Edinburgh: Edinburgh University Press.

Doek, J. E. (2006) The CRC and the right to acquire and to preserve a nationality. *Refugee Survey Quarterly*, 25(3), pp. 26–32.

Feinberg, J. (1980) A Child's Right to an Open Future. In Aiken, W. and LaFollette, H. (eds) *Whose Child? Parental Rights, Parental Authority and State Power*, pp. 124–153. Totowa, NJ: Rowman & Littlefield.

Gibney, M. (2006) A Thousand Little Guantanamos: Western States and Measures to Prevent the Arrival of Refugees. In Tunstall, K. E. (ed.) *Migration, Displacement, Asylum: The Oxford Amnesty Lectures 2004*, pp. 139–169. Oxford: Oxford University Press.

Kukathas, C. (2005) The Case for Open Migration. In Cohen, A. and Wellman, C. H. (eds) *Contemporary Debates in Applied Ethics*, pp. 207–220. Oxford: Blackwell.

Lenard, P. T. (2015) The ethics of deportation in liberal democratic states. *European Journal of Political Theory*, 14 (4), pp. 464–480.

Liao, S. M. (2006) The right of children to be loved. *Journal of Political Philosophy*, 14 (4), pp. 420–440.

Miller, D. (2010) Why immigration controls are not coercive: A reply to Arash Abizadeh. *Political Theory*, 38(1), pp. 111–120. DOI: 10.1177/0090591709348194.

Miller, D. (2005) Immigration: The Case for Limits. In Cohen, A. and Wellman, C. (eds) *Contemporary Debates in Applied Ethics*, pp. 193–207. Malden: Blackwell.

Moore, M. (2006) Cosmopolitanism and political communities. *Social Theory and Practice*, 32(4), pp. 627–658.

Raz, J. (1986) *The Morality of Freedom*. Oxford: Clarendon Press.

Rozzi, E. (2011) Undocumented Migrant and Roma Children in Italy: Between Rights Protection and Control. In Bhabha, J. (ed.) *Children Without a State: A Global Human Rights Challenge*, pp. 177–216. Cambridge, MA: MIT Press.

Silverman, S. J. and Nethery, A. (2015) Understanding Immigration Detention and its Human Impact. In Silverman, S. J. and Nethery, A. (eds) *Immigration Detention: The Migration of a Policy and its Human Impact*, pp. 1–12. New York: Routledge.

Villegas, P. (2010) Negotiating the Boundaries of Membership: Health Care Providers, Access to Social Goods, and Immigration Status. In Goldring, L. and Landolt, P. (eds) *Producing and negotiating non-citizenship precarious legal status in Canada*, pp. 221–237. Toronto: University of Toronto Press.

Wellman, C. H. (2008) Immigration and freedom of association. *Ethics*, 119(1), pp. 109–141.

15 Statelessness and the performance of citizenship-as-nationality

Katherine Tonkiss

Introduction

It is commonly posited in the literature on statelessness that the opposite of the stateless person is the citizen (cf. Bhabha 2011). The citizen, formally recognised in law as a member of a particular political community and therefore in receipt of all of the rights that this membership confers as well as the less tangible sense of belonging and security that it conveys, seems to have access to everything the stateless person is denied. While the binary nature of this definition may hold less convincingly in relation to identity and belonging, where citizens can find themselves on the outside if they do not represent the state's dominant ideal of the 'good citizen' (Aasland 2002; Carrera 2009; Tonkiss 2014), it is relatively non-controversial to claim from a legal perspective that stateless persons are excluded from 'the right to claim citizenship in a specific state' (Gibney 2009, p. 50), and indeed in international law a stateless person is one not recognised as a citizen under the operation of the law of any State.

Yet this legal categorisation runs into some complexity because typically the term 'citizenship' is used interchangeably with the term 'nationality'. While citizenship denotes a bundle of rights held by someone recognised as a citizen, nationality refers to specific socially constructed identity characteristics which are taken to denote membership of a national group (cf. Miller 1995). It is presumed, consistent with the dominant form of citizenship which currently exists in our international system of nation-states, that when we talk about access to citizenship for stateless persons we are actually talking about access to *national* citizenship, by which citizenship is conferred on an individual on the basis of their membership of a national group. As a result, the absence of citizenship for stateless persons is typically thought of in relation to the absence of a recognised nationality under international law, with the Universal Declaration of Human Rights (UDHR) declaring a right to nationality rather than a right to citizenship (United Nations General Assembly 1948; see also Batchelor 2006). The unquestioned and often implicit interchangeability of citizenship and nationality has been replicated in the academic literature on statelessness (e.g. Belton 2011; Blitz and Lynch 2011; Gibney 2009; Kingston 2013).

In this chapter, I seek to problematise this interchangeability of nationality and citizenship in academic and legal treatments of statelessness. Specifically, I argue that discussions of statelessness which draw on the language of nationality serve, through the reification of national group membership, to legitimise the very structures which drive and permit the exclusion of stateless persons. While these discussions may be arguing in favour of an end to statelessness, and so for the rights of stateless people, and are in turn arguing against the national citizenship regimes which permit statelessness, they nonetheless draw on the language of nationality to make these arguments. As a result, I therefore suggest that accounts advocating for the rights of stateless persons can only be partially successful if they draw on the language of nationality in order to make their claims. Finally, and based on this argument, I argue further that those working in the field of statelessness should do so from within a post-national framework which offers a basis for 'troubling' the exclusions permitted by nationality. Rather than calling for a rejection of nationality as a source of identity per se, I call for a reflexive problematisation of the reification of national group membership which acts as a barrier to the realisation of rights for stateless persons.

After first examining the treatment of citizenship and nationality in the statelessness literature and conceptualising this approach as what I will term 'citizenship-as-nationality', I then work to demonstrate the problems inherent in this approach by drawing on a literature in the field of political theory concerned with the defensibility of nationalism and the reification of national group membership (e.g. Abizadeh 2002; Miller 2000; Tamir 1993). Finally, I focus in on post-nationalism – and specifically the 'constitutional patriotism' approach (cf. Tonkiss 2013) – as an alternative approach to discussing, theorising and advocating for the rights of stateless persons, before offering some concluding remarks.

Citizenship-as-nationality

A mere glance at international law in the field of statelessness demonstrates the extent to which the rights of citizenship are understood through the prism of nationality in this field. Indeed, the Director of International Protection at UNHCR has described how, over and above citizenship, it is 'the formal legal bond of nationality' (Türk 2014) which is the key focus of work in the field of statelessness. It is the 'arbitrary deprivation of nationality' which is seen as at stake in statelessness (Equal Rights Trust 2014, p. 8), and it is nationality law within States which is seen as the primary vehicle for the realisation of the rights of stateless persons in these contexts (Institute on Statelessness and Inclusion 2014). As noted, the language of the UDHR rejects statelessness on the grounds that each person has the right to a nationality, and the two key UN conventions on statelessness also draw on this notion of a right to nationality rather than a right to citizenship. The 1954 Convention relating to the Status of Stateless Persons defines a stateless person as one 'not recognised as a national by any state under the operation of its law' (UN Convention 1954), while the 1961 Convention on the Reduction of Statelessness reiterates the right of every person to a nationality, supports safeguarding against statelessness through nationality laws in specific countries and sets specific provisions to ensure that children have the nationality of the country in which they are born if no other nationality is available to them (UN Convention 1961). Nationality is so central to understandings of statelessness that the UNHCR (2015) notes '[h]aving a nationality is something so natural that people rarely stop to think about what life would be like without it'.

What is evident in these treatments of statelessness through the prism of nationality is that, for international law, statelessness is not merely the opposite of citizenship. It is, rather, the opposite of specifically *national* citizenship. It is the right to nationality which frames the exclusion of stateless persons from the rights and responsibilities of citizenship, not citizenship itself. While the importance of nationality to the rights of the 'noncitizen' in all its guises is commonly discussed in the field of law, in academic literature on noncitizenship nationality is far less central, and citizenship is typically thought of in relation to nationalism only when it is explicitly the aim of the work to explore this relationship. It is therefore unusual that the growing academic literature on statelessness, while tremendously valuable and insightful across a myriad of disciplines and topics, has mirrored this conflation of citizenship and nationality, or the treatment of statelessness through the prism of nationality. While Kelly Staples advocates the terminology of 'membership' rather than nationality or citizenship on the basis that this language better captures the contours of inclusion and exclusion in the international system than the particularities associated with the latter terms (Staples 2012), this engagement with the complexities surrounding the use and conflation of nationality and citizenship is rare in the field. A far greater number of scholars draw on the language of nationality uncritically to speak to statelessness as it is described in international law. This implicit conflation of nationality and citizenship is particularly well illustrated in Blitz and Lynch's introductory treatment of statelessness in their edited volume on the subject (Blitz and Lynch 2011). They initially define statelessness in relation to nationality law, in keeping with the international legal conventions they cite, before beginning to use the phrase 'nationality and citizenship', and implicitly describing nationality as a gateway to citizenship as states 'have the sovereign right to determine how nationality, and hence citizenship, is acquired' (p. 4). Some paragraphs later, they then begin to define statelessness with regards to states and membership, before describing the status as the denial of citizenship (p. 5) and then as the denial of nationality (p. 6).

This tendency to use such terms interchangeably is a characteristic of the majority of writings on statelessness. This might be explicitly recognised, as in Kristy Belton's acknowledgement that 'in this article, nationality and citizenship are used interchangeably – a practice common in the literature on statelessness' (Belton 2011, n.1; see also Perks and de Chickera 2009), or the treatment might be far more implicit, drawing on the language of nationality in order to define statelessness. For example, in Lindsey Kingston's work, the notion of the 'arbitrary deprivation of nationality by the state' is central to the definition of statelessness (Kingston 2013, p. 75), Carol Batchelor refers to the importance of granting nationality to stateless persons, not citizenship (Batchelor 2006), and Matthew Gibney and others use the terms 'denationalisation' and 'denaturalisation' interchangeably to describe the revoking of citizenship status (Gibney 2013). This is perhaps not surprising given that accessing the rights of citizenship in the contemporary international system means belonging to a particular 'nation-state', which in itself means being the member of a national group and therefore holding a nationality. Yet my claim in this chapter is that if the rights of stateless persons are to be fully realised, we must 'trouble' this assumed relationship between citizenship and nationality and, related, the reification of national group membership as exempt from the kinds of protections against arbitrary discrimination which we hold other forms of group membership to.

To understand why the interchangeability of nationality and citizenship in international law and academic writing is problematic, it is necessary first to appreciate fully the socially constructed nature of citizenship. Far from the 'natural' characteristics which the UNHCR (problematically[1]) ascribes to nationality, scholars in the field of critical citizenship studies have made significant advances in demonstrating the inherently constructed characteristics of citizenship and their value in analysing the contours of inclusion and exclusion affecting populations. Nira Yuval-Davis' work has been particularly instructive in revealing citizenship as a performance of multi-layered and intersecting categories of rights, identities and belongings (Yuval-Davis 1999, 2006, 2007), and this notion of citizenship as a performance of a particular configuration of inclusion and exclusion has been central to the development of work on 'acts' of citizenship (Isin and Nielsen 2008; Nyers 2006) and on the ways in which citizenship is constructed and performed at the border, in the global city and in everyday life (e.g. Salter 2008; Sassen 2005).

The conflation of nationality and citizenship in international law and academic writing on statelessness is a particular expression of the performance of citizenship, and specifically the performance of what I will call 'citizenship-as-nationality'. Within this performance, nationality and citizenship are linked together so that the key criterion for access to the bundle of rights associated with citizenship is membership of a specific national group. This relationship is not foundational to the existence of citizenship; indeed, much has been made of the historical antecedents of contemporary citizenship before it became tied to the relatively modern notion of membership in a national group (see Habermas 1995; Viroli 1998), but it has attained a near hegemonic legitimacy in the contemporary global order to the point where, as noted, the UN describes it as 'natural'. This hegemonic legitimacy helps to explain why the conflation of nationality and citizenship in relation to statelessness has raised so few eyebrows. The performance of citizenship-as-nationality has deeply shaped societies, from the global order of states and the relationships between them, to the legitimate boundaries and borders of those states, to the everyday and unquestioned reproduction of the performance of citizenship-as-nationality by ordinary citizens (Billig 1995).

It is perhaps unsurprising then, given the hegemonic nature of the performance of citizenship-as-nationality, that the interchangeability of nationality and citizenship with regards to statelessness has passed by without significant problematisation. However, there are powerful reasons to suggest that this conflation is deeply concerning from the perspective of stateless persons. Georgio Agamben's notion of 'bare life' is semi-instructive[2] here, in that it draws attention in particular to the role of the performance of particular citizenship regimes in defining the exclusion of those deemed not to belong – in this case, the refugee (Agamben 2000). By reproducing citizenship-as-nationality, international law and academic writing adds legitimacy to this specific performance of citizenship and the exclusions it permits, but it is this very performance which produces significant problems associated with statelessness. It is this reification of national group membership and the exclusions that it permits over and above the exclusions permitted by other forms of group membership – which are commonly thought of as driving arbitrary deprivation – that shall be the focus of the remainder of the chapter.

Critiquing citizenship-as-nationality

My argument, therefore, on the basis of what I have said so far, is as follows:

1 If the existence of statelessness is viewed as indefensible,[3] and
2 If viewing citizenship through the prism of nationality is a contributing factor to the continued occurrence of statelessness, then
3 There are powerful reasons to move away from the reproduction of citizenship-as-nationality in international law and academic writing on the subject of statelessness.

In order to make this argument successfully, it is necessary to show why the performance of citizenship-as-nationality is particularly problematic from the perspective of statelessness, and this necessitates demonstrating why nationality itself is problematic. It is to this endeavour that I now turn.

The performance of citizenship-as-nationality bases exclusion from the State on the lack of membership of a specified national group. Membership of this national group is therefore a gateway to accessing the bundle of rights associated with citizenship. This exclusion is more significant in the case of stateless persons than in the case of other forms of noncitizenship, because stateless persons are not members of another State-recognised national group and so have no other recourse to citizenship rights. They are as such not only excluded from the national group of one particular State, but from all States, on the basis of the hegemonic performance of citizenship-as-nationality in the international system of States which cannot accommodate the primary group with which they identify. In this sense they are not just excluded from one State but fall through the cracks of the international system in its entirety. It is also more significantly problematic for stateless persons because their exclusion from citizenship rights may occur *in situ*, rendering them stateless within a State which does not recognise their rights claims due to not viewing them as co-members of the dominant national group. This means that they can be born into statelessness, or indeed that they may become stateless as a result of changes in nationality law, as in the case of Dominican Republic citizens of Haitian heritage (see also Blake, this volume, Belton 2011; Gibney 2009).

As such, the performance of citizenship-as-nationality has a profound impact on individuals' lives and the opportunities and deprivations which shape them. Yet nationalism is inherently a means of ascribing difference on arbitrary grounds, grounds which we would not find defensible in relation to other forms of group membership. It is not, for example, generally seen as defensible from a liberal perspective to deny rights to persons on the basis of membership of a particular ethnic group or a particular religion. While the inherently constructed nature of national identity is often more overtly stated than in the case of these other forms of group membership, membership of a national group is politicised and used as the basis for access to citizenship rights despite the fact that it is no more or less important than these other sources of collective identity (see Moore 1996). For example, groups that are smaller than the nation, such as families or smaller communities, and groups that are far bigger than the nation, such as religions which span international boundaries, may exert very strong feelings of allegiance (cf. Vincent 1997). In short, there is no specific reason to suggest that the nation offers any more or any less than these other forms of group membership which we would consider to be arbitrary memberships in considerations of justice.

It is not my intention to imply that scholars working in the field of statelessness find it defensible for people to be excluded from rights on the basis of membership of a national group. The literature shows that they find it as indefensible as exclusion on the basis of ethnic group or religious group membership. Yet, by implicitly supporting the performance of citizenship-as-nationality when advocating for the rights of stateless persons as was described in the preceding section, these scholars are legitimising the reproduction of the very system which serves to exclude stateless persons, and are contributing to the reification of this category of group membership above all others in questions of political organisation, the distribution of rights and the scope of justice. My argument is that claims for the rights and inclusion of stateless persons as legitimate members of political communities will be at least in part self-defeating if they do not challenge the nationally defined structures of citizenship which serve to exclude stateless persons.

National groups are an imagined social category of membership which have gained a prominence and political relevance within international society rarely granted to any other forms of collective membership; yet, they are no more or no less important than other kinds of collective membership based on other kinds of imagined shared characteristics. Stateless persons are as such denied rights associated with non-discrimination which would apply, from a liberal perspective, in the case of these other kinds of group memberships. For these other kinds of group memberships, the shared characteristics are typically viewed as ascribed, imaginary and arbitrary. The case of nationality is no different – the holders of the nationality are typically simply lucky to have been born into the particular set of characteristics that are taken to denote recognised membership; specifically, those associated with a particular national identity. The form of nationalism in question is irrelevant – whether this is ethnic, civic, cultural – the key point is that membership of a specific national group is an arbitrary characteristic and as a result ascribes difference on arbitrary grounds and ascribes access to the rights of citizenship on arbitrary grounds.

The obvious counter-argument to this claim is that national identity is in fact not arbitrary and that it is different to other forms of group membership in ways which matter to considerations of justice. Indeed, liberal arguments in defence of the performance of citizenship-as-nationality typically draw on the notion that shared national identity is a form of binding sentiment which is necessary for functioning liberal democracies. According to these 'liberal nationalist' arguments, shared nationality is distinct from other forms of group membership which make it non-arbitrary in considerations of justice; in other words, the good of maintaining national identity is taken as justification for the arbitrary exclusions it permits. It is argued that national identity provides the trust needed to support what I have termed elsewhere the 'willingness to lose' (Tonkiss 2013, p. 17) in democratic processes and to support the sacrifices needed to support a robust and well-functioning welfare state (Miller 1995, 2000). As Miller puts it, '[a] shared identity carries with it a shared loyalty, and this increases confidence that others will reciprocate one's own cooperative behaviour' (Miller 1995, p. 92). It is further argued that national identity provides a cultural context of meaning through which co-citizens develop shared ways of life together (Schnapper 1998; Tamir 1993; Walzer 1983), where 'a culture provides its members with meaningful ways of life across the full range of human activities' (Kymlicka 1995, p. 76).

Yet these claims to the non-arbitrariness of nationality in considerations of justice have been the subject of significant critique. Arash Abizadeh, for example, provides a highly nuanced account of the nature of trust and shared norms in diverse and international contexts to demonstrate that shared national characteristics are of little import to how people live together in robust and well-functioning liberal democratic welfare states (Abizadeh 2002). Abizadeh demonstrates the lack of coherence in the claim that national identity is necessary for trust and articulates critical instances of trust and shared norms emerging in diverse contexts, as well as the notion that the 'belief in another's general trustworthiness may be better explained by the other's previous *reputation* for trustworthiness, rather than by the fact of a culture shared by two parties' (2002, p. 501). He also shows that scholars who defend the performance of citizenship-as-nationality assume that the nation holds some 'concreteness' over and above other forms of binding sentiment between diverse peoples, but that this is a mistaken reification of the national group and further that for nationalism to be concrete it would have to fall back on the 'blood ties' or common ancestry which characterise ethnic nationalism and which are indefensible from the perspective of liberal political theory (Abizadeh 2004, 2012).

The wider body of research to which Abizadeh's theorisation belongs demonstrates that there are significant reasons to cast doubt over the value of shared national sentiment to the development of shared trust and meaning making and to the maintenance of liberal democratic institutions. These accounts highlight problems in the purported relationship between nationalism and trust (Follesdal 2000; Cabrera 2004), and cast doubt over the necessity of nationalism to liberal democratic institutions (Caney 1997; Müller 2007). If, as a result, we therefore reject these claims that the exclusions associated with (liberal) nationalism are outweighed by the instrumental value it provides, it is difficult to find grounds on which to defend a presumption in favour of nationality as a non-arbitrary form of group membership. In this sense there are no defensible grounds for the reification of national group membership over and above other kinds of group membership.

From a position where we reject arguments that nationality is non-arbitrary, it is clear that the exclusions affecting stateless persons constructed by the performance of citizenship-as-nationality are exclusions premised upon an indefensible form of arbitrary discrimination which allocates rights to some individuals and denies them to others based simply on the luck of holding a nationality that is associated with citizenship. This is an important argument to present in making the case for the rights of stateless persons more generally, but with regards to the more specific focus of this chapter, it points to the inherent problems with advocating for the rights of stateless persons drawing on the language of citizenship-as-nationality in order to make claims for those rights.

As Perks and de Chickera rightly note, 'recognition of nationality continues to serve as the key to many human rights, such as education, healthcare, employment, and equality before the law', and 'states continue to use national sovereignty arguments to impose limits on the rights of non-citizens even where these are unrelated to border control' (Perks and de Chickera 2009, p. 47). When basic rights of citizenship are tied to ascribing difference on the basis of arbitrary characteristics, this is rightly recognised as a form of indefensible discrimination. Yet the reification of nationality in international law and academic writing described in the preceding section means that these arguments can only ever be partially successful, because in themselves they legitimate the performance of citizenship-as-nationality which underpins this indefensible discrimination. It is as such my argument that we should not reproduce this hegemonic performance of citizenship-as-nationality when advocating for the inclusion and rights of stateless persons and further that the success of arguments in favour of the rights of stateless persons rests on a 'troubling' of that performance of citizenship-as-nationality.

A post-national alternative

Having set out my argument against drawing on the language of citizenship-as-nationality when advocating for the rights of stateless persons, in this final substantive section I offer a secondary claim that if we accept the premises of this argument, then we should explore alternative conceptualisations of the perform-ance of citizenship in which to base discussions of statelessness. In contribution to this endeavour, I suggest that a performance of citizenship based in 'post-nationalism' has much to offer those interested in realising the rights of stateless persons.

Theorists of post-nationalism suggest that it is commitment to abstract prin-ciples, rather than common national identity, which can and should be drawn upon to produce the binding sentiment traditionally associated with nationalism, in order to avoid the exclusionary logic that nationalism permits. While often associated with discussions of European integration and the emergence of insti-tutions at the supra-State level (for example Maas 2007; Scheuerman 2008), post-nationalism is primarily related to deconstructing the role of nationalism within society and suggesting alternative framings of identity and belonging to underpin more inclusive notions of citizenship. In this sense it advocates 'resist-ing particular identifications' associated with exclusive group membership (Markell 2000, p. 40) and promotes identification with universal principles of human rights, interpreted into the constitutions of particular States. As a result, many of these approaches have been termed 'constitutional patriotism' (Cronin 2003; Habermas 1998; Lacroix 2009; Müller 2007; Tonkiss 2013).

Scholars of constitutional patriotism do not advocate rejecting boundaries between States in order to build a global community of citizens,[4] but rather advocate a form of reflexive belonging about the ways in which a community of citizens as it exists in a non-ideal world embodies the ideal of universal prin-ciples of basic human rights. These principles are interpreted into a constitution through democratic processes, but rather than existing as a historical object to be reified it is *living*, subject to continual revision through those democratic pro-cesses in an open-ended quest to reach the ideal interpretation of those universal principles in that particular context. The approach does not call for people to renounce their nationality or for the complete rejection of national identity. Rather, it proposes a 'post-nationalist' approach (cf. Cronin 2003) which views national identity as one among many sources of self and group identity within societies on a par with other sources of identity (such as ethnic, linguistic, reli-gious, etc.) which should not have a direct bearing on access to citizenship rights. In this sense, under post-national approaches such as constitutional patri-otism, national identity is depoliticised and its reification as a defensible gateway to citizenship rights is challenged.

The performance of citizenship through the prism of post-nationalism offers a more defensible way of conceptualising membership of particular political com-munities than the performance of citizenship-as-nationality, because it involves an active 'troubling' of the exclusions driven and permitted by citizenship-as-nationality. Realising such a model of citizenship would challenge that hegemonic performance of citizenship-as-nationality which places nationality at the centre of defining access to rights, thereby reducing the capacity for persons to become state-less as a result of arbitrary identity characteristics associated with nationalism. It would also mean that reflexive political processes would challenge these arbitrary exclusions by continually developing the extent to which the political community and its constitution embodies universal principles of human rights, thereby working actively to deconstruct the exclusionary logics of citizenship regimes – whatever their relationship with nationality or other sources of exclusionary group membership such as ethnicity or religion – on an ongoing basis.

Once again, this argument is important to wider claims for the rights of stateless persons and how these can be realised in our existing system of States, but for the specific focus of this chapter on the language used by advocates of rights for stateless persons it has central relevance. As scholars working in the field, therefore, if (a) the existence of statelessness is viewed as indefensible and (b) the performance of citizenship-as-nationality is a contributing factor to the continued occurrence of statelessness, and (c) post-nationalism offers a means of thinking about citizenship and belonging without recourse to nationally defined citizenship rights, then (d) there are powerful reasons to suggest that we should move away from reproducing and legitimising citizenship-as-nationality towards a post-national approach which can 'trouble' this hegemonic performance. It is the performance of citizenship-as-nationality which prevents the realisation of the kinds of rights for stateless persons that are argued for from a normative perspective, and a more genuinely liberal, post-national variation of citizenship would be better placed to both acknowledge in practice that stateless persons have justified rights claims and to work towards the ending of statelessness in the longer term.

Opposition to this perspective could stem from the argument that there is still exclusion implicit in post-nationalism, one central example being the existence of non-liberal groups. If post-national approaches like constitutional patriotism are defined by liberal principles of human rights, then persons with illiberal beliefs could – the argument would go – be excluded and rendered stateless. This is related to the contemporary issue of (and another example of drawing on the language of citizenship-as-nationality in discussions of statelessness) 'denationalisation', which involves stripping an individual of their citizenship (Anderson et al. 2011; Gibney 2013; Graham 2004). This iteration of statelessness has become the subject of policy debate in relation to the contemporary securitisation of citizenship as a result of terrorism (see also Rygiel 2008; Walters 2004), with some proposing powers to denationalise individuals suspected of terror offences (Gower 2015).

However, post-nationalism would not permit processes of revoking citizenship status on the basis of membership of non-liberal groups regardless of its commitment to the realisation of liberal principles, in much the same way that any other liberal theory of citizenship would not permit anyone to be rendered stateless on the basis of the incompatibility of their views with the majority or over concerns surrounding national security (see also Barry and Ferracioli 2015; Gibney 2013). Of course there may be grounds to sanction individuals who may use violent means to threaten the liberal character of the State, just as anyone who falls short of the law, authored by the citizens, is subject to such sanction. This does not, however, include enforced and permanent exclusion from the citizenry in the style of statelessness. Post-nationalism involves a troubling of the binary oppositions between inclusion and exclusion which are mobilised by citizenship-as-nationality and an embracing of a more fluid, expansive and open means of living together collectively.

Conclusion

This chapter has conceptualised and sought to problematise the implicit legitimisation of the performance of citizenship-as-nationality in the field of statelessness, within both international law and academic writing on the subject. I have demonstrated how the way that we talk about statelessness, through the prism of nationality, serves to legitimise this performance of citizenship which in turn reproduces the structures which drive and permit the exclusion of stateless persons. On this basis, I have therefore suggested that accounts advocating for the rights of stateless persons can only be partially successful if they draw on the language of citizenship-as-nationality in order to make their claims, because this performance of citizenship will serve to undermine their arguments against statelessness.

Based on this argument, I have then further argued for those working in the field of statelessness to draw upon post-national alternatives as a basis for 'troubling' the performance of citizenship-as-nationality in theory and in practice. This approach is not calling for a rejection of nationality as a source of identity, but rather proposes a reflexive problematisation of the clash between the reification of national group membership and the universal principles which help us to realise the rights of stateless persons. As such, post-national approaches such as constitutional patriotism, I have argued, embody a critical challenge to, and troubling of, the hegemonic legitimacy that citizenship-as-nationality currently enjoys. This post-national framework is, therefore, a more defensible framework than nationality for those interested in ending statelessness to work within.

Hannah Arendt famously described how, in the case of refugees in the Second World War, '[t]he world found nothing sacred in the abstract nakedness of being human' (Arendt 1973 [1951], p. 299). With these words she is describing the relationship between rights and political community, and her resulting conceptualisation of citizenship of a political community as 'the right to have rights' has deeply shaped how we think about statelessness.[5] Yet how we think about statelessness is not simply as exclusion from a political community. I have, in this chapter, shown that it is conceptualised as exclusion from a *national* political community and that this has problematic consequences for advocating for the rights of stateless persons. My argument as such is that there is a space between the universalism of human rights and the reification of national group membership, which can offer us a useful way of thinking about how to realise normative claims for the rights of stateless persons. Rather than making such claims in isolation, it is necessary to challenge the structures which reproduce the exclusions faced by stateless persons.

Notes

1 See Tonkiss (2015 ch.1) for critique of nationalism as 'natural' rather than one of many socially constructed forms of group membership.
2 While the concept of 'bare life' has some relevance here in describing the exclusions that citizenship defines, it is not my intention to advocate the conclusions Agamben draws from his development of this concept. Space does not permit a critique of his position here, but Patricia Owens' critique covers important ground (Owens 2009).
3 As is problematised in Swider (this volume) and Bloom (this volume).
4 Although it may compel us to explore these ideas. For discussion see Tonkiss (2013, ch.2).
5 See Blitz (this volume) for further problematisation.

References

Aasland, A. (2002) Citizenship status and social exclusion in Estonia and Latvia. *Journal of Baltic Studies*, 33(1), pp. 57–77.

Abizadeh, A. (2012) On the demos and its kin: nationalism, democracy and the boundary problem. *American Political Science Review*, 106(4), pp. 867–882.

Abizadeh, A. (2004) Liberal nationalist versus postnational social integration: on the nation's ethno-cultural particularity and 'concreteness'. *Nations and Nationalism*, 10(3), pp. 231–250.

Abizadeh, A. (2002) Does liberal democracy presuppose a cultural nation? Four arguments. *American Political Science Review*, 96(3), pp. 495–509.

Agamben, G. (2000) *Means Without End: Notes on Politics*. Minnesota: University of Minnesota Press.

Anderson, B., Gibney, M. and Paoletti, E. (2011) Citizenship, deportation and the boundaries of belonging. *Citizenship Studies*, 15(5), pp. 547–563.

Arendt, H. (1973 [1951]) *The Origins of Totalitarianism*. New York: Harcourt Brace Jovanovich.

Barry, C. and Ferracioli, L. (2015) Can withdrawing citizenship be justified? *Political Studies*. DOI: 10.1111/1467-9248.12221

Batchelor, C. A. (2006) Transforming international legal principles into national law: the right to a nationality and the avoidance of statelessness. *Refugee Survey Quarterly*, 25(3), pp. 8–25.

Belton, K. (2011) The neglected non-citizen: statelessness and liberal political theory. *Journal of Global Ethics*, 7(1), pp. 59–71.

Bhabha, J. (2011) From Citizen to Migrant: The Scope of Child Statelessness in the Twenty-First Century. In Bhabha, J. (ed.) *Children Without a State*, pp. 1–40. Cambridge, MA: MIT Press.

Billig, M. (1995) *Banal Nationalism*. London: Sage.

Blitz, B. K. and Lynch, M. (2011) Statelessness and the Deprivation of Nationality. In Blitz, B. K. and Lynch, M. (eds) *Statelessness and Citizenship*. Cheltenham: Edward Elgar.

Cabrera, L. (2004) *Political Theory of Global Justice*. London: Routledge.

Caney, S. (1997) Self-government and secession: the case of nations. *The Journal of Political Philosophy*, 5(4), pp. 352–372.

Carrera, S. (2009) *In Search of the Perfect Citizen? The Intersection Between Integration, Immigration and Nationality in the EU*. Leiden: Brill.

Cronin, C. (2003) Democracy and collective identity: in defence of constitutional patriotism. *European Journal of Philosophy*, 11(1), pp. 1–28.

Equal Rights Trust. (2014) Equal Only in Name: The Human Rights of Stateless Rohingya in Malaysia. [online] Available from: www.equalrightstrust.org/ert documentbank/Equal%20Only%20in%20Name%20-%20Malaysia%20-%20Full%20 Report.pdf/ [Accessed 17 November 2015].

Follesdal, A. (2000) The future soul of Europe: nationalism or just patriotism? A critique of David Miller's defence of nationality. *Journal of Peace Research*, 37(4), pp. 503–518.

Gibney, M. (2013) Should citizenship be conditional? The ethics of denationalisation. *The Journal of Politics*, 75(3), pp. 646–658.

Gibney, M. (2009) Statelessness. *Forced Migration Review*, 32(April 2009), pp. 50–51.

Gower, M. (2015) Deprivation of British citizenship and withdrawal of passport facilities. *House of Commons Library Standard Note SN/HA/6820* [online].

Graham, N. (2004) Patriot Act II and denationalisation: an unconstitutional attempt to revive stripping Americans of their citizenship. *Cleveland State Law Review*, 52(2004–2005), pp. 593–622.

Habermas, J. (1998) *Between Facts and Norms: Contributions to a Discourse Theory of Law and Democracy*. Cambridge: Polity.

Habermas, J. (1995) Citizenship and National Identity: Some Reflections on the Future of Europe. In Beiner, R. (ed.) *Theorising Citizenship*. Albany: SUNY Press.

Institute on Statelessness and Inclusion. (2014) The World's Stateless [online] Available from: www.institutesi.org/worldsstateless.pdf [Accessed 17 November 2015].

Isin, E. F. and Nielsen, G. M. (2008) *Acts of Citizenship*. London: Zed.

Kingston, L. (2013) 'A forgotten human rights crisis': statelessness and issue (non)emergence. *Human Rights Quarterly*, 14(2), pp. 73–87.

Kymlicka, W. (1995) *Multicultural Citizenship: A Liberal Theory of Minority Rights*. Oxford: Oxford University Press.

Lacroix, J. (2009) Does Europe need common values? Habermas vs. Habermas. *European Journal of Political Theory*, 8(2), pp. 141–156.

Maas, W. (2007) *Creating European Citizens*. Plymouth: Rowman & Littlefield.

Markell, P. (2000) Making affect safe for democracy? On 'constitutional patriotism'. *Political Theory*, 28(1), pp. 38–63.

Miller, D. (2000) *Citizenship and National Identity*. Cambridge: Polity.

Miller, D. (1995) *On Nationality*. Oxford: Oxford University Press.

Moore, M. (1996) Miller's ode to national homogeneity. *Nations and Nationalism*, 2(3), pp. 423–429.

Müller, J. W. (2007) *Constitutional Patriotism*. Princeton: Princeton University Press.

Nyers, P. (2006) The accidental citizen: acts of sovereignty and (un)making citizenship. *Economy and Society*, 35(1), pp. 22–41.

Owens, P. (2009) Reclaiming 'bare life'? Against Agamben on refugees. *International Relations*, 23(4), 567–582.

Perks, K. and de Chickera, A. (2009) The silent stateless and the unhearing world: can equality compel us to listen? *The Equal Rights Review*, 3(2009), pp. 42–55.

Rygiel, K. (2008) Protecting and Proving Identity: the Biopolitics of Waging War Through Citizenship in the Post 9/11 Era. In Hunt, K. and Rygiel, K. (eds) *(En)Gendering the War on Terror: War Stories and Camouflaged Politics*. Abingdon: Routledge.

Salter, M. B. (2008) When the exception becomes the rule: borders, sovereignty, and citizenship. *Citizenship Studies*, 12(4), pp. 365–380.

Sassen, S. (2005) The repositioning of citizenship and alienage: emergent subjects and spaces for politics. *Globalisations*, 2(1), pp. 79–94.

Scheuerman, W. E. (2008) Global governance without global government? Habermas on postnational democracy. *Political Theory*, 36 (1), pp. 133–151.

Schnapper, D. (1998) *Community of Citizens: On the Modern Idea of Nationality*. New Jersey: Transaction.

Staples, K. (2012) *Retheorising Statelessness: A Background Theory of Membership in World Politics*. Edinburgh: Edinburgh University Press.

Tamir, Y. (1993) *Liberal Nationalism*. Princeton: Princeton University Press.

Tonkiss, K. (2015) *Migration and Identity in a Post-National World*. Basingstoke: Palgrave Macmillan.

Tonkiss, K. (2014) What's so bad about citizenship testing? *E-International Relations* [online] Available from: www.e-ir.info/2014/11/28/whats-so-bad-about-citizenship-testing/ [Accessed 17 November 2015].

Tonkiss, K. (2013) *Migration and Identity in a Post-National World*. Basingstoke: Palgrave Macmillan.

Türk, V. (2014) Ending Statelessness: An Imperative for the 21st Century. *United Nations High Commission for Refugees* [online] Available from: www.unhcr.org/5416d1619.html [Accessed 17 November 2015].

UN Convention on the Reduction of Statelessness. (1961) [online] Available from: www.unhcr.org/3bbb286d8.html [Accessed 17 November 2015].

UN Convention relating to the Status of Stateless Persons. (1954) [online] Available from: www.unhcr.org/3bbb25729.html [Accessed 17 November 2015].

UNHCR (United Nations High Commissioner for Refugees). (2015) *Stateless People,* [online] Available from: www.unhcr.org/pages/49c3646c155.html [Accessed 17 November 2015].

United Nations General Assembly. (1948) The Universal Declaration of Human Rights. [online] Available from: www.un.org/en/documents/udhr/index.shtml [Accessed 17 November 2015].

Vincent, A. (1997) Liberal nationalism: an irresponsible compound? *Political Studies*, 45(2), pp. 275–295.

Viroli, M. (1998) *For Love of Country: An Essay on Patriotism and Nationalism*. Oxford: Oxford University Press.

Walzer, M. (1983) *Spheres of Justice: A Defence of Pluralism and Equality*. New York: Basic Books.

Walters, W. (2004) Secure borders, safe haven, domopolitics. *Citizenship Studies*, 8(3), pp. 237–260.

Yuval-Davis, N. (2007) Intersectionality, citizenship and contemporary politics of belonging. *Critical Review of International Social and Political Philosophy*, 10(4), pp. 561–574.

Yuval-Davis, N. (2006) Belonging and the politics of belonging. *Patterns of Prejudice*, 40(3), pp. 197–214.

Yuval-Davis, N. (1999) The 'multi-layered citizen'. *International Feminist Journal of Politics*, 1(1), pp. 119–136.

16 Insider theory and the construction of statelessness

Phillip Cole

Introduction: the radical role of theory

Many of the chapters in this edited collection are very applied and practical, examining empirical evidence and policy development around migrancy and statelessness. This chapter, in contrast, works at the level of political theory in what may strike some as a very abstract level. It is, in a sense, *radically* theoretical, in that it looks at political theory itself as a subject for study, and at statelessness, not as a phenomenon in the world, but as a theoretical concept. What I want to examine is the way in which liberal political theory gives statelessness its shape and content. It is important, I believe, to look at theory, because even the most applied essay is drawing on a set of ideas and concepts such as the state, the citizen and the nation, and while those ideas are reflected in political practice they also have a theoretical history, and to the extent that our task in all of our essays is evaluative and critical, not merely descriptive, we are drawing on that theoretical background.

It is theory that enables evaluation and critique to take place, because it is at the level of theory that we can imagine alternative possibilities to the current order, and so ask why that current order persists when there are superior possibilities available to us. This means that our discussions are not limited by states, citizenship or nations as we find them in the world, but can explore alternatives as we use theory to imagine different political orders. And if some respond by saying our work is not rooted sufficiently in the real world, we should also remember that the systems of citizenship and exclusion that are actually practised by states are, in an important sense, not part of the real world, but are themselves constructs. Current political practices of membership are contingent, perhaps even arbitrary, and are mostly very recent developments, and so there is no good reason why they should constitute the limits of our thinking about migration, membership and statelessness. Indeed, what we should keep in mind is that statelessness is a condition created and sustained by those contingent, arbitrary and recent political practices, and so thinking beyond them is an urgent necessity. This chapter is, therefore, radical in a second sense, in that I want to push our imagination as far as possible beyond the current political order, and imagine what a just world would be like even if that means radically revising practices of citizenship, migration and nation-states.

One question we have to consider, though, is whether there are any practical limitations on our thinking when it comes to imagining different possible political orders. Joseph Carens (2013) asks this in his discussion of the ethics of immigration.[1] He makes a distinction between what he calls the Just World Presupposition and the Real World Presupposition. The Just World Presupposition imagines what a just world should be like with the idea of justice as unqualified and absolute. Among other things, 'an exploration of what justice ideally entails with respect to immigration should take the whole world into account' (p. 301). The Just World Presupposition allows us to critique the current world order to the extent that it fails to meet ideal standards of justice, but Carens points to the disadvantage that we are in constant danger of losing our bearings. In looking at what justice ideally demands in relation to statelessness, we will find that we need a wider moral theory dealing with the human good in general. We can't propose what the right to membership ideally demands without a general theory of human rights, and we know that it is notoriously difficult to ground a general theory of human rights.

The Real World Presupposition constrains us to thinking about what justice demands with respect to statelessness in the context of the world as we find it, both institutionally (a world of nation-states) and ethically (a world in which certain principles are taken for granted, such as nation-state sovereignty when it comes to membership). This Real World Presupposition is on the continuum near to where things actually are but is not right at the end, as there is still room to criticise how things stand – it is not merely descriptive. The advantage is that our arguments will be relevant to policy debates, but the disadvantage is that we may not see deep structural injustices. Carens argues that his own approach, which he calls the Democratic Principles Presupposition, lies somewhere between these two 'extremes'. I will not discuss his approach here,[2] but simply recognise that my work takes place within the space constituted by the Just World Presupposition, and that the Real World Presupposition itself, as Carens says, opens up *some* critical space between practice and possibilities. Once that space is opened, it seems to me, we, as theorists, should see how far we can go.

However, my primary focus in this chapter is liberal political theory and so I will say little about current political practices and possible alternatives, however radical. In a sense, this chapter is the groundwork for that radical vision, by exposing and therefore overcoming limitations on our imagination that are embedded at the level of theory. I argue that liberal theory is itself a practice, and as such has limits which could be, on examination, exposed as contingent, and perhaps even arbitrary. It is not a 'pure' space free of contingent limitations upon how we think, and so those limitations must be exposed and critically examined to see if we ought to move beyond them. And so the object of my enquiry is liberal theory itself, and the concept of statelessness it constructs.

The conceptual argument is that the concept of statelessness is a space which has boundaries and a shape. It stands opposed to the opposite space of citizenship, which itself has boundaries and a shape. Indeed, we might argue that it is the space and content of citizenship that defines the space and content of state-lessness. The stateless lack the properties necessary to enter the space of citizen-ship, and so are confined to the space of statelessness. But what is it that they lack? Certainly, it looks as though our attention should be on the concept of cit-izenship, to see whether it is drawing boundaries in an arbitrary manner, but that is hard to do and draws us away from theory towards practice, as there is no single agreed theoretical model of citizenship that states are using in their prac-tices. And so the reasons why people are confined to the *political* space of state-lessness are diverse. What work can we do here at the level of theory, beyond imagining an ideal model of citizenship which would not create statelessness? That work is important, once we realise that it is how we construct citizenship that creates the stateless (the stateless as an externality of citizenship). However, in this chapter I want to do something quite different.

I want to focus on the *figure* of the stateless person in theory, and ask if there is something about them that leads them to be confined to the theoretical space of statelessness. It may be that they *lack* certain properties, but they may also *possess* certain properties that lead to their confinement – they possess certain undesirable properties that have to be positively excluded from the realm of cit-izenship. It may be that this figure is constructed at the level of liberal political theory in ways that are contingent, arbitrary and non-rational, and, possibly, irra-tional. And while some would argue there must be space in political theory for the contingent, arbitrary and non-rational,[3] my argument in this chapter is that there are elements of the construction of the stateless figure that take us into the realm of the irrational. And so this claim is more than that political theory must take into account the non-rational and irrational, in the form of the emotions of fear and anger, for example, but that political theory itself is formed, to some extent, by the non-rational and the irrational, and we can witness this by examin-ing the shape and form and role of the stateless in political theory.

Residual or structural statelessness

In international development theory there are, broadly speaking, two ways of understanding global poverty, known as the residual view and the structural view. The residual view largely emerges from neo-liberalism, and sees the global poor as a leftover from the international economic system – a residue. But this residue is not created by the economic system: it is simply unable to absorb it. The solution is to make the economic system more efficient so that it does absorb this leftover element. And so where national economies lie outside of the global economic order, barriers need to be deconstructed so that those economies become incorporated into the international system. Or, where certain sections of a national economy that is incorporated into the international system remain on the outside, then reform has to take place such that they are included. The inter-national system as it were moves in and soaks up the poor so that they become part of the global order. The presupposition is, of course, that it is better to be inside the capitalist economic order than outside of it.

The structural approach comes out of the Marxist critique of liberalism, and sees the global poor as a product of the global economic order. For the neo-liberal position, the global poor are simply on the outside of that order, but for the Marxist, they are produced by how the system is structured – the order itself produces the economic inside and the outside. And so the solution to global poverty cannot be to make the economic order more efficient, because that may have the effect of *increasing* the numbers in extreme poverty. Rather, the solution has to be to radically change the economic order so that it no longer produces an inside and an outside, because all are genuinely included in an egalitarian system of production and consumption, a system in which they are free and equal (autonomous) producers and consumers. These two forms of analysis can be applied to many issues, such as the position of women, ethnic minorities and the physically disabled, and not only in relation to the economic system, but also all kinds of political and social systems. Either these groups lie outside of those systems because of factors that have nothing to do with those systems or because there is a minor inefficiency in the system that can be tweaked, or those systems *produce* an inside and an outside such that the order is structured around the exclusion of certain others.

The stateless can be understood in this way, again not in relation to the global economic order but in relation to the global political order. We can see them as a leftover residue lying outside of the international system of sovereign states, either nothing to do with that system or because of some minor inefficiency of that system that can be tweaked. Or we see them as a structural failure, a product of that order, such that finding a solution to statelessness means asking radical questions about the international political order. This is not so much a dispute between neo-liberals and Marxists, but between reformists and radical critics of the nation-state system. Carens can, to an extent, be seen as taking the former position, in that he believes his approach to the migration and membership is compatible with the nation-state system more or less as it stands. For example, in his discussion of refugees he explains the obligation nation-states have to refugees in terms of the normative presuppositions of the nation-state system. That system organises the world so that everybody ought to be assigned to a nation-state. However, in some cases that does not happen when states fail people either deliberately or through incapacity. 'Because the state system assigns people to states, states collectively have a responsibility to help those for whom this assignment is disastrous' (Carens 2013, p. 196). It does not take much to apply this argument to the stateless, and the clear implication is that the failure does not arise from the nation-state system itself, but from certain nation-states failing to behave, either deliberately or through incapacity, as we believe nation-states should.

The theoretical inside/outside

But while we have an interesting line of argument about moral responsibility for the stateless – whether we should see it as a systemic failure or a domestic one – I am not going to pursue this here. My focus in this chapter is not how people become stateless but how the idea of statelessness is produced, not how the political system constructs an inside and an outside, but how liberal political theory constructs an inside and an outside. My main contention is that these two approaches – the residual and the structural – are embodied at the level of political theory itself. What we should notice is that not only are certain groups excluded from economic, political and social systems, but that they are excluded at the level of theory, from theoretical systems. Certain groups such as women, the physically disabled, non-white 'ethnic' groups, migrants and the stateless, have been excluded from liberal political theory. This, of course, is not news. Political theorists have been aware of this for decades and many have addressed it. But the point is to notice that we can understand that exclusion either as residual or structural. If residual, all we need to do is tweak our theory a bit to include them, and then carry on more or less as before. If structural, then we have to radically rethink our political theory in order for it to be genuinely exclusive, and that may involve rethinking everything – we cannot go on as before. My contention in this chapter is that this exclusion is structural; the inside and outside is produced by theory itself, and business as usual is not an option.

I first noticed exclusion at the level of political theory many years ago while working on my PhD and looking at the work of John Rawls in relation to the physically disabled. Rawls explicitly acknowledges that his theory applies to what he describes as the 'normal range'. He says: 'it is reasonable to assume that everyone has physical needs and physiological capacities within some normal range', and his theory is for 'those who are full and active participants in society, and directly or indirectly associated over the course of a whole life' (Rawls, 1978, p. 70, note 9). His theory therefore explicitly excludes those who are excluded from full and active participation in society. Although he suggests that he may be able to 'attempt to handle these other cases later', it is extraordinary to realise that liberal political theory, as Rawls understands, is not for everybody, but only for the included.

And so what we have here is a double exclusion, from practice and from theory, and the exclusion from theory reflects and is based upon the exclusion from practice. Rawls, though, obviously takes the residual view, with the supposition that we can ignore these difficult subjects for now, but once we have worked out the theory for the 'normal' we can bring them in later – all we need do is tweak the theory a little to include the excluded and we can go on much as before. The implication has to be, I think, that this is how the problem can be tackled in practice: We can make the practice work better from the point of view of justice for all those included in the practice, and at a later date tweak that practice to include those who have been excluded from it.

However, my view is that this is entirely mistaken and what we have here is a deeply structural challenge. Part of the problem is that when we come to include the excluded, we are attempting to include them within a theory that has been actively structured around their exclusion. This reflects the problem at the level of practice. If our practices have been fundamentally constructed around an idea of what it is to be 'able-bodied', including the physically disabled within them through some 'tweaking' is going to be highly problematic. What is needed is a fundamental rethink of those practices from the ground up, treating all as equal members with no prior distinction between the 'able-bodied' and the 'disabled', and that may mean radically different practices. The same holds for theory.

What we realise is that theory has a topology, a shape. Historically, liberal theory has simply excluded the 'other', whether they be the physically disabled or in our discussion the stateless. It has not acknowledged their existence at all and has presented a false universalism. This means that their presence within theory becomes deeply disruptive and disturbing because, if I am right, it cannot be business as usual only now with the 'outsider' on board. The theory we have ended up with is exposed as deeply flawed and in need of radical critique.

My proposal is that this is how we should see the concept of the stateless in liberal political theory. Liberal political theory has notoriously been structured on the assumption that we are dealing with members of a nation-state (and Rawls shows us how, in fact, the focus is much narrower than that, as feminist theorists and those working on the concept of 'race' and other identity positions have pointed out more critically). This is an assumption that I have confronted in my work on migration, arguing that the migrant should be an equal figure with the citizen in any ethical discussion of immigration, rather than the interests of the citizen dominating theory. But equally, international political theory, when it does address the ethics of migration, is equally structured on the assumption that people, even if they are migrants, are members of *some* nation-state. And so while we have confronted the fact that the migrant was not included within liberal political theory, we now have to recognise that the stateless are not included within international political theory, however cosmopolitan we believe that theory to be.

The obvious reply to this critique is, of course, that we *are* addressing that absence, otherwise we would not be here now discussing the stateless. But my point is that we can't simply apply the political theory we have to the problem of statelessness, because the political theory we have does not acknowledge their existence, or rather it can only acknowledge their existence in a particular way. Even if we direct the theory towards statelessness as an issue, the theory constructs statelessness as a specific kind of problem, and keeps the stateless at the margins of theory, not allowing them to become the central problem of theory. It has to do this, because if it did allow the stateless to become the central problem of theory, they would expose that theory as fundamentally structurally flawed and incoherent.

When I wrote my book *Philosophies of Exclusion: Liberal Political Theory and Immigration* in 2000, the major aim of my argument was not, in fact, for open borders, but to show that addressing the question of membership has the potential to undermine the entire coherence of liberal political theory. Immigration is not some marginal question which we can add on to theory, but goes to the heart of that theory and exposes it as fundamentally flawed. My conclusion to that book was that liberal theory had a choice, either to embrace open borders or embrace its own incoherence, and since then many liberal theorists have indeed embraced that incoherence and tried to make sense of it rather than accept the open-borders implication of their theory. Whether they have succeeded or not is a matter for their readers.

The topography of theory

The question of statelessness reveals that the structural flaws go much deeper than I accounted for in *Philosophies of Exclusion*. The problem we face is that liberal political theory has been an 'insider theory', a body of theory that privileges the voice of the insider, the one who possesses statehood, the citizen. That privilege, at the extreme, has meant that this is the only voice acknowledged as existing, but even if we recognise the existence of the stateless as a problem for political theory, it may still be that the voice of the citizen is acknowledged as the only legitimate voice to be heard. The stateless are included in the theory, but as a problem for the citizen, a problem that must be solved in the interests of the citizen. Any solution of that problem has to keep the interests of the citizen at the centre, in the same way that the theory has always been structured around the interests of the citizen.

Rawls tells us, unwittingly perhaps, that the problem is even worse than this, that the theory has been constructed around the interests of a particular *kind* of citizen, one who is a member of the 'normal range' however we construct that range. But my contention in this chapter is that the problem is even worse than this. Not only has liberal theory been 'insider theory' with a specific *topology*, theorising from inside a nation-state, it has also had a specific *topography*, theorising from inside a particular *kind* of nation-state in a particular area of the world. Liberal theory has a *geographical* shape, as a body of theory structuring a viewpoint on migration and membership centred upon the interests not only of those who already have membership of a state, but membership of a particular kind of nation-state in a particular location in the world. This means that any solution to the problem of statelessness theory produces will be structured around the interests of those specific members. So the relationship we are trying to understand here is not simply between statelessness and citizenship, but between statelessness and citizenship of liberal democratic states in the Global North.

This topography of theory means that any solution to the question of statelessness constructed within liberal political theory even in its international form cannot be genuinely inclusive and egalitarian, because the negotiation on which that solution is based cannot take place on an equal basis. Indeed, it is likely that any negotiation will still only be between those on the inside, with the stateless remaining on the outside, excluded as participants in any negotiation of a solution. There is still a core and periphery of theory, with the other – in this case, the stateless – confined to the periphery and the core structured around the interests of the insider, the citizen of a particular kind of nation-state in a particular location. They have to be so confined because, as we saw earlier, to bring them to the centre shows the theory to be deeply flawed, and shows the subject – the citizen/member – at the centre of the theory, the subject whose interests it priori-tises, as equally deeply structurally flawed. The integrity of the subject depended on the exclusion of the 'other', and their position, identity, interests and power still depend on the confinement of the 'other' to the periphery even if we acknowledge their existence.

The psychology of theory

The presence of the 'other' in political theory – that against which the core iden-tity is defined – is therefore theoretically disturbing and disruptive. First, it reveals that the core identity is not universal, but particular – it exposes what Vron Ware and Les Back describe as the 'unwitting' solipsism of the 'individual unaccustomed to questioning the idea that she or he occupies a privileged polit-ical and cultural category' (Ware and Back 2002, p. 5). Second, it reveals that the core identity is not a pre-theoretical given, but a theoretical construct, which can therefore be deconstructed. Third, it reveals that the core identity is flawed – the process of exclusion of the 'other' creates tensions and antagonisms which cannot be resolved without a radical, ground-up revision of the entire theoretical landscape. In the words of Marx and Engels, all that is solid melts into air. Therefore the presence of the 'other' must be tightly controlled and confined – the problem of the 'other' must be solved, but in a way that maintains and even strengthens the position of the core identity.

I want to argue that we need to acknowledge not only theoretical but also psychological disruption, and indeed that these two are connected. Imogen Tyler, drawing on Julia Kristeva (who in turn is drawing on Jacques Lacan who is drawing on Sigmund Freud), has written about 'revolting subjects', using the core concept of abjection (Tyler 2013). The abject is precisely that revolting residue we saw in the neo-liberal approach to the global poor. Barbara Creed writes that the sources of the abject are those things that disrupt the boundary between the living body and its own death, such as bodily wastes and decay. These are things that threaten our identity as a member of humanity, such that we wish to expel them behind a border which will protect us from them. However, they are part of who we are, so that the expulsion has to be constant and the border is constantly threatened. Because of this constant need to repel, ritual becomes centrally important to maintaining the boundary between the human and the non-human, and that ritual has to become more detailed, complex and intense. Creed says that the abject has to be radically excluded and 'depos-ited on the other side of an imaginary border which separates the self from that which threatens the self' (Creed 1993, p. 9; see Cole 2006, pp. 113–117).

There is much more to be said about the abject and Imogen Tyler's use of it, but for now I want to point to the small conceptual leap in applying this to the politics of membership and migration as boats of desperate humanity crossing the Mediterranean are constructed as abject and to be repelled, for some at all costs, likened recently to cockroaches by a columnist in the United Kingdom newspaper the *Sun*[4]; and to those gathered at Calais, described by United

Kingdom Prime Minister David Cameron as a 'swarm' of migrants threatening to overwhelm the United Kingdom.[5] Although the United Nations High Commissioner for Human Rights, Zeid Ra'ad Al Hussein condemned the *Sun* for the article,[6] the attitude in Europe continues to darken, with French Prime Minister Manuel Valls claiming that the European Union may 'die' if the current levels of refugees entering the region continue.[7]

Tyler applies the notion of the abject to travellers, rioters, the poor and asylum seekers as well as migrants. The additional conceptual leap I am suggesting here is to apply the idea of the abject as a critique not only of political practice but also of political theory and its construction of – for the purposes of this discussion – the stateless. Indeed, the stateless present an even more radical challenge. If we assume that migrants have membership of some other state then they have a home and we need not allow them to enter ours. The stateless have no home, and so to place them at the centre of theory destroys the border that constitutes the integrity of the core subject in a radical way and so disrupts the subject itself as it loses any property that distinguishes it from the 'other'. Any acceptable solution to the migrant crisis in political theory or practice must be one that strengthens the boundary between the inside and outside rather than dissolves it. At the level of practice the European Union's ten-point programme for dealing with the unfolding tragedy in the Mediterranean was certainly aimed at strengthening the border, for example including proposals to destroy the boats used by people smugglers; and the response by the British and French governments at Calais was to build more fences, and we build fences at the level of theory as well. But this strengthening of the border, either in practice *or* theory, makes no sense in response to the challenge of statelessness, because the very notion of the state to be defined by the fence makes no sense. The stateless are abject in the extreme – psychologically and theoretically *revolting*.

And so the neo-liberal residual approach reduces the stateless to a revolting residue. The challenge for the structural approach is how to build a genuinely inclusive theoretical context within which all have equal voices in reaching an egalitarian settlement based on universal principles of justice. This approach is based on a realisation that everything has to be up for negotiation – there can be no fixed points, because what we take to be fixed points have been fixed by the old topology/topography of theory, and it is those fixed points that are the problem, and to think that we can arrive at a solution to statelessness based around those fixed points is the mistake. The core idea of this discussion is not in fact statelessness, but membership – it is our idea of membership that constitutes and constructs the idea of statelessness, because it is the way in which membership is constructed in theory and practice that dispossesses those who do not meet its criteria. At the level of theory, it is not the idea of statelessness that is the problem, but the idea of membership itself. And that means that at the level of practice, it is not the stateless who are the problem, but those of us who possess membership.

The meaning of membership

And so the theoretical basis for discourses of membership and mobility must be challenged and transformed. What membership means has to be fought over, rather than taken as our starting point. The fight is not just *for* membership, but also for its meaning. And what we realise is that its meaning will be determined not by theorists and policy makers, but also by the stateless themselves acting out these ideas in their everyday lives. What is needed is a dialectic between theory and lived experience. This has always been how moral and political concepts have been determined – not through abstract thought, but through political and practical struggle, and through ordinary people seeking to improve their lives and the lives of those around them in conditions of political and economic oppression. Political theory must become cosmopolitan in the true sense of the word, by providing space for all these voices and experiences by embracing our common humanity and dissolving the boundaries that separate 'us' from ' them'. Only then can we negotiate the terms of membership as equals.

The way in which the privileging of the voice of the insider is deeply ingrained within political theory is shown by Seyla Benhabib's use of discourse ethics to establish a human right to membership. Her discourse between the insider and the outsider goes as follows (note that from the beginning she, as the speaker, is the insider):

> If you and I enter into a moral dialogue with one another, and if I am a member of a state of which you are seeking membership and you are not, then I must be able to show you with good grounds, grounds that would be acceptable to each of us equally, why you can never join our association and become one of us. These must be grounds that you would accept if you were in my situation and I were in yours. Our reasons must be reciprocally acceptable; they must apply to us equally.
>
> (Benhabib 2004, p. 138)

In order to be acceptable, such grounds would be to do with qualifications, skills and resources (Benhabib 2004, p. 139). But note that the crucial aspect of the discourse is that *these must be grounds that you would accept if you were in my situation.* In other words, the outsider must think from the perspective of the insider, and so once more the perspective of the insider is privileged. The sentence should at least read: *These must be grounds that you would accept if you were in my situation and I would accept if I were in yours.* As it stands, there is no reciprocity here. If the grounds for exclusion are to be genuinely 'acceptable to us equally', then they have to be acceptable to the outsider *as outsider*. And equally importantly, they must be contested against grounds for *inclusion* which must carry equal weight in the exchange.

Lori Watson points out:

> The emphasis on reasons we could not reasonably reject as the standard of moral justification requires us to recognize that such reasons have the character

they do, in part, because they are reasons we can share – as moral equals. Acknowledging that immigrants stand in a political relationship vis-à-vis the state of intended migration requires acknowledging that the state is obligated to offer justifications that could not be reasonably rejected for its principles. This, however, also requires acknowledging the immigrant as a reason-giver in this context, and as an equal.

(Watson 2008, p. 988)

But in order for the migrant or, for the purposes of our discussion today, the stateless to be an equal in this exchange, we must be able to give our reasons from positions of equality, and to make this possible we have to be prepared to think outside of the conventional political frameworks that position the stateless as the 'problem' figure in this relationship. It is not the stateless who are the problem, but the relationship itself, a relationship which privileges the reasons of the 'insider' and renders the 'outsider', in this case the stateless, silent.

Notes

1 See Carens (2013).
2 See Cole (2014) and Cole (2015).
3 See Galston (2010) and Rossi and Sleat (2014).
4 See www.theguardian.com/global-development/2015/apr/24/katie-hopkins-cockroach-migrants-denounced-united-nations-human-rights-commissioner
5 See www.bbc.co.uk/news/uk-politics-33714282
6 See www.theguardian.com/global-development/2015/apr/24/katie-hopkins-cockroach-migrants-denounced-united-nations-human-rights-commissioner
7 See   www.telegraph.co.uk/news/worldnews/europe/france/12114438/French-Prime-Minister-Migration-crisis-could-kill-off-the-European-Union.html – and see my 'Europe's Response to Migrant Tragedy in the Mediterranean', Politics in Action, www.e-ir.info/2015/04/27/europes-response-to-migrant-tragedy-in-the-mediterranean/

References

Benhabib, S. (2004) *The Rights of Others*. Cambridge: Cambridge University Press.

Carens, J. H. (2013) *The Ethics of Immigration.* Oxford: Oxford University Press.

Cole, P. (2000) *Philosophies of Exclusion: Liberal Political Theory and Immigration*. Edinburgh: Edinburgh University Press.

Cole, P. (2006) *The Myth of Evil*. Edinburgh: Edinburgh University Press.

Cole, P. (2014) Carens and the problem of method. *Ethical Perspectives*, 21(4), pp. 600–607.

Cole, P. (2015) At the borders of political theory: Carens and the ethics of immigration. *European Journal of Political Theory*, 14(4), pp. 501–510.

Creed, B. (1993) *The Monstrous Feminine: Film, Feminism, Psychoanalysis*. Abingdon: Routledge.

Galston, William (2010) Realism in political theory. *European Journal of Political Theory*, 9(4), pp. 385–411.

Rawls, J. (1978) The Basic Structure as Subject. In Goldman, A. and Kim, J. (eds) *Values and Morals*. Dordrecht: Reidel.

Rossi, Enzo and Sleat, Matt (2014) Realism in Normative Political Theory. *PoliticalCompass*, 9(10), pp. 689–701.

Tyler, I. (2013) *Revolting Subjects: Social Abjection and Resistance in Neoliberal Britain.* London: Zed Books.

Ware, V. and Back, L. (2002) *Out of Whiteness: Colour, Politics, and Culture.* Chicago: Chicago University Press.

Watson, L. (2008) Equal justice: comment on Michael Blake's immigration and political equality. *San Diego Law Review*, 45(4), pp. 981–988.